Gods of Play

SUNY Series, The Margins of Literature

Mihai I. Spariosu, Editor

Gods of Play

Baroque Festive Performances as Rhetorical Discourse

Kristiaan P. Aercke

State University of New York Press

Published by
State University of New York Press, Albany

Printed in the United States of America

For information, address State University of New York Press, State University Plaza, Albany, N.Y., 12246

Production by Laura Starrett
Marketing by Nancy Farrell

Library of Congress Cataloging-in-Publication Data

Aercke, Kristiaan P., 1959–
Gods of play : baroque festive performances as rhetorical discourse / Kristiaan P. Aercke.
p. cm. — (The margins of literature)
Includes bibliographical references and index.
ISBN 0-7914-2049-3 : $59.50. — ISBN 0-7914-2050-7 (pbk.) : $19.95
1. Theater—Europe—History—17th century. 2. Theater—Semiotics. 3. Europe—Court and courtiers. I. Title. II. Series: SUNY series, the margins of literature.
PN2174.A35 1994
792'.094'09032—dc20 93-31052
CIP

10 9 8 7 6 5 4 3 2 1

For Muriel

En fait, de la façon la plus universelle, isolément ou en groupe, les hommes se trouvent constamment engagés dans des processus de dépense. La variation des formes n'entraîne aucune altération de caractères fondamentaux de ces processus dont le principe est la perte. Une certaine excitation, dont la somme est maintenue au cours des alternatives à un étiage sensiblement constant, anime les collectivités et les personnes. Sous leur forme accentuée, les états d'excitation *qui sont assimilables à des états toxiques, peuvent être définis comme des impulsions illogiques et irrésistibles au rejet des biens matériels ou moraux qu'il aurait été possible d'utiliser rationellement (conformément au principe de la balance des comptes). Aux pertes ainsi réalisées se trouve liée . . . la création de valeurs improductives, dont la plus absurde et en même temps celle qui rend le plus avide est la* gloire.

—Georges Bataille, "L'Insubordination des faits matériels"

Contents

Acknowledgments

Among those who have guided my work, I would like to thank, first and foremost, the late Frank J. Warnke, who, at the University of Georgia, introduced me to Comparative Literature and to the Baroque. I am grateful to my colleagues at the Department of Comparative Literature, University of Wisconsin-Madison, in particular to Jane Tylus, for her time and her valuable suggestions on early drafts, and to Hazel Carter, Department of African Studies. This book also owes much to the fair criticism of Giancarlo Maiorino (Indiana University), Margaret Rich Greer (Princeton University), and an anonymous reader for SUNY Press. Mihai Spariosu's work on play has influenced me, as the notes to some chapters will indicate. These notes, as well as the main discourse, record my debt to numerous scholars and critics—too numerous, of course, to list here; I hope that their ideas have not been misrepresented in the following pages, and that I have acknowledged them all.

Thanks go also to the University of Wisconsin-Madison: the Graduate School Research Committee awarded me a summer research grant to write a substantial portion of this book. An award from the Hilldale Faculty-Research Fellowships Committee allowed me to work with Comparative Literature senior Kevin Carollo in the early research phase; Kevin proved a very able and dedicated bibliographer. The staff of the Interlibrary Loan Department at Memorial Library has invariably been both efficient and courteous.

At State University of New York Press, I would like to express my great appreciation to Mihai Spariosu, series editor, for his efficiency in dealing with my revised manuscript despite his very busy schedule in the summer of 1993; to Carola Sautter and Cari Janice; and to Laura Starrett, production editor.

I am much indebted to the Archivio Segreto of the Vatican, Vatican City State, through whose kind services I obtained a copy of the text of *Sant'Alessio*. The following have allowed me to reprint copyrighted materials, for which I thank them: Editions Gallimard (Paris, France) for permission to reprint a passage from Georges Bataille, "L'Insubordination des faits matériels" in "La notion de dépense," in *Oeuvres complètes* vol. 1 (1970) 302–20; the editors of *Rhetorica* (Texas A&M University) for permission to reprint from Brian Vickers,

"Figures of rhetoric/Figures of music?" (*Rhetorica* 2.1 1984: 31–33 passim); the Crossroad Publishing Company (New York, New York) for permission to reprint passages from Hans-Georg Gadamer, *Truth and Method* (2nd revised ed., 1989); and the Pendragon Press (Stuyvesant, New York) for permission to reprint material from Edward Lippman, ed., *Musical Aesthetics: A Historical Reader* (1986) vol. 1. The quotation on page 70 is reprinted from Edward A. Lippman, *Musical Aesthetics: A Historical Reader.* Copyright Pendragon Press. The quotation on page 71 is reprinted with permission from Brian Vickers, "Figures of Rhetoric/Figures of Music?" *Rhetorica* 2.1 (1984). Copyright Texas A & M University.

In what follows, all translations are mine, except when indicated otherwise. Of course, I am solely responsible for the errors that doubtlessly remain in *Gods of Play*.

Prelude: The View from Above

When the late June sun has finally set over Madrid, King and Council board their gold-covered gondolas; floating peacefully on brightly shimmering lakewaters, they admire the gorgeous illuminations in the gardens of the new pleasure palace. As the fragile vessels drift toward an artificial islet, the waters, now put in motion by invisible machines, whisper and murmur, then rise and fall. Suddenly a splendid sea chariot, plated with silver, appears out of nowhere, pulled by two gigantic dolphins from whose mouths jets of water, fountainlike, shoot up high in the air. In the chariot stands a goddess, Aqua herself, robed in silver. Shiny rivulets form her hair; her left hand holds a silver urn, filled with fish of many species, which she pours into the now torrential waters. In Aqua's wake, a chorus of twenty nymphs—fountains, springs, and rivers—sing and play their instruments. Approaching the king, Aqua motions to the waters to come to rest, then addresses the monarch with a panegyric on Madrid. As Aqua speaks, the islet gradually comes to life with light. Scores of cleverly hidden lamps and torches reveal a multitude of treelike humans, or humanlike trees, covering a rugged, lofty mountain in the center. Cantilating her last lines, Aqua bows and withdraws with her train, as magically as she has appeared. Then, another tempest whips up the waves. With tremendous noise—shrill cries for help, fiery gunshots, blaring trumpets—a damaged golden bark struggles into view, with streaming banners and swollen sails, heading for the safety of the island bay. The anchor is dropped, the sails are furled, the crew appears on deck: here comes Ulysses with his companions, and as they speak, the play begins . . .

Throughout the seventeenth century, and during its middle decades in particular, Baroque Europe was racked by incessant religious and political strife and violence, struck by a sapping succession of economic disasters and by starvation and disease (including several major outbreaks of the plague), and stirred profoundly by intellectual, philosophical, and scientific discoveries of enduring importance. In the present study, some of the serious political, philosophical, and artistic problems and achievements of Baroque Europe will be approached from an unusual angle, that is, in a context of play—although it will gradually become clear that this playfulness is of a rather serious kind. I am interested in the première performances of particularly majestic and splendid musical-dramatical spectacles at the courts of absolute rulers: performances given on the occasion of specific events, for selected courtly audiences, and especially in the middle decades of the seventeenth century. I consider the première performances of operas, machine plays, ballets, and any large-scale, costly entertainment in which elaborately patterned dances, innovative instrumental and sung music, complex stagecraft involving huge machines, and dramatic performance by armies of highly trained artists collaborate to express a coherent mythological, fabulous, or legendary story, the purpose of which was primordially to serve the nation's controlling institution: the absolute monarchy. These performances served specific social functions within the community of each court that hosted them, as well as, in a larger perspective, within the organized political competition of the Continent.

The Baroque frame in which we will move was singularly complex as a historical period, as an intellectual movement, and as an artistic style.[1] Numerous arguments in favor of or against the Baroque have been made, and it is not my task to list them all and make my own case for or against critics and concepts—although some of these arguments will inevitably surface in the course of the discussion or in the notes.[2] My topic is specific and interpretative. Like other students of the Baroque, I have tried to capture the essence of this multifaceted object of study in an all-encompassing formula, in a symbol of its ethos. The first two chapters of the book provide an historical and theoretical framework for the notion that the ethos of the Baroque era and its sensibility was crystalized most succinctly in the majestic, splendid festive performance, that is, in *the festive expression of the spirit of play*, at the court of the absolute ruler. Such performances were of course not the only form of serious play available to the rulers and their courtiers. For example, in spite of the extreme seriousness of courtly life, and life in general, in the seventeenth century, precisely the people who were most powerful in this age and most actively involved in shaping it would not dream of being seen in public and executing their tasks . . . without a fashionable periwig.

Now, can one possibly imagine an article of apparel that is more inherently and intensely playful than the long, irregularly curled, profusely powdered and beribboned peruke of the Baroque? In *Homo Ludens* (1938), a study of culture *sub specie ludis*, the Dutch philosopher–historian Johan Huizinga argues that the periwig (he does not mention festive performances) should be taken as the symbolic epitome of the spirit of play in the Baroque period—the equivalent, perhaps, to the mask in the Renaissance (chapter 11).[3] True: powdered and beribboned periwigs became first fashionable in the 1620s and reached their most exuberant forms in the 1660s and 1670s (thus the fashion coincided with the heyday of the grandiose performances). With its endless fantastic variations, the peruke was nothing less than an arrogant attempt by Artifice to outdo Nature, an hyperbolic statement of excess and profusion, an extreme signifier of the control of Illusion over Reality. Thus, Huizinga seems somewhat justified in considering this icon of fashion the most concrete expression of the Baroque obsession with exaggeration and role-playing.

Although Huizinga's playful argument is very interesting, I would maintain that the Baroque age, and its spirit of play, was far too complex to be summarized in a single, idiosyncratic object—whether one prefers to single out Huizinga's curly periwig, Montaigne's "fleeting thoughts," *trionfi* (intricate sugar sculptures that served as banquet table decorations), Bernini's spiraling columns, Bach's soaring fugues, or the "writhing martyr" paintings that the Jesuits commissioned as pedagogic devices for their seminaries. Each of these elements, together with many others, merely contributes to a total picture. It is not in one single (art) form or object conceived by and for the personal taste of an individual that one can hope to recover to some extent the complex, Baroque spirit of play. Instead, I would argue that the latter—which is also the spirit of the era under consideration—materialized in *total* works of art: in the splendid festive performances in which all the arts, crafts, and ideas of the age were combined to celebrate and memorialize specific events that were, at the same time, unique-ephemeral (as in a specific dynastic marriage) as well as monolithic-sempiternal (the continuity of the line and the balance of power).

But let us first return briefly to the descriptive opening paragraphs, for they provide an excellent example of what we will be discussing. It matters but little that the nymph Galatea rather than the goddess Aqua addressed King Philip IV of Spain at the beginning of Calderón's *El mayor encanto, amor* (Love the greatest Enchantment), when its festive première was given with great pomp in the spring of 1635 in the gardens of the new pleasure palace "El Buen Retiro."[4] Calderón's three-act mythological *comedia* represents how Ulysses becomes the victim and enchanted lover of the beautiful witch Circe;

when Ulysses is finally able to tear himself away from her and escape with his crew, the wrathful Circe destroys her palace and her island. All in all, *El mayor encanto, amor* is a highly characteristic example of the central problem that this study will address. On the one hand, Philip and his inner council were enjoying a clever, well-prepared show, created at enormous cost in an extravagant setting that had been built on purpose for this sort of occasion. On the other hand, in June, 1635, Spain's economy was in shambles, and likely to get worse: only weeks before, a war had broken out with France that promised to be both very long and very expensive. The armies went hungry in the field, and the once redoubtable Armada remained badly equipped. In spite of these distressful times, the king had taken up residence in his pleasure palace rather than in the Alcázar (the official royal residence and office-palace) where everybody knew he was indulging in sundry entertainments such as Calderón's mythological-theatrical production with a few intimates.

At first sight, such festive performances as that of *El mayor encanto, amor* appear as whimsical, frivolously "Baroque" trifles, self-congratulatory acts on the part of an absolute ruler. Actually, these performances were designed as serious enterprises, which, as I have suggested, can greatly contribute to an understanding of some of the real, serious problems of the period. The possibility of the misunderstanding stems largely from an undeniable histori-cal-cultural shift in point of view. Indeed, people in general who live in a democratic society and whose views on the relationship between, for example, leisure and work have been formed after or because of the solidification in the western/northern mind of the so-called work ethic (whether Protestant or not is immaterial), could be expected to hold what I will call "a view from below." In effect, they might tend to condemn play of the kind that we are about to discuss as irrelevant, "mere play," and the people who indulge(d) in it as childish, or, less kindly, as ostentatious and insensitive to the plight of the general populace. I wish to argue here that the Baroque absolute rulers who sponsored such celebrations, as well as their courtly satellites, held the contrary "view from above" and considered their splendid performances in terms of a different and very serious form of play, the functional "play of cult."[5]

Much like the modes of consumption that Bataille has labelled *expenditure* (*dépense*)—in effect, those modes of consumption that emphasize an economic "*loss* that must be as great as possible in order for that activity to take on its true meaning" (1970, vol. 1: 305; "The Notion of Expenditure" 118)—this form of play could on occasion consume all available resources (time, labor, talent, materials) without sustaining positively the economic system of the nation in general.[6] Such an energetically and intensely pursued production of loss is likely to be the first characteristic of this sort of play activity to strike a modern audience.[7] But I have introduced the word "cult," and if we look at the splendid performance from this angle, we might argue that because of its pregnant symbolisms, this form of all-consuming play was actually not unproductive, because it had a multifaceted (though primordially political) end beyond itself. As behooves a cult, such a sacrifice of various kinds of resources amounted, in the etymological sense of "sacrifice," to the production of "sacred things" (Bataille 1970, vol. 1: 306). The "sacred thing," then, was the symbolically pregnant status of the sponsor-ruler in whose circumscribed domain the so-called "loss" was produced; the perception of this status both within the organizing court and abroad had concrete consequences that far surpassed the fleeting entertainment value of the performance. In fact, the combined creation of this status by all the circumstances of the performance and the perception thereof was itself a cultic element, in that it did constitute "le fait spécifique du mouvement communiel de la société" (that is, of the court society), which constitutes for Bataille the definition of "le sacré" (1970, vol. 2: 302). The occasion of the splendid performance acted as one of the most powerful agents that could draw a court together (and thereby define the microcosm of that court-world vis-à-vis the macrocosm of the world beyond) in an at least temporarily stable communion around the figure of the sponsor-ruler, who alone could provide the sort of "mediation" that Bataille considers a necessary factor in the interattraction between people (1970, vol. 2: 309–11). We might say that an essential fear of the ruler kept the court together, and that the splendid festive performance served as an unusually privileged and significant means of placating the shared source of fear—which leads us back to the notions of serious (even cultic) play and sacrifice.

The first chapter, "Feasts, Allegories, and Politics," is diachronic and takes off from the fact that dynastic celebrations of various sorts had been staged in splendid fashion in western Europe from at least the fifteenth century onward. I will therefore need to point out both the continuity of these celebrations into the seventeenth century, as well as the shift that occurred in festive habits of courts under absolute rule. Let me clarify this point somewhat further. Such dynastic festivities were largely determined by philosophical (especially Neoplatonic) concerns and rhetorical procedures; by means of the latter, the makers of the feast could systematically transform a community event into a political statement that served as an affirmation of the power and cohesion of the city and, increasingly, of the personal ruler. As the first sections of this chapter will demonstrate, Renaissance rulers and their feast designers used playful celebratory forms that were primarily public and still close to a mythic community spirit, and they sponsored these forms of sacred play according to a liturgical calendar or when special occasions called for them: pageants, royal Entries, masques, ballets, theatrical performances, and the like. Baroque rulers did not abandon such traditional, mostly public forms of (dis)play, but they generally began to highlight important dynastic (that is, national) celebrations by means of "private" play: grandiose performances in enclosed spaces to which only a selected group of spectators (who often also became performers) had direct access. Such splendid performances were hardly ever isolated, whimsical play-moments or events in the life-rhythm of a Baroque court. On the contrary; one could probably reconstruct much of the history of the Continent throughout the Baroque period by determining the personal, causal, chronological, and geographical connections between the numerous festive performances given at its courts. Given by a powerful sponsor—petty prince, queen, empress or pope—in the private setting of a court and for a privileged audience, the majestic festive performance was the occasion on which not only all a society's arts and crafts, but also all the ideologies which governed it, were combined and re-presented in a physically tangible form in order to recall from the past (or a willfully recreated past), reiterate for the present, and preserve for future memory the political and philosophical concerns of the age. Such organized play served several functions within the communities for which it was enacted.[8] Most fundamentally, it was a crucial strategy in the ongoing process of dynastic self-representation or self-affirmation in stability, which is itself, perhaps, the essential feature of the very principle of absolute rule. For that reason alone, the principles that guided the labors of the participating artists-craftsmen in various media can with justification be called rhetorical. It was their task, of course, to persuade the nation or community, and, perhaps most important of all, its neighbors, of the sponsoring ruler's power and wealth; not less importantly, they praised and affirmed the ruler's validity and place in history.

I have already used the word "rhetoric" several times. In the second, synchronic, chapter, which is entitled "Rhetoric and Baroque Festive Performances," the transition is made from discussing the historical-political purpose of the splendid celebrations as explained in chapter 1, to exploring their practical-functional execution. The Baroque age was very interested in Aristotelian rhetoric, not only theoretically, but on many levels of practical conduct and experience. I argue, then, that private splendid performances of the type discussed in the first chapter are, for all practical purposes, rhetorical constructs. After all, fewer occasions were ever better suited for the kind of rhetoric that Aristotle calls epideictic. Thus, under the heading "Rhetoric and Festive Performances," I extend some of the philosophical and cultural notions introduced in the first chapter and discuss applications of the allegorical program (the text) in praise of the dynasty. Next, under the heading "Invention, Disposition, Elocution," I introduce contemporaneous (as well as ancient) views on the mimetic, affective, and ethical powers of music, and also discuss rhetorical techniques of singing and acting. This section incorporates aspects of the history of opera, an aristocratic and philosophic art form when it was purposefully created in the very early seventeenth century. In the third section, "The Rhetorical Mise-en-scène," we will examine aspects of stage architecture, scene design, and the use of complex machinery.

Many of the artists that we will encounter in the following chapters, far from being merely entertainers, were the historiographers and sometimes even the architects of absolute rule. Ultimately, the greatest of all these artists was the absolute ruler. Capable of incorporating every mode of thought and expression and every form of the arts, the festive performance that served such a monarch was also nothing less than a scale model—a microcosmos—of Giordano Bruno's new vision of the world—the macrocosmos. Its rhetorical formalization (disposition and elocution) intended to affect the ethos of the audience-participants, and the literary-visual-aural program (Idea; invention) concerned the praise and celebration of the sponsor-absolute ruler over that new world.[9] A key principle in the doctrine of absolute monarchy was precisely the proposed assumption of a direct, though metaphorical ("as if") relationship of filiation between the ruler and a divine system. The function of the courtly nobility was, then, to serve the absolute monarch with ritual ceremoniousness. At the same time, the ruler was depersonalized, subjected to the collective ideal of a state, and metamorphosed into the protagonist of a social drama of power: each time the ritual is carried out, the power of the protagonist is confirmed, or vice versa: the ritual needs to be repeated endlessly, rhythmically, for the protagonist to remain in power. Rites do not celebrate an individual, but rather a collective force, embodied in the depersonalized figure of the monarch.

Such splendid performances as will be discussed here thus served a decidedly political (and therefore, social) function in the absolutist-courtly culture that invented and stimulated them. Not only did they serve to assure the continuation into the early modern world of ancient, perhaps even mythic patterns of communal behavior; they also produced a "sacred thing" (in the sense mentioned before) and represented what might be called the climax of the cultic celebration, dating back to earlier times, of the spirit of play as a serious social-political activity. Indeed, this kind of play involved much more than the mere technical organization of a spectacle, the performance of an opera, the dancing of a ballet. The general point of the second chapter, then, is that the aspects of invention, disposition, and elocution to be discussed constitute the solidly thought-out rhetorical basis for a ritual celebration, even amounting to worship, of the sponsor-ruler.

The considerations made in these two chapters lead up to the hypothesis which is proposed in the Interlude, and then to the discussion of specific, representative festive performances in chapters 3 through 6 which will, I hope, confirm the validity of the hypothesis.

In the Interlude, entitled "The Gods of Play," I argue that the rhetoric of grandiose festive performances was created to enable the Baroque absolute ruler to cast himself or herself, via an organized ritual of play in which he or she was the key player, in a role that had hitherto and curiously enough remained vacant in the West: the embodied spirit of serious festive play, the

God(dess), or tutellary deity, of play. Indeed, as Huizinga notes, the antique western pantheon referred to many gods as playing or playful but never went quite so far as to designate a specific deity to preside over play. Play may well be the single essential human activity or need which never had a tutelary deity—until (*horror vacui*) the arrival of the absolute sponsor-ruler of the Baroque grandiose performance. The initiated courtiers were forced into a quasipermanent celebration of the rites of this sponsor-ruler, as one feast followed upon another. I will argue that these rites can be interpreted as intending to overcome operative Reality principles and the tension between "love" and "duty" (for and to the absolute ruler-sponsor become god), in order to create a playful civilization that is charged with eroticism and that amounts to something more than the sum of the individual talents and interests of its members (including its magnetic kernel, the sponsor-ruler).

At that point, I would have the reader take possession of the monarch's throne, and, comfortably seated on purple cushions, assume this august personality's "view from above." Indeed: from this position, the splendid Baroque festive performance does not seem a form of trivial play but rather very much like a serious, even mythic, type of play, something like the "unified play" concept that has been posited as having existed from primeval times also in the western (read: Greek) consciousness—until, that is, Plato, Aristotle and afterward the early Christian writers broke up that mythic concept into supposedly "mere" or gratuitous play on the one hand, and supposedly "serious" or pedagogically useful play on the other, while privileging, it goes without saying, the latter as an ethical tool. From the mid-seventeenth-century on, Cartesianism, Protestantism, and the rise of the work ethic combined to contribute to a further erosion of this concept of unified play.

My point is that in feasts and festive performances of the types that form the subject of this study, "work" and "play" were still closely related, even intertwined "categories." In other words, the splendid festive "play" performance of the Baroque court constituted a political and philosophical program that was potentially as intense as (and, as many students of the seventeenth century will agree, probably more entertaining than) many contemporaneous political treatises or tracts on absolutism. But it would be fallacious to assume these feasts were merely so many forms of political discourse; they were also, quite simply, festive celebrations, elaborate games, forms of play for a limited number of players. One of the objectives of the game was to prove, time and time again, that the Baroque ruling class could indeed correct what it perceived to be the principal defect in Nature: namely, the upsetting fact that without the accouterments invented by Art and Artifice, it is usually impossible to distinguish a king from a valet or a princess from a peasant. The Baroque sensibility thus created a complex strategy to emend Nature's relative egalitarianism. Together with exuberant perukes and stunning experiments with three-dimensional clothing, the grandiose festive performance was part and parcel of this playful yet serious strategy. It is perhaps because of a distaste for the obviously "undemocratic" nature of the Baroque festive game that modern theorists of play (that is, "modern" beginning with the Romantics, and with Schiller in particular, who gave again serious attention to the spirit of play and who regretted the separation in the West of the "playful" and the "serious" impulses) have ignored the playful aspects of the theory and practice of Baroque festive performances.

In a conventional rhetorical scheme, invention, disposition, and elocution are followed by the actual execution. In chapters 3 through 6, I therefore present individual applications of the theoretical points made so far by means of a discussion of selected splendid première performances. The performances retained for analysis are Rospigliosi and Landi's opera *Sant'Alessio* at the palazzo Barberini (Rome, 1631, 1633, 1634), Calderón de la Barca's mythological *comedia El mayor encanto, amor* for Philip IV of Spain (Madrid, 1635), Cavalli and Buti's machine opera *Ercole amante* for Louis XIV and Maria Theresa (Paris, 1662), and Molière and Lully's *comédie–ballet La Princesse d'Elide* for Louis XIV and Louise de la Vallière (Versailles, 1664). Each of these performances was created to celebrate a unique event; each inaugurated also a newly designed, private theatrical space. The selection of these performances was partly determined by the fact that they were all interconnected by means of specific historical personalities as well as by the patterns of dynastic history itself. My aim is to illustrate what was obviously a trend. For each splendid performance selected, ten, or even scores of other ones like it could have been substituted: many were designed as grandiose events of which the memory was to survive in future history. The philosophical question to be addressed is, then, whether these private courtly performances, given their function in the ritual of the court and its rhetorical nature, gradually became "sacred plays," "as if" acts of worship of their sponsors, the absolute rulers, and effective ways of instructing the world of the court in the principles of ruler worship. After all, play (including *mousikè*) is also the most effective educational principle in Plato's *Laws* (Book I) as well as in his *Republic*: play not only teaches one how to function in the Republic, but also how to rule or to be ruled according to one's role. The argument can be applied equally well to the Baroque courts in question, their rulers, and their courtly satellites.

The subject of the concluding chapter, entitled "Ne Plus Ultra," is the feast opera *Il pomo d'oro*, which was originally designed for the wedding of Leopold I of Austria and the Infanta Margareta Theresa in 1666, but which was not performed until the summer of 1668. The examination of this work fully deserves to form the climax of the book, for *Il pomo d'oro* was designed to be unsurpassable—and so it turned out to be. All the theoretical principles and ideas, all the allegorical-rhetorical subtleties, all the artistic craftsmanship that we have seen developing in the preceding chapters/decades come together in this virtually unperformable work. No artist-courtier working in the context of an absolutist court could hope to surpass librettist Francesco Sbarra, who, with a stroke of genius, changed the hackneyed plot of the "Judgment of Paris" *muthos* and had Juno, Pallas and Venus grant the contested golden apple to Empress Margareta Theresa. Thus avoiding the need for (the Trojan) war, the three principal goddesses of the Greek pantheon directly recognize the young Empress as their superior—as the "goddess" who provides the occasion for virtue and power, wisdom and strength, beauty and love, to merge in sacred play—until, that is, the Reality principle (in the form of history, and more particularly in this case, the Ottoman Empire) entered the arena, intent on spoiling the game. As we will see, it succeeded remarkably well in Vienna as elsewhere, leaving nothing intact of the true Idea of the grandiose festive performance save some lifeless props: gilded putti, dusty libretti, static engravings of sets, some drawings for cloud machines, scattered reports. Working mainly with these, we will try to reconstruct the cult of the "gods of play."[10]

Notes

1. For the purposes of this study, I denote with the term "Baroque" a shared awareness in Europe, during a sliding historical period roughly between the 1580s and the 1680s, of a common set of philosophical, political, and aesthetic norms, as well as the various expressions thereof in any medium. First manifesting itself in Italy and France, the Baroque sensibility expanded over the Continent (and its colonies), gradually travelled north and eastward, and reached the Slavic nations toward the end of the seventeenth century. Thus it corresponds roughly to the Spanish *siglo de oro*, the Dutch *Gouden Eeuw*, the French *grand siècle* (including much of the reign of the Sun King Louis XIV), the late-Elizabethan, Jacobean, Interregnum, and early Restoration periods in England, the German period that was dominated by the specter of the Thirty Years War and its aftermath, and the Russia of Czar Peter the Great. To delineate literary or artistic periods is always difficult, especially if one assumes a comparative viewpoint. Time lags are largely responsible for this: countries or cultures do not develop synchronously or simultaneously. In other words, when the fruit was still fairly green in the German-speaking lands, it was perfectly ripe in France and Spain, and already quite overripe in Italy.

Although Rubens, Rembrandt and Poussin may seem to us worlds apart, as do Montaigne, the later Shakespeare and the early Corneille, or Donne, Crashaw, and Milton, all of these artists represented in their own ways the shared awareness which I have labeled the "Baroque sensibility." In its very essence, the Baroque sensibility amounted to the systematic examination of a new world by means of new parameters. To this sensibility contributed the allegorical awareness of the age, the absolutist character of its political organization, its quasi–unprecedented interest in science, mechanics, and machinery, its love of formal display, its even greater passion for play and formalized feasting, its ambivalent attitudes toward spirituality and sexuality, and, more often than not, its abysmal fear of failure and dissolution. All these elements were formally expressed in old and new artistic media, and especially so on the theatrical stage. Transition and change, even crisis and disorder, and more than anything else, an obsession with the phenomenon of movement, were central concepts.

2. A bibliography of works devoted to the concept of Baroque in European literary history and scholarship is, of course, immense. The following represents a fair, chronologically arranged selection of interesting studies, some rather general, others quite specialized.

H. Wölfflin, *Renaissance und Barock* (1884; trans. rpt. 1967) and *Principles of Art History* (1915; 7th edition 1929; English trans. 1932.; rpt. 1951); B. Croce, *Storìa dell'età barocca in Italia* (1925); P. Hankamer, *Deutsche Gegenreformation und deutsches Barock: Die deutsche Literatur im Zeitraum des 17. Jahrhunderts* (1935); H. Schöffler, *Deutsches Geistesleben zwischen Reformation und Aufklährung* (1940; 1956); N. Heuser, *Barock und Romantik: Versuch einer vergleichenden Darstellung* (1942); G. de Reynold, *Le XVIIe Siècle: Le classique et le baroque* (1944); R. Wellek, "The Concept of Baroque in Literary Scholarship," *Journal of Aesthetics and Art Criticism* 5 (1946): 77–109, and "Postscript 1962" in René Wellek, *Concepts of Criticism* (New Haven, 1963): 69–127; E. Orozco Diaz, *Temas del barroco* (1947); H. Hatzfeld, "A Clarification of the Baroque Problem in the Romance Literatures," *Comparative Literature* 1 (1949): 113–39; M. Raymond, "Propositions sur le baroque et la littérature française," *Revue des Sciences Humaines* 55 (1949): 133–44; special issue on the Baroque of *Revue des Sciences Humaines* 55–56 (1949); H. Haydn, *The Counter-Renaissance* (1950); J. Tortel, *Le Préclassicisme français* (1952); E. D'Ors, *Du Baroque* (1953); J. Rousset, *La Littérature de l'âge baroque en France: Circé et le paon* (1954); H. Hatzfeld, "The Baroque from the Viewpoint of the Literary Historian," *Journal of Aesthetics and Art Criticism* 14 (1955–56): 156–64; W. Sypher, *Four Stages of Renaissance Style* (1955); M. Raymond, *Baroque et renaissance poétique* (1955); F. Strich, "Die übertragung des Barockbegriffs von der bildenden Kunst auf die Dichtung" (1956), in W. Barner, ed., *Der literarischer Barockbegriff* (1975); I. Buffum, *Studies in the Baroque from Montaigne to Rotrou* (1957); G. Hocke, *Die Welt als Labyrinth* (1957); D. Alonso, *De los siglos oscuros al de oro* (1958); R.A. Sayce, "The Use of the Term Baroque in French Literary History," *Comparative Literature* 10 (1958): 246–53; T.

Schüssel, *Kultur des Barock in österreich* (1960); A. Angyal, *Die slawische Barockwelt* (1961); C. Hill, *The Century of Revolution, 1603–1714* (1961); R. Mandrou, *Introduction à la France moderne (1500–1640): Essai de philosophie historique* (1961); P. Sage, *Le Préclassicisme* (1962); H. Hatzfeld, *Estudios sobre el barocco* (1964); J. Mazzeo, *Renaissance and Seventeenth-Century Studies* (1964); H. Peyre, *Qu'est–ce que le Classicisme?* (1965); R. Alewyn, ed., *Deutsche Barockforschung* (1966); M. Kitson, *The Age of Baroque* (1966); P. Charpentrat, *Le mirage baroque* (1967); J. Rousset, *L'Intérieur et l'extérieur: Essais sur la poésie et sur le théâtre au XVIIe siècle* (1968); A. Boase, "The Baroque Syndrome," *Essays in French Literature* (1969): 1–17; W. Friederich, "Late Renaissance, Baroque or Counter Reformation?" *The Challenge of Comparative Literature and Other Addresses* (1970); R. T. Petersson, *The Art of Ecstasy: Teresa, Bernini and Crashaw* (1970); F. J. Warnke, *Versions of Baroque: European Literature in the Seventeenth Century* (1972); C. Dubois, *Le Baroque: profondeurs de l'apparence* (1973); A. Marino, "Essai d'une définition du 'Baroque littéraire'," *Baroque* 6 (1973): 43–61; J. Baiche, *La Naissance du baroque français* (1975); W. Barner, ed., *Der literarischer Barockbegriff* (1975); C. Hill, *The World Turned Upside Down* (1975); S. Sarduy, *Barocco* (1975); W. Bahner, *Renaissance, Barock, Aufklärung: Epochen—und Periodisierungsfragen* (1976); J. Hook, *The Baroque Age in England* (1976); G. Bazin, *Baroque: Principles, Styles, Modes, Themes* (1978); P. Skrine, *The Baroque: Literature & Culture in Seventeenth-Century Europe* (1978); D. Klebaner, *L'Adieu au Baroque* (1979); A. Buck, et al., eds., *Europäische Hofkultur im 16. und 17. Jahrhundert* 3 vols. (1981); J. Lafond and A. Stegmann, *L'Automne de la Renaissance 1580–1630* (1981); T. Reiss, *The Discourse of Modernism* (1982); E. Harth, *Ideology and Culture in Seventeenth-Century France* (1983); J. M. Benoist, ed., *Figures du Baroque* (1983); R. Nicolich, "Mannerism and Baroque: Further Notes on Problems in Transfer of These Concepts from the Visual Arts to Literature," *Papers on French Seventeenth–Century Literature* 10 (1983): 441–57; M. Bircher, et al., eds., *Barocker Lust–Spiegel: Studien zur Literatur des Barock* (1984); H. Rüdiger, "Deutsche Barock–Autoren und ihre Werke," *Arcadia* 19 (1984): 175–83; A. Battistini, "L'età barocca," in E. Pasquini, ed., *Guida allo studio della letteratura italiana* (1985) 319–45; W. Godzich and N. Spadaccini, eds., *Literature Among Discourses: The Spanish Golden Age* (1986); José Antonio Maravall, *La cultura del Barroco* (1975), trans. T. Cochran, *Culture of the Baroque: Analysis of a Historical Structure* (1986); J. Varloot, ed., *Du Baroque aux Lumières* (1986); S. Vjetta, *Literarische Phantasie: Theorie und Geschichte: Barock und Aufklärung* (1986); G. Dotoli, *Littérature et société en France au XVIIe siècle* (1987); P. J. Smith, *Writing in the Margin: Spanish Literature in the Golden Age* (1988); G. Maiorino, *The Cornucopian Mind and the Baroque Unity of the Arts* (1990); J. Steadman, *Redefining a Period Style: "Renaissance," "Mannerist," and "Baroque" in Literature* (1990).

3. Johan Huizinga, *Homo Ludens: A Study of the Play-Element in Culture* (1938; English trans. Boston, 1955).

4. I have condensed and rephrased the description of Aqua's appearance from a long document entitled "Circe," which was found in the Biblioteca Nacional, Madrid; published by Don Casiano Pellicer, *Tratado Historico sobre el Origen y Progresos de la Comedia y del Histrionismo en España* 2 vols. (Madrid, 1804) 2: 146ff.; reprinted by Hartzenbuch in his edition of Calderón, *Biblioteca de Autores Españoles* (Madrid, 1848) 7: 385ff.; and translated into English by Denis Florence Mac-Carthy in *Love the Greatest Enchantment; The Sorceries of Sin; The Devotion of the Cross, from the Spanish of Calderon* (London, 1861) 5–14, 5–7. Unknown still to Mac-Carthy, the document entitled "Circe" was Cosme Lotti's *memoria* or blueprint for what would become *El mayor encanto, amor*, rather than a different play. In the actual performance, the nymph Galatea took the place of Aqua.

5. The reaction of a modern visitor to, say, the Hall of Mirrors in Versailles may very well consist of a combination of such judgments as "how gorgeous," "what a fantastic monument of western culture," "what megalomania" and "I couldn't live a day in such a setting," all spoken at the same time and with perfect sincerity. It is probable that quite a few of the people who actually constructed the Hall of Mirrors (begun in 1679 by LeBrun), or went about their daily business surrounded by its opulence, felt exactly the same. But most likely these people were in a position to grasp the *function* of the Hall in its entirety and to interpret its opulence in a total ideological context, which allowed them to suppress (at least in public) their personal judgment of taste as rather irrelevant and interpret the Hall of Mirrors according to its intended function. It is precisely this capability of functional empathy that I label the "view from above." The splendid performances that are the subject of this study are in many ways related and comparable to the Hall of Mirrors.

6. Georges Bataille, *Oeuvres Complètes*, ed. Denis Hollier (Paris, 1970) 13 vols: "La Notion de Dépense," in Vol. 1: 302–20, and "Collège de sociologie," in Vol. 2: 291–374. All translations from Bataille that follow are mine.

7. Modern observers (taxpayers in general), accustomed to scant governmental support for "the arts," may be either impressed or scandalized by the astronomical budgets that were made available (so easily, it seems) for the festive manifestations of the spirit of play in the late sixteenth and seventeenth centuries, especially given the fact that the Baroque period might be adequately defined as the "Renaissance under the strain of inflation" (the phrase is from Trevor-Roper, in August Buck, et al., eds., 1: 11–23, 21). Indeed, toward the end of the sixteenth century, prices of most commodities suddenly rose sharply all over Europe, and few, if any, nations or states could boast a

stable economy. For example, the giant nation Spain was almost entirely dependent on a diminishing trickle of American precious metals. This economic crisis continued well into the seventeenth century.

It is therefore easier to tone down the enthusiasm of those who are unduly impressed with the festive budgets than to soothe those who are scandalized. True, the enormous cost of the splendid performances was somewhat offset by the massive employment of artists and highly as well as lowly ranked craftspeople. But consider what these gifted people might have produced if circumstances had been different (see Richard Alewyn, "Feste des Barock," in Richard Alewyn, et al., eds., *Aus der Welt des Barock* [Stuttgart, 1957] 101–11). Moreover, the virtually unlimited budgets of the splendid festive performances hardly ever interfered directly with military spending: absolute rulers or totalitarian governments of the Baroque age could, and always would, simply increase the burden of taxation in crisis situations. Thus the lower and middle classes ultimately paid for the wars as well as for the entertainments of the Continental courtly aristocratic class, since the latter was almost universally tax-exempt for most of the seventeenth century.

But the underlying pressures of this phenomenon are of course virtually universal. Bataille suggests that human poverty has never compelled societies to emphasize conservation over unproductive expenditure, because the classes that expend are also the classes that hold power (1970, vol. 1: 308).

8. In the context of this paragraph, the following consideration is essential. It is a critical mistake to detach a Baroque work of art from its setting, its locus, and from its intended functions. For example, one cannot properly understand Jesuit martyr painting without considering also the missionary boom that followed the Council of Trent (1545–1563) or the seminary setting in which these paintings were used as teaching tools. Or, one cannot simply lose oneself in the vortex of an illusionistically frescoed church or palace ceiling without taking into account the ideology of the absolute faith or the absolute ruler. Likewise, a *comédie-ballet* demands to be enjoyed, or studied, in the context of the total concept of Versailles.

My general point is that the post-Romantic, middle-class concept of "art" as the product of an individual creative genius simply does not apply to the Baroque. Only the poet, as an artist working alone, enjoyed prestige—much more so than the popular dramatist, who often collaborated. (Shakespeare saw to it that his poems were published but did not care about the plays.) True: from the very end of the fifteenth century on, Leonardo's artistic intellectualism had begun to set an example for artists. Nevertheless, in the late sixteenth and the seventeenth centuries, a painter in the service of a sponsor (and almost all painters aspired to that condition) still had little control over what he would do. For example, a painting was often not even commissioned by subject; instead, its future location determined the subject, and the number of figures to be represented set its price. Likewise, music was primarily composed for purposes of worship, for theatrical entertainments, or simply for background. It is a commonplace that the prince kept composers and musicians just as he kept a groom and stable. Art for Art's sake did not exist.

9. A word of clarification is in order here. Originality of subject matter ("invention," in the rhetorical sense) was perhaps an even less important concern to the Baroque artist-craftsman than it had been to his Renaissance colleague. In southern Europe, the latter had profited much from the support of powerful Neoplatonism, which, among other things, fostered the notion that the artist who succeeds in representing the essence, rather than the mere outline, of the object of mimesis, touches the sublime, has a divine gift, is a genius (*ingegno*) (see Gérard LeCoat, *The Rhetoric of the Arts 1550–1650* [Bern; Frankfurt, 1975] 38, on Tasso). Giordano Bruno, for example, gave originality precedence over conformity, and he blamed the Aristotelians, as imitators and traditionalists, for the theoretical and practical problems in the arts (Maiorino 48). By contrast, in the seventeenth century, the influence of Aristotle in this and in other matters was far greater than Plato's. Still, the Baroque artist could express true originality but primarily so by reworking with unusual intensity familiar materials into new, unfamiliar, unconventional forms. By finding new meanings in old material, the good artist was thought to be capable, still, of stirring the emotions by means both sensuous and intellectual, and, via the emotions and the intellect, of affecting the ethos of the audience. To achieve these two related goals (the latter via the former) was in fact the principal aim of all Baroque art, which was therefore, in a sense, always rhetorical (see LeCoat chapters 1 and 2).

And this is where I am leading up to. Baroque art in general can be said to have intended to "move" the audience: to lead the reader, spectator, or auditor from one passion or condition to another, and to achieve an emotional or ethical metamorphosis. In other words, Baroque art did not simply favor metaphor as a rhetorical figure; it was itself, literally, a meta-phor, a translation, a means for the artist (both in the Platonic-Classical sense of "maker" and in the Judeo-Christian sense of "creator") to ferry the audience from one thought, or opinion, or passion, or deed, to another one. The mythological characters Circe—the witch who enchants others and metamorphoses them—and Proteus—the man who constantly metamorphoses himself—were used time and time again as proportionate analogues to, or models for, the Baroque artist in real life as well as on the theatrical stage. (For example, see Prospero in Shakespeare's *The Tempest*, 1610–11, and Alcandre in Corneille's *L'Illusion comique*, 1636.) Regardless of the medium, Baroque art could never forget its audience.

Always involved in a rhetorical type of discourse, such a Baroque artist had in effect two distinct audiences: a sponsor-patron, who provided the ideology and the means for its execution, and an ultimate target-audience, whom the sponsor wanted to convince of her own opinions or move in harmony with his own passions and actions. The parameters of such a discourse are obvious especially, but not exclusively, in the art of the Counter Reformation. Thus, the typical Baroque artist-craftsman and his work of art—the product of an intellect, a creative sensitivity and much artistic skill—were both go-betweens or interlocutors, charged, first, with constructing a bridge for the passions and actions of the sponsor-patron to cross over into the hearts and minds of the target-audience, and, second, with influencing the ethos of the latter. This important function of the artist-craftsman in the political-ethical organization of his environment helps to explain why it was necessary for an artist anxious to succeed to possess, besides talent, a solid formal education, good manners, and a certain "class." High birth itself was not a prerequisite for success, and certainly by the end of the sixteenth century, it had become perfectly possible for an artist to move up dramatically in the patronage society by virtue of art, education, and dedication to the sponsoring ideology. Many achieved exactly this, which contributed to the new self-awareness of the artistic professions as being socially valuable (which in its turn, paradoxically enough, helped pave the way for the Romantic concept of the artist as an independent genius).

The system of patronage was obviously a two-edged sword. On the one hand, the totally dependent artist-craftsman was at the beck and call of the sponsor-patron and faced humdrum political problems, favoritism, and the sponsor's humor and whims. Cellini's Renaissance *Autobiography* (begun 1558 but not published until 1728) gives us an idea of these very real problems. And even at the height of his European fame in the Baroque period, Bernini was not free to work as he wished or for whom he wished but was constantly in need of the consent of his principal patron, Pope Urban VIII. On the other hand, the sponsor-patron and the individual artist-craftsman needed one another: the former depended on the latter as much as the latter on the former. Though of uneven rank, they could develop something like a symbiotic relationship: as paired-off partners, each could only express himself via the other. For example, whoever thinks of the Milanese Sforza thinks almost automatically of Leonardo, and the same is true for Maria de'Medici and Rubens. Similarly, the memory of Charles I conjures up Anthony Van Dijck and vice versa. It is not different with Bernini and Urban VIII, with Velazquez and Calderòn vis-à-vis Philip IV, and with Molière and Lully vis-à-vis Louis XIV.

The artist-craftsman who enjoyed such a relationship with the sponsor-patron actually served as the patron's historiographer, immortalizing not so much the mere chronicle and the nitty-gritty facts of the patron's career and reign as the idealized concept, the Idea of the patron's significance to the

Nation and to history *sub specie aeternitatis*. (See on this subject for example Louis Marin, *Le Portrait du Roi* [Paris, 1981]; trans. Martha M. Houle, and Tom Conley, foreword, *Portrait of the King* [Minneapolis, 1988].) The courtly art of the artist-craftsman did not only "move" the artist himself upward in a mobile society, but, by "trans-lating" the patron-sponsor's real or assumed importance into the terms of a superior significance, it also "moved" the latter upward onto a different, a higher level of meaning. Hence the great emphasis that was placed, in this sort of art, on fables and mythic precedents of artists who transform themselves or others (Circe, Proteus), and on humans who are promoted to superhuman status (saints, demigods). It is precisely this particular function of courtly art that we will highlight in the discussion of the festive performances.

10. I am ruefully aware of the evidently self-contradictory nature of this study, in which I am forced (1) to present *in abstracto* matters that were essentially extremely concrete, and (2) to rely exclusively on *printed* and engraved materials for the discussion of an enterprise that was not only primarily aural and visual but that even deliberately defied fixed media. This self-contradiction can scarcely be avoided, however.

1

Feasts, Allegories, and Politics

Public Play and Festive Forms

From the fourteenth century onward, Europe's courts and cities routinely celebrated important religious and political occasions with splendid feasts.[1] This policy was instituted simultaneously in the two wealthiest and most culturally developed areas of the Continent, the Burgundian realm and the northern half of the Italian peninsula, and within a century or so had spread all over Europe.[2] Like the religious and secular occasions themselves, their public festive expressions remained very much the same throughout the Renaissance and Baroque periods. Among the quasi-religious occasions, one thinks first of carnival rites, but numerous feasts were organized on the liturgical calendar as well: to highlight processions, canonizations (such as the canonizations of Ignatius of Loyola and St. Francis Xavier in Rome, 1622; Fagiolo dell'Arco 296) and various special events (such as Christina of Sweden's spectacular conversion to Catholicism following her abdication in 1654). Political occasions for public celebration (which cannot always be clearly distinguished from the religious ones) included dynastic events and various matters of state: visits of foreign dignitaries, the signing of peace and other treaties,[3] state funerals,[4] the handing over of the keys of a city to a conqueror or new ruler, and, especially, the Entries of the ruler in a city. The latter were consciously modelled after antique models combining public entertainment with the serious business of the state (the triumphal processions of Roman generals or emperors), and they required the construction of (mostly) temporary or (more rarely) permanent triumphal arches and similar devices in the streets through which the procession passed.[5] Also revived were antique-style mock battles, including *naumachiae* (naval battles on flooded city squares).[6] At some European courts, elaborate masquerades (*personatorum grex*) were a specialty.[7] And finally, tournaments (with blunt lances, wooden swords and ingenious *imprese* or coded heraldic devices marking the participants) were staged, which aimed at expressing the essential rituals and functional arrangements of feudal–chivalric society and which were, consequently, usually inspired by themes from texts characteristic of the literary revival of chivalry in the Renaissance, such as Ariosto's *Orlando furioso* (1532).[8] Almost always, the "fighting" on these occasions was prearranged and staged according to elaborate allegorical scenarios, designed to grant the ultimate victory to the primary participant: the prince. Interestingly enough, they occasionally assumed the form of a caricature of the originally serious medieval joust.[9]

The organization of such festive events was stimulated by the ceremonial consciousness that structured the political life of the community—which could be the court, the city, or the budding nation—and by the competition among such communities. The memory of enough feasts has survived in descriptions by visitors and ambassadors, in engravings or paintings, to leave an impression of their splendor and their elaborate ritualistic character. Such festive events could take place in the street, on the marketplace, or in ephemeral architectural structures erected specifically for the purpose within an existing structure or locus. They can be considered "public" because, at least in their origins, they were relevant for, and largely accessible to, the entire polis. An important contributing factor to the public nature of most of these celebrations was the fact that they were movable and travelled, in processions, through the polis.

Characteristically, the festive celebrations of the public type directly involved the ruler (with the court) as a participant, indeed, as an actor.[10] The ruler danced in the ballet, rode through the city as the crowning part of an itinerant procession, or participated in the tournament *à thème*; in funeral ceremonies, the deceased ruler was undeniably still the chief actor. Thus, the sponsor-ruler was a participant in the public celebration, on display, and visible to the entire city. By turns participating in the equestrian ballet (a revival of a Greek practice) or *carrousel*; proceeding on horseback or in a decorated coach through the permanent and ephemeral gateways of the city;[11] enjoying a sleigh-ride in northern Europe, or a regatta or a gondola race on real canals or on artificial lakes in the south—in all these situations the ruler projected onto the crowd a three-dimensional image of himself or herself.[12] At least in theory, the members of the polis had the opportunity to observe their ruler frontally and in profile, from behind and from above as they watched, perched on rooftops, trees, or poles, as well as from below, as they jostled each other in the streets or in front of the raised dais. More than a presence, the sponsor-ruler was also a ceremonial representation of the Idea of the ruler-in-attendance, and the public celebration was therefore also an occasion to express visually (via clothing, horsemanship, retinue, and the like) the existing class structures within the polis as they were perceived and approved by the ruling class.[13]

During public celebrations of these types, the entire city—its squares, streets, churches, palaces, and fountains—was temporarily metamorphosed into a theatrical, festive space. Besides sheer entertainment, these festivities offered the participants and witnesses an imitative assessment (imitative by allegorical means) of the wealth, the education, and the religious devotion of the sponsor-ruler and the polis as opposed to other poleis. In addition, the celebration, with its multiplication of symbolic accouterments, was also a rhetorical vehicle that could be adapted to communicate a judgment on the state of the community or the nation as well as a judgment on the ruler's function therein. And finally, in all their details as well as in the whole, these festive rituals were also the symbolic expressions of religious, philosophical and deeply rooted mythic concerns. After all, Renaissance and Baroque artists were also, to some extent, philosophers. Whatever the specific occasion, such feasts could be considered the literal and metaphorical expressions of a community or dynastic spirit in action, whether they took place in the streets, in the church or the courtyard of the palazzo. It has been said that "the feast was a privileged moment for polis or court to express itself in its hierarchically articulated entirety and with all the material and symbolic means it had at its disposal" (G. Stefani in Fagiolo dell'Arco 11). Perhaps that was precisely the original purpose of the feast or festive performance: the ritualistic symbolic formulation by a community of its identity as a polis. On the occasion of a shared event, the community rallied together in such a way that it must have been difficult to distinguish between "performers" and "public" (though not between the classes) in an outdoor feast or even in an indoor performance (Fagiolo dell'Arco 287, 431–38). In order to obtain a maximum of "marvels" (*meraviglie*), the concrete details of the initial realization were left to professionals: engineers, artists-craftspeople, laborers, and, in its first stage, men of letters.

The latter provided an intellectual, even philosophical, foundation for the festive enterprise, and the specific nature of that foundation should come as no surprise. Steadman has written that

> many of the external (and sometimes superficial) aspects of the literature and painting of the age—the copiousness of mythological allusions, the imitation of classical figures and motifs and decorative ornament, the frequent glorification of the sages and heroes of antiquity, and indeed the concern for the service of the state and pursuit or bestowal of secular glory—

were in part attributable to the kind of schooling that poets and their patrons were receiving and the character and aims of humanist pedagogy (54).

The dominant philosophical trend that had touched the lives of these men of letters and their patrons was Platonism. With its doctrine of the two worlds, Platonism and its various adaptations, which are known as Neoplatonism, formed a fundamental presence in the formative centuries of western civilization and remained so for more than a thousand years.[14] In fact, Christianity itself was deeply permeated with it. Its interpretive principles structured the creative imagination of men of letters and their patrons, and helped to found the ceremonial festive expression of mythic-political values in symbolic patterns. At the heart of these Neoplatonic adaptations or movements was the shared central notion that an inner reality is half concealed and half revealed by the outer reality. Essentially, Neoplatonism always explored the symbiosis of a fictional semblance on the outside and a veiled truth within (that is, veiled by means of allegory and symbolism), in which the latter refers to archetypes open to subliminal recognition.[15] The Neoplatonic emphasis on images and on the interpretation of visual forms (an emphasis which, as we will see, can also be applied to music) probably originated in Plato's argument that language (*logos*, discursive speech) is an inferior tool for the revelation of truth. From this argument it was inferred that *visually represented* images can lead more swiftly—because more directly—to higher knowledge than language (Gombrich 1972: 147).[16] Hence the crucial function of visual, allegorical emblems in the practical execution of the festive celebrations: "The visual symbolism must be got right, or it will not work," writes Donington (58). The fact that Renaissance intellectuals and many artists were informed by a Humanistic tradition combining Scholasticism and Neoplatonism provided the basis for their ability to engage playfully in complex allegorical cross-referencing.[17] Essentially, the game consisted of encoding and decoding the very diverse but mostly pagan imagery that expressed the symbolical implications comprising, within Neoplatonic thought, the veiled significance of art. For with the Neoplatonic philosophy came also the notion that an image can at the same time represent (surface realism), symbolize (conscious allegory), and express (subconscious meaning) (Gombrich 1972: 123–24).

Perhaps we can best illustrate some of these ideas by means of a contemporaneous, albeit irreverent, application. Jack Wilton, the roguish narrator of Thomas Nashe's novel *The Unfortunate Traveller* (1594), explains the allegories contained in the armor of participants in a mock joust:

> His armour was ill intermixed with lilies and roses, and the bases thereof bordered with nettles and weeds, signifying stings, crosses and overgrowing encumbrances in his love; his helmet round-proportioned like a gardener's

> water-pot, from which seemed to issue forth small threads of water, like cittern strings, that not only did moisten the lilies and roses, but did fructify as well the nettles and weeds, and made them overthrow their liege lords. Whereby he did import thus much, that the tears that issued from his brains, as those artificial distillations issued from the well-counterfeit water-pot on his head, watered and gave life as well to his mistress' disdain (resembled to nettles and weeds) as increase of glory to her care-causing beauty (comprehended under the lilies and roses). The symbol thereto annexed was this: *Ex lachrimis lachrimae* [editor's note: "From tears, more tears"]. . . . A third, being troubled with a curst, a treacherous and wanton wife, used this similitude. On his shield he caused to be limned Pompey's ordinance for parricides, as namely, a man put into a sack with a cock, a serpent and an ape, interpreting that his wife was a cock for her crowing, a serpent for her stinging, and an ape for her unconstant wantonness, with which ill qualities he was so beset that thereby he was thrown into a sea of grief. The word, *Extremum malorum mulier*: "The utmost of evils is a woman."[18]

The iconological novelties that are applied in these far-fetched trappings and *imprese* are explained with the sense for detail that was characteristic of contemporaneous iconographical manuals of Neoplatonic inspiration, such as the mythological encyclopedias and emblem books, which, originally written in Latin, were quickly translated into the European vernaculars.[19] As Nashe's text indicates, they soon surfaced in a context where they could be appropriately and easily applied: the political (and religious) sphere of festive celebrations. The textual and visual memorials of the festive celebrations clearly indicate that the creation of patterns of visual symbolism was a principal concern of the artists who designed and executed them.[20] The first stage in the creation of a festive celebration was thus heuristic and can be compared to the first phase in the construction of a rhetorical discourse: the stage of "invention." A theme for the celebration must be found, or a specific application of a theme devised, as well as the best arguments to advance and communicate the theme. Motifs were gathered from mythological, Egyptian, Christian, historical, literary and scientific sources. Translated and reinterpreted, or "actualized" according to the specific context and for the particular occasion (which involved, in many cases, the superimposition of a required happy ending—a *lieto fine*—on the fable or allegory), the most suitable motifs were subjected to amplification in a literary and visual program that was supposed to be visually attractive and as erudite as the artist-compiler could possibly make it.

This program usually represented a selection of ideas and motifs derived from the philosophical, scientific, and other movements of its period and space (Fagiolo dell'Arco 55). For example, text and decoration could refer to symbolically charged elements from the concrete world of plants and animals as well as from the scientifically or theologically abstract, artistic, or humanistic strata of knowledge. Thus, fruits and flowers in the program suggest fertility and abundance in the state, especially when linked with dynastic genealogical trees. The four elements have their own sets of connotations, as do examples of metamorphosis drawn from the Great Book that is Nature.[21] And so forth. In the festive celebrations, these elements were combined in redundance, and presented visually in service to the Ideas that structured the performance and provided its occasion—such as the expression of the identity of the polis, and especially, the ruler's identification with the stable polis. For example, the great contemporaneous interest in exoticism (artistically, with bizarre objects; philosophically, with different societal systems; religiously, with the missions; politically, with embassies) could emerge in festive events because its symbolically charged motifs could become part of, at the same time, utopianism and religious propaganda (see Fagiolo dell'Arco 60).[22] Likewise, the constituent elements of the feast or performance also reflected the new science, for the allegorical apparatus and the illusionistic techniques of decoration, architecture (in particular, artificial perspective with single vantage point), and stage devices (new forms of movable scenery) incorporated the era's sense of the infinite, the dynamic, and the new concept of space.[23] Regardless of its sources, however, a well-defined, coherent, and challenging program was always considered a necessity. For example, on the subject of royal Entries, de Pure writes that,

> il faut qu'il y ait un dessein, un poinct principal, un noeud mysterieux qui d'une façon ou d'autre appartienne si precisement au sujet, et s'étende si naturellément à toutes les parties qui le composent, qu'il ne puisse estre appliqué à autre chose qu'à ce qu'il est destiné. Ce point peut estre ou historique & reel, ou allegorique (205).[24]

And ultimately, the translation (metamorphosis, metaphorization) of external objects drawn from all spheres (that is: figurative or textual emblems) into internal states (into archetypes even), still followed from the central Neoplatonic metaphor: the human being is the small equivalent (microcosm) of what the universe is in large (macrocosm). Similarly, the festive celebration can be interpreted as a microcosm of the world, which was a manner of equating the sponsor-creator of the celebration with the creator of the world (see Strong 1973: 39–41).

Given the specified raisons d'être of the festive celebrations, the reinterpretation of motifs in their literary-visual-aural program was closely linked with politics (Donington 57). With this I mean that the artistic and artificial expression of allegories and symbols, which amounted to an extensive cultural repertory, was manipulated time and time again for reasons of political and religious propaganda, that is, in order to manipulate the audience's conscience and thought, and to persuade, convince, and especially, to praise.[25] In such obviously political art, visual symbolism was (and remains today) a crucial factor. The symbolic values of all the artistic components of the performance had to be combined harmoniously, just like the arts/crafts themselves: the union of the arts/crafts symbolized the union of the nation. The desire for stability within the polis or realm, under an increasingly centralized princely rule, was perhaps the principal motif of Renaissance and Baroque public celebrations. Part of the rhetorical function of the latter was to convince the polis and the world at large of this desire. The perceived need to publicly express such ideas in a festive form may well have followed directly from the era's keen awareness of unprecedented political, religious, social and intellectual instability.

The framework of the communal festive event was thus adapted in order to express contemporaneous Ideas. The literary-visual program and the practical details of the occasion served as allegorical reminders of the existence of a higher world of Ideas (including the Idea of the polis, its desire for stability, its place in the temporal and eternal scheme of things). All the concerns and problems that intrigued the era's intellectuals and philosopher-artists were translated into the allegorical motifs that surfaced in every part of the celebration, in which the details were designed to work together to produce a principal meaning. Supplemented with other forms of knowledge known to members of the polis, the allegories merged in the ceremony and its festive expression, and became available for interpretation according to the level of understanding of each individual observer-participant. Allegoresis ruled supreme in these feasts and festive performances; representations drawn from the outer world served, in effect, as expressions of the archetypal consciousness of the polis. The method of allegorical presentation heavily drawn upon on these occasions employed textual or figurative emblems to serve, simultaneously, the purposes of decoration (half revealing the Ideas) and allegoresis (half concealing the Ideas), and also to create a sense of magnificence appropriate to the ruler and the polis. Triumphal arches, fantastic statues and pyramids, and complex floats—why not, as in Florence, 1661, construct a float with a large pond complete with island and beautiful nereids and playful tritons? (Baur-Heinhold 17)—as well as texts of performances, details of processions and pageants, and geometrical figures (appropriately called hieroglyphs) performed in dances or equestrian ballets: all of these inherently transitional, itinerant media were loaded with symbolic evocations of the seasons, the zodiac, the planets, the elements, and the whole or parts of sacred, mythological and secular history. After all, in spite of the beginning shift of opinion that we have detected in Ripa's manual, the learned consensus still held that "truth" could be represented better in images than in words—even, in a sense, according to the Aristotelians themselves, for whom "thought consisted of forms which are received by the mind as images" (see Strong 1973: 28). For example, in the complicated figures of dances, the Pythagorean belief survived that the cosmic harmonies could be concretely reflected in visual representations of measures and numbers.[26]

The carnivals, feasts, pageants, tournaments *à thème*, and performances arranged along these lines can indeed be called triumphs of deeply entrenched allegorical mechanisms, producing ever more complex results. Of all the forms, equestrian ballets offered perhaps the most grandiose occasions for display. At an especially grandiose *carrousel*, held in Versailles in 1662, Louis XIV was officially inaugurated as the Sun King. He was dressed like a Roman Imperator, and his shield, embossed with a sun dispersing the clouds, bore the devise *Ut vidi, vici*; each of the participating noblemen informed the sponsor-ruler-imperator of his specific attachment by means of allegorical representations and devices, many of which implied or assimilated the need for the sun.[27] As the ceremonial expression of the social organization of the cities, the *poleis* and the courts, such festive events could hardly emerge spontaneously any longer.

Doubtlessly, the creators of the festive celebrations (sponsor, man of letters, composer, engineer, craftsman, and last but certainly not least, architect) counted on their future audience to be somewhat familiar with Neoplatonic theory and allegorical interpretative strategies, both when planning the formalization of the political goals and when making extensive use of symbolism that was based upon antique philosophies and the more recent versions thereof. Much of this symbolism may have been fairly well known as a shared and often seen codex of images and conceits that were classified accordingly in Neoplatonic manuals, which were repertories of symbolic and allegorical motives (Carandini 283). Yet, the more obscure symbols and references were clearly available only to the more sophisticated among the audience–participants.[28] But although the *hoi polloi* did not have access to the profundities of Neoplatonism, we may presume that even the less educated could have access to at least some of the meanings the designers wanted to impart, even if only through a visual familiarity with frequently recurring motifs. In addition, the intended symbolic argument was often explained in relatively easily available libretti or epilogues.[29] Thus, the allegorical complexity did not necessarily prohibit understanding and enjoyment or appreciation of rich materials, brilliant colors, intricate designs, harmonious sounds, and graceful movements. Also, the technique of subjecting symbols to allegorical interpretation was not restricting and did not contradict the desire for openness and movement that is a prime characteristic of the Baroque sensibility. On the contrary, symbols were not endowed with one single meaning; even for the Neoplatonists, "ideas" were not fixed, but changeable, always open for improvement and reinterpretation (Maiorino 80).

Finally, it seems paradoxical that festive celebrations of the types discussed were designed to be ephemeral, and were yet consciously imbued with an air of permanence (Carandini 280; Strong 1973: 21–22). This seeming paradox requires further explanation. On the one hand, the festive "event" (such as the performance) is to be distinguished from the "feast" proper, in that the latter was the occasion (in many cases, a recurring one) and the former an (ephemeral) event; yet, the occasion was to be remembered by the event. On the other hand, the symbolism applied to the events was designed to give the impression of a conscious quest for the ephemeral. For example, symbols and imagery pointed at the brevity of life, and occasionally the destruction of the event site was part of the event itself—perhaps testifying to the truth of the assumption that the ritual sensibility acts cumulatively, in the sense that "all further growth requires the immolation of that which was fundamental to an earlier stage."[30] But at the same time, the event was also and simultaneously designed to be permanent. For the actual sensuous experience of the festive event, whether public or private, was partly provoked and partly commented upon by elements that were intended to remain behind as permanent relics of the occasion: historiographical texts, libretto books, engravings, printed illustrations, eyewitnesses' reports in letters and diaries, dedications, properties, architectonic structures, etc. The fairly stable recurrence, in catalogue form, of specific features in written descriptions of festive celebrations, for example, may even lead us to consider such descriptions as a "genre" proper—the verbal equivalent of the detailed engravings or oil paintings that also made the feasts and celebrations permanent.[31] These features characteristically include "inexpressibility topoi" (see Curtius 159–62); the full titles and complete description of the sponsor(s) and participants; a pseudonaive narrator who feigns astonishment and who, for reasons of dramatic immediacy, switches tenses from the historical present to the past and back again; dramatic, epic, and novelistic stylistic and compositional features; and, most likely, authorial inventions and embellishments.[32] Thus, the feasts and celebrations did not only represent the sponsor-ruler and the interests of the polis, but were themselves represented.

Baroque Festive Forms and Private Performances

In the late sixteenth century (the transitional era from the Renaissance to the Baroque), the festive forms by which the city was temporarily transformed into a theatrical space were supplemented with (but not replaced by) new ones, among which the French *ballet de cour* and the English court masque rank first in importance.[33] These forms were organized in more private festive environments, and they reflected the ceremonial rules and circumstances of courts that were in the process of becoming both larger and more absolutist. In other words, festive celebrations like masques and ballets no longer only expressed an "aspiration toward political order" but rather began to pretend that the aspiration had actually been achieved and that the order had been established in the figure of the increasingly absolute prince (Strong 1973: 171).

The sponsor-ruler continued to participate in these new forms of courtly celebration. Of course, the ceremonial organization still represented dialectically the hierarchical differences between those in attendance: the sponsor-ruler occupied the central position in the entertainment (for example, situated at the apex of the pyramidical pattern of court-ball dances) just as he or she did in real life. Indeed, to emphasize this central position of the ruler vis-à-vis the courtly nobility, and to illustrate the quasi-impossibility of distinguishing between the "play world" and the "serious world," were principal functions of ceremonious festive forms. To this end, the textual-visual-aural program of these new forms remained mainly allegorical and Neoplatonic; dance patterns were still (though more complexly than before) "moving geometrical hieroglyphs" (Menestrier, in Strong 1973: 61). But rather novel was the fact that the participating sponsor-ruler was no longer on display for the *entire* polis.[34] Such ballets and masques were generally celebrated for a select audience in a private context (essentially, the court) and in a fixed, secluded location (a specific room, hall, or "theater"). Thus, on occasion, even the tournament *à thème* moved indoors.

The ballet, which could be ordinary or equestrian (*carrousel*), was a modern successor of the medieval tournament and joust (see further Strong 1973: 57–61). De Pure defined it as "une representation muette, où les gestes & les mouvemens signifient ce qu'on pourroit exprimer par des paroles . . . ce divertissement est destiné presque uniquement pour les yeux" (210).[35] The required skills to excel in the ballet reflected the change that had occurred in court ceremonial and in the functions of the ruler and the court: elegance and grace, rather than muscular force and dexterity, were now the accouterments of the courtier. Such ballets were performed all over Europe, but nowhere with more seriousness of purpose than in France between 1581 and 1672, where a tradition of organized court dances had existed since the end of the fourteenth century but really took off only by the middle of the sixteenth.[36] One of the most famous was the *Balet comique de la Reyne*, given at the Palais du Petit Bourbon on 15 October, 1581 to celebrate the wedding of Mlle de Vaudemont (the sister of King Henri III) and the Duc de Joyeuse. Designed by Balthasar Beaujoyeux (actually Baltazarini), with music by Lambert de Beaulieu and Jacques Salmon on a text by La Chesnaye and painted scenery by Jacques Patin (who also designed the costumes), it is the earliest such ballet of which the music was preserved.[37] Its name was derived from the fact that the queen performed in person, along with numerous ladies of first rank loaded with precious stones, who danced as naiads. In this ballet, as in many other ones, Circe was the protagonist and her magic island (complete with men transformed into wild beasts but transported entirely to a French château) provided the setting; the characters included deities from the Greek pantheon who spoke or sang like late sixteenth-century courtiers. The main point of the program—which was actually sung as much as it was danced—was to indicate that Circe (the official embodiment of chaos, disorderly imagination, unreason, unproductive creativity, and whatever else brings ruination to a realm by enslaving its [male] forces) will only surrender to the French king, the supremely rational and benign force of the universe, a more powerful signifier of Order than Jupiter himself: "Et si quelqu'un bientôt doit triompher de moy, C'est ce Roy des François, et faut que tu luy cèdes, Ainsi que je luy fais, le ciel que tu possèdes (8)."[38]

Here, as in many similar works performed later at the courts of Christian rulers, the pagan setting obviously served to avoid any charges of blasphemy. According to Donington, the many allegories of this particular spectacle, which lasted well over five hours, and which made use of complex technical devices such as cloud machines and a large, partly hidden orchestra, were designed to

> convey the impression (all the more emphatic since it was not in accordance with the facts) that a prosperous and beneficent and perfectly stable monarchy was giving freely of its bounty to a contented court and populace; that all outstanding enemies other than the purely mythological Circe had already been satisfactorily defeated; and that when she, too, yielded, general reconciliation must needs be achieved (57).

Another wishful expression, or "confirmation," of the nation's desired stability under its all-powerful monarch.[39] Other famous examples are the *Balet de la Nuit* (Paris, 1653), in which the fifteen-year- old Louis XIV, dancing together with Lully, anticipated his future role as the Sun King; in 1654, Louis appeared again in the *Balet du Temps* (a production, as always, of Benserade and Lully), in which roles were danced by the Minutes, the Hours, the Day, the Night, the Weeks, the Months, the Years, and the Ages. But such thematic ballets were also danced elsewhere; a case in point is the *Ballett der sieben Planeten* (Dresden, 1678), created for the visit of the parents of Johann Georg II. Magnificent equestrian ballets were given also in Florence (for example, *La guerra d'amore* for the Grand Duke of Tuscany in 1615, and *La guerra di belleza* for the prince of Urbino in 1616). Perhaps the most splendid equestrian ballet ever was *La Contesa dell'Aria e dell'Acqua*, designed by Sbarra with music by Bertali, which involved floats large enough to be equipped with ponds and complete ships, and which was performed in Vienna, January 1667, as part of the festivities celebrating the marriage of Emperor Leopold I and the Infanta Margareta Theresa (see also the concluding "Ne Plus Ultra" section). The masque was the English equivalent to the French court ballet.[40] Both forms remained rooted in Neoplatonic symbolism and had the same functions. Their designers, in addition to entertaining the court and privileged visitors (*divertimento*), were supposed to testify to the power and wealth of the sponsor-ruler and serve as historiographers. Their task was to immortalize the idealized, or Ideal, concept of the sponsor-ruler's significance for the Nation and in History *sub specie aeternitatis*, and to convince their contemporaries of this concept and claim's validity.

Special occasions in the life of the polis or the court continued to be celebrated with festive events that were either public and movable, or more private and circumscribed. But a third, additional type of festive form had meanwhile come to fruition in the more private circles of European courts. Unlike in the former two types, the sponsor-ruler did not necessarily participate personally in these new, complicated, and expensive festive forms: opera, the machine play, the heroic-gallant comedy,[41] and the *comédie-ballet*, performances of which were increasingly seen as the ideal climax to specific celebratory occasions—most obviously, dynastic weddings. The practice of presenting, in a relatively private courtly setting, new plays with varying degrees of musical involvement and spectacle, as part of the prolonged series of festivities that marked such occasions, had existed for a long time, first at the richer courts of Italy and Burgundy, and later elsewhere. But these events, though fascinating objects of study in themselves, were not always splendidly produced, or very grandiose, or conceived as guessing games pregnant with Neoplatonic-political significance. Among the more memorable examples of this earlier type were the "Labors of Hercules" on the occasion of the wedding of Charles the Bold and Margareth of York in Bruges in 1468, and the variegated ceremonial festivities that Leonardo da Vinci designed for Gian Galeazzo Sforza's marriage to Isabella of Aragon in Milan, 1490. Such relatively private performances continued to be held throughout the sixteenth and seventeenth centuries, and gradually a number of them became more splendid and were produced according to the latest technological developments and with the best available artists. Usually, they formed the climax of a complex program of festive celebrations that could last from a few days up to several months. From a vast number of examples, I will merely pick a few. The première of *La Confanaria* (a comedy by Francesco D'Ambra and executed by Vasari) took place for the wedding of Francesco de'Medici with Johanna of Austria in Florence, 1565; the opera *Euridice* (by Jacopo Peri on a libretto by Ottavio Rinucci) was first performed for the wedding of Ferdinand de'Medici with Christina of Lothringen, also in Florence, 1600; at the same court, the 1608 wedding of Cosimo II with Maria-Magdalena of Austria was fêted with the première of the opera *Il Giudizio di Paride*. This fashion was certainly not restricted to the Medici courts. In Castle Hartenfels near Torgau, for example, the wedding of Princess Eleonore with Landgraf Georg III of Hessen-Darmstadt was celebrated in 1627 with the première of *Daphne*, the first truly German opera (composed by Heinrich Schütz on a libretto by Martin Opitz).

No matter how much money and talent were spent on the production of such works, they could always be outdone . . . in the theater of the mind. On occasion, contemporaneous poets acted like architects, engineers, and producers, introducing the type of the splendid private performance as a motif in their work. Probably the most impressive example is provided by Giambattista Marino in the fifth canto of his once celebrated epic *L'Adone* (Paris, 1623). In a "gilded theater" that has somehow been fitted into the "colossal hall" of Venus's elaborately described palace, Mercury has prepared "a courtly spectacle" to entertain Venus's guest Adonis. In total privacy, sitting on golden chairs, Venus and Adonis watch a lengthy performance of Ovid's tragic tale of Diana and Actaeon by "histrions," not one of whom, characteristically enough, "would deign to act before/ a vulgar and commercial audience."[42] Live beasts run from the stage-forest to the startled but merry couple, there is music, and the many decors are rich and complex. Marino outdoes the actual stage engineers and architects by providing a curious revolving stage for numerous quick and astonishing scene changes (Priest trans. 92–93).[43] His long epic was enormously successful, in part perhaps because the "vulgar and commercial audience" could not yet otherwise satisfy its interest in theatrical extravaganzas of the kind described in the fifth canto.

The most interesting phase in the development of these increasingly splendid private courtly performances—clearly, I use the adjective "splendid" to indicate the scale of expense involved, the profusion of talent employed, and the total desired effect of the performance—was the period that immediately followed the publication of *L'Adone*, stretching from the 1630s through the early 1670s.[44] (Interestingly enough, this was also the most violent and brutal part of the seventeenth century.) And of the splendid performances within this period, the most magnificent ones—produced with no eye to cost and eclipsing anything that had been shown before—were première performances of total works of art that had been designed to inaugurate a new, permanent auditorium, a symbolic locus or focal point for the power of the sponsor-ruler in times to come.[45]

Thus, the 1631 carnival season in Rome was highlighted with the première performance of *Sant'Alessio*, an opera created by Rospigliosi and Landi especially for the occasion, in the brandnew Barberini palace. A different version of *Sant'Alessio* was given on similar occasions, in 1632 and 1634. In Madrid, the 1635 inauguration of the Hall of Realms in Philip IV's Buen Retiro palace was the occasion for the first performance at the Retiro of Calderón de la Barca's *El mayor encanto, amor*. In the Palazzo Pitti, Florence, 1637, the wedding of Emperor Ferdinand II with Vittoria de Urbino was feasted with the première of *Le Nozze degli Dei*, an opera with music by Ferdinand Saracinelli and decorations by Alfonso Parigi. In Davenant's private residence in London, Rutland House, the first operatic performance of any kind in England was held in 1656, prior to the return of King Charles and perhaps in order to test Puritan policies toward theatrical entertainment. Performed on that occasion was the first part of Davenant's *The Siege of*

Rhodes.[46] In the Grande Galérie of the Louvre, Paris, 1660, the wedding of Louis XIV and the Infanta Maria Theresa was celebrated with Cavalli's opera *Xerxes*. In Munich, 1661, on the occasion of the birth of Princess Maria Anna, the festive opera *L'Erinto*, by Kerll, Bissari, and Santurini, was first performed. Also in Munich, 1662, in the opera house on the Salvatorplatz, the birth of Max Emmanuel, heir to the Bavarian Electorate, was the occasion for the performance of the opera *Fedra incoronata*; the performance was followed by a tournament with pageant, which continued the Phaedra theme (*Antiopa giustificata*), and by *Medea vindicata*. In the Salle des Machines in the Tuileries, Paris, 1662, the opera *Ercole amante*, composed by Cavalli on a libretto by Buti and with machines by Vigarani, was performed to celebrate the Peace of the Pyrenees (1659), as well as (belatedly) the wedding of Louis XIV and Maria Theresa. Again in Paris, 1664, the Park of Versailles was inaugurated with the first series of the "Plaisirs de l'Ile enchantée," which lasted three days and included ballets, festive dinners, fireworks, tournaments, and performances—including, on the second night, the première of the *comédie-ballet La Princesse d'Elide* by Molière and Lully. And in Vienna, 1668, the new theater "Auf der Cortina" was the setting for what would go down in history as the most splendid show of the century: the two-day, extremely costly performance of *Il pomo d'oro*. In Paris, the Académie Royale de Musique was inaugurated in 1671 with the opera *Pomone*, composed by Robert Cambert on a libretto by Pierre Perrin. And the list goes on and on.

Functionally and practically, the splendid private festive performance still had much in common with the public festive celebration as well as with the masque and ballet. Certainly since the *Balet comique de la Reyne*, the primary subject and main purpose of all these forms had become the praise of the ruler by means of his or her representation in a heroic or gallant-heroic role as the (real or desired) provider of stability for the realm.[47] Their designers strove to achieve this goal in two ways: first, via intellectual means that were originally informed by Neoplatonic theory (thus, their success or failure depended on the application of the habits of allegorical interpretation that had been part of the western cultural imagination at least since the Middle Ages), and secondly, via the use of time-honored mimetic-rhetorical techniques for representing these Ideas and emotions and affecting the audience's ethos. Just like the public celebratory forms, the splendid private performance was, indeed, a *rhetorical discourse* between the sponsor-ruler, the artists, and the audience. Indeed, in the sixteenth and seventeenth centuries, theoreticians and practising artists in all media reapplied the principles of traditional rhetoric to poetry (which includes drama), to music (the connection between music and rhetoric was suggested first in Quintilian's *Institutiones*), and even to the visual arts. They did so in order to imitate more naturally the passions and deeds of Man (mimesis)—which Humanism considered the common goal of all the arts.[48] I use the term "rhetoric" as it was understood in the seventeenth century, that is, as an *organon*: a practical tool to reach the hearts of men, "a science of persuasion" (Fagiolo dell'Arco 58).[49] Of the three types of rhetoric that Aristotle described in the *"Art" of Rhetoric*, the epideictic type seemed the most relevant: it is mainly intended to praise (or blame), does not aim at transmitting new facts or developing new areas of thought, and does not even intend primarily to persuade or dissuade.[50] The conception and execution of private as well as public festive performances thus concurred with Aristotle's opinion that the master discipline controlling all the arts and sciences, is, ultimately, politics.

But the splendid and usually private festive performances differed from the public festive celebrations, and from the masques and the ballets, first of all, in the sheer size of the enterprise, and also in the fact that the rhetorical purpose was far more evident and expressed with much greater concentration in these total works of art. Leonardo's rhetorical approach to art (see n. 48) may guide us through this point. If painting, poetry, and music are all seen as directly related, in that they all address the intellect, then it can be said that the function and end of all art, whether pictorial, plastic, or literary, is to move the affections. From this, it follows that the artist's ultimate emphasis must be not so much on the content (Idea) as on the form (mimesis)—which confirms our previous suggestion that for the Baroque artist, originality of subject (invention) was less important than the masterful re-presentation of the subject (disposition, elocution) in a new context (*materia superat opus*; Argan, in Castelli ed., 11). From a strictly rhetorical viewpoint, "total works of art" such as the splendid festive performance, which uses all artistic media and matter available, can thus more effectively persuade, dissuade, or praise than any single medium by itself. For unlike the latter, the splendid festive performance addresses all the senses at once and therefore penetrates the intellect more efficiently.[51] The festive performances created after these models ranged from Florentine-style *intermedi* to *comédies-ballet*, "machine plays," and full-fledged opera—forms that all thrived on ostentation. The point is that in its attempt to incorporate every artistic element available, the splendid festive performance was for all practical purposes the culmination of the venerable philosophical-theoretical attempt at blending the arts, which the Humanists had reemphasized in their discussion of the ancient topos of *ut pictura, poesis*. Such private celebrations amounted even less to a celebration of the community spirit than had been the case in the transitional forms of the private ballets or masques. Obviously, the enclosed space affected the policy of admissions as well as the perception of the presence of the ruler. Instead, the focus of the festive event was exclusively the person and function of the sponsor(s)-ruler(s). No longer a collective occasion, and circumscribed within the limits of a specific locus, the private celebration really became a "performance" in the modern sense—but a performance from which the general community was almost totally excluded and which ceased to hold direct relevance for the members-at-large of a polis (unless they were involved in it as craftspeople or derived their income from it). It is highly characteristic, for example, that unlike the public forms described in the preceding section, the private splendid performances under examination here were usually staged at night, when the commoners and the laboring folk were supposed to be asleep. The nocturnal setting emphasized the exclusion of those who led a working life, and at the same time celebrated the unrestricted freedom of the ruling class to substitute its own schedule for the natural, temporal organization of the cosmos.[52]

In addition, the enclosed site of the splendid performance (theater, opera house, pleasure garden) symbolically confirmed the power of the sponsor-ruler by its architectural arrangements and the organization of the stage, by applying the linear, "peep show" perspective with a single, or "absolutist" vantage point, and by exploiting the symbolic effects of the great machines.[53] The new forms (machine play and opera) were developed in symbiosis with these developments in theater and stage architecture. Like a true *rey planeta* or Sun King, the sponsor-ruler promoted the court as a microcosm of the universe in which he occupied the center and the courtiers served as satellites. Still redolent of Neoplatonic symbolic strategies, the private festive performance emphasized and confirmed the status quo in the relationships at court. These magnificent performances of new machine plays or operas were, at the same time, an invention of the absolutist Baroque age, the best synthesis of the period's intellectual, political and artistic concerns, and, perhaps, the culmination of the organized spirit of play in the West.

We might justifiably interpret these entertainments both as an ironic comment on the dreadful events of the time and as a deliberate flouting of the reality surrounding the court or its theatrical locus. Symbolic and arrogant celebrations of the power of the sponsor-ruler (who paid) and the artist-craftsman (who created), the performances expressed a deep contempt for the forces that succeed in imposing intellectual and physical restraints on ordinary humankind. Contrary to all practical or rational sense, they required "loss" expenditures of money, creative energy, and labor so huge as to seem to later observers rather out of proportion to their own ultimate significance and to their context. By means of their machines, the designers and the participants pretended to defy the laws of gravity and the separation of the cosmic realms. Such courtly festive celebrations became, in a way, somewhat pathetic substitutes for court life itself—equivalent in function to the heavily ornamented spaces in which the court functioned in its regular organization. The proverbial courtly-Baroque opulence in ornamentation may well have been an overcompensation for a crushing sense of worthlessness and a neurotic fear of annihilation and of the void. Unable to tolerate the emptiness and the distance between a project and its execution (Alewyn 1957: 107), the courtly Baroque demanded instant gratification (Alewyn justifiedly calls the Baroque "eine ungeduldige Kultur. Es kann nicht warten").[54]

A further significant characteristic of the private splendid festive performances was the opportunity they gave the sponsor-ruler to withdraw personally from the action on the stage. Instead of participating in play-in-performance, the sponsor-ruler observed "performed play."[55] Instead of appearing as an agile person on display, he or she became a static function while (often but not always) remaining on (deliberate) display. The ruler's relative rise in status—from Renaissance prince of a city-state with or without outlying territories, to Baroque absolute monarch—made it often (though not always) impossible for him or her, as sponsor, to play personally. Instead, he or she only presided over the performance, placing the spirit of play under his or her aegis. Staged *for* rather than *with* the sponsor-ruler, the private splendid performance was, in content and execution, the ruler's metaphysical, symbolic expression. For example, the gradual changes in theater architecture and stage design reflected, or were even occasioned by, the fact that the sponsor-absolute ruler did not necessarily wish to be on permanent display. The advent of perspective with a single vantage point coincides with the withdrawal of the sponsor-ruler as an active participant: the whole stage is arranged in perspective from his or her vantage point in perfect symmetry—the world is ordered, the ruler is the fixed point of reference, the embodiment of stability heads the state. Again, the *Balet comique de la Reyne* anticipates this development: the king himself did not participate (though the queen did), and an engraving, done around the time the work was performed, shows him sitting in the theatrical space as it was codified half a century later by the influential Sabbattini:

> Let [the prince's seat] be placed as close as possible to the focus point, and on a level with the vanishing point, let it be surrounded by a balustrade of stout wood so that no harm may result from the press of the people, who on such occasions are used to take little consideration. About it may be placed seats for his courtiers or for the soldiers of his bodyguard, as they may please.[56]

In spite of its fixed setting, the splendid festive performance was limited neither spatially to the narrow confines of the theater, opera house, or pleasure garden, nor temporally to the actual duration of the performance. Instead, it outlasted its sensuously perceived execution: perhaps for reasons of propaganda, it allowed a ratiocinative discussion of itself and of its creator(s), sponsor(s), and participants. This discussion was part of the structure of the celebration and was built into its very fabric. For this reason, the splendid festive performance cannot be studied in isolation from its context, nor only through its literary program. As a ritual, it consisted of a set of phases which had to be gone through completely. In fact, the words "perform" and "performance" are derived from Old French *parfournir*: "to carry through completely" (Turner 12ff), "to accomplish entirely, complete, achieve" (*OED*). A performance did not begin when the first line of the prologue was spoken or sung, nor did it end with the last line of the epilogue. Rather, the performance proper included the occasion, the organization, the construction of the specific site, various festive activities (including the central event, the ephemeral performance of machine play or opera), as well as the (typically Baroque) paradoxical effort of making the ephemeral permanent, by means of material records, enduring physical structures, and the lasting reputation of the event and its sponsors, audiences, and artists.

An interesting point for consideration is the fact that the splendid performance was only a part (though usually the climax) of a series of fluently connected events, all of which were in a sense incorporated into a total rhetorical scheme. For example, a coronation or wedding mass was followed by a banquet, which could itself lead into a ballet, after which could follow a presentation of awards or distinctions, which itself might occasion a theatrical performance of some sort, which could be concluded by a fireworks display. All these events were intricately connected in time and space by the presence of the participants, as well as by the deployment of related symbolical-allegorical schemata. The point is that the several aspects or stages of the celebration were often not clearly distinguishable from each other. The entire event was, indeed, a "performance:" the completion of an elaborate set of rituals.[57]

The etymology of the word "performance" leads to a related consideration. If a performance, strictly speaking, demands "to be carried out completely," it follows that there is a finale, or rather, that the performance in the large sense, as the total series of events, *is* the finale, the conclusion, the final stage. A double emphasis can be distinguished, then: first on the process, which corresponds with the Baroque obsession with movement, and second, on the implied "sense of an ending." Carrying the latter notion somewhat further, one can argue that the splendid festive performance, in its large as well as in its limited meaning, was always the posited culmination, even the required ending, of a total series of other events. Not infrequently, this culmination constituted a challenge of sorts, setting in motion another social drama, another series of events (see the Interlude for a discussion of potlatch; Bataille 1970, vol. 1: 309). For example, in 1659, the war between Spain and France was concluded with the signing of a peace treaty (the Peace of the Pyrenees), which was in turn confirmed by the marriage of representatives of the two dynasties involved, in turn celebrated with a "performance" (in the large sense), which culminated in the splendid performance (in the limited sense) of the opera *Ercole amante*. First the war, then the peace treaty, then the dynastic marriage, and finally the splendid private performance of the opera formed a quadrangular series of events that we, as observers looking back in time, can hardly afford to dissociate. These events were inextricably connected parts of a complex social drama, or interwoven sets of social dramas, which—as is typical of social dramas—had their origin in an initial breach and which were resolved in a conclusive reconciliation (Turner 92ff). The operatic performance was thus the culmination, the *lieto fine* of the total social drama, in which the original breach was not only redressed but in which the participating dynasties were symbolically raised to a level superior to the level they occupied before the social drama began, or, in the case of the example given, to the level of the demigods (Hercules). This elevation was, of course, the true climax of the entire series of connected events. The organization of the whole corresponds nearly exactly with the order of four elements represented in a complete ancient drama: the *agon* between the old and the new fertility principle; the sacrificial death; the *anagnorisis*, or recognition of the king to be followed by the latter's initiation and reincarnation; and then the feast or marriage in honor of the young god, to be followed by a procession with songs of joy.[58] Another example of a performance with such a "sense of an ending" was the première of *Tartuffe* at Versailles in 1664. After the court had already engaged for several days and nights in the elaborate costuming and fanciful mythmaking that constituted the first series of "Plaisirs de l'Ile enchantée," the appearance of Tartuffe toward the end of these festivities, was extremely shocking. Dressed in a simple, black robe—probably the first "real" dress that the participants had been exposed to since "Les Plaisirs" had begun—this villain was suddenly introduced as the signifier of the "real" world, and therefore as a dangerous intruder. My point is that an understanding of *Tartuffe* and the contemporaneous controversy which it generated would be enhanced by considering the play in its total setting as a composite of rhetorical strategies, as a well-placed feature in the structural organization of "Les Plaisirs," and as a pawn in the service of a specific artistic-ideological purpose.

To the ritualistic minded Baroque sensibility, a complex series of events, be they historical or fictional, simply would not have been complete without a festive performance giving the events of the drama a higher meaning. It has been argued that no experience, whether personal or social, can be called complete until it has been "performed," until meaning has been squeezed out of it ("ex-pressed") and transferred to terms intelligible to others: via words, song, dance, architecture, or any other medium of communication (see Dilthey, quoted in Turner 13ff). This means that the splendid festive performances were not seen by their Baroque sponsors and makers as mere decorative appendages or whimsical entertainments that necessitated real expenditures (the cost of the theater, the artists' fees, among others) but, more importantly, also as *sacrifices* (by means of economic "loss" creating sacred things), as symbolic expenditures (Bataille 1970, vol. 1: 306–7). As the ritual culmination of series of social events or dramas, the festive performance was an absolutely necessary catharsis of the lived drama and the formulation of the meaning that the series of events was, in retrospect, perceived to hold.

Yet another reason for studying the entire "event" of a festive performance, rather than simply the text of the performed opera or play, is supplied by the iconological tradition of the Renaissance. Artists worked according to what Gombrich has called "the principle of intersection" (Gombrich 1972: 8). When artists selected subjects—usually from antique sources, although in the Renaissance they added a miscellany of contemporaneous objects and motifs, such as symbolically pregnant clocks or spectacles—they intended these subjects to have specific, contextually significant meanings. We must bear in mind that for the sixteenth- and seventeenth-century artists who worked with images and for the audiences who were asked to interpret them, the image and even the specific subject were closely determined by the occasion for which they were used and the place where they appeared.[59] Thus, a story or fable or image or symbol did not have one set and fixed meaning but was intended to be interpreted, allegorically and pragmatically, according to its specific context. In other words, when Circe appeared in a performance given for Philip IV of Spain, we cannot expect automatically that she would be perceived as having the same functions as in a late sixteenth-century French *ballet de cour*.[60] Symbols are open-ended, diachronic semantic fields, very much linked to continually changing social life itself (see Turner 21–23). Similarly, when characters or events were lifted from the texts of pagan antiquity (especially, from Ovid's *Metamorphoses*) and inserted into the symbolic world of the festive performances, they acquired new and constantly changing connotations. This principle, though it is basic, has been largely ignored in the scant criticism that exists of plays or operas created as Baroque festive performances.

For all these reasons, any study of the splendid festive performance, like the study of iconology itself, must start with the institution and the event rather than with an isolated analysis of the specific image, symbol, or text. Likewise, because the Baroque festive performance cannot be studied in isolation from its context, the student must not overvalue individual factors (the creative process) at the expense of social factors (the communication process). Indeed, the latter is probably the more important of the two, since it provides the true raison d'être of the festive celebration. Renaissance Humanists maintained the notion of antiquity that representational art is always communication, a form of "discourse," since each work of art establishes a relationship between what does the representing and what is being represented (LeCoat 30). The celebration of festive events was likewise a serious discourse, a communication of truths (real or fictional) between a sponsor-ruler, numerous artists and craftspeople, and a specific audience. It has been said that for Renaissance Humanists truth was readymade, whereas

Baroque truth was dialogic, "born between people committed to mutual interactions" (Maiorino 55). Baroque art apparently had an "implied reader" who was also a "participant, whose role in the formative experience of the art work was seen as active" (Maiorino 98). And surely, Solf is right when she writes that "der Barocke Mensch . . . als Figur des Zeremoniells wird . . . objektiv konstituierender Bestandteil des Rahmens, unbedingt notwendiger Akteur an der 'Peripherie'."[61] In a way, Baroque art, or Baroque truth, was always art or truth "in the making," since the addressee was asked, even obliged, to discover meanings.[62] Such a dichotomy located in a difficult chronology may sound rather simplistic, and at first sight seems to contradict the absolutist and dogmatic context of the grandiose performances. But the contradiction vanishes when we accept that the literary and visual-aural program of the splendid performances (the "truths" to be transferred) contained many connotations and hidden layers of meaning, mainly related to the ruler, which were inserted for the audience to discover according to their relative degree of understanding and sophistication. In this sense, the total truth of the performance was dialogic (though certainly not in the Bakhtinian sense of that term), because its expression involved a rhetorically structured process of communion—though not necessarily of communication.[63]

Private splendid festive performances were thus dialogic, rhetorical acts (just as public festive celebrations). But were they also a form of "communication?" Let us briefly review the mechanics of Roman Jakobson's model of communication. This model requires the following components or functions: *sender* (the individual or collective sponsor), *creator* (the poet, composer, architect, engineer, ballet master), and *receiver* (the sponsor, the audience, the recorders of the event). The communication refers to a *world* (the mythic-allegorical frame, the political and/or religious setting) in a specific *form* (a *Gesamtkunstwerk* of text, music, dance, dress design, stage effects, architecture).[64] Without the cooperation of the receiver, the communication process is mutilated, for the addressee bears a complementary function of interpreter. Obviously, a festive performance cannot take place if no one hears or observes its address.[65]

In spite of the general phrasing of the previous paragraphs, we must maintain a clear distinction between public festive celebrations and private splendid performances. The kind and degree of dialogic discourse that each form allowed differed substantially. In the public celebrations, the sponsor-ruler was present three-dimensionally, and he or she often participated actively, in which case the functions (in the Jakobsonian sense) assumed by the partners in the communication process were difficult to separate. In spite of the strict ceremonial that was rigorously observed, the communication was to a certain extent "open." Although class barriers were of course never truly lifted, in some forms the monarch joined the actor or the dancer on the stage; the actor became the substitute monarch for the duration of the feast; and the artist-technician (the architect or designer in particular), by virtue of his skill and talent, ruled over monarch and actor alike. Moreover, the symbolisms and the mythic relevance of public festivities, in the Renaissance as well as in the seventeenth century, still pertained to the entire polis. (In such a form as the royal Entry, it was even the polis who effectively addressed the visiting prince and expected a response, not the other way round.) And finally, the attendance and participation of the audiences was to a large extent voluntary. In sum, we can say that the public festive event, with all its technologies and allegories, constituted a genuine act of communication. For this sort of discourse, the rhetoric of persuasion and dissuasion was obviously most appropriate.

The situation was very different in the case of the private splendid performances, which were controlled by another model of discourse. As we have seen, in these festive forms the sponsor-ruler did not communicate directly with the carefully screened audience. (We might consider to what extent these audiences were truly "voluntary.") Numerous contemporaneous engravings or paintings, which preserve the memory of the splendid festive performances (given both indoors and outdoors) of the 1630s and later, serve as evidence.[66] Almost invariably, the sponsor-ruler sits in the center of the theater, bright lights illuminating him or her, and stiffly faces the performance.[67] The ruler's back is turned to the audience. The stage is perspectively arranged in perfect symmetry from the vantage point of the ruler, who serves as the fixed point of reference and presides and officiates over the clearly ordered world of organized play. (We will return in more detail to stage arrangements.) This is not the same as saying that the sponsor-ruler did not or could not communicate with the audience; but it followed from the standard arrangement described that the performers on stage served as interlocutors and intermediaries, delivering the ruler's message to the court over his or her head. In fact, on such occasions the audience saw the ruler simultaneously twice: first, represented larger than life frontally on the stage, and second, in his or her actual presence, from the back. Paradoxically, during the festive performance the living sponsor-ruler is an "image," a "function," whereas the "image" is "alive." Instead of a communication, there is a *communiqué* which rules out a creative response. The audience could merely interpret, admire and applaud, and all the stage techniques and machinery were directed to achieve precisely that response.[68]

Of the three types of rhetoric (forensic, deliberative, and epideictic) discussed by Aristotle in his *"Art" of Rhetoric*, the epideictic type obviously corresponds best to the requirements of the grandiose festive performance. To paraphrase Aristotle briefly: besides the blame of vice and the disgraceful, the subject of epideictic rhetoric is mainly the praise of virtue and nobility before an audience that does not need convincing and that already knows the "facts of the case" (Aristotle discusses at length what exactly constitutes "nobility").

Confronted with epideictic rhetoric, the audience is mainly asked to judge the ability of the speaker. The relative merit or demerit of the subject's actions that are being praised or blamed is usually not the issue, although the question of the subject's honorable behavior is an important one. It is also very important that the choice of subject be adapted to the particular audience. The criterion of epideictic rhetoric is beauty, and its principal argumentation is the figure of amplification (which implies the modes of hyperbole, repetition, metaphor, and qualification). This means that if the subject proper does not furnish the speaker with enough material for praise or blame, the comparison with other subjects affords ground for amplification.

The figure of amplification, with its appendant modes, was an extremely valuable tool in the praise of the absolute sponsor-ruler in the context of the splendid festive performances, especially because the programs of the latter were so deeply rooted in Neoplatonically inspired models of allegoresis. The subjects chosen for the literary program of Baroque splendid festive performances— whether they were drawn from mythic, sacred, or secular history— were allegorical and demanded to be interpreted in the light of the contemporaneous situation. Regardless of the particular source, the choice of subject almost invariably fell on unique characters of epic dimensions who had faced difficult tests and miraculously overcome personal and circumstantial limitations. These saints and heroes had ably demonstrated their ability to prove unequivocally that they had a vocation, that this vocation was authentic, and that they were entitled to superhuman status for successfully rising to their character. It is this central theme that the creators of Baroque festive performances—these allegorical celebrations of the person and the functions of the absolute sponsor-ruler—wished to enhance and asked the audience to recognize in the context of the specific performance. The participatory role of the audience in this rhetoric of the *communiqué* was primarily restricted to recognizing and applauding the allusions made in the literary program—allusions designed to reflect the contemporaneous claims and the recent achievements of the sponsor-ruler (Solf 27–32). This kind of activity partakes of the nature of ritual, in which one "lives through," "relives" or "performs" events of magnitude, the deeds of saints or heroes. In order to make these claims and achieve the audience's participation, the creators of festive performances called upon rhetorical principles. How they did this will be discussed in the next chapter.

Notes

1. See, for example, O. Cartellieri, *The Court of Burgundy* (London, 1929). On the role of the medieval heritage, see Roy Strong, *Art and Power:*

Renaissance Festivals 1450–1650 (London, 1973, 1984) 115ff. A very well illustrated survey of all forms of festive activity in Baroque Rome (but of which the conclusions and implications are relevant for other cities and regions as well), is Maurizio Fagiolo dell'Arco's two volume *L'effimero barocco: strutture della festa nella Roma del' 600* (with Silvia Carandini; Rome, 1977; all references are to vol. 2). I am much indebted to Strong and Fagiolo dell'Arco for the first section of this chapter.

2. The Italian princes were the first to attract professional musicians and composers to their courts. The first French monarch to imitate them was François I (1494–1547), an eager patron of the arts who contributed much to the development of the Renaissance in France. The numerous court balls and tournaments François—and his immediate successors—organized, were enlivened by professional musicians imported from Italy.

3. An example is offered by the grandiose festivities at the Vienna Congress of 1515. See Stephan Füssel, "Kaiserliche Repräsentation beim 'Wiener Kongress' 1515 im Spiegel der zeitgenössischen Darstellungen," in August Buck, et al., eds., 2: 359–68.

4. For example, for the funeral of Francesco de'Medici in Florence, the San Lorenzo church was transformed into a supernatural scene with gigantic silver skeletons (1634). On this type of celebration in Rome, see further Fagiolo dell'Arco 24–29. For France, see Ralph Giesey, *The Royal Funeral Ceremony in Renaissance France* (Geneva, 1960).

5. Strong 1973 provides a survey with examples of the royal Entry (7ff), as well as numerous primary and secondary sources (186–87). Among the early particularly splendid Entries were that of Johanna of Burgundy in Brussels (1496) and that of her son Charles V in Bruges (1514); the wealthy citizenry organized magnificent parades, replete with allegorical-symbolical *tableaux-vivants* based on biblical and classical material, to welcome their Habsburg rulers. In spite of the title of his book, Thomas E. Lawrenson includes pre-seventeenth-century royal Entries in France, in *The French Stage and Playhouse in the Seventeenth Century. A Study in the Advent of the Italian Order* (1957; New York, 1986) 60ff.

Seventeenth-century Entries were, if possible, even more splendid than they had been previously and the most successful artists contributed to these celebrations. For example, Rubens designed and directed the grandiose Entry of the Cardinal-Infante Ferdinand of Spain in Antwerp, 1635 (see M. Rooses, "L'entrée solemnelle du cardinal Infant Ferdinand à Anvers en 1635," in *L'Oeuvre de Rubens* [1886] 3: 292–336; the arches themselves are described in detail by Strong 1973: 49ff. Likewise, Arcimboldo designed festivals for Emperor Rudolf II (see Strong 1973: 143). One of the most famous Entries of the century was organized by Mazarin for Louis XIV and his bride Maria-

Theresa in Paris, on August 26, 1660. Its conventional features included the succession of triumphal arches (mostly fabricated from cardboard) replete with allegorical motifs. An unusual element was the crossing of the Notre Dame bridge, where Louis passed the medallions of his ancestors (and his own as well), thus symbolically entering History as the next member of the dynasty. Upon entering the Place Dauphine, the procession faced a view in which the laws of science (perspective) and the rules of allegoresis were combined: through Le Nôtre's magnificent triumphal arch, the statue of Henri IV could be seen standing far away on the Pont-Neuf. This was all very clever, but one is left to speculate how much the young French monarch would have understood these allegorical refinements, given his well-known lack of interest in books of any kind at this stage in his life. (For a further description of this 1660 Entry, see Jean-Marie Apostolidès, "L'entrée royale de Louis XIV," *L'Esprit Créateur* 25 [1] 1985: 21–31.) It is noteworthy that Abbé Michel de Pure dedicated to Louis XIV his extensive description of triumphal processions, entries, and other types of public celebrations: *Idée des spectacles anciens et nouveaux* (1668; Genève, 1972).

6. Aquatic festivals were continued, at least locally and sporadically, until well into the eighteenth century; for example, in 1756, one such festivity was performed on the Piazza Navona in Rome. See Giovanni Paolo Pannini's remarkably detailed oil painting of that event, as reproduced in Margarete Baur-Heinhold's wonderfully illustrated study *Theater des Barock: Festliches Bühnenspiele im 17. und 18. Jahrhundert* (Munich, 1966); trans. Mary Whittall, *Baroque Theatre* (London, 1967), monochrome plate 6. See Part 1 of de Pure's *Idée des spectacles anciens et nouveaux* for elaborate descriptions of circuses, amphitheaters, theaters, *naumachiae*, and triumphal entries.

7. Such was the case at the court of Sophie Elisabeth, Duchess of Braunschweig-Lüneburg, in the middle of the seventeenth century. See Hans-Gert Roloff, "Die höfischen Maskeraden der Sophie Elisabeth, Herzogin zu Braunschweig-Lüneburg," in August Buck, et al., eds., 3: 489–98.

8. For examples of such tournaments, see Strong 1973: 11–16; Strong calls them "mostly a northern festival form." An important contemporaneous French source for descriptions of such public occasions is Claude-François Menestrier, *Traité des tournois, joustes, carrousels et autres spectacles publics* (Lyon, 1669). Note that Menestrier calls all these forms "public." Interesting also is Charles Perrault, *Courses de testes et de bagues faites par le roi* (Paris, 1670). See also F. H. Cripps-Day, *The History of the Tournament in England and in France* (London, 1918), and Richard Barber, *The Knight and Chivalry* (London, 1970).

In *Homo Ludens*, Huizinga argues that the codes and practises of chivalry, as they were maintained for centuries in the Christian West, were mutations or remnants of initiation rites, which themselves originated in the serious sacred play of primeval times. It would therefore be possible to establish a (direct or indirect link) between this primeval form of sacred play and the allegorical Baroque court ballet, which was the successor of the Renaissance tournaments *à thème*. See further section 2 of the present chapter, and see also the Interlude.

9. For example, the tournament given in Munich on February 24, 1568, as part of the festivities for the wedding of Crown Prince Wilhelm of Bavaria and Princess Renata von Lothringen, featured participants in mock-exotic, pastoral or fake antique costumes and with animal masks (the full reference of Massimo Troiano's 1569 *relation* of this event is given by Klaus Lazarowicz, "Konzelebration oder Kollusion? Über die Feste der Wittelsbacher," in August Buck, et al., eds., 2: 301–17, 316 n. 3). Another famous actual mock-tournament, with much military display, was given in Dijon, 1656 (*Les Armes triomphantes*); it was concluded with a fireworks display. In his satirical novel *The Unfortunate Traveller, or, The Life of Jack Wilton* (1594), the English journalist Thomas Nashe provided a hilarious description of a fictional Florentine mock-joust (see also further).

10. In general, rulers of northern courts (Lorraine, Valois, England) seem to have begun participating personally in such celebrations earlier than in the south (Medici Florence), where the so-called *intermedi* remained mainly professional performances until the end of the sixteenth century (see Strong 1973: 141). Kivy defines *intermedi* as "the predominantly musical interpolations between the acts of Italian Renaissance dramas, which sometimes actually become unified enough in plot and character to achieve the status of 'play within a play.' These musical performances were truly musical theatre, both elaborate and sophisticated" (Peter Kivy, *Osmin's Rage: Philosophical Reflections on Opera, Drama, and Text* [Princeton, 1988] 23).

11. Fagiolo dell'Arco defines the elaborately constructed and decorated coach very aptly as "une vera forma simbolica del secolo dinamico e proiettato verso la comunicazione" ("a truly symbolic form of this dynamic century, projected [outward] toward communication"; 121).

12. See Baur-Heinhold, "The Courts" (9–32).

13. Cf. the *sophrosyne* inherent in Plato's Republic—or at least in Socrates' view of the ideal Republic as reported by Plato. See Mihai Spariosu, *God of Many Names: Play, Poetry and Power in Hellenic Thought from Homer to Aristotle* (Durham; London, 1991) 145. Arthur W.H. Adkins, in *Merit and Responsibility: A Study in Greek Values* (Oxford, 1960), defines *sophrosyne* as "the acknowledgement of the rulers that they should rule, of the defenders that they should defend, and of the rest that they should acquiesce" (288; reference from Spariosu 1991: 145).

14. Neoplatonism originated in Alexandria and Athens in the third century A.D. and was continued via the early centuries of Christianity and the Middle Ages straight into the Renaissance. I am much indebted to Strong 1973 (chapter 2: "Removed Mysteries"), and to Robert Donington, *The Rise of Opera* (New York, 1981) 21–39, for illustrative data given in this section.

15. Thus, Donington writes that the Neoplatonic view of art was that of "a veil which half reveals, in the very act of half concealing, deeper meanings than its surface shows," or, of something that is "outwardly enjoyable, inwardly suggestive" (21). All things visible suggest things invisible—but, it is understood, each visible thing represents many invisible things, for, at least prior to the eighteenth century, allegories were not designed to carry only one meaning, to be in effect a "decorative pictograph" (Ernst Hans Gombrich, *Symbolic Images: Studies in the Art of the Renaissance* [London, 1972] 123). From such a perspective, art can never be considered truly original, for only God creates *ex nihilo*. Myth and ritual were perceived as capable of suggesting deeper, inner meanings through their outer representations—the former, it was understood, being reserved for the initiates. Holy matters, it was thought, are couched in misleading symbols to prevent them from becoming easily accessible. This idea was Platonic in the sense that the emphasis was placed especially on the Idea, not on mimesis.

16. This idea also resulted at one time in the mistaken belief that Egyptian hieroglyphs, as visual images, were still very close to the original, higher world of Ideas and therefore were likely to contain prelapsarian wisdom. Hence for example the *Hieroglyphica* (1419; first printed 1505, and often reprinted during the sixteenth century), an emblem book attributed to "Hor Apollo," which generated emblematic representations by means of Egyptian symbols. But we must remember that for Plato himself, images made through art and perceived through the senses are very deceptive (see further Gombrich 1972: 146ff).

17. One reason for the success of the Humanist movement in Renaissance Italy was precisely that it had trained successive generations of aristocrats and gentlemen in the aesthetic and moral values of classical literature, thereby creating a potential audience and patronage for the writings of the Humanists themselves (Steadman 27). It must be added that, in the wake of the creative resurgence of Neoplatonic thought, the sixteenth and seventeenth centuries did not necessarily see Greco-Roman history-mythology as competing with the Judeo-Christian tradition. On the contrary, it was in the judicious combination of these two epistemological and historical-mythological systems that the sum of all knowledge was supposed to rest. Protests were occasionally raised in the Baroque era against the frequent use of pagan subjects to cross-refer to Christian ideas.

18. Thomas Nashe, *The Unfortunate Traveller and Other Works*, ed. J. B. Steane (Harmondsworth, 1985) 316–22 passim.

19. Boccaccio's *Genealogia deorum gentilium* (approx. 1350) was such a crucial document for Renaissance Neoplatonism. Reprinted many times in the sixteenth century, the *Genealogia* was a syncretic compendium of pagan symbols, deities and ideas not only Hellenic, but also Hellenistic, Egyptian and cabalistic in origin. According to Steadman, "Boccaccio went out of his way to denounce the superstitions of the Gentiles even while extolling the moral doctrines hidden under the veil of myth and allegory" (18). Regardless, the book was so successful partly because it served a need in that period when the ceremonial celebrations and festive performances were being developed as rhetorical concepts. Artists and philosophers could dabble in these matters on the ground of the simple but convincing excuse that such pagan elements serve not only to entertain but also to instruct and teach: the more one is initiated, the more one learns. Thus, in practical terms, the *Genealogia* was a sort of Neoplatonic bible for generations of artists; it informed them how to conceal truth (truth about the outer world and especially about inner man) in a fabulous and seemly covering. Another important manual that combined many sources, Egyptian and medieval, was Piero Valeriano's encyclopedic *Hieroglyphica sive de sacris Aegyptiorum aliarumque gentium literis* (1556; Strong 1973: 24 ff. discusses applications from Valeriano, for example, in the work of Ben Jonson). Cesare Ripa's eclectic *Iconologia* (1593) became perhaps the most frequently used encyclopedic codex of images and their allegorical meanings. Ripa's book documents how the great interest in Platonism was slowly waning by the late sixteenth century, with Aristotelian rhetorical principles in the ascendant. For example, the first two editions (1593, 1602) were not even illustrated, and even when illustrations appeared in the subsequent editions, these images remained subordinate to the text (see further Gombrich 1972: 143). A selection of entries from the *Iconologia* is available to the modern reader in a Dover edition (ed. Edward A. Maser; New York, 1971), which combines the illustrations of the famous 1758–60 Augsburg "Hertel" Ripa edition with extracts from Ripa's own explanations and Maser's commentaries drawn from various sources. Though not truly scholarly, this Dover edition is a beautiful and fascinating compendium of several centuries' worth of iconography. Other important manuals were Scipione Bargagli's *La prima Parte dell'Imprese* (Siena, 1578), Henri Estienne's *The Art of Making Devices* (trans. T. Blunt; London, 1646), and Père le Moine's *De l'Art des devises* (Paris, 1666).

Iconologists such as Ernst Hans Gombrich and Erwin Panofsky (*Studies in Iconology: Humanist Themes in the Art of the Renaissance* [London; New York, 1939]) have shown that the visual images contained in the manuals mentioned were designed to be translated by the beholder: the greater one's familiarity with the codex, the more meanings (half revealed, half concealed) one could gather. This ideology relates to the fact that abstraction had become more important in the theory of artistic mimesis since the late sixteenth century. The artist's task was not to represent an object realistically and for its own sake, but rather to execute such a representation for the sake of an "idea," an "essence"—for example, to express a person's movement in such a way that the rationale for the movement is clearly the real issue, or a facial expression in such fashion that the psychic reason for that expression is suggested. Ignoring more or less the mere imitation of externally visible meanings, the Neoplatonic aesthetic served the idea that "art" is not a carrier of a single meaning with validity only in our outer world, but rather a sacred object that contains many levels of interpretation and many symbolisms. Regardless of its value, this conception of art did help to keep pagan mythology and the habit of personification alive, and it was able to preserve the mythopoeic faculty at least until well into the seventeenth century. By that time, aesthetics (in the modern, philosophical sense) began to replace mythopoeia and an awareness of definable beauty was substituted for the sense of mystery (Gombrich 1972: 123–24). For a survey of the practical influence of the manuals on the various arts, see J. Seznec, *The Survival of the Pagan Gods* (1940; New York, 1953) 279–326.

Incidentally: in literature, Neoplatonism seems to have especially affected the pastoral "mode"—perhaps because the pastoral was originally linked to Orpheus, whom the Florentine Neoplatonists considered a kind of proto-Neoplatonist by anticipation. See further Harry Levin, *The Myth of the Golden Age in the Renaissance* (Oxford, 1969) 107ff; and Donington 47.

20. See Hélène Leclerc's essay, "Du Mythe platonicien aux fêtes de la Renaissance: 'L'Harmonie du Monde,' Incantation et Symbolisme," *Revue d'Histoire du Théâtre* 11 (1959): 109–71.

21. On the topos of "Nature as a book," see Ernst Robert Curtius, *European Literature and the Latin Middle Ages*, trans. W. Trask (Princeton, 1953) 319–25.

22. The abundant use made of exotic costumes in such celebrations can thus be explained. Numerous illustrations can be found in Baur-Heinhold, passim.

23. The infinite, the dynamic, the new concept of space were all crucial notions that were first suggested by developments in the budding natural and physical sciences and that greatly contributed to the notion of instability characterizing the Baroque as a historical period and an artistic style and movement. Since the sixteenth century, science had mainly occupied itself with "breaking the circle," with opening up and decentering the universe (the phrase, as applied by Maiorino 3, was taken from Marjorie H. Nicholson's

The Breaking of the Circle: Studies in the Effect of the "New Science" Upon Seventeenth-Century Poetry [1960]). Copernicus had attempted to end geocentrism, and in *De Immenso et Innumerabilis* (1590), Giordano Bruno had argued for the infinite universe (for which he was consequently arrested by the Inquisition in 1593 and burnt in 1600) which Galileo's telescope had served to prove.

Briefly, this age saw the hesitant transition from superstition and allegoresis to science. I will merely refer to Michel Foucault's (arguably problematic) *Les Mots et les Choses* (1966), in which he essentially argues that toward the middle of the seventeenth century a new episteme was introduced, a new order of understanding by means of discrimination and classification, which put itself squarely against the old way of interpretation which, so Foucault claims, worked by means of analogy, or interpretation through resemblance or identity. In other words, by the middle of the seventeenth century, the inquiring mind starts to separate things instead of drawing them together. A study that in some ways parallels Foucault's but which is more rewarding in our present discussion is Svetlana Alpers' *The Art of Describing: Dutch Art in the Seventeenth Century* (Chicago, 1983).

Not entirely unlike Foucault, Alpers discerns in the middle decades of the century a phase of transition between two modes of scientific thought, two syntagmata. Slowly on the way out was the system that Alpers calls "textual," which contained everything related to the so-called Italian order of thought. In this rhetorical system, which favored text-based scholarship related to the abstract sciences (the mathematical) as well as to Christian Humanism (the symbolic, the allegorical), "new knowledge" was to be gained primarily through disposition and elocution—working with existing textual or iconographic material—rather than through invention. The Neoplatonic system, as applied to the celebratory occasions we have been discussing, is directly aligned with what Alpers calls the "textual" or "Italian" or "rhetorical" syntagmata. In the middle decades of the century—which was, perhaps not incidentally, the period when the most grandiose festive performances were staged at absolutist courts—a new system was already making an impact on inquiring minds, and primarily so in northern European middle-class cultures—those that were least predisposed to hosting grand celebrations of the types described. This new syntagmata was "visual" (Alper's word) rather than "textual," and it was related to the Anglo-Dutch order of thought as exemplified by the work of such men as Hooke (*Micrographia*, 1664), Bacon, Huygens, Leeuwenhoek, and Comenius (*Orbis Sensualium Pictus*, 1685, the first illustrated schoolbook). This new system favored the world in which seeing is believing, as well as techniques related to the applied sciences—observation, empiricism, the need to visualize—and craftsmanship, rather than genteel scholarship. It was in the context of this system that Kepler theorized the relativity of vision and conceived a system of ellipses rather than circles in order to understand the cosmic machine. Indeed, the northern

European scientists, professionals as well as amateurs, did not need Archimedean levers and stable points to lift and decenter the earth and even the cosmos itself, but only thin, curved glass lenses. A drop of water from a canal or a river was revealed to contain an entire world, and Earth was discovered to be moving with unimaginable speed through an immeasurable cosmos. What, then, was humankind's position relative to the great and the small? Or that of the microcosm to the macrocosm?

These discoveries were of course known throughout the Continent, and the psychological effects thereof on educated, sensitive people must have been staggering. In view of this universal instability, the completion of any project must henceforth have seemed impossible if not altogether irrelevant. (See Thomas S. Kuhn, *The Copernican Revolution: Planetary Astronomy in the Development of Western Thought* [Cambridge, 1966].) Thus, completed works became somehow suspect; stable forms that incorporate or represent stasis were avoided; and calm emptiness was scrutinized as a freak of nature; it is, incidentally, for this reason, and with the benefit of hindsight, that the Baroque has been defined as a *Stil des Werdens* (Becoming) rather than as a *Stil des Seins* (Being) (Weisbach, in Maiorino 2).

I would argue in this context that the arrangements of the festivities may be seen as the aristocracy's way of countering this sort of self-reflexivity that can—and did in documented and literary cases—lead to scepticism and despair in the seventeenth century. For in spite of all the "movement" that is involved in their production, the ritualized abundance of the festive celebrations and, later, of the splendid performances, emphasizes first and foremost a comforting stability, embodied first in the spirit of the celebrating community, and increasingly, in the patriarchal (or occasionally matriarchal) figure of the absolute ruler. The new scientifically derived concepts and techniques were incorporated in the old patterns of thought and imagination in an attempt to conquer them and render them harmless. Yet, the cult of the "god(dess) of play" was not an anodyne, as I hope to demonstrate further, but a serious political undertaking.

24. "It is absolutely necessary that there be a design, a principal point, a mysterious knot [or node] which, in some or other fashion relates so precisely to the subject and connects in such a natural way all the elements that constitute it, that [this design] could not possibly be applied to any other subject than the one for which it was intended. This point can be historical and real, or allegorical."

Note the similarity to Aristotle's description of a good tragic plot, from which no elements can be deleted or changed position without damage being done to the whole (*Poetics* VIII).

25. See Silvia Carandini, "La festa barocca a Roma," *Biblioteca teatrale* 15–16 (1976): 276–308, 276ff.

26. See Isabel Rivers, *Classical and Christian Ideas in English Renaissance Poetry* (London, 1979), chapter 13: "Numerology"). The application of such learned theories represented a drastic sophistication of the popular dances, which were, after all, a source from which the aristocratic ballets were derived. For example, a Poitou country dance was the origin of the minuet, which became the most royal dance of all, and which conquered, via Versailles, all of civilized Europe.

27. See Jean-Marie Apostolidès, *Le Roi-Machine: Spectacle et politique au temps de Louis XIV* (Paris, 1981) 42–3; see also further, chapter 5.

28. It is probably exaggerated to claim that every observer or participant was a card-carrying Neoplatonist who claimed that outward action or outward representation must be understood first in its inner meaning before it can truly have an impact. To many (or most), the festive celebration must simply have been enjoyable for its "outward" effects. This includes courtly audiences as well; the degree of intellectual cultivation of the majority of these audiences should not be overestimated; obviously, only the brightest or otherwise most interesting minds of the period have addressed us with their work across the centuries. By contrast, even although most courtiers and aristocrats could probably speak and read a few languages, they were not necessarily very well read beyond the classics, and probably had not much general knowledge. Indeed, "the organizers [of especially complex events] could not possibly hope anybody but themselves to understand all of [the equipment of properties and symbols] . . . e.g., the learned allusions or costumes, cars etc., all of which were not static but only there for a fleeting moment" (Gombrich 1972: 176). After all, the Abbé Menestrier needed no fewer than nineteen folio pages to explain all the allegories he had crammed into a single triumphal arch of his own design on the occasion of the entry of the grandson of Louis XIV into the city of Grenoble; see Richard Alewyn and Karl Sälzle, *Das grosse Welttheater: Die Epoche der höfischen Feste in Dokument und Deutung* (Hamburg, 1959) 21. Ben Jonson, who made it quite clear that the true meaning and beauty of his entertainments and masques were deliberately reserved for an elite audience (see Stephen Orgel and Roy Strong, *Inigo Jones: The Theatre of the Stuart Court* [London: 1973] vol. 1: 105–14), was criticized for that very reason. Strong (1973: 27) records contemporaneous criticism of the allegorical complexities of Jonson's "Haddington Masque" (1608) and of Vicenzo Borghini's "Genealogia degli Dei" (1565–66).

29. For example, a week before the grand Entry of Louis XIV and Maria Theresa in Paris, the citizens could purchase booklets in which the itinerary of the procession was outlined and the allegories of the triumphal arches were explained. See Marie-Christine Moine, *Les Fêtes à la Cour du Roi Soleil 1653–1715* (Paris: 1984) 14.

30. See Victor Turner, *From Ritual to Theater: The Human Seriousness of Play* (New York, 1982) 84.

31. See for example, the evolution of the Medici festival books, in Cesare Molinari, "Delle Nozze medicee e dei loro cronisti," *Il Teatro dei Medici. Quaderni di Teatro* 2 (7) 1980: 23–30. For similar sources on other celebrations see many references in Strong 1973, for example, 210. For visual information I refer to Baur-Heinhold, like Strong 1973 a veritable treasure-trove.

32. For a good example, see the poet Wekherlin's description of celebrations in Stuttgart, 1616, given by Christian Wagenknecht in "Die Beschreibung höfischer Feste: Merkmale einer Gattung," in August Buck, et al., eds., 2: 75–80).

33. Some of these new forms, along with previous types, were described in detail by Michel de Pure in the second part of his *Idée des spectacles anciens et nouveaux* (1668).

34. Occasional examples of earlier private celebrations in specifically reserved or created environments can of course be found. Strong 1973: 36–37 lists as one of the earliest the "Festa del Paradiso," which was staged for the marriage of Isabella of Aragon at the Sforza court of Milan in 1490.

35. "[A] mute representation, in which the gestures and the movements signify what one might express by means of words . . . this entertainment is intended almost exclusively for the eyes."

De Pure claims that he is only the first author to discuss "les Lois du Balet" (214). Eager to make up for the lacuna, he devotes more than one third of his entire book to it (Chapter 11: 209–318); by contrast, he only spends forty pages on "comedie," "bal," "feux de ioye," "ioustes," "courses de bagues et de testes," "carozels," "mascarade," and "exercices ou reveües [militaires]" combined under the general heading "Spectacles nouveaux." The length of his "balet" section is a good indication of the relative importance of the ballet at the French court since the late sixteenth and throughout the seventeenth century. After a brief discussion of the etymology of the word and its present definitions, he treats the following topics: subject and title; the composition in parts, entries, and *liaisons*; steps and figures; appropriate types of music, sung *récits*, and instruments; the skills required of the dancers, and suitable costumes and masks; parts in verse; the introduction of machines; and the differences between fixed and mobile theaters for the spectacle.

Ingrid Brainard supplies many interesting facts on dances and ballets, and especially on the distinction between the "artistic performance" dance and the "participation-ballroom" dance: "Der Höfische Tanz. Darstellende Kunst und Höfische Repräsentation," in August Buck, et al., eds., 2: 379–94, 387–8. See further references to the ballet in my chapter 5.

36. The change in taste from tournament to *ballet de cour* can be noted in Mme de Lafayette's *La Princesse de Clèves* (1678). This "historical" novel is set mainly in the reign of Henri II and describes how that monarch died as the result of an eye injury incurred in a tournament (1559). More than a century after the death of Henri II, it had become inconceivable for Louis XIV to expose himself to serious physical danger for the sole purpose of play. Instead, the highly stylized, symbolic ballet form offered him the chance to excel in the execution of elegant, quasi-ritualistic dance patterns. A similar change in role affected the courtiers, who, from chivalric knights, became courtly cavaliers. Thus, although the taste for the tournament *à thème* had certainly not died out in the seventeenth century, it had mutated.

37. Quotations are from Balthazar de Beaujoyeux, *Le Ballet-Comique de la Reine* [sic] Chefs-d'Oeuvre Classiques de l'Opéra Français 1 (New York, [s.d.]).

38. "And if someone must soon triumph over me,/ It will be this King of the French, and you will have to yield to him,/ Just as I yield to him, the heavens that you rule."

39. Specifically on the *Balet comique de la Reyne*, see further Rousset 1954 (chapter 1). Donington summarizes contemporaneous explications of the allegories expressed in the program of this ballet (58–61).

40. A first-rate source on the masque is still *Twentieth-Century Criticism of the English Masques, Pageants and Entertainments: 1558–1642*, ed. David M. Bergeron (San Antonio, Texas, 1972). In his chapter "Illusions of Absolutism," Strong 1973 discusses Stuart court masques; many sources are listed on pp. 211–12.

In spite of the grandiose ceremonial in which they were encapsulated, the festivities that we have been discussing were not always "dignified" in our modern, middle-class sense. A case in point, famous but probably not unique, was the masque presented at the court of James I in the honor of King Christian IV of Denmark. On this occasion the performing courtiers were even more inebriated than they were, apparently, on other occasions. The ladies representing Hope, Faith and the Queen of Sheba were so drunk that they fell down on their Royal Highnesses and were violently sick in the hall; only Charity could more or less hold up her role (Robert Ashton, *James I by his Contemporaries* [London, 1969]; reported by Ronald D. S. Jack, "James VI and I as Patron," in August Buck, et al., eds., 2: 179–85, 184).

41. Caspar Stieler's six "Rudolstadt Festspiele," written and performed between 1665 and 1667, provide very good examples of this genre. See chapter 4 in Judith Aikin, *Scaramutza in Germany: The Dramatic Works of Caspar Stieler* (University Park; London, 1989) 17–54.

42. Harold Martin Priest, trans., *Adonis: Selections from "L'Adone" of Giambattista Marino* (Ithaca, 1967) 90–91. Priest also provides an excellent introduction to Marino and his extraordinarily long epic poem. All the translated phrases from *L'Adone* that follow are from Priest.

43. See Harold M. Priest, "Marino, Leonardo, Francini, and the Revolving Stage," *Renaissance Quarterly* 35 (1) 1982: 36–60; and Susanna Peters Coy, "The Theatre and the Stage of Marino's 'Adone:' Canto V," *Modern Language Notes* 98 (1) 1983: 87–110.

44. These dates are merely indicative. Indeed, some students of this subject argue that the private performances reached their most opulent forms and acquired their most magnificent dimensions only toward the end of the century or, in eastern Europe, even at the beginning of the eighteenth century. See Baur-Heinhold 9, but compare Trevor-Roper 22. In his excellent study of "Renaissance Festivals, *1450–1650*" (my emphasis on the dates), Strong 1973 does not mention these grandiose festive performances among the festival forms with which "art and power" were celebrated.

45. Remarkably, though, the architectural details of the permanent sites of private performances were often heavily influenced by the conventions of the structures designed for the celebration of ephemeral festive events—mainly floats, triumphal cars and arches.

46. Few grandiose festive performances were organized at the English court in those years, as compared to the activity on the Continent. At the heyday of the Baroque, the court of Charles II Stuart did not even have the theatrical facilities that would have made such performances possible. The "Cockpit at Court" in Whitehall, which was called from 1665 onward the "Hall Theatre," was "just a stage and auditorium modestly equipped for plays to be performed by amateur courtier actors or by professional players by royal command" (Peter Skrine, "Court and Theatre in Restoration England," in August Buck, et al., eds., 2: 329–34, 330). By contrast, many a ruler of a petty German or Italian principality could boast a well-equipped theater. And the Polish House of Wasa (the Wasas ruled Poland from 1587 until 1668) knew a very active theatrical (especially operatic) life throughout the 1640s (see Władisław Czapliński, "Das Theater am Hofe des polnischen Wasas," in August Buck, et al., eds., 2: 295–300).

47. In exceptional cases, the rhetoric was purposefully not designed to praise. Perhaps the most poignant case was the Entry of the Cardinal Archduke Ferdinand in Antwerp, 1635. Several arches commissioned by the city and designed by Rubens indirectly criticised the Archduke and his brother King Philip IV, by presenting a gloomy picture of the city's present and future situation as a result of the blockade of the river Scheldt and of

trade embargos imposed by Philip. (The arches are described in detail by Strong 1973: 49ff.)

48. I acknowledge my great debt to Gérard LeCoat in this section; he is an excellent guide for this matter. An important account of the influence of rhetoric on *music* in the period under examination is Brian Vickers' essay "Figures of rhetoric/Figures of music?" *Rhetorica* 2 (1) 1984: 1–44 (see also further).

It is relevant to note that Humanist art critics translated the values of the *figurative* work of art into the values of the *literary* work: forms were like nouns, compositions like verbs, color like adjectives, and all these aspects were called upon to contribute to the imitation and expression (Giulio Carlo Argan, "La 'Rettorica' e l'arte barocca," in Enrico Castelli, ed. *Retorica e Barocco. Atti del III Congresso Internazionale di Studi Umanistici, Venezia 6/1954* [Rome, 1955] 9–14, 10). One might wonder, hence, if the notion of "poesis" in the traditional tandem "pictura/poesis" did not simply acquire the meaning of "eloquence" at this point. This suggestion requires further explanation. In *De Pictura* (1435; trans. C. Grayson, *On Painting* [Harmondsworth, 1991]), the *cinquecento* theoretician Leon Battista Alberti did advocate a style of narrative painting in which the artist emphasized the natural imitation of human passions and actions by means of motion and in order to move the spectator's affections. And in his *Trattato*, Leonardo da Vinci, too, claimed that painted figures are only praiseworthy if they actually express the emotion they are supposed to feel. (Leonardo's *Trattato*, or "Treatise on Painting," a collection of notes in Italian and French, dates from 1498; it was widely known before its publication in 1651. See Leonardo's *Libro di pittura*. Facs. ed. [Princeton, 1956] fol. 17; reference from LeCoat 14). Leonardo in effect advocated a rhetorical approach to art as well as to science when he emphasized the necessity of a precise sequence of steps in order to proceed toward experience.

49. Rhetoric, being a means of persuasion, dissuasion, praise or blame, obviously does not present itself primarily as a tool for exploring new knowledge and conducting speculative research. This function was best filled by a different epistemological tradition: dialectic, which was destined to become the most precious instrument of a later period and a different intellectual movement. Although the Baroque sensibility turned first and foremost to rhetoric, dialectic was by no means nonexistent in the seventeenth century. For this reason I would hestitate to subscribe to the dualism that is sometimes perceived to have existed between "la voie spéculative—qui mène au Classique—et la voie oratoire—qui est le Baroque" ("the speculative way—which leads to Classicism—and the oratorical way—which is the Baroque;" Francastel, in Castelli ed., 59).

50. Aristotle, *"Art" of Rhetoric*, trans. J. H. Freese (1926; Cambridge; London, 1982) I: 1355a-1368a passim (Loeb edition).

51. Witness Vasari (1565) and Buontalenti (1589), who were the first "mannerists" to occupy themselves seriously with scenography and the organization of feasts and performances as events to be interpreted allegorically (see Hans Tintelnot, "Annotazioni sull'importanza della festa teatrale per la vita artistica e dinastica nel Barocco," in Castelli ed., 233–41, 236; see also Fagiolo dell'Arco, passim, who has much interesting information on Bernini in this role).

52. The major exception to the rule of exclusion was the fireworks display, often the climax of a grandiose festive celebration, which the organizers of the feasts, whether they liked it or not, could not prevent the commoners on the other side of the gates and fences from enjoying. The magnificent fireworks displays at Versailles are best known, but spectacular displays were held everywhere, in London as well (the Royal Fireworks). For example, in Dresden, 1665, a series of feasts was concluded with a firework display representing, ironically enough, the scriptural parable of the rich man and poor Lazarus. A famous handbook for pyrotechnical displays was Vannuccio Biringuccio's *Li diece libri della Pirotechnia*, 1540; Fagiolo dell'Arco 389. While it is true that occasionally the general public was admitted to the private setting for a repeat performance of the festive event (as in the Retiro), this practice in fact emphasized the "exclusivity," for it fostered the keen awareness that only the "première" really "counted" and had "sacred value"—if only because the sponsor-ruler was present on that occasion only. Duplications of successful "sacred play," even when very "faithful," never have the same power as the first enactment, the "première," which is unique precisely because it can never be repeated.

53. These new arrangements, which constitute the so-called "Italian order," will be discussed further on (see also Lawrenson 1986). The earliest experiments with illusionistic design and a single vantage point probably date from 1586 and 1589, at the Medici *intermedi* in Florence (see Strong 1973: 140, and see further in the present chapter).

54. ". . . an impatient culture; it cannot wait." For a brief but very interesting presentation of the alternative, *anti-courtly* Baroque attitude, see Erika A. Metzger and Michael M. Metzger, "Courtly and Anticourtly Literature," in Gerhart Hoffmeister, ed., *German Baroque Literature: The European Perspective* (New York, 1983), 250–69.

55. Let me repeat that the sponsor-ruler remained on display also in the "public" festive events, which continued throughout the century as they had in the Renaissance. For example, at several Roman carnivals in the 1660s, the

Barberini had Christina of Sweden sit by their side in a prominent box to watch equestrian ballets and other events on the Piazza di S. Marco and the Corso. Moreover, as we have seen, the ruler and his or her circle continued to participate in some events: dancing, hunting, acting. But most of these occasions were private and cannot be compared to the splendid festive performance with its principal literary-visual program (such as we find it in the feast opera or machine play), which is the subject of this study. It is significant that Louis XIV refrained from personally participating in the ballets from 1670 onward.

56. Nicola Sabbattini, from chapter 4 of *Pratica di fabricar scene e machine ne' teatri* (Ravenna, 1637–38); quoted in translation by Baur-Heinhold 36.

57. If the grandiose festive performance was part of an event which must be studied in its entirety (arguably, such study was even part of the program of the event itself), then the Baroque festive performance may perhaps also be called a "chronotope," in the sense developed by Bakhtin ("Forms of Time and of the Chronotope in the Novel," in *The Dialogic Imagination. Four Essays*, ed. M. Holquist, trans. C. Emerson and M. Holquist [Austin, 1981] 84–258) for its power of revealing the "intrinsic connectedness of temporal and spatial relationships that are artistically expressed" in a total work of art (suggested by Maiorino 84). See also Hans-Georg Gadamer, "Play as the Clue to Ontological Explanation," in *Truth and Method*, trans. Joel Weinsheimer and Donald G. Marshall (New York, 2nd. rev. edition 1989; all following references to Gadamer are to this edition/translation and are reprinted here with permission from the (c) Crossroad Publishing Company): "The performance of a play, like that of a ritual, cannot simply be detached from the play itself, as if it were something that is not part of its essential being, but is as subjective and fluid as the aesthetic experiences in which it is experienced. Rather, it is in the performance and only in it—as we see most clearly in the case of music—that we encounter the work itself, as the divine is encountered in the religious rite . . . The work of art cannot simply be isolated from the 'contingency' of the chance conditions in which it appears, and where this kind of isolation occurs, the result is an abstraction that reduces the actual being of the work" (116). Gadamer actually goes so far as saying that a work of art is "play" when "its actual being cannot be detached from its presentation and that in this presentation the unity and identity of a structure emerge" (122). This statement relates well to my view, to be developed in the Interlude, that the grandiose festive performance is a celebration of the cult of the sponsor-absolute ruler, the "god of play."

58. Francis L. Lawrence, *Molière: The Comedy of Unreason* (New Orleans, 1968) 14.

59. Renaissance documents testify to this interpretation. See e.g. Book 6 of Lorenzo's *Trattato*, as given by Gombrich 1972: 7.

60. The same is true for *imprese*; for example, the figure of Hercules changes meaning according to the context or the specific book in which he appears. For an interesting study on the subject, see Sebastian Neumeister, "Höfische Pragmatik. Zu Baltasar Graciáns Ideal des 'Discreto'," in August Buck, et al., eds., 2: 51–60.

61. "the Baroque person [. . .] as ceremonial figure is turned into [. . .] an objective constitutive ingredient of the background, an implied, necessary actor in the "periphery." Sabine Solf, *Festdekoration und Groteske. Der wiener Bühnenbilder Lodovico Ottavio Burnacini: Inszenierung Barocker Kunstvorstellung* (Baden-Baden, 1975) 29.

62. Baroque writers explicitly demanded such a participation—which helps to suggest that for the Baroque artist, the work of art was open-ended and could never be finished since new meanings were always to be found. If the audience was indeed an active participant, we must speak of Baroque art as being rhetorical. (For a thoughtful development of this idea, see Maiorino 98.)

63. For Bakhtin "[a] word, discourse, language or culture undergoes 'dialogization' when it becomes relativized, de-privileged, aware of competing definitions for the same things. Undialogized language is authoritative or absolute" (*The Dialogic Imagination* 427). My use of the term is thus practically the reverse of Bakhtin's, for it implies the installation and affirmation, rather than the subversion, of power.

64. This model is adapted from Roman Jakobson's model of communication as set forth in his essay "Linguistics and Poetics," in T. A. Sebeok, ed., *Style in Language* (Cambridge, Mass., 1960) 350–58.

65. For instance, Lazarowicz speaks of the "latente Formen" by means of which an (or any) audience must participate in the discourse of a (or any) performance for the performance to exist: the sensory, imaginative, and cognitive acts that, together, constitute the audience's engagement in the presentation (Lazarowicz, in August Buck, et al., eds., 2: 313).

66. Manifestations of the phenomenon that is described in this paragraph had occasionally occurred previously, especially in Medici Florence.

67. See the evidence of many contemporaneous illustrations in Baur-Heinhold (11, 15, 123, 124, 129, 164, ff.).

68. At this point, I merely want to raise the question whether the successful development of the perspective stage for grandiose performances

(the so-called "Italian order") was the cause *or* the result of the fact that the sponsor-ruler no longer wished to be on display. Perhaps the question is not very pressing, yet the fact remains that the period of unchallenged domination of perspective stage architecture (with a single vantage point) from the early 1630s onward coincided with the gradual withdrawal of the sponsor-ruler as active participant and with the great success of the private performances (machine play, opera). For the *communiqué* that the private festive performance had become, the only possible rhetoric was the rhetoric of praise: the epideictic type. I refer again to Marin's *Portrait of the King*, a difficult but very rewarding discussion of epideictic strategies in forms of discourse used to address Louis XIV.

2

RHETORIC AND BAROQUE FESTIVE PERFORMANCES

Rhetoric and Festive Performances

As we set out to apply concepts of traditional rhetorical discourse to the splendid festive performances at Baroque courts, it is useful to remember, first, that rhetoric has no subject proper but serves all possible subjects and, second, that ancient theory, which was crucial to the Renaissance and the Baroque, did not firmly separate "rhetoric" from "art."[1] No less than the *cinquecento*, the Baroque sensibility was fascinated by the interaction of the theory and practice of the various modes of expression, and was therefore very receptive to theories of rhetoric and their practical applications. Since antiquity, rhetoric had never ceased to be a fundamental part of a good education—and a solid Humanistic education was almost a necessity for artists to succeed in the world of patronage in the sixteenth and the seventeenth centuries.[2] In the Baroque period, Aristotle's *"Art" of Rhetoric* actually became a more influential textbook than his *Poetic*.[3] Likewise, Cicero's *De Oratore* and Quintilian's *Institutiones* both exercized an enormous influence (see Vickers 4). It is not accidental that, at least on the Continent, the many rhetorical manuals of the time were produced mainly by Jesuits. When Aristotle's rhetoric officially became part of the Jesuit curriculum in the wake of the Counter Reformation, it was thus immediately in a position to affect, directly or indirectly, the lives and mentality of a sizable portion of the European population—and not only its intelligentsia. The basic manual in Jesuit schools (and, presumably, elsewhere), was P. Cipriano Soarez' *De arte rhetorica libri tres ex Aristotele Cicerone et Quintiliano deprompti*, a practical anthology aimed at mastering the techniques of composition and delivery.[4]

In the Baroque period, rhetorical strategies permeated all aspects of the arts and intersected with societal and cultural strategies. Worldly and spiritual authorities and their spokesmen easily found specific applications for the conventional purposes of rhetoric: to convince, to persuade, to praise and to blame. This particular historical context afforded much practical use for rhetorical strategies and oratorical skills, which did not remain limited to the spoken or written word, but which could be, and were, transferred to all available media: print, painting, music, architecture, dance, clothing, gesticulation. For example, as early as the sixteenth century, theorists of literature (Daniello, Tasso), of the visual arts (Dolce, Lomazzo) and of music (Zarlino) had seemingly effortlessly adapted conventional rhetorical schemes for constructing a discourse for their respective fields. Rhetoric was thus a practical art, a *ciencia usual*, to be acquired in school as well as through practice. It was thought that, with some adaptations, the general rules for an effective discourse could be applied toward the creation of an effective work of art, be it a poem, a painting, or a musical composition, a festive celebration, and even an effective mode of personal conduct at court (LeCoat 30ff).

Since we are dealing in this study with a complex art form devised by and for courtiers, the latter point merits some attention. Indeed, in the courtly-political discourse of the sixteenth and seventeenth centuries, the courtier could even be seen as a rhetorical figure in the flesh: more specifically, as a metaphor, given the fact that one's main strategy for survival and success at court was *dissimulatio*, the translation and representation of one's natural character into the required forms and accidents of rigidly structured court life. It was a commonplace that one changed one's nature when at court.[5] Courtiers were expected to control themselves under any circumstances, and to apply to any given situation the correct expressions or gestures they had gradually acquired and codified—much as they had been taught at school to accumulate collections of topoi or commonplaces for use in polite conversation or in letters. The courtier was a breathing work of art! Interestingly, connections have also been pointed out between characteristic verbal and stylistic elements of Renaissance and Baroque court poetry on the one hand, and the courtier-poet's dissimulating role-playing or stylized self-metaphorizing in the context of model courtliness on the other. Thus, in his *Arte of English Poesie* (1589), the Elizabethan Puttenham had already argued that

> writing poetry can be an extension of good courtiership since many of the poet's characteristic figurative devices give him the opportunity to display the graceful indirection and subterfuge so admired in proper court conduct.[6]

The relevance of the subject is further suggested by the discussion throughout the Baroque period of the concept of the *honnête homme*. This concept was derived from Castiglione's *cortegiano*, gradually blended with ideas from Jansenism, *préciosité* and neo-Epicureanism, and ultimately proposed as a modern alternative to the type of the Machiavellian courtier.[7]

But let us begin by considering the conventional rhetorical scheme for linguistic discourse proper as it entered the Baroque. Usually five stages were distinguished in the proper construction of such discourse: (1) invention (*heuresis*, which implies finding the theme and its most efficient arguments, and which requires creative power (*ingenium*); (2) disposition (*taxis*), which depends on the faculty of judgment (*iudicium*), and which concerns itself with arranging the parts of the discourse (exordium, narration, confirmation, digression, epilogue) in the most efficient order for the task of teaching, pleasing, and moving to the best advantage; (3) elocution (*lexis*), which is the process of giving the discourse the most appropriate style and choosing the most appropriate words, figures and tropes; (4) memory, which is learning the text and its most suitable performance aspects by heart; and (5) action (or, aptly in Greek, *hypocrisis*), which is the rehearsal of all of the above and its concrete execution in front of an audience. (Thus the adroit courtier was, literally in the rhetorical sense, a hypocrite.) Appended mainly to the phase of elocution was a theory of styles that became increasingly complex. Originally, this theory was derived from Cicero's three *genera dicendi* (manners of saying): the *genus grande* (the high style, corresponding to elevated subjects), the *genus medium* (about which Cicero has not much to say), and the *genus tenue* (the low style) (see also Steadman, chapter 2). Cicero's limited and rigid scheme was made more flexible in the second century by Hermogenes, who presented in his *Peri Ideon* ("On Ideas") no fewer than seven "ideas" with an appropriate style for each.

In his second chapter, LeCoat demonstrates in great detail precisely how these antique schemes were not only incorporated in Renaissance and Baroque thought but were also adapted to the arts of poetry, music, and painting, which, therefore, can be said to have developed under the aegis of rules developed specifically for the Word.[8] For example, the poet Tasso, the musical theoreticians Mei and Mersenne, and the painter Poussin each made versions appropriate to their own medium.[9] And Monteverdi added to the two existing levels of musical discourse (*molle*, or soft, and *temperato*, moderate) a third, higher level of his own invention, *concitato* (agitated), specifically suited for the representation of epic (battle and heroic) scenes.[10] The more complex stylistic schemes that resulted from these efforts stimulated artists in various media to create gradually a wider range of expressions of ideas and affects, and therefore encouraged the invention (*heuresis*) of creative approaches to the judicious rearrangement and presentation (disposition and elocution) of existing matter, which remained to sixteenth- and seventeenth-century artists and interpreters of rhetoric (the distinction is not always clearcut) the most important phase in the creation of a work of art. Thus new methods could become available to affect the passions and the ethos of the audience appropriately and effectively, by means of the useful and beautiful objects which the artist-craftsman could forge from some existing material. Tasso and Poussin were among many who subscribed to the view that any old subject matter could generate new interest, as long as it was presented in a way that revealed the excellence and *ingenium* of the artist (LeCoat 33).

We recall that the subjects chosen for the festive celebrations and the splendid performances were almost never original at the base—they were drawn from mythic fables, or from secular and sacred history. What mattered was not suspense or plot denouement, but rather the most appropriate presentation of the generally known material and the twist given to it by the genius of the artist, who worked within the requirements of the occasion and the sponsor. Before anything else, the artist had to construct an appropriate and exquisite design in which all the parts fitted harmoniously together, as in a well-arranged discourse. For example, in his definition of the *carrousel* as "un Jeu, et un Spectacle representé sur des Chariots" (191), de Pure emphasizes that "*un parfait Carosel comprend un dessein amoureux & guerrier, & fait porter ses Troupes, marcher ses Chars, & eslever ses Machines, avec une continuelle relation à son Jeu & à son dessein*" (194), and that, regardless of anything else, this design is the most important element:

> la richesse des habits, la fierté des Chevaux, & le nombre des Soûtenans n'eust pas eû tout son éclat, si le sujet & le dessein n'eussent esté accompagnez d'un esprit secret & d'une fine intelligence, tant au choix & à la distribution de ses diverses parties, qu'à l'expression & qu'à la justesse de la representation (192).[11]

De Pure then gives an example of a possible *carrousel* on the subject of the abduction of Helen, a typical example of the hackneyed material to which the artist needs to apply his *ingenium* and which he must make appealing and interesting by means of "marvels" (*meraviglie*): ingenious developments, multiple interpretations, clever applications, stupendous machines. All in all, the event became a carefully composed and planned conglomerate, a total work of art constructed according to the stylistically most appropriate decorum, in which nothing happened haphazardly, although on occasion complex machines created the impression that much was improvised (fires, floodings, apparent errors in the execution of the production) and which was designed to surprise the audience and affect its ethos. Thus, the rhetorical strategies, whether applied by a speaker or by a painter, architect, or stage designer, were attempts, first, to make contact with the audience and second, to act as levers on the audience's affects.

From the sophisticated, even unwieldy, rhetorical classifications of subject matter and corresponding styles available to them, the makers of the festive performances considered the *genus grande*, the style of grandeur, as most appropriate to their general subject matter, their occasion, and their target audience. Cicero had suggested that this "high style" was to be used for subjects expected to be generally known to the reader or spectator—as was the case for the subjects of the performances, and for matters pertaining to epideictic rhetoric in general. The principal reason for this choice was that in such cases it was not the ostensible content (the facts) of the story that mattered but rather the artist's skilful and creative presentation of these facts and, correspondingly, the effect on the passions and the ethos of the audience. The passions of the typical heroes of the high genres that go with this style (epic, tragedy) are, literally, greater than life; they are thus magnified or amplified (*auxeisis*).[12] All this was true for the festive performances, the creators of which painstakingly observed the rhetorical law of decorum, in effect, that the mode of expression (*verba*) should be appropriate to the matter expressed (*res*).

Sixteenth- and seventeenth-century artists considered *figurae* the principal instruments of rhetoric and the most powerful aids for persuasion, and it is a common opinion that the consistent use of a number of figures actually constituted a common European language in the Baroque age. Originally, such figures were linguistic transpositions of mental conceits. But in the context of the new interest in correspondences among the arts, and especially in the context of feasts and festive performances, the term can be extended to cover the transpositions of mental conceits in other media as well: machines, stage sets and decoration, costumes, vocal music, and gesticulation. The figures that best expressed the concerns of the Baroque sensibility were those that the Piemontese Jesuit and teacher of rhetoric Emanuele Tesauro, in his *Cannocchiale aristotelico* ("The Aristotelian Telescope," 1654) called *figure ingegnose* (rhetorical ingenuities). In this textbook, a practical manual intended for preachers and orators but used by an audience including the composers of inscriptions and the designers of festive programs, Tesauro classified figures, images and symbols. The principal *figure ingegnose* were hyperbole, oxymoron, antithesis, anastrophe, metonymy, ellipsis, and, still the most prominent of all, metaphor, with its inherent dynamism that renders possible the translation of names and characteristics of one object to another (Fagiolo dell'Arco 232ff).[13] All these figures functioned prominently in the texts of the plays or operas written for the splendid performances, and they were also put to useful service in the non-verbal part of the feast or festive performance. Their total effect was essentially dynamic (expressing movement), since they forced the audience's intellect to pass from one concept to another.

These rhetorical figures could, indeed, be applied concretely to festive celebrations and performances.[14] Specific elements of the performance, architecture, or decoration were juxtaposed and made to contradict one another in oxymoronic fashion. Or they could be exaggerated hyperbolically and accumulated. Hyperbolic repetition, augmentation, accumulation, redundancy, and the multiplication of allegorical elements were all characteristic of the complex performances—as they are of epideictic rhetoric in general. Furthermore, in matters of thematics and formal presentation, Baroque feasts and festive performances explored the various tensions between the microcosmos and the macrocosmos—individual versus polis; the identity of the polis or nation versus other communities; humanity versus the rest of the cosmic creation—in other words, the tensions between the whole and the parts, which is essentially a metonymic concern (as well as a central tenet of Neoplatonism). This tension between what is perceived as a hierarchical difference between the whole and its parts can often produce an inversion of these hierarchies, a rupture with normal social or cultural patterns, which can be likened to certain forms of syntactic anastrophe. And antithesis was always present in the deliberate opposition of parts, themes, styles, allegorical terms, or artistic solutions and techniques (such as the function of machines in the performance and the impact they are supposed to have on the audience).

The essential function of these rhetorical figures was to construct the imaginary—that is, the Platonic Idea, the literary program of the performance to be played—in a code *and* to decode it. The true purpose of the festive performance, the essential purpose underlying the accidental liturgical or dynastic occasion, was the self-representation of a (courtly) society via the praise of and for the society's ruler and the stability derived from the ruler's power, as well as, occasionally, via the presentation of unpleasant truths.[15] The project of the performance was to translate that occasion—in other words, to devise a metaphor for it—in a system of signs and codes, and therefore in a form of discourse: a communication, or, more often in the splendid performances, a communiqué.

The importance of the artist-technician in this discourse was crucial, for the rhetorical explicitness of a performance discourse depended greatly on the capacity of, for example, the scenery, the machines, and the dancers to perform *meraviglie* in abundance, and, in general, on the capacity of all performers to please by teaching, teach by pleasing, and present the program in such a way that the audience could discover its meanings and thereby flatter itself as well as the sponsor-ruler. This shared exercise in taste and discrimination was rather more important than any willingness to suspend disbelief, which is an anachronistic concept in this context. The principal figure of any such festive discourse was precisely that of metaphor (I use the term in the general sense given above).

By metaphorical means, the technicians of the Baroque imagination—poet, stage engineer, architect, designer of machines, composer, ballet master, costume designer—tried to bring disparate elements together. The bringing together of disparate elements (*concordia discors*) is precisely what was implied in the title of Tesauro's treatise: the Aristotelian telescope (*cannocchiale*). Telescopes (invented in the sixteenth century and perfected and popularized in the next) effect a movement, bringing near what is far and vice versa. Thus the telescope is an excellent emblem to describe the actual function of a metaphor, a trans-lation: to "carry over" or "carry across" (in this case, by means of an intellectual leap), or to ask the mind to make swift comparisons. The dancing master brought together the world of the raised stage proper and the world of the auditorium by having members of the audience join the dancers on stage. The machine engineer, with cloud machines, opening skies, and techniques to let the earth open in a sea of flames, effected a movement as well: the immediate, swift and amazing connection, both physical and spiritual, between the heavens, the world, and the netherworld. To phrase it differently: while pursuing the allegorical representation (mimesis) of an Idea, the machine engineer blatantly contradicted "unities" and psychological verisimilitude. The poet, then, confronted the audience with conceits, asking it to incorporate simultaneously quasicontradictory notions. And the architect or stage designer, who constructed perspective decors, asked the audience to believe that things that are really very near are actually far away. Such intellectual leaps are pleasing, said Tesauro (who, admittedly, spoke only of poetic conceits), because they "cause movement from deceit to truth," and such "a method of learning . . . is unexpected and, therefore, pleasing" (Maiorino 107).

Tesauro's work is of specific importance in the present context. It purports to reconcile by means of an intellectual leap the Neoplatonic world of Ideas with Aristotelian modes of expression. This combination of Ideas (content) and rhetoric (mimesis, content imitated and represented through leaps of thought) eventually determined the theory and the execution of the Baroque splendid performance in general and that of opera in particular. In the next section, we will therefore first examine the gradual convergence in the early Baroque period of some Neoplatonic and Aristotelian principles, and then the subsequent emergence of the new ceremonial forms designed to praise the sponsor-ruler as a present but essentially passive absolute monarch.

Invention, Disposition, Elocution

The starting points of this section are twofold: the content of the private spendid performance was an Idea (or several Ideas) relating to the sponsor-ruler, and the formalized representation (mimesis) of this Idea was an epideictic-rhetorical undertaking.

It should be reiterated that for the Renaissance and the Baroque, mimesis (as defined by Aristotle) was the common denominator of all the arts (LeCoat 14). *Quattrocento* humanism had begun to emphasize such matters as personal experience, concrete reality as perceived by the senses, and the notions of movement and actual history which can be shaped in its representation by man's own logic and order. Since then, the common goal and denominator of the arts had become precisely the representation (mimesis) of man's feelings and actions. All the classification and cataloguing that occupied the rhetoricians (schemes and hierarchies of genres and appropriate styles, prosody, gesticulation or facial expression, among other things) actually came to constitute a vast database of information, available to artists, on how to imitate "naturally" the passions and deeds of man and how to affect the passions and ethos of the audience.[16] True, this Humanistic interest, furthered by rhetorical techniques, at first sight seems to contradict the trend among contemporaneous religious-philosophical systems (such as allegorical Christianity, medieval Scholasticism, Renaissance Neoplatonism) to deal with higher matters, inner realities, and to ignore the artistic imitations of human passions and deeds that are made for their own sake and that do not reflect the higher order, the laws of the universe (Curtius 224).

But the contradiction is illusory. Philosophers and theoreticians consistently maintained that the task of the mimetic arts was not to reproduce mere external realities for their own sake, but rather the psychic processes of thought or feeling, or the true nature of the represented objects themselves.[17] In the sixteenth century, scientific laws were eagerly researched to find formulae to realize this purpose, and artists were praised whose mimesis was the product of mathematical laws, or who were able to represent the essence of a given passion and therefore the motif of the passion, the motivation of the represented action. This tendency also partly illustrates and partly explains the growing importance of abstraction in representation. The formal, "realistic" mimesis of external elements (prosody, gestures, facial expression, folds of an article of clothing) was facilitated by a familiarity with rhetorical procedures. The function of this applied rhetoric was, ultimately, to represent higher matters, inner realities, the soul and the psyche.[18] In the Baroque festive performance, which was the most synthetic and syncretistic event of the age, these concerns, partly artistic-technical and partly philosophical-theoretical, were executed on a vast scale, with the cooperation of all artistic media. Mimesis was attempted for the sake of an Idea.

We are now moving into stormy waters, for we are about to explore the relationship between text and music, and the supposed powers of music to imitate, which remain among the thorniest issues in musicological/opera scholarship and criticism. Approaching the subject from a literary rather than a musicological angle, I will try not to engage too deeply in the many tricky arguments that musicologists such as Win, Lindenberger and Kivy have explained with grace and subtlety.[19] Limiting myself for the time being to text and music, I merely posit that the construction of a splendid festive performance called first for the creation of a libretto with Neoplatonic, allegorical layers: a text proposing ideas relevant to the festive occasion via textual and figurative emblems designed for exegesis by the "audience" (in the widest sense of the word). In a second stage, the composer set to work on this program, giving it physical expression, representing the ideas (mimesis), endowing them with the incipient life of the represented human utterance.[20] Together with the text (which could be changed at the composer's request) and the other constitutive elements of the production to be discussed below, the music was designed to arouse the sentiments of the audience and to engage it in a moral or ethical response—which is also a function of Aristotelian mimesis, since the term mimesis itself means "expression, bringing forth" (from the auditor) as well as "imitation, representation."[21] I say: *together* with the text. Because, whatever might have been the case for Venetian public opera houses (where all sorts of transactions unrelated to what was happening on the stage took place in the boxes during performances) or for later, post-Baroque opera (on which most of Lindenberger's arguments focus), the literary program of the private festive performance at courts in the seventeenth century was not intended to be drowned out by the music, but to be taken very seriously and *heard* and *understood* by the audience. This is precisely where rhetoric comes in to join mimesis.

Let us then first examine music, and more specifically, its attributed powers to represent as well as produce strong emotions and psychological affects, for herein resides its principal rhetorical function in the discourse of the Baroque festive performance. The creation of music to fit the previously made literary program corresponds to the phases of disposition and elocution in the composition of a rhetorical discourse. These phases encompass the stylistic formalization of the ideas contained in the program of the discourse, in order to represent the subject and arouse the audience's emotions and direct its ethos. The two fundamental questions, at this point, are the following: (1) Can music represent the outer, clearly visible manifestations of human emotions or ideas, as well as, on a psychological level, the invisible emotions and ideas that indicate the inner life of humans? In seventeenth-century interpretations, mimesis typically encompassed both.[22] And (2), perhaps the thornier problem: can music arouse an audience, either emotionally or ethically?[23] In the prologue to Monteverdi's *pastorale L'Orfeo*, the allegorical character "Musica" answers both questions with a lyrical, "yes":

> Io la Musica son, ch'ai dolci accenti
> So far tranquillo ogni turbato core,
> Et hor di nobil'ira hor d'amore
> Poss'infiammar le più gelate menti.
> Io su cetera d'or cantando soglio
> Mortal orecchio lusingar tal'hora
> E in questa guisa a Marmonia sonora
> De la lira del ciel più l'alme invoglio.[24]

Plato, Aristotle, and Renaissance writers (and Rousseau after them, as in his *Essai sur l'origine des langues*) were much concerned with these problems, and so should we be, for the solutions of the latter, which were achieved in part via a painstaking application of rhetorical principles such as figures, led directly to the creation of opera.[25] It was not accidental that opera became the most splendid festive form and the most rhetorically pregnant, playful expression of the sponsor-ruler's ideologies. If each of the arts was considered capable of representing and arousing, then opera, as the organically integrated combination of all these arts, could represent and arouse as effectively as all of them combined. As Lindenberger phrases it,

> the notion behind the *Gesamtkunstwerk* takes for granted that "more" is obviously better. When Wagner comes to define the *Gesamtkunstwerk*, he allows its superiority to lie not simply in the broad array of arts it is able to include but also in the inclusiveness of the communicative process he expects to take place between work and audience (97).[26]

Restricting ourselves for the moment to music, we must note that festive entertainments and theatrical events had already incorporated music to a significant degree in the Middle Ages and even more so in the Renaissance, when courtly performances employed music as an essential part of the event. For example, the Florentine *intermedi* were predominantly musical interpolations between the acts of dramas, which were sometimes developed enough to become "plays within the play."[27] In general, instrumental music accompanied dances or provided ornamentation; however, vocal music existed to convey the textual ideas. Thus, there was already a distribution of function in place, one suggesting that vocal music could be seen as superior to instrumental music. In the secular drama of the Renaissance, music was largely instrumental and ornamental, but not everyone was convinced that historically, the role of music in the theater had always been thus limited, nor that the power of music, and of the theater, could not be expanded dramatically. Especially in sixteenth-century Florence, the gentlemen musicians who made up the so-called "Camerata," a Neoplatonist academy of music (and painting) which duplicated literary academies, looked to Greece for inspiration and created their own musical myth.[28] Sharing a central concern of sixteenth-century Humanism, they too, like the members of the Pléiade, attempted to recreate the hypothetical, intimate union of all the arts to which was attributed the celebrated mastery in classical times over strong and specific emotions. For example, the Camerata knew that the Aristotelian view of "music" (*mousikè*) incorporated, or was even at one with, the temporal and corporeal arts of poetry and dance. In Greek drama, unlike Renaissance secular drama, music had fulfilled a vital function. As practising musicians as well as scholars devoted to theoretical and philosophical research, the members of the

Camerata attempted to describe Greek theatrical performances, starting from the conviction that Greek drama was sung:

> It has been the opinion of many . . . that the ancient Greeks and Romans, in representing their tragedies upon the stage, sang them throughout. But until now this noble manner of recitation has been neither revived nor (to my knowledge) even attempted (Rinuccini, dedication to *Euridice*; translated in Lindenberger 99).

The Camerata posited that the great success of that drama (as suggested, though with varying degrees of appreciation, in the writings of Plato and Aristotle) was due to its ability to harmoniously unite the arts of poetry, song, and dance. Forced to theorize because no examples of actual Greek music had survived, the Camerata were especially interested in thinking through the musical applications of Platonic and Aristotelian theory, the combination of which seems, in retrospect, to have offered useful insights into a possible resolution for the music-text relationship.

They found that in ancient thought, music passed for a mimetic art; their crucial problem was the nature of the musical imitation (mimesis) of visible and invisible ideas and emotions.[29] From Plato's dialogues, they learned that music "imitates" human character and emotional states by imitating the inflections of the human voice that indicate specific character traits and emotions. Moreover, they found that music was considered to have a moral and psychological function, and that the effects of the mimesis (because of its two-pronged meaning: imitation-representation and expression-bringing forth) by means of music on the spectator-auditor as well as on the performer were to be taken very seriously. Briefly, if there was to be any music at all, then it was to be "vocal music," the combination of poetry and music, which Plato deemed superior to instrumental music as a means of education. As his Athenian Stranger maintains to Cleinias, if there are words, it is easier to find out what precisely is being imitated:

> music is more celebrated than any other kind of imitation, and therefore requires the greatest care of them all. For if a man makes a mistake here, he may do himself the greatest injury by welcoming evil dispositions . . . yet the poets go on and [unlike the Muses] make still further havoc by separating the rhythm and the figure of the dance from the melody, setting bare words to metre, and also separating the melody and the rhythm from the words, using the lyre or the aulos alone. For when there are no words, it is very difficult to recognize the meaning of the harmony and rhythm, or to see that any worthy object is imitated by them. And we must acknowledge that all this sort of thing, which aims at only swiftness and smoothness and a brutish noise, and uses the aulos and the lyre not as the mere accompaniments of the dance and song, is exceedingly coarse and tasteless (*Laws* II.669; translation in Lippman ed., vol. 1, 19–20).[30]

Like Plato's remarks on music, those of Aristotle do not seem very concrete in relation to music as it was understood in the sixteenth and seventeenth centuries, or as we might understand it (Kivy 32ff). The principal topic of *Poetics* is of course drama, although we must keep in mind that the drama that Aristotle discusses was sung. In the *Poetics*, Aristotle treats music, under the same rubric as tragedy and comedy, as one of the arts that imitate, or represent, by means of rhythm and language and tune (or, in the case of instrumental music, by means of tune and rhythm alone). In *Politics* VIII, Aristotle, like Plato, insists on musical performance and composition as part of the education of the citizens, and he, too, considers rhythm and melody capable of imitating and representing human character and emotions and of potentially affecting the souls of listeners and performers. But Aristotle departs from Plato when he writes that

> and moreover everybody when listening to imitations [music dramatically expressing various states of emotion; Loeb ed.] is thrown into a corresponding state of feeling, *even apart from the rhythms and tunes themselves* . . . and it is the case that whereas the other objects of sensation contain no representation of character, for example the objects of touch and taste . . . , pieces of music on the contrary do actually contain in themselves imitations of character; and this is manifest, for even in the nature of the mere melodies there are differences, so that people when hearing them are affected differently . . . (my emphasis; *Politics* VIII.5–8 passim. Loeb ed. 657–59).

This means, I take it, that objects of sound (the voice, musical objects) can literally and directly imitate mental traits (such as moral character and feelings), rather than merely copy the expressions of these traits or emotions, as Plato says they do. For Aristotle, objects of sound are therefore superior to, say, sculpture and painting (objects of sight, figures and colors), which can only imitate mental traits by proxy via the physical manifestations of these states (Kivy 34–35).

The influence of ancient Greek thought on Renaissance musical and artistic thought and practice can be gauged from letters Girolamo Mei (1519–1594) sent between 1572 and 1579 to his friend Vincenzo Galilei (1520–1591). Mei's letters in fact contributed much to the philosophical foundations of the Florentine Camerata (Lippman x–xi; Kivy 38–40).[31] He considered poetry and music (vocal music, particularly) sister arts. Both are superior to the plastic arts, he argued, because they represent ideas (or passions, or actions) directly, whereas the plastic arts can only represent bodies that execute actions. (Let us recall that, in Mei's time, painting and sculpture were virtually exclusively figurative.) Mei was thus actually closer to the (then recently rediscovered) thought of Aristotle than to Platonism. Vincenzo Galilei, the father of Galileo, was a professional composer and performer, and, in addition, the theorist who translated the aesthetic principles of Mei's letters into a musical program (Kivy 40–43).[32]

What particularly interested Mei, Galilei and their colleagues was text-setting and the remarks of the ancient theoreticians relevant to the great powers of music over the emotions and characters of men (*melopoeia*). The Camerata were namely of the (mistaken) opinion that the (mainly, polyphonic) music of their own time failed miserably in this respect; music had become degenerate, failed to properly represent the emotions and made it difficult simply to follow the text. Given the fact that Plato and Aristotle had both ascribed such amazing powers of arousal to the music of their time, then that music must clearly have been non-polyphonic, in other words, monophonic with a "definite melody" (Mei's phrase; Lippman ed., vol. 1. 98):[33]

> what chiefly impelled me and made me arrive at this belief that the whole chorus sang the same melody was the observation that the music of the ancients was considered a powerful means of exciting the affections, as one discovers through the many incidents related to us by their authors, and the observation that that of our musicians is, as is commonly said, more readily adapted to everything else. Now all this is necessarily a power which arises from the opposed and contrary qualities which each of them possesses by nature, of which those of ancient music are adapted and naturally suitable to accomplish what they do, and in contrast, those of modern music to impede it (Mei, *Letter on Ancient and Modern Music* [1572]; translation in Lippman ed., vol. 1, 91–92.)

Thus dabbling in abstractions, the members of the Camerata answered the questions "can we be moved by what we hear if (1) we do not recognize what we hear (because of all the different melodies that are maintained simultaneously), and (2) the composer did not empathize with the emotions or characters he tried to render?" briefly, and naively perhaps, with a resounding, "no." Though the Camerata were misguided, their sincere theoretical occupation with the problems of the representation of visible and invisible emotion and the arousal of the listener was a crucial stimulant to the creation of opera.

This art form emerged (after its theory had been devised) as the partial solution to a philosophical problem: how to relate, in the context of a festive event, the (Platonic) symbolism of Ideas and the (Aristotelian) musical expression (mimesis) of human speech and emotion? Although Neoplatonism and Aristotelianism both contributed to the ultimate musical-formal solution (as distinguished from the textual content) of opera, the latter probably contributed more to this solution than the former. The reason for this is that, as was mentioned before, Neoplatonic thought considered the work of art much like a sacred object, whose many hidden levels of interpretation and symbolisms (Ideas) are more important than its externally visible meanings (mimesis). Applied to musical drama and its constituent parts, the Neoplatonic interpretation would hold that music does *not* simply try to imitate or represent, by means of external sound and rhythm, whatever emotions the text suggests; on the contrary, the music has a value independent from the text. The Aristotelian viewpoint is quite different: art, as mimesis, directly represents meaning: since the forms represented by art have no concrete reality of their own, the particular, outer representation of the form is truly the essential reality. Applied to musical drama, this means that musical sound and rhythm therefore can, and do, "naturally" represent natural human speech and emotions, and that the musical setting of a text is to be determined by the text itself. For the humanist musical philosophers of the Camerata, *logos*, the text, came first and foremost—as it had, indeed, for Aristotle.[34] The music must imitate the passions and represent the emotions that the text, or the literary program, contains.[35]

We are now coming to the point of this sketch of the gradual genesis of the philosophical-theoretical justification of the new art form, opera, and the consequent appropriation of this art form by the festive cult of the absolute ruler. A consensus was gradually created in some circles that it was desirable to establish an art of musical drama that would be able to represent and imitate emotions and actions (visible and invisible) *and* that would also be able to arouse emotions and an ethical response.[36] Once this consensus had been achieved, the attention shifted toward considerations of a more practical nature: how can musical drama best represent emotion in order to arouse emotion and generate an ethical response? The answers to this question were suggested, of course, by rhetoric, many principles and figures of which were being applied to musical theory and practice (Vickers 1–22), although not everyone who dealt in these matters recognized the inherent common sense limitations of such transferrals:

> the general conclusion so far is that the model from rhetoric can be applied to music only partially, by an analogy or *tertium comparationis* that preserves just one element of the complex contained in the rhetorical figure . . . the formation of a musical rhetoric takes the form of a theorist looking at a rhetorical textbook in order to find a figure in rhetoric that applied, or could be adapted, a musical effect or structure. . . . All the figures based on semantic properties face . . . difficulties. Some theorists recognized this early on, in that they never attempted to apply to music tropes, which involve the transference of sense from one area to another (Vickers 31–33, passim).

Indeed, Renaissance and Baroque composers experimented with the representation of the passions by means of the manipulation of rhythm and melody, a vogue that would give rise to curiously pre-psychological rhetorical codices listing numerous rhythmical and melodic figures that were capable, it was hoped, of expressing every shade of emotion.[37] The Camerata stayed on somewhat more solid ground and were primordially interested in rhetorical problems of declamation. An important document was *"Art" of Rhetoric* (III: sections 1 and 7), in which Aristotle discusses correspondences between passions and such outward signs as gesticulation, facial expression, and sound, and goes into the necessity of distinguishing between "universal" and "eccentric" actions and passions. Ancient poets had often pointed out that the choice of meter must be made to depend on the emotion to be represented (rapid rhythms for excitement, slow ones for languor, careful balancing of high pitch versus low pitch, and so forth), or, in Plato's often quoted words, "the notes and the rhythm ought to follow the speech" (*Republic* III: Donington 72; Donington 77, LeCoat 18). The main problem that the Camerata faced regarding the rhetorical problem of declamation was related to this issue: when action moves slowly and the represented sentiments do not run very deep, singing is not really difficult, but what does one do when action moves swiftly and the feelings alternate quickly?[38] To appear natural as well as dramatically convincing, the representation of passionate, swiftly developing feelings must be passionate and swift. The music, in other words, must approach the modulations of flexible speech; at the same time, it must also remain recognizably musical, that is: disciplined and controlled.[39] The beginning of a solution was found, first, with monody in a declamatory, reciting style:

> that sort of melody, which can suitably, and gracefully be recited, that is, be sung by one alone in such manner, that the words are understood, whether this is done on the boards of the stage, or in Churches, and Oratorios in the manner of dialogues, or indeed in private Chambers, or elsewhere; and finally, [...] every sort of Music, which is sung by one alone to the sound of some instrument, with little duration of the notes, and in such manner, that it approaches common speech; but however with feeling" (G.B. Doni, *Trattato della musica scenica* [c. 1635]; translation in Donington 91),

and then, as the technique became gradually more sophisticated, with recitative proper (Donington 83–100). The Camerata advised composers to observe actors at work and to study their techniques for representing passions in declamation—techniques such as the manipulation of duration and pitch of sound according to the feeling to be represented. The most effective representation is the one that arouses most. Fundamentally, the performers of the new art form had to master prosody and rhetoric.

It was characteristic of seventeenth-century performances of musical drama (and of performances well into the eighteenth century) that the singers as well as the audience paid very close attention to the text, to the declamation of individual syllables, vowels and consonants. This tendency had actually begun in the sixteenth century as the result of the development outlined in the preceding paragraphs. For example, one of the principal theoreticians of the Camerata had given the then modern advice that

> in composing, then, you will make it your chief aim to arrange the verse well and to declaim the words as intelligibly as you can, not letting yourself

> be led astray by the counterpoint like a bad swimmer who lets himself be carried out of his course by the current and comes to shore beyond the mark that he had set, for you will consider it self-evident that, just as the soul is nobler than the body, so the words are nobler than the counterpoint.[40]

Like a muscular swimmer, the words should not be carried away by the stream of music with its strong currents in which it is easy to drown. The primary function of the declamation techniques was to achieve dramatic expressiveness by a close observance of the rules of rhetoric. Actors learned precise rules for adapting the manner of speaking (for example, determining the length of individual letters or sounds) to the content of the speech, and these rules were lifted directly from rhetoric. Singers were advised by their manuals to consider themselves actors first and singers second, and to observe how stage actors executed the rules of prosody and rhetoric and then to imitate them (see also Rogerson 72). In this respect, a very important source for seventeenth-century training is Marin Mersenne's treatise, in which it was advocated that melody ought to closely follow speech and prosody as they indicate passion.[41] In practice, this meant, for example, that singers in training for musical drama at the Paris conservatory first learned their roles without music, in order to match the prosody with the content—like a regular actor would; only afterward did they add the musical score, attempting to preserve the acquired prosodic patterns. This training procedure resulted in the so-called *déclamation lyrique*.[42]

Rhetorical strategies could obviously be applied particularly well to the narrative parts of the musical performance (the recitatives) but for arias, too, singers' manuals suggested rules directly derived from rhetoric (Barnett 335–36). As we might expect, the first and fundamental rule held that recitative is a matter of declamation rather than music; the composer as well as the singer formed their performance style after the styles of theatrical declamation. Another basic rule dictated that, in matters of speed (tempo), emphasis (accent), and timbre, the recitative was to be sung as if it were a pronounced declamation—which means that tempo, accent and timbre were not dictated by the musical measure but by the content.[43] Briefly, the musical score was to be regarded as a general guide or a vehicle, rather than an absolute dictate; the words and the content which the music expressed had preeminence over the music itself. The interpretation by the actor-singer of the text dictated the performance, and not, as is generally the case in post-Baroque musical drama, the director's baton or the *chef d'orchestre*'s bow. In the seventeenth century (and well into the eighteenth), the orchestra followed the directions of the actor-singer, and the latter followed the rules of prosody and rhetoric.

If typical seventeenth-century stage declamation would appear strange to us precisely because of its rhetorical nature, it is not different with the acting and gesticulation techniques. These, too, were rhetorically determined, and related to the delivery, or "action," of the discourse. The manner in which a dialogue was typically represented on stage, for example, indicates that the primary concern of actors or singers was to communicate something to the audience and to elicit its response. As the speaker advanced on the stage, s/he faced the audience rather than the interlocutor. Once the lines were recited, the speaker turned away from the audience, at which point the interlocutor advanced and repeated the process. Especially given the fact that the auditorium was usually lighted (particularly for private performances at court), a speaker can thus be said to communicate with the audience rather than with the interlocutor on stage.

Gesticulation and facial expression were rhetorical means of communication only second to declamation or singing itself. In fact, just like voice, gesticulation was considered in the seventeenth and the eighteenth centuries at least as important as the music proper. For aesthetic reasons and for the purpose of mimesis, actors were trained to vary their poses and facial expressions. For there is a rhetoric of gesticulation just as there is one for prosody, and, just like prosody, gesticulation can represent the meaning of the words and the feelings they express in order to move the audience.[44] In countless paintings, etchings, or sketches that show actors rehearsing or performing, this corporeal eloquence speaks directly to the viewer (even in those sketches which served primarily as costume designs). In fact, seventeenth-century actors and actresses in musical drama were praised more frequently for their gesticulation skills than for their singing qualities. The publication of many books throughout the Baroque period and well into the eighteenth century on dramatic technique indicates that there was a great awareness that the moving body and facial expression could be used for rhetorical purposes, and that there is such a thing as corporeal eloquence. For example, writing about gesticulation suited to singing, the singer and theoretician Bérard insists that

> l'action en général, telle qu'on doit l'entendre ici, est l'Art de peindre les idées et le sentiment des gestes, par tout le maintien du corps, et sur-tout par l'air du visage. L'action dont il s'agit, est le même art appliqué aux paroles mises en musique, aussi le jeu des Acteurs qui chantent, doit varier autant que ces dernières, c'est-à-dire à l'infini.[45]

In such manuals, the same point recurs often: the actor must know, first of all, how to render visual (*peindre*) a feeling or the content of the words by means of the appropriate prosody and gesticulation. Actors learned the appropriate prosody from "speaking" the role first; in the same manner they often studied appropriate gesticulation and facial expression from statuary and the visual arts. Indeed, Baroque painters such as Rubens insisted on the fact that muscles must move for a body to function, and that all the physiological details of such movement need to be shown. All the arts shared certain rhetorical rules of expression, which were determined by the need to create natural but decorous expressions (imitations) of emotions and actions. These rules were intended to give the artist the persuading power of the *rhètor*, and the composer and the singer, the painter and the sculptor, the poet and the actor, the choreographer and the dancer, were all familiar with them.[46] The exact position of a wrist vis-à-vis the total body, or the angle of the knee or the thigh, had symbolic relevance. For the study of appropriate facial expressions, eighteenth-century actors could benefit from the works of Le-Brun, whose illustrated book for the use of painters, *Méthode pour apprendre à dessiner les passions* (posthumously published in 1698) was the most widespread manual for and codex of the expression of emotions in the graphic arts.[47] Earlier works that could be applied to the same purpose were still available, such as Caroso's *Il Ballarino*, which was published in 1581, the same year in which the *Balet comique de la Reyne* was performed at the French court. When actors wanted to study gesticulation, they also could, and did, turn to sculptured representations, such as statues and busts by Bernini and others. Even the exact manner of arranging one's hair or the folds of one's clothing with significance and decorum could be studied from paintings and statues.[48] All this amounts to a codification of gesture, a rhetoric and a prosody, a limiting and cataloguing of a number of appropriate gestures matched with appropriate expressions to serve the imitation (mimesis) of certain ideas or feelings.[49]

The rhetorical techniques of singing-declamation and acting-gesticulation that shaped seventeenth-century musical drama, and *a fortiori* the splendid Baroque festive performances, may well seem unnatural to us, but they served rhetorical purposes: to persuade or convince the audience of an Idea and to engage it in an emotional or ethical response. Nothing was allowed to stand in the way of the thought that must be expressed (mimesis). Everything visible or audible on the stage had to contribute to the thought and its mimesis: the theme of the performance, the text, the order and arrangement of the performance events (prologues, succession of arias and recitative, interjected ballets or interludes apparently unconnected with the main subject, epilogue), the singing technique—and, as we will see in the next section, also the architecture of the theater itself, the décor, the sets, and the machines. For unlike Aristotle, who argued in favor of plot over performance, the makers of the grandiose festive performance created a rhetoric which functioned as much by means of scenic opsis as by means of the opsis of the mind.[50]

The Rhetorical Mise-en-scène

The concrete artistic mise-en-scène of the literary program in the courtly private theaters can also be considered a rhetorical act.[51] The architectural setting of the discourse had rhetorical value in itself. In the early seventeenth century, considerable changes occurred in theater architecture and stage design in response to the new forms of festive celebrations and the functions of the splendid performance.

First of all, as I suggested in the previous section, the actors faced their audience, which perceived them frontally. This was a relatively new development in stage technique, which occurred first in private and/or courtly theaters (those where the "Italian order" prevailed). Previously, in the classical period, in the Middle Ages, and during most of the Renaissance, audiences characteristically surrounded the stage during daylight performances. In the open air, public theaters (such as improvised stages in inns, courtyards, *corrales*), a version of this "surround stage" remained in effect.[52] The first new private theater of importance, and the oldest surviving theater of modern Europe, was the Teatro Olimpico in Vicenza. It was begun in the late 1570s by Palladio (then already famous for his examination of ancient monuments) and completed by Scamozzi in 1584.[53] Palladio was heavily influenced by the Vitruvian tradition—or the interpretation thereof by the Roman Academy—when he designed the Olimpico. The stage and auditorium of this theater are connected: there is no open proscenium separating the stage and the audience. The narrow acting area is in front of a background with five open, narrow "streets" (the central one being wider than the others) and offers a very deep perspective with dramatically foreshortened buildings. Palladio provided neither a curtain nor a ceiling or floor apparatus to allow changes of sets during the performance. Clouds were painted on the ceiling. The theater was mainly intended for daylight performances: the hall which encapsulates the auditorium had windows. In fact, the Olimpico leaned very heavily upon antique Greek stage design: clearly recognizable is the semicircular, rising amphitheater with a permanent back structure with many niches, in which were placed mythological statues representing (all-male) subjects (Baur-Heinhold 161). Although it did introduce the synthesis of plastic and painterly elements that was to be so important for the Baroque stage, the Olimpico was actually more an anachronism than a true innovation in theater architecture.[54]

The "Italian order" in seventeenth-century theater design (as represented, for example, by the theaters of Scamozzi, Aleotti and Sabbattini) placed the spectacle in front of the audience. The usually rectangular room had an elevated stage facing the audience and separated from the audience by a scenic frame, a proscenium arch; in the course of the century, a curtain was added. This picture frame enclosed a single perspective; its framing devices also served to hide the increasingly complex machinery. Yet, scene changes often still occurred in full view of the audience (as they did in Inigo Jones's theater). The production of visual effects was a paramount concern for the Baroque stage (auditory effects too, but these were easier to achieve). An important visual difference from the previous stages was the changeable background for the action. The novelty principally resided in the (three-dimensional) application to the stage of the principles of linear perspective that had been derived from research and experiments in the (two-dimensional) visual arts, and, ultimately, from architecture.[55] The painted stage sets that were put up in perspective constituted a rhetoric of eloquence of their own. These sets were conceived as a codex, containing symbolic representations of all possible geographic scenes on earth, in the heavens, or in the underworld, and as a tool for translating one milieu into another. Thus the stage became a flexible geographical metaphor with, at least in theory, endless possibilities.[56] A painted set was like a topos or commonplace, fixed in usage by certain conditions of decorum, determined by allegorical and mythological connotations, adding the power of the image to the power of the words. The task of the stage designer was to manipulate these topoi eloquently and efficiently, according to the required decorum of the context, and in order to affect the emotions and ethos of the audience. For example, one might argue that in *gloire*-scenes, the machines lifted the spectators figuratively just as they lifted the protagonists literally for the final apotheosis.[57]

Machines had been used for centuries to highlight festive and theatrical occasions, both outdoors and inside. In the sixteenth century, machines had been experimented with in public movable street celebrations, as well as in private indoor performances, but in these forms, the machinery had been secondary to the characters and the text.[58] The Baroque sensibility applied technology and built moving machines as a pretext for satisfying a desire for variety, for showcasing technical virtuosity by emphasizing scenic movement and metamorphosis within Nature herself (clouds, storms, fire, light effects, rocks opening to reveal inner settings), and, why not admit it, for alleviating some of the boredom that spectators of the often extraordinarily long performances must have felt on occasion.[59] Underlying such technology was the paradoxical obsession with the visual confusion of what is static and what is not, and with the representation of that confusion. Just as architectural tricks (Bernini) made static structures appear ephemeral and capable of movement, and vice versa, the world of the theater made systematic use of static, artistic structures and machines precisely to represent, multiply, repeat, and amplify the most ephemeral, dynamic phenomena of nature: clouds, fire, water, and light. Many machines were designed (usually in Italy) to represent these elusive phenomena—a development that occurred alongside the rapid development (not accidentally originally also in Italy) of the science of hydraulics.[60] In Baroque festive celebrations and performances, machines were devised to represent fire, water, clouds and the effects of their dynamic interaction more than any other natural phenomenon.[61] The interest in these elements may be explained in part by their allegorical adaptability. Clouds, fire and water are vehicles that allow an immediate communication between the world, the heavens, and the netherworld. With floods, the heavens can signify disapproval; by means of clouds, denizens of the heavens can descend to earth, or, conversely, humans ascend to the heavens; fire refers to the underworld, or, alternatively, to the heavens. Clouds and cloud machines in particular were crucial elements in plays and operas and even in pageantlike performances, representing the forces of dynamism, instability, change, and metamorphosis itself. The Baroque representation by means of stage machines of these cosmic powers of movement had primarily metaphysical (allegorical), rhetorical (amplification, repetition), and, perhaps most important, psychological purposes, demonstrating the power of technology to "move" (figuratively and in some cases literally) the audience into a psychological reaction. Bernini's theatrical activity can be quoted as a good example of the latter purpose. Bernini's intentions were psychological, in that he aimed at spectators' participation in the action by means of the created illusions.[62]

Add to all of the above the fact that in the Italian performance order the play area was isolated and separated from the audience vertically, that is, by the raised, frontal stage with proscenium arch, and, in the case of festive performances in parks or gardens, horizontally (often by water).[63] The combination of this new frontal setup of the private theaters and the themes of magic, illusion, enchantment, folly, dreams, and transformation and the like that were so often performed in them, has led Jean Rousset to conceive of the Baroque stage as a "magic cube" or "illusionistic box," which he describes as facilitating the "aesthetic of illusion," a prime characteristic of the Baroque.[64] There is much to be admired in Rousset's phenomenological theory, which works very well to shed interesting light on a number of Baroque plays—plays such as *The Tempest*.[65] Rousset's pathbreaking work remains crucial to students of the Baroque (and not only of the French Baroque). However, given that his aesthetic of illusion rather contradicts my interpretation of the performance process as rhetorical discourse, I must argue against it—or rather, indicate why the key points of his argument are not relevant for the splendid festive performances. Participants (which includes spectators) in the latter, and more generally, in plays performed on an Italian-style stage, were never really able to simply let go and forget themselves.[66] On the contrary, the Italian order actually facilitated and emphasized the rhetorical functions and principles of the performances that were staged there, for its actors consciously and directly addressed the audience. The acting methods were not "natural" ("natural" in the sense of not drawing attention to themselves—the sort of acting that would eventually lead to method acting) but firmly grounded in rhetoric, demanding that a very deliberate prosody and technique of declamation, along with a well-defined stock of set facial expressions and physical gestures, be learned and maintained by the actor. The new theatrical and stage architecture favored a rhetorical delivery of speeches. Regardless of whether the speakers stood on a (separating) raised stage with a (separating) proscenium arch, or on an island stage in the middle of (separating) waters, they faced the audience frontally and directly. Even while they spoke, actors kept facing the audience; thus they did not really address one another, but rather the audience. Moreover, the speakers-singers-actors faced first and foremost the passive sponsor-absolute ruler for whom the new stage was designed. This method was not likely to induce in the spectator the type of suspension of disbelief that the aesthetic of illusion requires; rather, it was a method very proper to rhetorical discourse, in which the *rhètor* presents arguments for the audience's judgment or approval.[67] Rousset interprets Chapelain's statement (1630) that it is desirable to "ôter aux regardants toutes les occasions de faire réflexion sur ce qu'ils voient et de douter de sa réalité,"[68] as a testimony to his aesthetic of illusion. Chapelain's words, however, also support my rhetorical interpretation: the purpose of the *rhètor* is precisely to persuade the audience into accepting as true the *rhètor*'s words and nothing else. The succesful speaker thus obliterates the boundary between truth and performance.[69] Furthermore, the auditorium was usually lighted just as the stage was, meaning that the actors could see the audience as well as the audience could see the actors—with considerable consequences for the rhetorical function of the performance.[70] There is also the fact that the machines—even the least complex ones producing simple flight effects—were quite clumsy, often imposed long intervals between scenes, and on occasion squeaked so loudly that, in spite of all the good intentions and training of the performers, it was difficult to hear what was being said or sung on stage. And in spite of curtains and proscenium arch, scene changes were often executed in full view of the audience. What I am saying is that the entire program and all those involved in its execution seem to have worked together to prevent the spectator from forgetting even for a moment that a politically inspired, rhetorically constructed performance was in the making. And finally, rather than creating an "illusion," the designers of Baroque grandiose performances often created a *desillusion*, by playing tricks on the audience's expectations. Thus curtains were deliberately raised unexpectedly or too early, plays sometimes began supposedly at the wrong moment, and all sorts of "accidents" were faked or provoked precisely in order to expose the theatrical nature of the entire enterprise (Alewyn 1959: 67).

Regardless of this difference in interpretation, Rousset remains a crucial source for those who believe that the Baroque stage, which accommodated the splendid festive performances with its symmetrical perspectives, its scenes that constantly became more complex and yet easier to change, and its machines that allowed amazing connections, both physical and spiritual, between the heavens, the world, and the netherworld, was absolutely incompatible with the so-called "classical" theater, which strove to represent the unities of time, place, action, and tone. Let us not forget that in the seventeenth century, these unities, derived from Aristotle, were developed primarily for the public stage and for a specific purpose, that is, the pursuit of psychological verisimilitude. The latter, understandably enough, was hardly a concern of the makers of the splendid festive performances. On the contrary, these artists were interested in representing to the court, by means of rhetorical representation and allegorical strategies of interpretation, the very Idea of the monarchy and the glorification and apotheosis of the sponsor-ruler.

In this chapter, we have (all too briefly) introduced basic relevant rhetorical concepts; investigated the creation of opera as a primordially philosophical undertaking; considered some conventions of elocution and disposition; examined the connections between the rhetoric of singing-declamation and mimesis in the framework of Platonic, Aristotelian and Renaissance thought; and studied the connection between the rhetoric of gesticulation and mimesis. We have looked also at the essential functions of the actual mise-en-scène in the splendid festive performance as a rhetorical discourse. It will now have become clear why the most grandiose festive performances were precisely those of operas: opera was the most ideal medium for the absolute monarchs to advertise and celebrate their new status in a festive, playful mode, because of the new art's unparalleled power to combine an Idea-content (linked to allegoresis) and an ethical appeal (determined by the rhetorical execution). Exploiting quasi-infinite artistic resources for the symbolic expression of an ideology, the splendid festive performance of such a work can be considered a private relative of the Catholic High Mass. Very rhetorically structured and ideologically determined phenomena both, the festive performance and High Mass were the lone survivors of "true Ritual," which has been defined as

> richly textured by virtue of . . . varied interweavings of the productions of mind and senses . . . all the senses of participants and performers may be engaged: they hear music and prayers, see visual symbols, taste consecrated foods, smell incense, and touch sacred persons and objects. They also have available the kinesthetic forms of dance and gesture, and perhaps, cultural repertories of facial expression, to bring them into significant performative rapport" (Turner 81).[71]

In the following chapter, I will introduce the notion of ritualistic play to argue that the rhetorically designed splendid festive performance at the Baroque court represents a significant change in the consciousness of "play" in western culture: that is, the appropriation by the absolute sponsor-ruler of the spirit of play in his or her own service. The ruler becomes truly the "god(dess) of play."

Notes

1. Benedetto Croce, of course, divorced rhetoric and art, but then, Croce also despised "the Baroque" (see further Gombrich 1972: 222 n. 17).

2. See Curtius 224. On rhetoric in Renaissance education, see W. H. Woodward, *Studies in Education during the Age of the Renaissance 1400–1600* (Cambridge, 1906). Useful is also Wilfried Barner, *Barock-Rhetorik. Untersuchungen zu ihren geschichtlichen Grundlagen* (Tübingen, 1970).

3. It was translated by Annibale Caro (1570). The Humanistic transmission of Aristotle and the adaptations of his work in the Baroque are discussed in great detail by Guido Morpurgo Tagliabue, "Aristotelismo e Barocco," in Castelli ed., 119–95.

4. Miguel Batllori, "Gracián y la Retórica barroca en España," in Castelli ed., 27–32, 29 gives Coimbra, 1561 as data for the first edition; Vickers 4 gives 1568. Regardless, Soarez' manual was published in more than one hundred editions and in dozens of European cities within two centuries. Other important manuals were composed by the learned preacher Leonard Cox (*The Arte or Crafte of Rhetoryke*, 1530); the politician Thomas Wilson (*Arte of Rhetorique*, 1553); Puttenham (*Arte of English Poesie*, 1589); the Jesuit Baltasar Gracián (*Agudeza y arte de ingenio*, 1642); and by many others: the list of Renaissance and Baroque texts on rhetoric comprises more than 3000 items. See James J. Murphy, *Renaissance Rhetoric: A Short-Title Catalogue* (New York, 1981).

5. Among the relevant texts of the period, see Nicholas Faret, *Honneste homme ou l'art de plaire à la court* (Paris, 1630). On court ceremonial, see, for instance, Theodore Godefroy's *Le ceremoniel françois* (Paris, 1649), and on the distinction between "state ceremonial" and "court ceremonial," see Hubert Ehalt, "Zur Funktion des Zeremoniells im Absolutismus," in August Buck, et al., eds., 2: 411–19. For an interesting study of the relevance of Gracián's treatise *El Discreto* (1646) on court life, see Neumeister, in August Buck, et al., eds., 2: 51–60.

It is paradoxical that the artistic and philosophical emphasis in the Baroque period on the representation of themes and forms of movement, freedom, and the imagination, was counterbalanced by stringent official, political, and religious views of the world as closed, defined, and unfree. The Baroque, after all, witnessed the entrenchment of nationalisms, the triumph of absolutism, the reemphasis on firm doctrines in matters of religion, and the first real scientific laws (the matters proven by a scientific law are "fixed" until disproven). Crucially important in this development were the middle decades of the century, which constituted truly a period of conflict between the contrary tendencies of movement and stability—and which, perhaps not accidentally, also witnessed the most magnificent feasts and festive performances.

Absolutism, for example, did not mark the beginning of the modern state but was rather the culmination and end-phase of a previous form of state organization, that is, aristocratic-feudal society. In *Le Roi-machine. Spectacle et politique au temps de Louis XIV*, Jean-Marie Apostolidès sees the absolute ruler as the transitory reincarnation of a sacred function (12) and emphasizes the identification of the ruler with the nation. Hence, "celui qui verse le sang royal détruit le corps à travers lequel la nation s'incarne" ("he who sheds the royal blood destroys the body through which the nation incarnates itself;" 15). On the education of rulers, see Le Mothe le Vayer (tutor to Louis XIV), *De l'instruction de Monseigneur le Dauphin* (Paris, 1640). See also Potier de Morais' heroic-galant novel *Discours des Divertissements, Inclinations, & Perfections Royales* (1644), which was actually written as a pedagogical tool for the use of the young Dauphin, later Louis XIV; further, Bossuet's letter "De l'instruction de Monseigneur le Dauphin" to Pope Innocent XII (1679); and Fénelon's *Télémaque* (1699), which was also written for the education of the Dauphin. Trevor-Roper writes that "after 1660, though absolutism might continue, it no longer claimed a total monopoly of culture and religion, science and philosophy," a view that seems a bit extreme, especially because of the stated conclusion that the effects of the War "taught the prince that it was wiser to leave culture to private enterprise" (23). It is true, though, that, by the end of the rule of Louis XIV, Versailles had very little to offer; bourgeois Paris was taking over as the center of power and innovation. Court entertainment had, perhaps, proven to be quite pointless and sterile.

6. In Daniel Javitch, "Poetry and Preferment at Elizabeth's Court. Some Preliminary Observations," in August Buck, et al., eds., 2: 163–69, 163.

7. Oskar Roth, "Höfische Gesinnung und *honnêteté* im Frankreich des 17. Jahrhunderts," in August Buck, et al., eds., 2: 239–44; see also Gerhard Schröder, " 'Courtisan' und 'honnête homme.' Zum Problem der Entstehung eines bürgerlichen Bewusstseins im 17. Jahrhundert," in August Buck, et al., eds., 2: 245–48.

8. See on this also Annabel Patterson, *Hermogenes and the Renaissance* (Princeton, 1970).

9. For example, the theoretician of painting Gian Paulo Lomazzo wrote in his *Trattato de la Pittura* (Milan, 1584; facs. ed. Hildesheim, 1968) that "the various components of the landscape, such as trees, clouds, flowers, etc. are capable of expression, as all things that move" (179 ff; reference from LeCoat 60). Likewise, a principal thesis of Ripa's *Iconologia* is precisely that inanimate things are emblematic expressions of the passions and have a mute rhetoric. Thus, architectural orders and forms, too, are rhetorical. The poet Tasso reworked Cicero's generic "high style" into a scheme that contained the options of grandeur, beauty, splendor, gravity, asperity, ethos, vehemence; for the "middle style," Tasso suggested gracefulness, suavity, "dolcezza," pleasantness, and for the "low style," acuteness, subtleness, and humor. John

Porter Houston studies the applications of these *genera dicendi* in sixteenth- and seventeenth-century poetry, in *The Rhetoric of Poetry in the Renaissance and Seventeenth Century* (Baton Rouge; London, 1983). See also further LeCoat 35–36.

10. Monteverdi, "Eight Book of Madrigals" (1638), in Oliver Strunk, ed. *Source Readings in Music History* (New York, 1950) 413–15; reference from Lindenberger 81.

11. "a perfect carrousel ['a Game and Spectacle performed on chariots'] is built around an amorous and warlike design; its participants, its chariots, and its machines all bear a continuous relationship to its Game and the design" (194) and "the rich costumes, the splendid horses and the numerous supporting participants would not have appeared so brilliant, if the subject and the design had not been produced with such a cleverly searching wit and refined understanding, both in the selection and distribution of the various elements and in the expression and exactitude of the representation thereof" (192).

12. Gadamer argues that every imitation is an exaggeration, and thus a form of *auxeisis*: "Imitation and representation are not merely a repetition, a copy, but knowledge of the essence. Because they are not merely repetition, but a 'bringing forth,' they imply a spectator as well. They contain in themselves an essential relation to everyone for whom the representation exists. Indeed, one can say even more: the presentation of the essence, far from being a mere imitation, is necessarily revelatory. In imitating, one has to leave out and to heighten. Because he is pointing to something, he has to exaggerate, whether he likes it or not" (114–15).

13. Baroque poetics had to abandon the simile as the favorite figure of expression—for, in principle at least, similes (so diligently pursued by "Renaissance" poets) assume that a stable harmony exists between elements and that it is indeed possible to reach an objective understanding of phenomenological reality via the senses. Instead, the Baroque favored metaphors, and, more particularly, conceits: the kind of metaphor which, disguised through wit, makes intellectual jumps and moves the reader with its *obviously* artificial, violently forced imagery. In music, new concepts were created to express the same irrepressible sense of urgency: crescendo, rinforzando, diminuendo, fugue, pathos, and dynamism.

14. I am much indebted to Fagiolo dell'Arco 231–39 for this argument.

15. In her article "Art and Power in the Spectacle Plays of Calderón de la Barca," Margaret R. Greer uses two discussions of seventeenth-century political emblems to indicate that poets occasionally manipulated figures and fables to present "unpleasant truths, not just to the prince, but to the public

at large", thus creating a "polyvalent discourse" (in *PMLA* 104 [1989]: 329–39, 330–31). This point is very valid but should not create the impression that in the splendid festive performances *vituperatio* was ever deliberately allowed to outweigh *laudatio*; if this was ever the case, then changing historical circumstances rather than artistic-moralistic intention were the dominant cause. *Ercole amante* provides an excellent case in point (see chapter 5).

16. See LeCoat 14; and Erwin Panofsky, *Meaning in the Visual Arts* (1955; Chicago, 1982) 52.

17. Among these philosophers were Plato, Plotinus, and Butcher (LeCoat 15).

18. LeCoat 15ff discusses this issue in depth and gives numerous references.

19. James Anderson Winn, *Unsuspected Eloquence: A History of the Relation of Poetry and Music* (New Haven, 1981); Herbert Lindenberger, *Opera: The Extravagant Art* (Ithaca; London, 1984). Much of Lindenberger's book deals with various aspects of the movement of opera "back and forth between two extremes—on the one hand, a dramatic emphasis in which musical values serve the interests of the text; on the other, an emphasis on performative features such as vocal virtuosity and sumptuousness of spectacle" (56). The focus of the book, however, is clearly on nineteenth- and twentury-century opera, in spite of occasional, very well informed gestures to the first century of the "extravagant art." I hope to suggest in the course of the following chapters that, precisely in the splendid, private festive performances of operas at the absolute courts in the middle decades of the seventeenth century, the oscillation that Lindenberger describes in the passage quoted above and throughout his book, was less pronounced than at any later point in the history of the art.

20. See on this D. P. Walker, "Musical Humanism in the Sixteenth and Early Seventeenth Centuries," *The Music Review* 2 (1941): 1–13, 111–21, 220–27, 288–308; 3 (1942): 55–71. Vickers 8–10 provides examples.

21. See further F. Angelini, *Il teatro barocco* (Rome; Bari, 1975) 70–1; and Spariosu 1991: e.g., 114, 143, 155–58, 195–97, 203.

22. For more detail on these matters, see LeCoat 44–45 and 52; Vickers 12; and Steadman 44–45.

23. Spariosu 1991 (23ff.) discusses Plato's and Aristotle's uneasiness with the archaic mimetic experience that underlies both Dionysian ritual and artistic performance (*rhapsodein*), and the subsequent attempt of these two philosophers to divorce the ritual and the artistic performance by redefining mimesis in logo-rational terms.

24. "I am Music, who know with my sweet accents how to quiet every perturbed soul and can, now with noble ire, then with love, inflame the coldest hearts. Sometimes I sing to the accompaniment of my golden cithara [lyre] to delight mortal ears, yet inspire rather the soul by virtue of the sonorous harmony of my heavenly lyre" (Claudio Monteverdi, *Tutte le opere*, ed. G. Francesco Malipiero [Asolo, 1930], vol. 11: 4).

25. We will not be concerned with medieval theoreticians (such as Augustine, in *De musica* [six books, A.D. 391]), because they were not primarily interested in imitating human emotions, or in appealing to them; rather: music had to please God, and could be used for all sorts of practical effects, including exorcisms (see examples in LeCoat 18). This does not mean that their work is not important or interesting. The reference to Rousseau is from Lindenberger, who discusses the primacy of the passions and the relationship between passions and music as central to Rousseau's theory of the origin of language (148–50).

26. Was the ideologically determined and rhetorically structured splendid festive performance at the Baroque absolute court a well-functioning prototype of the late nineteenth-century Wagnerian *Gesamtkunstwerk*, or of the incorporation thereof by the early twentieth-century aesthetics of fascism? Another field of inquiry opens up.

27. On *intermedi*, see Donald J. Grout, *A Short History of Opera* (1947; New York, 1988) 3rd. ed., 30–35.

28. See Kivy 29–36; and Edward A. Lippman, ed., *Musical Aesthetics: A Historical Reader*, 2 vols. (New York, 1986) 1: x. I have drawn much from Kivy's book in the following pages.

29. For a sophisticated treatment of the subject that extends beyond my present objective and period-frame, I refer to Lindenberger 127–44 ("Opera and Mimesis").

30. Reprinted with permission from (c) Pendragon Press. Besides *Laws* II (654ff.) and VII, other relevant texts are *Ion* and *Republic* III. Although Plato studied music for its function as a social, ceremonial experience (Lippman 3; Kivy 28–29; also Spariosu 1991: 184ff), he did not spurn its purely aesthetic value. Plato basically distinguished between the "metaphysical" study of music, which sees music as a sensuous, harmonious embodiment of ideal mathematical forms, and the "ethical" study of music, which sees music as a potentially positive influence in the lengthy educational process in the course of which the citizen's character is built. These two views are related: the former, ideally, is the outcome of the latter. Likewise, music can be a metaphor for the ideal, harmonious society; music is thus related to the Good.

The central point in Plato's musical remarks seems to be that music gives true pleasure when it is educationally valuable—in other words, when it contributes to one's education. Music teaches when it imitates, through its tones and rhythms and words, those things that are worth imitating because they are educationally valuable—such as virtuous emotions and behavior. These notions are certainly very puzzling, for, how can music imitate emotions, and, if we accept it can do that, how can it teach, in other words, change one's character (just like gymnastics or religion—the other elements of the citizen's education—can)? Moreover, we must be aware that if music can make one virtuous or brave, it can also do the opposite: make the virtuous man depraved and the brave man cowardly (Lippman 3; Kivy 29). Plato's (or to be more precise, Socrates' alleged) answer to these puzzling questions is fairly straightforward: music can "imitate" human character and emotion states by imitating the inflections of the human voice that indicate these character traits and emotions. Thus music cannot really "represent" bravery itself, but it can represent the ways a brave man would speak. According to Plato's moral psychology (which he shares with Aristotle), a man will gradually become brave, as it were by practice, if exposed long enough to the behavioral expression, for example through musical representation, of examples of bravery in other men. The same goes for the performers of the musical representations of human character and emotion states; the latter rub off, so to speak (Kivy 29–31). Imitations, heard or performed, grow into habits and change one's original nature. There can be great benefit in this, as well as great danger, which is why music must be regulated by laws (Kivy 30–31).

31. Girolamo Mei, "De modis veteris musicae libri quattuor" (1574), and *Discorso sopra la musica antica e moderna* (Venice, 1602). See Claude Palisca, ed., *Letters on Ancient and Modern Music* (American Institute of Musicology, 1960). Mei's musical aesthetic shows some influence from the Neoplatonists—especially from Ficino, who followed Plato (*Laws* II: 669) in associating poetry and music, because both appeal to the ear by means of melody and rhythm (LeCoat 18)—but more from the then new wave of Aristotelian thought and from the *Poetics* in particular (Kivy 28).

32. Vincenzo Galilei, *Dialogo della musica antica e della moderna* (Florence, 1581; facs. ed. New York, 1967).

33. Mei thought that in monophonic music tones are sounded in unison, and that only such music could produce the behavior modification which Plato and Aristotle claimed the music of their time could achieve (Kivy 29 and 35). Polyphonic music, which since the fourteenth century had become increasingly and exceedingly complex, can only astonish and delight, so the Camerata argued, but not imitate or represent human character and emotions; it cannot imitate or represent speech and other expressive behavior; it does

not resemble human speech at all, for in reality people who want to be understood do not speak all at the same time. And for reasons of counterpoint, it cannot represent the fact that the human speaking voice differs in range, rhythm, tones and accents under the influence of different passions: high or rapid tones supposedly express excitement and arousal, whereas lower tones and a slow rhythm express abjectness or sluggishness. Thus the message and the represented emotions get entangled in the flowery arrangements which call attention to themselves. For that reason, polyphony lacks the potential power of music over the soul and character of men. I acknowledge my debt to Kivy (chapters 1 and 2) and Donington 82ff. in this section.

34. In *Politics* VIII: 1341, Aristotle rejects the flute for educational purposes, mainly because playing it prevents one from using *logos* (words, the voice).

35. See V. Galilei in LeCoat 19, and Tasso ibid. 44. In the Renaissance, this attitude came to be associated with the *musici poetici*, the "moderns," and it was to be repeated over and over again in the early seventeenth century. The *musici poetici* fought the excessive use of polyphony in which the harmony dominated the words (in Monteverdi's phrase, the *prima prattica*); they were determined to make "the words the mistress of the harmony" for the sake of mimesis (*seconda prattica*; Monteverdi, preface to *Quinto libro de'Madrigali* [1605, reference from LeCoat 21]). By contrast, the *musici mathematici* of the old school clung to the view that a work of art reflects a supernatural order and that the musical composition in particular is a *speculum naturae*, the mathematical proportions of which relate the microcosmos to the macrocosmos (LeCoat 17, 19).

36. The one question that really matters: whether music (or any art) actually and truly arouses emotions, is one that we cannot answer here. One of the principal indictments that since antiquity has been raised against certain works of art, namely that they corrupt, seems to suggest that the capacity of art to arouse has never been truly questioned. The numerous writers who developed and kept adapting the Orpheus myth throughout the centuries may have been guilty of pious wishful thinking when they wrote about song/poetry that has the power of shaking trees and melting hearts hard like rock, for it is this very ancient problem of intentional arousal-via-mimesis that is captured in the crucial literary myth of Orpheus. In fact, the more literature (or art in general) arouses its audience, the more it is genuinely Orphic. For some, "poetry and lovemaking are essentially analogous" (Malcolm Bradbury, "*Fanny Hill* and the Comic Novel," *Critical Quarterly* 13 (1971) 263–75: 270). Which leads us to conclude that what is generally referred to as pornography—the representation of sexuality and nudity that intentionally aims at sexually arousing the audience and at inducing it to like

behavior—actually fulfills most efficiently the originally stated function of the mimetic arts. "Probably the only Orphean music we ever hear, the only literature we ever read which realises the classical myth of the poetry that could make trees dance, is the first piece of pornography we are ever taken by" (John Hollander, "The Old Last Act: Some Observations on *Fanny Hill*" *Encounter* 21 (1963) 69–75: 69).

37. One of the early examples of such a list was Jan Albert Ban's *Dissertatio epistolica De musicae natura* (Leyden, 1637; reference from Brewster Rogerson, "The Art of Painting the Passions," *Journal of the History of Ideas* 14 [1953] 68–94, 82–83).

38. See Kivy, chapter 4.3.

39. This problematic is precisely the subject of Peter Kivy's *Osmin's Rage*.

40. Giovanni Bardi, *Discorso sopra la musica antica e'l cantar bene* (c. 1580); translation in LeCoat 20.

41. Marin Mersenne, *Quaestiones celeberrimae* (Paris, 1623). LeCoat 53–54 quotes Mersenne's interesting but somewhat fastidious theory on determining the expressive value of musical intervals by means of five pairs of opposites.

42. See Dene Barnett, "La rhétorique de l'opéra," *Dix-Septième Siècle* 33 (1981) 335–55: 343.

43. In other words, in the execution, the singer replaced the written, measured notes with the rhythm of the words. Thus, the tempo and accent of the declamation were governed by the passions that needed to be expressed according to the text, not by the measure of the written notes. For example, if the words changed in refrains or strophes, it was considered necessary to change the notes from the second strophe onward, in order to respect, for example, the expressive length of sounds in the new words. For a contemporary source, see Bacilly, "Application du Chant aux Paroles Françoises," in *Remarques curieuses sur L'art de bien chanter* (Paris, 1668) 350; reference from Barnett 341. Timbre, too, depended on the text. If tender feelings were to be expressed, the words would be pronounced/sung accordingly; the same was true for hard or unpleasant feelings. Excellent pronunciation skills were therefore paramount.

44. In terms of semiotics, the codex of poses and expressions available to such actors was comparable to that of the famous dancers of Bali, Burma and Thailand, and their mastery of this codex was appreciated by contemporaneous audiences as much as we appreciate southeast Asian dance today—with the difference that we applaud the latter as sophisticated, whereas many would reject the former as artificial. But acting technique in the seventeenth century,

and well into the eighteenth, was precisely that: "artificial," studied, rhetorical, and expressive. If you dance, writes Michel de Pure in his section on "le Bal,", "tous vos pas & toutes vos actions sont tributaires aux yeux des Spectateurs, & leur exposent & le bien & le mal, dont l'Art & la Nature ont favorisé ou disgracié vostre personne" ("all your passes and all your actions are dependent upon the eyes of the Spectators and expose to them both the good things and the bad things with which Art and Nature have graced or disgraced your person;" 178).

45. "the action in general, in the sense that one must understand it here, consists of the Art of painting the ideas and the feelings of the gestures, by means of the entire pose of the body, and especially by means of the expression of the face. The action that is dealt with, is the same art that is applied to words set to music, and the play of the Actors who are singing must vary just as much as these words do—which means, infinitely much." From a treatise by Bérard, a singer at the Opéra, "De l'action propre au Chant" in *L'Art du Chant* (Paris, 1755; quoted in the original in Barnett 344–5). Barnett provides other interesting examples. In *Quaestiones celeberrimae*, Marin Mersenne devoted an entire chapter specifically to the movement of the body, the face and the hands, which he says must be adapted to the "poesie," "sans cela la musique sera imparfaite, et incomplète" ("without that, the music will be imperfect, and incomplete;" 346). Mersenne specifically refers the actors to Cicero, Quintilian and other rhetoricians for instruction. A century later, in *Dissertatio de actione scenica* (Munich, 1727), the Jesuit Franciscus Lang proposed as a model the gestures of polite society and the tones of natural speech, and he, too, gave exact advice on how to represent specific emotions by modulations of the voice and movements of the limbs (346).

46. It is therefore perfectly legitimate to compare techniques of expression in, say, Poussin and Corneille. See Renselaer Lee, *Ut Pictura Poesis: The Humanistic Theory of Painting* (New York, 1967) 28.

47. In LeBrun's manual, "Descartes' psychology was virtually put on the tip of the young painters' brushes," says Rogerson 75.

48. Conversely, Poussin studied wax models, theatrically arranged, for the composition of his historical paintings. The Dutchman Gerard de Lairesse, an etcher and painter, published his *Groot Schilderboek* (Amsterdam, 1707; trans. John Frederick Fritsch, *The Art of Painting in All its Branches* [London, 1738]), in which drawings illustrate the techniques of theatrical gesticulation and indicate the semantic differences between vulgar and polite manners, poses, and gestures.

49. In the eighteenth century, observation and judgment rather than

codified rhetorical figures were gradually called upon to represent the passions. As a result, a more "natural" acting style was developed—the gist of which was actually already contained in Hamlet's advice to the actors (*Hamlet*, 3.3). See, for example, Aaron Hill, *The Art of Acting* (1746), Thomas Wilkes, *General View of the Stage* (1759), and Diderot, *Paradoxe sur le comédien* (c. 1778). For a survey of principal acting styles in the eighteenth century, see Alan S. Downer, "Nature to Advantage Dressed," *PMLA* 68 (1943) 1002–37.

50. Spariosu defines "opsis of the mind" as the visual ability of perceiving not movement and discontinuity, but continuity and sameness in things (1991: 215). This ability stems from concentrating on the abstract or visual aspects of lexis—in our case, the allegorical content and images in the literary program of the performances.

51. On the connection between rhetorical eloquence and theatrical representation, see also Solf 23–24 and Baur-Heinhold 121ff.

52. In the twentieth century, these two systems coexist once again, although the order of perceived modernity is now exactly the reverse.

53. See L. Magagnato, "The Genesis of the *Teatro Olimpico*," in *Journal of the Warburg and Courtauld Institutes* 14 (July-Dec.) 1951. Palladio's design was a deliberate attempt to recover for modern times the stage architecture of Vitruvius (c.50–26 B.C.), whose manual *De Architectura*, in ten volumes, was heavily influenced by Hellenistic building conventions. Vitruvius, who probably knew the late Hellenistic theater from personal experience, was considered the supreme authority on architecture during the Renaissance, and numerous manuscript copies of his treatise are said to have circulated throughout Europe already before the Renaissance (unillustrated *editio princeps* 1486; see Lawrenson 21–23). In 1548, the Academia della Virtù was founded in Rome to study Vitruvius' work, which marked the new Renaissance attitude toward reconstruction. Section 8 of Book V of *De Architectura* in particular was a crucial source, serving as a bridge between the ancient theater and that of the modern world (in the same book, Vitruvius included baths and other public buildings). It is in this section, namely, that Vitruvius introduces his famous distinction between the "tragic," the "comic," and the "satyric" scenes; this triad, with its codified characteristics, was to influence theater architecture and stage design throughout the Renaissance and the Baroque. For example, in Book VIII of his influential *De Re Aedificatoria* (Florence, posthum. 1485), Leone Battista Alberti discussed the ancient theater according to Vitruvius and fixed its characteristics for the next century. A more important steppingstone toward the Baroque stage was the summarizing treatise by Sebastiano Serlio, *Architettura* (Paris, 1545). The stage design that is today considered "typically Baroque" was proposed and canonized by Nicola Sabbattini in his *Pratica di fabricar scene e machine ne'teatri*

(Ravenna, 1637-'38). For completeness' sake, we must add that in the interlude between Serlio and Sabbattini the Uffizi theater in Florence (in other words, the official Medici stage) had already witnessed experiments (in 1586 and 1589) with so-called "Baroque" perspective and proscenium arrangements.

54. See Lawrenson 36ff. Because the Olimpico was designed for reconstruction performances of antique plays rather than for splendid festive performances directly relevant to the Baroque, I will not discuss its inauguration performance in this study.

55. See Strong 1973: 32ff for the invention by Brunelleschi (in 1425) of the artificial perspective—the principle of the centric ray—that concerns us here. In his *Della Pittura* (1435), Alberti applied the new principle to the visual arts. In a third stage, the principle was combined with the revived theatrical architecture of Vitruvius. The perspective principle was almost immediately applied to the aristocratic palace theaters, where various techniques were designed for swiftly turning sets or changing scenery.

56. Theoretically, that is, rather than practically. See Serlio's three "stages," and Menestrier's fifteen categories (*Des Représentations en musique anciennes et modernes*, 1681).

57. The *gloire* was perhaps the most popular machine effect of all: the descent or ascent of characters upon a cloud. Its direct ancestor, and pictorial source, is to be found in religious paintings of the Renaissance (Lawrenson 44).

58. "Machines" and engineering techniques were already put to use in medieval productions (the liturgy, mysteries, banquets). See Villard de Honnecourt's *Sketchbook*, ed. T. Bowie (Bloomington, 1959). And the festive celebrations, pageants, and performances of the Renaissance (and, most likely, especially the *intermedi*) had seen experiments with more sophisticated machines.

59. These new motifs, which appeared equally prominently in the visual arts and in literature, favored those aspects of nature that had not been previously cultivated for their own sake by the arts: changing skies, tempestuous seas, wild nature, ruins. Baroque thinker-artists were fundamentally interested in movement: in *natura naturans* rather than *natura naturata*, and in changing rather than in stable humankind. Paradoxically, these favored images of instability created a rather stable and closed codex of symbols that could be recalled instantly to suggest transience, fluidity and openness.

60. Besides Bernini, the master of machines was Sabbattini, o.c. On seventeenth-century hydraulics, see G.-B. Aleotti, *Idrologia overo Vaso delle*

Scienze et Arte dell Acque del ben regulare le acque (5 ms. vols.; Aleotti was also the builder of the Teatro Farnese. References from Lawrenson 45). Renaissance and Baroque mechanics were anticipated and greatly influenced by the scientific work done at the School of Alexandria (especially famous for Hero), which had then been recently rediscovered. See on this A. G. Drachman, *The Mechanical Technology of Greek and Roman Antiquity* (Copenhagen: 1963) 18ff and 197–98. Vitruvius, in Book X of *De Architectura*, also discusses machines for building and for creating the kind of special effects that were pursued by the makers of the festive celebrations and performances. Furthermore, see Bertrand Gille, *Engineers of the Renaissance* (Cambridge, Mass., 1966).

61. Cesare Molinari, *Le Nozze degli Dèi: un saggio sul grande spettacolo italiano nel seicento* (Rome, 1968), 117–19.

62. Thus he "set fire" to the theater in the production of his play "The Fair" (before 1645): as the audience was evacuating the room in a panic, the scene changed into a delightful garden. (Compare also with the trickster-god Dionysus in *Bacchae*, whose play with lightning sets fire to a palace without burning it down.) The fairly sophisticated pyrotechnical devices necessary for the special effect had in fact been developed earlier for court spectacles, mainly in order to represent scenes set in Hell. On another occasion, for the performance of his "Inundation of the Tiber," Bernini seemingly caused the theater to flood; once more, the audience panicked. In two publications (*Bernini and the Unity of the Visual Arts* [New York; London, 1980] 1: 146–57; and a review of C. d'Onofrio's edition of an untitled play by Bernini that was named "Fontana di Trevi" after the manuscipt book in which it was accidentally found, *Art Bulletin* 46 [1964] 568–72), Irving Lavin emphasizes that Bernini's importance for the history of Roman theater was only minimally the result of his mechanical skills and machines, for all his "tricks" had been experimented with before in courtly spectacles; more important was what he did with them. Indeed, Bernini was not too fond of the machines themselves; his interest in improvized *commedia dell'arte* did not really have room for elaborate machines, which he considered too cumbersome and too slow. His secret was to avoid doing things that would not succeed perfectly, and he preferred putting up spectacles in his own house.

Bernini's "Fontana di Trevi" is actually a comedy of which the protagonist is a malfunctioning "cloud machine;" this unfinished play was translated, with a very useful introduction and notes, as *The Impresario* by Donald Beecher and Massimo Ciavolella (Carleton Renaissance Plays in Translation 6; Ottawa, 1985). My point is that when Saint-Evremond complained about the dullness of opera in the 1670s, he was probably not talking about the sort of rhetorically structured, ideologically determined festive performance that we are discussing here, but about the next generation of totally sung opera in which verisimilitude and realism was a much more pregnant issue (see Lindenberger 206; see also chapter 5).

I would like to draw attention to the twentieth-century incarnation of this playful Bernini, namely the eccentric director-producer William Castle, known in the 1950s and 1960s as the "King of Gimmicks." For an exhilarating survey of Mr. Castle's remarkable achievements in B movies and showbusiness, see chapter 2: "Whatever Happened to Showmanship," in John Waters, *Crackpot: The Obsessions of John Waters* (New York; London, 1986) 14–23.

63. The awareness that movement (a formal change, a metamorphosis) is an inescapable reality of nature, was reflected in the feasts and performances of the age. This awareness was especially visible when nature and art were made to meet—and when nature and architecture, in particular, were made to interact, such as in the artificial arrangement of space in the curious (outdoors) "hedge", "ruin", and "rock" theaters (see Baur-Heinhold 136–39 for a list of famous outdoors theaters of these various types). When an elaborate feast was staged or a complex performance held in a natural setting (gardens, parks) or a pseudo-natural setting (a *piazza* flooded and transformed into a lake), the latter was made to function as if it were an architectural construct; conversely, the architectural component (scene, stage, arches, fountains) was integrated in the natural setting. Thus an attempt was made to have forms and materials of architecture harmoniously exchange use and value with the forms and materials of nature. In the rhetoric of the celebratory occasion, architecture became a metaphor for nature, and vice versa.

64. See Jean Rousset, *L'Intérieur et l'extérieur: Essais sur la poésie et sur le théâtre au XVIIe siècle* (1968; Paris, 1976) 165–82. The separation between audience and actors is effected, Rousset argues, in order to create the illusion that the performed events happen in a reality of their own. Further, Rousset claims, the audience has no access to this reality and must therefore willingly suspend its disbelief, that is, its normal consciousness of real time and place. In other words, an atmosphere of enchantment is created, in which the spectator is considered to be absent and in which the actor hides behind the character. The aesthetic of illusion also implies that both actor and audience subscribe to a notion of folly. The actor must play as if nobody were there to hear or see, as if one is really the character that one embodies and in the location that one pretends to be in. The purpose is for the audience to be engulfed totally in this hallucination—which amounts in fact to a case of collective and systematic folly: "l'accès d'aliénation mentale auquel on convie le spectateur est souvent donné pour un rêve éveillé, accompagnant un sommeil artificiellement provoqué par l'envoûtement de la scène" ("the bout of mental alienation in which the spectator is invited [to participate] is often presented like an alert dream, occurring in the course of a slumber artificially

induced by the spell of the scene;" 172). The representation is, indeed, literally a "dream" (*songe*, or *rêve*, although these words mean different things in French). Furthermore, Rousset writes on the subject of the illusionistic theater of the "magic cube," that "nous sommes ainsi préparés à comprendre la présence, dans la pièce même, des magiciens et magiciennes opérant sous les yeux des spectateurs, avec la complicité des machines, ces 'merveilles' qui se donnent à la fois pour réelles et pour théâtrales; l'illusion est consentie, mais le spectacle illusoire met tout en oeuvre pour faire oublier momentanément aux trompés qu'ils sont au théâtre" ("we have thus been prepared to understand the presence within the play itself of magicians at work before the very eyes of the spectators, with the assistance of machines, those "marvels" that pretend to be real and theatrical at the same time; the illusion [the suspension of disbelief] is granted, but the illusory spectacle tries its best to let the duped ones forget momentarily that they are in the theater" 170–71). The myth that the scene or place of representation is an "enchanted island" was very much developed in the first half of the seventeenth century. It fitted the aesthetic of illusion perfectly: the place of the performance is perfectly separated from the audience. The island (or its equivalent) was a place of exception, circumscribed, isolated by a protective zone from the profane world, ideal milieu for the "songe tenu pour réel," "the dream considered reality," of the performance.

65. See Kristiaan P. Aercke, " 'An Odd Angle of the Isle': Teaching the Courtly Art of *The Tempest*" in Maurice Hunt, ed., *Approaches to Teaching Shakespeare's "The Tempest" and Other Late Romances* (New York: MLA, 1992) 146–52.

66. Rousset interprets the dramatic development he describes solely by means of play texts and stage directions and rather indiscriminately blends private (courtly) and public theaters in his discussion; he does not discuss the context of the performances, their occasion, and their value as total events.

67. Interestingly, seventeenth-century portrait painters, too, preferred to depict their subjects frontally—as if ready to engage in a rhetorical communication with the viewer—rather than in profile, as was more common in the Renaissance and again in the middle-class eighteenth-century (Alewyn 1959: 40).

68. "to allow the spectators no occasion whatsoever to reflect on what it is that they are seeing or to doubt its reality." Rousset (170) quotes from Chapelain, *Opuscules critiques*, ed. Hunter (Paris, 1936) 115–16.

69. Equally interesting is D'Aubignac's statement in the *Pratique du théâtre* (1657), also quoted by Rousset, that the total spectacle should convince the senses and the imagination like magic, so that the spectator thinks that

the spectacle truly is identical with the "reality." True, this amounts to asking the audience to suspend its disbelief—but in this instance it follows from the magic of the rhetorician whose true function and merit as *rhèthor* resides, according to Aristotle, in finding, for each possible subject, the existing means of persuasion and in applying these means appropriately and successfully (*"Art" of Rhetoric* I: 1355b).

70. The aesthetic of illusion absolutely requires the audience to be in the dark, facing a lighted stage, whereas the rhetorical function of the performance is certainly served by a lighted auditorium but not drastically threatened by a dark one. According to the scholarly consensus, the auditorium was generally well lighted—which clearly works against the aesthetic of illusion. According to Baur-Heinhold, "until the end of the eighteenth century, nearly all performances at court took place with the auditorium as brightly lit as the stage. The spectator wanted to be seen and to play his own part" (34). And also according to Barnett, auditoria were "toujours éclairée," "always lighted" (335). Both the stage and the auditorium were lighted with candelabra; in addition, oil lamps served as footlights. (Interestingly, the only exception was in the opera houses in Venice, which were public.) In spite of the evidence, Rousset constantly implies that the audience was sitting in the dark; for example, in his brief discussion of the 1664 *Plaisirs de l'Ile enchantée* (174), he withholds the very important information that the gardens were brilliantly illuminated.

71. For a complementary view on the same matter ("only the Catholic courts favored the festive performance"), see Trevor-Roper.

Interlude: The Gods of Play

So far I have attempted to describe as rhetorical discourse the splendid festive forms that the Baroque ceremonial consciousness developed in order to confirm and praise the sponsor-ruler in the new role of present but *passive* absolute monarch. The final development of the theme depends on the awareness of a sense of ritual, and ritualistic play in particular. Let us begin with a fairly stable description of the phenomenon of play. Though much has been written on play and the theory of play since *Homo Ludens*, Huizinga's definition has lost little of its usefulness.[1] Huizinga considers play a voluntary action or activity, which is limited in place and time, and which follows rules that are freely accepted but nevertheless hold absolute authority. Play has a goal *an sich,* and the players must experience feelings of tension and pleasure alike. They are conscious of doing something that somehow differs from "daily life" activities. Moreover, play is also gratuitous in the sense that material or useful connotations are usually not characteristic of genuine play—although this is not the same as saying that such play is also gratuitous in an ideological sense.

Furthermore, play can be repeated, but none of the replays will ever be exactly the same; each time this happens, something of the playful repetition remains in the consciousness, as a spiritual re-creation. And the fact that play is separated from "daily life" has much to do with the fact that it requires a separate locus: a specific, originally sacred space is meted out both for the sake of isolation and to protect the act of playing against influences or threats from the nonplaying world outside. The delimitation of such a space is the initial stage of any sacred action. And perhaps most important of all is the fact that play creates order: it is order itself. Play is thus a considerable civilizing force, because, in an imperfect world, it stimulates, at least temporarily, the firm belief that a limited perfection can be achieved (Huizinga, chapter 2).

In the West, play that was formalized as performance or drama originally belonged to the sphere of ritualistic, sacred activity. The sacred representations in antiquity or in archaic civilizations in general were originally ludic reenactments—in the form of dancing, for example—of the order of the universe and of the position of humankind in that universe.[2] Moreover, play was also perceived and expressed as an instrument of power (a leitmotif in Spariosu 1991). In this aspect at least, play is very close to rhetoric. In "playful" sacred performances as in ancient liturgical games, a ludic element was maintained as the community spirit re-enacted (performed, represented mimetically) the civilizing process. Both in form and in essence, the participants (the actors, that is, the officiating priests, and the spectators, i.e., the responding audience) were temporarily transported, in a sense, to another sphere. As long as it was felt that the playful sacred activity had a direct effect—as in the playful seasonal rites that ancient peoples perform(ed) in order to confirm and impersonate (play) the order of nature—play was extremely serious and on occasion required death for its finale.[3] Such play was thus a productive social activity, assisting toward the conservation and furthering of the community, and greatly outweighing in importance "mere pleasure" play, if such a notion existed at all (see Bataille 1970, vol. 1: 303).

But Greek thinkers gradually began to discern in play a psychological, aesthetic dimension (*paidia*), as separate from its social, ethical dimension (*agon*; Miller 101–16). As a result, from the fifth and fourth centuries B.C. onward the notion of *paidia*, or play as a pleasurable activity for its own sake, was present in the Greek habit of thought as well as in the Greek language (Spariosu 1991: 92). When Plato formalized the link between play and sacred activity (in *Laws* VII: 803), he essentially affirmed an already existing dichotomy between, on the one hand, "noble" play and, on the other, gratuitous aesthetic pleasure (see also Aristotle, *Politics* VIII: 1339a). The distinction between these two forms of play, which can be rephrased as the opposition between mere or gratuitous play (which society needs to curb, for its excessive enjoyment borders on or leads into the pathological) on the one hand, and the serious play of cult on the other, is not without relevance for my present thesis.[4]

I argue, again, that the Baroque sponsor-absolute rulers and their satellites, holding a view "from above" and drawn together in an at least temporarily stable communion around the mediating figure of the sponsor-ruler, considered their splendid performances in terms of the very serious play of cult (Bataille 1970, vol. 2: 309–11).[5] This argument concurs with Gadamer's critique of the "leveling process of aesthetic consciousness," with which he means the tendency resulting from eighteenth-century aesthetics to consider a work of art—in our case, a performance and all its surrounding circumstances—an "object that stands over against a subject for itself" (102). Instead, the work of art is an experience of creation which can, theoretically at least, change its makers and those at whom it is directed. Let me say, then, that the splendid festive performance of the Baroque was not a form of trivial play but instead the final resurgence of sacred play and perhaps even its culmination in western culture, a microcosmos of the "new" macrocosmos, intended to affect the ethos of the audience-participants via the praise and celebration of the depersonalized, collectivized sponsor-absolute ruler, for whom an "as if" relationship of filiation with the divine system was reconstructed by means of the repeated rite.[6] In the seventeenth century, Church and State often collaborated to reinforce this assumption. It was therefore probably not accidental that festive performances were organized especially at Catholic courts.[7]

Of course, the various types of Renaissance festive celebrations, too, were serious playful activities in the old-fashioned sense, for they were redolent of pagan rituals as well as of the rituals of Christianity. For example, the sense of ritualistic sacrifice, consecration, and initiation were part of the carnival mystique. However, such celebrations were usually still relevant for the entire community, and the sponsor-ruler not only officiated over them but also participated in them personally—just as the priest officiated over the sacred play of the liturgy.[8] By contrast, festive performances in the Baroque were generally private: organized in a closed space, they did not any longer address the entire community or polis, and from the private (theater, play) space followed the notion of exclusion. Much of the pleasing seduction, or power, of play resides precisely in the players' (including, the audience's) feeling of "belonging," of being together in an atmosphere that is "exceptional" (different from "routine") and that forges a common bond among the participants, pitting them against those outside the world of the play, or outside the play-circle of the court—a form of escapism, which, however, is also characteristic of true play. Sacred play activity has always to some extent excluded the Other (the noninitiated, the permanently or temporarily "unclean"), but it was probably a notion peculiar to the early modern western world that the exclusion be determined primordially by the social class structure.[9]

As a rhetorical discourse, the Baroque festive performance thus addressed a small, fairly well educated group, not any longer a community or polis.[10] The initiated participants knew very well that what was presented was an allegorical construction, an illusion, but they were nevertheless prepared to go along temporarily with it.[11] In fact, this tendency may signify an attempt at cultural-historical regression. In archaic Greece, power was originally situated in the aristocratic *oikos*, and the singer of tales (the player) performed his art (inevitably an art in praise of the aristocratic system) for the closed court circle, the center of which was the "king" (epic poetry). In the later classical phase, the powerbase was reorganized in function of the *polis* or city state, in which entertainment was directed at the community and was closely tied to religious events or beliefs (fifth-century dramatic festivals) (Spariosu 1991 passim). The general context of the Renaissance festive celebrations reminds one of the classical Greek phase, whereas the advent and the rhetorical exploitation of the Baroque splendid performance seems to signal a return to the preceding archaic phase.

The philosophical question then remains whether the private courtly performance, given its function in the ritual of court and its rhetorical nature, gradually became "sacred play:" an "as if" act of worship of its sponsor-absolute-ruler, the production of the latter as an irrefutably sacred object, the kernel of a community, which was transformed (metamorphosed, translated) via the program and the rhetoric of the performance from an object of shared fear (*sacré gauche*) to an object of exaltation (*sacré droite*; for these terms, see Bataille 1970, vol. 2: 316–17, 330ff). A sacred object is always perceived to be surrounded, or protected, by barriers, to be in part repulsive to the worshipers because of its awesome power of excitation over their life, or fate, or death, or because some sacred objects are essentially controlled by taboos; it is partly because they are invested with the repulsive that such objects are attractive to the worshipers. It is not different with the sacred role that the absolute monarch played as the *roi thaumaturge*, as the god-appointed healer of loathsome diseases; it is not different with the Catholic doctrine of Transsubstantiation—which may well provide another reason for the fact that the truly grandiose festive performances seem to have been celebrated at Catholic courts. The absolute monarch was the magnetic lodestone that bound the courtiers together by their shared fear and interests. By virtue of its allegorical program, the festive performance was one important way of transforming such fear into exaltation, of turning the repulsive into the attractive (in chapter 5 we will examine a clear example of this sort of attempted metamorphosis, when we look at *Ercole amante* for Louis XIV), of metamorphosing the potential motives of the sponsor-ruler into half revealed, half concealed statements about the monarch, the court, and the world. Such an enterprise of sacred play was political, and it could not do without external splendor. In the words of the experienced Bossuet: "les dépenses de magnificence et de dignité ne sont pas moins nécessaires pour le soutien de la majesté aux yeux des peuples."[12] All the rituals with which the absolute ruler surrounded himself or herself were inherently cultic in the sense of sacred play (see, again, the concept of the *roi thaumaturge*).[13] Can the absolute ruler who sponsored splendid performances then be said to have filled the hitherto vacant position of the god(dess) of play, if only "as if?" I have already referred to Huizinga as noting that the antique western pantheon did not designate a specific deity to preside over play, hence leaving play as the only elementary human activity or need which may never have had a tutelary deity.[14]

The "as if" concept of play theory, and, interestingly enough, also of myth theory, is an important one. In *The Masks of God: Primitive Mythology* (New York, 1959), Joseph Campbell argues that the logic of myth and the logic of play are essentially the same; both follow the logic of "as if" (see Miller 20). The central notion of the "as if" concept, which has been analyzed in depth by Hans Vaihinger, is that humans have always felt the need to create fictions in order to shape and arrange their lives; politics, religion, and art, among other forms, result from this need. Originally it entailed role-playing and simulation, as well as, in the more advanced stage of philosophy, the tendency to act on the premise that we can at least pretend that truth is available to us, "in the 'as if' play of Reason" (Spariosu 1989: 20–21). Even in the seventeenth century, no educated person in his or her right mind would mistake the absolute ruler for a deity of any sort, no matter how complex the allegorical programs and how stunning the visual-aural flourishes of feasts and spendid performances. But as vehicles of a power-oriented rhetoric, the festive performances reinforced the symbolic "as if" claim that is also an original feature of genuine play—in this case the claim that only the absolute monarch was responsible for, and capable of, realizing the common desires of the court and the nation: stability and abundance.

Renaissance rulers claimed nothing of the sort; they can be likened to high priests in the service of mysteries of a different order than their own, sponsoring or presiding over forms of sacred play according to a liturgical calendar or when special occasions called for it. They did not maintain a permanent atmosphere of play. Far from restricting the playful activity to a private area, they emphasized the public places: streets, squares, the market place. Their artists were not merely the receptacles or instruments of the semidivine words. Giordano Bruno, Renaissance neoplatonist par excellence, saw the artist as an inventor, as an actually creative force (following Plato's idea, of course, that good poets are active and *do*, or create, something, as the verb *poiein* implies). And the courtiers of such Renaissance sponsor-ruler-priests were not perpetual actors in their rulers' own service. The settings in which the rites took place did not systematically favor the ruler's sole vantage point with intricately arranged perspectives.

By contrast, in the private festive performance, the presiding absolute ruler occupied the center front position as the guarantor of order (which at times made his/her situation also a precarious one). Precisely this fact, this presence, contributed to make some performances more grandiose and majestic than others, for the ruler always had the option of simply retreating, secluded and invisible, into the royal box. But on certain occasions, he or she came out. Back turned to the audience, this sponsor-ruler-become-god communicated an ideology (a *communiqué*) to the select and initiated courtly audience by means of the actors and other artists—the "priests," interlocutors and intermediaries, the successors to the joker-player via whom the medieval lord allowed "truth" to be known to the court.[15] Or, in another analogy, the artists and creators of such Baroque festive performances can be likened to the poets whom Plato *did* allow to reside and work in the (undemocratic) Republic, to serve there as mouthpieces for the (semi)divine rulers and to utter what the Muse (including the sponsor, or the polis) impelled them to express.

The ruler's new theater, opera house, or magnificent garden, was the temple especially designed for such ritualized worship. The constant use of mythological subjects provided the symbolic vehicle for the sponsor-ruler's divinification, the pagan aspects conveniently invalidating potential charges of blasphemy. The machines symbolized her metaphysical grandeur or his pretended control over the elements, over time and space. The initiated courtiers were forced into a permanent celebration of these rites as one feast followed upon another, for, like any Olympian before him, the god of play could—and as we will see in the next chapters, very often *did*—disregard the dire economic, political, and social realities of the age. These performances can thus perhaps be seen as a compulsive celebration of rites, that is, the rites of the gods of play. Indeed, the ruler was "interested in keeping his festivals going in order to keep himself entertained" (Spariosu 1991: 129, writing about Dionysus in Aristophanes' *Frogs*). And at the same time, such sacred and socially determined *play* (including *mousikè*) was a most effective way of instructing the world of the court in the principles of ruler worship.

The rites of the sponsor-ruler-god of play required the participants, or worshipers, to submerge themselves completely in the celebrations and to ignore the calls of a "Reality principle" which were present, on the extradiegetic level of the performances, in the form of, for example, sermons preached at court (in which the orator necessarily and, literally, "hypocritically" reminded the ruler and the court of the vanity of earthly things),[16] in occasional and timid oppositions to absolutism (Apostolidès 1981: 34), or, sometimes, in the hidden meanings embedded in the literary program of the festive performances themselves. But in general, such prosaic reminders of the needs of the real world were taboo and even irrelevant in the context of the splendid private festive performances at Baroque courts. In part, the rites of the gods of play aimed at overcoming operative Reality principles, and, by overcoming the tension between love and duty, at creating a playful and erotic civilization—a short-lived restoration and practical execution, perhaps, of the unified, pre-Platonic concept of play in the West.[17]

With this I mean that the courtiers' duty demanded loyalty to the "family" (the court) and love for and absolute obedience to the family's awesome head: the father-sponsor-absolute ruler-god of play.[18] Required to subject their own desires to those of the sponsor-ruler, who provided in most of their immediate and long-term needs, these courtier-players were compelled (at least in theory and when the sponsor-ruler-god[dess] could see them, which was most of the time), to "work" by an external necessity, to assume their role and perform their part in the rhetoric of play, which was the worship of the ruler-god. This duty affected everyone within the walls and gates of the court, and it rendered the demands of the real world invalid, as courtiers were actively discouraged from doing any "real work" other than "play-work." At least for the duration of each festive celebration (of which there were very many, and most of which lasted very long), love-*eros* and duty-*ananke* were happily and harmoniously conjoined in the romance world of the court. Appropriately enough, this utopian world was often directly inspired by the topoi of Renaissance mock-chivalric *romanzesco*-epics. That is, it was represented as an attractive, vibrant and definitely erotic world—a world, moreover, that hinged upon the sponsor-ruler's visible generosity of excess, the sort of expected *noblesse/richesse oblige* generosity that characterizes a feudal-aristocratic society and that was immediately thrown out of the window when the bourgeoisie, with its strategies for dissimulating wealth behind closed doors, took over power (see on this also Bataille 1970, vol. 1: 312–13). The "view from below," which is therefore irrefutably bourgeois, rejects these magnificent performances and celebrations of sacred creative play as childish or unprofitable, thereby rejecting the practical execution of a utopia: a rather adolescent utopia perhaps, but a utopia nevertheless, in which happiness is actively pursued and play truly rewarded, and which is charged with eroticism.[19]

Were these performances insane enterprises? It is useful to recall, again, the Protestant work ethic and its relevance for the growth of modern, rational capitalism.[20] For not only does the existence of a Protestant philosophy of "work ethic" and "economic consciousness" provide yet another possible reason why the truly grandiose festive performances seem to have been celebrated only at Catholic courts; it also helps to explain the fact that, from our modern (i.e., post-Platonic, post-Aristotelian, middle-class, industrial) point of view, which not only officially praises work over play, but which also praises moderation and democratic restraint, the Baroque festive performance may indeed appear a rather odd undertaking.[21] The actual expenditure of energy, money, and supplies seems totally out of proportion, first, to the actual value or function of the occasion, and secondly, to the rapid consumption of all that energy. But then, don't *we* belong to the band of those permanently excluded from these splendid feasts and performances, whose obstructed view is obviously that from below? Better, we could argue that the participants in the splendid festive performance of the Baroque still knew how to *feast* in a deeply rooted mythic sense, that they still knew how to be "concelebrants" in a ritual with sacred origins. Lazarowicz pertinently reflects on the state of affairs in our modern theater and feast culture, which he describes as extremely depressing, because

> wenn Konzelebration und Kollusion nicht mehr funktionieren, verkümmert die Fest– und Theaterkultur. Dann tritt an die Stelle von ehemals produktiven Haltungen und Tätigkeiten der schiere Konsum von Kunst und Glamour. Zu den Konsequenzen dieser Konsumtion gehören Sattheit, Müdigkeit und Langeweile. Unsere zeitgenössischen Theatermacher und Festival-Veranstalter haben diese Lähmungserscheinungen bisher nicht kurieren können (315).[22]

All of the elements discussed in the preceding pages lead up to a definition of the splendid festive performance at Baroque absolute courts in terms of a form of exchange (production, acquisition, expenditure) that has been identified as characteristic of archaic economic institutions in many places of the world: potlatch. This sort of exchange, which amounts actually to the opposite of bartering, occurs in a festival setting and is a marker of important rites of passage in the life of the individual (the possessor of power and therefore of wealth, or vice versa; it makes no difference) who initiates it—rites of passage such as marriage, increase in status, treaties. As characterized by Marcel Mauss in 1925 and fruitfully incorporated by Georges Bataille in his "notion of expenditure," potlatch means gift-giving with the purpose of challenging and/or humiliating the recipient as well as obligating the latter to produce a more splendid gift in return: *do ut das*, in effect, in a context which is festive but which nevertheless preserves much of the competitive *agon* that Huizinga deems characteristic of genuine play.[23] Another recorded form of potlatch expenditure, besides gift-giving, is the grandiose display of wealth (which may include human beings), and more particularly, the voluntary destruction thereof in a splendid festive setting as a grand gesture that the challenged individual (or community) is invited not only to match but even to surpass in order to preserve honor. Such a deliberate pursuit of loss must seem to the bourgeois hunters and gatherers of wealth-to-be-hidden an insanely unproductive expenditure, but seen "from above" rather than "from below," potlatch activity is in fact quite something else. It is a sacred activity that brings communities together in a playful context of potentially endless rivalry and that places aristocratic personal status (that is, how the giver of potlatch is perceived) through honor far above mere personal status through material possessions. It is also an activity that borders on delirium, from any point of view, and that theoretically has the potential to upset the stability within the domain of the potlatch giver, who may be willing to stage ever grander displays of loss until victory is reached, until the opponent can no longer compete and fails to return the gift. In a sense, to have the most chips left is to incur humiliation and to lose the game.[24] I would argue, then, that the splendid festive performances at Baroque absolute courts were a direct descendant of such exacerbated potlatch poker, its last revival, perhaps, before different, bourgeois, economic principles channelled the playful loss-expenditure of wealth into secular, less glamorous, and certainly less potentially destabilizing directions. We will return to this subject in the next chapter, for I believe that it is precisely the notion of potlatch that provides the key to an understanding of the apparently self-contradictory performance of *Sant'Alessio* at the Barberini court.

Before concluding this "Interlude," I wish to emphasize the importance of the première and/or inauguration aspect of the festive performances. In the sacred play of ritual as well as for the splendid performance, setting is of primordial importance: establishing the locus actually initiates the ritual and is the first playful act. Without a designated locus, play is seriously hampered or even downright impossible. The Baroque pleasure palace, with its indoor or outdoor theater, furnished the logical extension of this concern, and, moreover, visual evidence of the antagonistic, even antisocial desire of separation (setting oneself apart, or rather, above) that stems from engagement in potlatch activity (Bataille 1970, vol. 1: 314–15).[25] Consider that the truly splendid festive performances were the première performances of machine-plays or operas, created for the inauguration of a new locus or theatrical space within the pleasure palace or on its adjacent grounds.[26] Such occasions were obviously rare, and therefore especially interesting in a consideration of the performance as sacred play.

It is for this reason that I have selected for further discussion in the following chapters splendid performances that were also inaugurations of significant, new play spaces. The mythic, or sacred implications of this double "newness" are staggering. The playful aspect of the plastic and durable arts, painting or architecture, says Huizinga, is found in the phenomenon of the inauguration.[27] The opening of an exhibition of paintings or sculptures provides even today an occasion for a festive celebration. Likewise, such activities as breaking the ground for a new building and the laying of the first brick, crowned by the consecration, are still accompanied by rituals that originate in play. The inauguration of a new permanent structure (court theater, court opera house, pleasure palace, pleasure gardens on the palace grounds) carried playful, festive connotations: the value of the première performance as sacred play was increased dramatically when it was also the première for the locus of the performance. In fact, the special value of the "first enjoyment" is even deeply rooted in the originally feudal context of absolute rule (*ius dominis*). Moreover, let us also not forget that many, if not most, of the relatively few truly splendid performances were performed only once: the première was thus also the majestic finale of a complex process. Designed and executed with an enormous investment of energy, creativity, and money, the genuinely lavish performances derived much, if not most of their magic from the quasi-uniqueness of the occurrence—from the "occasionality," to use Gadamer's term.[28] The final paradox of it all is that these events, which were destined to be the most memorable of all, were also the most transient—precisely because their cost and complexity forbade duplication. Such uniqueness was in general an important part of the mystique that was created around the figure and the function of the absolute ruler.[29]

Finally, I would like to build in a *caveat* to the hypothesis developed in this Interlude. On occasion (periods of mourning, for example), the courtly world did call for a temporary pause in the feasting. But the fact that such interruptions were usually faithfully recorded suggests that they were abnormalities and that the festive atmosphere, the rule of sacred play, was the norm. Thus, the Baroque courtly atmosphere, in which the activity of play was prescribed and carefully directed as a substitute for the activity of useful work, can be considered neurotic. When play becomes the only reality or a permanently enforced substitute for reality, does it not cease then to be *ludic* (like play), and does it not run the danger of becoming, instead, *ergic* (like work), if not a neurotic obsession? An essential element of authentic play seems to be lost in such a situation: in effect, the consciousness exists, even if only in the background, that one is acting "as if." Perhaps the very nature of feasts as such changed when the festive performance, the celebration, became something like an neurotic addiction. Court propaganda (via the *gazettes* and similar publications) succeeded effectively in reinforcing the notion that participation in court life and its feasts meant to be truly alive. Exclusion or absence from court, and thus from its continuing cycle of celebrations, was represented as a form of death; it was certainly perceived as such by aristocrats forced to dwell in the provinces, by exiled courtiers.[30] To the permanently excluded (such as the crowds gaping through the garden fences at the feasts in Versailles), the royal playhouse became, indeed, an illusionary world, a setting for unrealizable dreams and aspirations. At the most, the crowd was given the crumbs of the table.[31]

I am actually leading up to the question whether one can still speak of play and feasts when these become the norm and a substitute for real life, and when there are so many feast days to be marked in red on the court calendar that there is hardly enough time to prepare for them. In *L'Impromptu de Versailles*, produced before Louis XIV and the court at Versailles on October 14, 1663, the "marquis ridicule" Molière goes right to the heart of the matter, when he replies to Mademoiselle Béjart's complaint that, even for such a limited performance, their *troupe* was still not given sufficient time to prepare:

> Mon Dieu, Mademoiselle, les rois n'aiment rien tant qu'une prompte obéissance, et ne se plaisent point du tout à trouver des obstacles. Les choses ne sont bonnes que dans le temps qu'ils les souhaitent; et leur en vouloir

> reculer le divertissement est en ôter pour eux toute la grâce. Ils veulent des plaisirs qui ne se fassent point attendre, et les moins préparés leur sont toujours les plus agréables. Nous ne devons jamais nous regarder dans ce qu'ils désirent de nous; nous ne sommes que pour leur plaire, et lorsqu'ils nous ordonnent quelque chose, c'est à nous à profiter vite de l'envie où ils sont. Il vaut mieux s'acquitter mal de ce qu'ils nous demandent que de ne s'en acquitter pas assez tôt; et si l'on a la honte de n'avoir pas bien réussi, on a toujours la gloire d'avoir obéi vite à leurs commandements. Mais songeons à répéter, s'ils vous plaît.[32]

Hence the pressure on artist-technicians; hence the need for an ever greater expenditure of energy, technical marvels, complex programs, and outlays of cash to produce festive events when there actually was a genuine, an authentic reason for celebrating an event that did indeed transcend in importance the occurrences of daily life. And finally, hence also the relative scarcity of *truly splendid* festive performances in which artist-technicians were called upon to outperform themselves in an attempt to make the celebrations pertaining to the event truly memorable. It is on the occasion of such really majestic, splendid festive performances that we witness the Baroque sense of play at its most neurotic, and that the threat and the consequences of failure must have been most oppressing. In the next chapters, we will examine in detail five of the most splendid performances of the century in their total context. Please be seated on the purple velvet of the ruler's throne.

Notes

1. On play, see the following studies (in addition to Huizinga): the "Game, Play, Literature" issue of *Yale French Studies* 41 (1968); the "Game and the Theories of Game" issue of *Canadian Review of Comparative Literature* 12 (1985); Roger Caillois, *Les Jeux et les hommes* (Paris, 1958); Harvey Cox, *The Feast of Fools: A Theological Essay on Festivity and Fantasy* (Cambridge, Mass., 1969); Eugen Fink, *Spiel als Weltsymbol* (Stuttgart, 1960); Freud, "The Relation of the Poet to Day-Dreaming," *Neue Revue* 1 (1908); Gadamer, "Play as the Clue to Ontological Explanation," *Truth and Method* (1960; trans. New York, 1975; rev. ed. 1989), and *Die Aktualität des Schönen: Kunst als Spiel, Symbol und Fest* (Stuttgart, 1977); Margaret R. Greer, *The Play of Power* (Princeton, 1991); Karl Groos, *The Play of Man* (New York, 1901); Ingeborg Heidemann, *Der Begriff des Spieles* (Berlin, 1968); Thomas Kuhn, *The Copernican Revolution* (Cambridge, 1967); Harvey C. Lehman and Paul A. Witty, *The Psychology of Play Activities* (New York, 1927); Herbert Marcuse, *Eros and Civilization* (Boston, 1955); Louis Marin, *Utopiques: Jeux d'Espaces* (Paris, 1973); Susanna Millar, *The Psychology of Play* (Harmondsworth, 1968); David

Miller, *Gods and Games* (New York, 1973); Robert Neale, *In Praise of Play: Toward a Psychology of Religion* (New York, 1969); R. B. Onians, *Origins of European Thought* (Cambridge, 1951); Jean Piaget, *Play, Dreams and Imitation in Childhood* (New York, 1951); Michel Picard, *La lecture comme jeu* (Paris, 1968); Josef Pieper, *Leisure: The Basis of Culture* (New York, 1952); Hugo Rahner, *Der spielende Mensch* (Einsiedeln, 1954); J. C. F. Schiller, *On the Aesthetic Education of Man* (trans. London, 1954); from Mihai I. Spariosu, besides *God of Many Names* (1991), also his earlier works *Literature, Mimesis and Play* (Tübingen, 1982) and *Dionysus Reborn: Play and the Aesthetic Dimension in Modern Philosophical and Scientific Discourse* (Ithaca; London, 1989); Hans Vaihinger, *The Philosophy of "As If"* (1924; trans. C. Ogden, 2nd ed. [New York, 1935]); Ludwig Wittgenstein, *Philosophical Investigations* (Oxford, 1953).

In recent decades, a fair number of important—mostly philosophical—studies of play and the theory of play have been published. The general tendency among these seems to be to discuss play by what it does rather than by what it means. It is a curious but interesting fact that none of these works devote much, if any, space to an analysis of play in the Renaissance and Baroque periods. For example, in *God of Many Names* (1991), Spariosu discusses theories of play from Homer to Aristotle, whereas his earlier *Dionysus Reborn* (1989) developed a theory of "play and the aesthetic dimension in modern philosophical and scientific discourse," beginning with Kant. Other scholars and philosophers (for instance, Miller) trace the concept of play from Greek antiquity through the Fathers of the Church, and then continue their chronology with Nietzsche and Schiller; they apparently see little of interest regarding the theory of play in the century of Descartes. Huizinga's remarks on play in the Baroque are very limited as well.

Huizinga argues that in the early to mid-seventeenth century—the climactic period for the Baroque sensibility—the spirit of play was voiced more clearly than in any other period, and that the ludic character of (political, social) life was recognized without reservations, for example in the celebrated topos of the world as a stage, which was glorified more in this particular era than in any previous one. On this topos, see also Curtius 138–44, and chapter 4, "The World as Theatre," in Warnke's *Versions of Baroque*. This topos is at least as old as Plato, and it existed in many versions prior to its Baroque development (Luther, Ronsard, Ralegh, Shakespeare, among others). But in all these earlier versions, the topos surfaced merely as a metaphor, to communicate a moral through an analogy: "All the world's a stage,/And all the men and women merely players,/They have their exits and their entrances,/ And one man in his time plays many parts" (*As You Like It* 2.7.139–42). By contrast, the Baroque version of the topos (which includes its appearance in Shakespeare's high comedies and romances) went deeper, since it considered "the theater . . . in its essential nature as metamorphosis and conflict, an absolutely valid projection of the inner reality of earthly experience. To see the world as a theatre is to see it as it is—not because life, in its 'dramatic' texture, sometimes *resembles* a stage spectacle, but because life, recognized as a conflict of opposites and as a shifting phantasmagoria of appearances, is fully identifiable with a stage spectacle" (Warnke 69). After all, the seventeenth century was the Golden Age of European drama, and the concept "the world as a stage" justified the conception of "the stage as the world," thus giving the art of drama the status of reality. Moreover, in the Baroque, the topos was not confined to drama, but also surfaced in lyric poetry and in prose writing to express the fundamental notion, the radical Baroque conviction, that the phenomenal world is an illusion. Of course, not all Baroque plays "embody the theatre-topos in its full sense as a metaphysical questioning of the ultimate reality of the phenomenal world" (Warnke 83).

In spite of the general awareness of the importance to the Baroque of the "world is a stage" topos (which is essentially a manifestation of the spirit of play), I perceive a certain reluctance among theoreticians of play to determine the relative importance of a "Baroque" spirit of play. Although Huizinga notes the frequency with which the commonplace appeared in the seventeenth century, he claims that it had mainly an ethical function, namely to highlight the vanity of earthly things. In other words, he finds no genuine concern in the Baroque with the deepgoing interconnections between play and "culture." I would argue, however, that in the splendid, courtly festive performance of the middle decades of the seventeenth century, play and "culture" (the continuation of the political-social consciousness and the artistic expressions related thereto) were interconnected more tightly than ever before or after. In their planning and execution, these festive performances were obviously very intensely related to the topos "life is a play, the world is a stage," but the philosophy of the topos was carried decisively further than in any previous versions—even so far that it was reversed. Of course, the world is a stage, but the stage of the sponsor-absolute ruler was interpreted to encompass the world. And it was on the theatrical stage that the sponsor-ruler's power over the world was made manifest in more complete form than on any other occasion of state (see the essays in Section 7, "Der Hof im Drama," ed. John Lindberg, in August Buck, et al., eds, 3: 521–80).

2. See also Gadamer: "The classical theory of art too, which bases all art on the idea of mimesis, *imitation*, obviously starts from play in the form of dancing, which is the representation of the divine" (113).

3. See, for example, the origins of the Morris dance, or events surrounding the summer solstice, or the rebirth of the world in spring or the rebirth of the god, or many of the rituals that Frazer describes in *The Golden Bough* (12 vols, 1890–1915). See also Gadamer: "Seriousness is not merely some-

thing that calls us away from play; rather, seriousness in playing is necessary to make the play wholly play" (102).

4. On violent pleasure-play as pathological, see Bataille 1970, vol. 1: 302). In *Myth and Cult among Primitive Cultures* (1953; trans. 1963), Jensen corrects Huizinga's view that play is the basis of all culture, when he states that play is only one aspect of cult, and cult is only one aspect of culture. Jensen would like to see a distinction between "mere play" (such as the games of children) and the more serious "play of cult" (reference from Miller 21–22).

5. Spariosu argues that "any prerational, aristocratic mentality will invariably favor [effortless, pleasurable, and free-movement] play over work, regarding the latter a severe limitation of power-freedom. On the other hand, a predominantly rational, middle-class mentality will tend to favor work over play" (1989: 22).

6. See in this context the concept of the *roi thaumaturge* as it was celebrated in Europe from the Middle Ages until the Enlightenment. Briefly, the concept refers to the allegorical-typological habit of representing the ruler as a sacred person, an embodiment of virtues, and a type—or at least a direct representative—of Christ on earth. See James the First's treatise *Basilikon Doron*, written for his son, Prince Henry. See also Strong 1973: 8–10, 159; and especially, Apostolidès 1981.

7. See further Norbert Elias' celebrated *The Court Society* (1969), trans. E. Jephcott (New York, 1983).

8. Interestingly, this was the case even when the sponsor-ruler was dead and the "celebration" was occasioned by the funeral.

9. In the case of foreigners, admission depended in addition on carefully scrutinized letters of introduction, without which few travellers would leave their native country in the first place (see the cases of Jean-Jacques Bouchard and of Milton at the Barberini court, in chapter 3).

10. An instructive comparison can be made between the fairly open "Renaissance" court of Elizabeth I and the rather closed "Baroque" court of James I. Unlike the former, the latter monarch virtually limited his court to Whitehall, and his "Progress" was much reduced.

11. The very word "entertainment" contains the notion of exclusion: it comes from Old French *entre-tenir*: to hold apart, or to create a space in between. "To go along with the illusion" may perhaps be likened to the analogy of the lodestone which Socrates introduces in *Ion*: "the archaic audience totally identifies with the singer of tales through *methexis*, mimetic participation, or an ecstatic trance similar to that caused by Dionysian

intoxication. Such ecstatic trance often results in catharsis, a pleasurable relief of dammed-up emotional tension" (Spariosu 1991: 21). In this case, the lodestone is the allegorical presence of the ruler's identity, with which the audience becomes infused.

12. "the [necessary] expenditures to maintain splendor and dignity are not less necessary to sustain majestic status in the eyes of the peoples;" *Politique tirée des propres paroles de l'Ecriture sainte*, ed. J. Le Brun (Genève, 1967), X.1.1: 381.

13. In a way, this self-representation of the ruler by means of rhetorical performance-play enacts yet another play definition of Gadamer's: "inasmuch as it is a structure, it is, so to speak, its own measure, and measures itself by nothing outside it. Thus the action of a drama—in this respect it still entirely resembles the religious act—exists as something that rests absolutely within itself. It no longer permits of any comparison with reality as the secret measure of all verisimilitude. It is raised above all such comparisons—and hence also above the question of whether it is all real—because a superior truth speaks from it" (112).

14. Without ever saying it explicitly, Spariosu makes a case for Dionysus as the god of play (see especially chapter 3 of *God of Many Names*, in which he examines *Bacchae* and *The Frogs* in the light of ancient play theory and philosophy). Miller, too, refers *en passant* to Dionysus when mentioning Nietzsche's Zarathustra (131). But instead of identifying Dionysus as *the* god of play, it is probably safer to consider him a playing god, or a god who makes play possible, or who creates playful effects, or something of that nature. His pranks in *Bacchae*, for example, anticipate the stage effects produced by Bernini.

15. The role of the audience cannot be overestimated. As I have already mentioned, without an audience, there can be no performance in the strict sense. In the context of the "rhetoric of the performance" that I have been suggesting, it may be useful to quote Gadamer at length: "The presentation of a god in a religious rite, the presentation of a myth in a play, are play not only in the sense that the participating players are wholly absorbed in the presentational play and find in it their heightened self-representation, but also in that the players represent a meaningful whole for an audience. Thus it is not really the absence of a fourth wall that turns the play into a show. Rather, openness toward the spectator is part of the closedness of the play. The audience only completes what the play as such is. This point shows the importance of defining play as a process that takes place 'in between' [in my terms, a dialogic, a rhetoric]. . . . The player experiences the game as a reality that surpasses him. This is all the more the case where the game is itself 'intended' as such a reality—for instance, the play which appears as

presentation for an audience. . . . But however much a religious or profane play represents a world wholly closed within itself, it is as if open toward the spectator, in whom it achieves its whole significance . . . the play itself is the whole, comprising players and spectators" (Gadamer's emphasis, 109).

16. Margaret R. Greer provides interesting examples of "plain-speaking" preachers and other moralists in the service of Philip IV—such as the nun María de Agreda, a faithful correspondent of the monarch, who referred to herself as a "médico" and to her worldly ruler as an "enfermo" (330).

17. See Freud's curious interpretation of civilization in *Civilization and its Discontents* (1930). Freud argues in this text that the conflict between *eros* (love) and *ananke* (duty, or necessity) leads to some of the many discontents that we recognize in our so-called civilization. *The Standard Edition of the Complete Psychological Works of Sigmund Freud*, trans. James Strachey, with Anna Freud, vol. 21 (1927–1931), (London, 1961), 100ff.

18. On the absolute ruler as "father" of the *oikos* of the state: see Jean-Marie Apostolidès, "Image du père et peur du tyran au XVIIe siècle," *Revue française de psychanalyse* 44 (1980): 5–14. See also Paul Münch, "Haus und Regiment—Überlegungen zum Einfluss der alteuropäischen Ökonomie auf die fürstliche Regierungstheorie und-praxis während der frühen Neuzeit," in August Buck, et al., eds., 2: 205–10. Important contemporaneous statements occur in Luther's *Grossen Katechismus* (1529), Calvin's *Institutio Christianae Religionis* (1559), Petrus Canisius' *Catechismi Latini et Germanici* (1560), Jean Bodin's *Six Livres de la république* (1576), James the First's *The Trew Law of Free Monarchies* (1598), and Robert Filmer's *Patriarcha or the Natural Power of Kings* (1680). For a contrasting view, see Immanuel Kant's "Über den Gemeinspruch" (1793).

19. As noted before, it was not until Romanticism that western thought began once more to pay serious attention to the spirit of play and the regrettable separation in the western (sub)conscious of the playful (Dionysian?) and serious (Apollonian?) impulses (Schiller, *On the Aesthetic Education of Man* [trans. London, 1954]).

20. See, of course, Max Weber's *Protestant Ethic and the Spirit of Capitalism* (New York, 1958).

21. See further Miller 101–17; and on the relationship between work and play in the pre-industrial versus the post-industrial age, see Turner 30–36.

22. "When concelebration and collusion have ceased to function, then the culture of feasts and theater shrivels up. At that moment, modes of behavior and occupations that were once productive must give way to the

mere consumption of art, and to glamour. The consequences of this consumption include the slaking of appetite, weariness, and boredom. So far, our contemporary theater producers and festival organizers have not been able to cure these symptoms of paralysis."

23. Marcel Mauss, *The Gift: Forms and Functions of Exchange in Archaic Societies*, trans. I. Cunnison (New York, 1967); Bataille 1970, vol. 1: 309–12.

24. I would also argue that the notion of potlatch does not extend only to the splendid festive performances themselves, but to the setup and daily organization of the court itself, which was a never-ending, collective expenditure on a microcosmic scale. This is particularly obvious in the case of the court at Versailles, where each courtier was drawn into the game by being forced to "squander" (a "view from below" term) his or her ancient, inherited possessions in order to function properly at court and participate in its daily operation, with the ultimate goal of raising, on a macrocosmic scale, the status of the absolute monarch vis-à-vis his European competitors.

25. It would be interesting to pursue the connections between the rhetorical functions of, on the one hand, the Baroque pleasure palace, which inevitably incorporated a locus for festive performances, and, on the other, the rhetorical topos of the *locus amoenus* or "pleasance," which was one of the fixed commonplaces in the great aristocratic theme of the "Golden Age"—a theme that was also especially dear to the Baroque sensibility (see Curtius 195–200). After all, the Virgilian Elysian Fields, to which the commonplace was usually traced back by the rhetorical manuals which standardized it, was employed by Christian poets for Paradise (Curtius 200); this would fit in nicely with the theory that the splendid festive performance was in effect the ritualistic celebration of the sponsor-absolute ruler. See also Levin, *The Myth of the Golden Age in the Renaissance*. For a poetic application, see the description of Venus's complex pleasure palace in Marino's *L'Adone*—a description that starts in Canto II and takes up a very large portion of that inordinately long poem.

26. Again, Gadamer's *Truth and Method* provides an interesting gloss: "works of art can assume certain real functions and resist others: for instance, religious or secular, public or private ones. They are instituted and erected as memorials of reverence, honor, or piety only because they themselves prescribe and help fashion this kind of functional context. They themselves lay claim to their place, and even if they are displaced . . . the trace of their original purpose cannot be effaced. It is part of their being because their being is presentation. If one considers these special forms as possessing exemplary significance, one sees that certain forms of art become central which, from the point of view of Erlebnis art, are peripheral: namely all those whose own

content points beyond them to the whole of a context determined by them and for them. The greatest and most distinguished of these forms is *architecture*. . . . A building is never only a work of art. Its purpose, through which it belongs in the context of life, cannot be separated from it without its losing some of its reality. . . . Architecture gives shape to space. Space is what surrounds everything that exists in space. That is why architecture embraces all the other forms of representation: all works of plastic art, all ornament. Moreover, it gives a place to the representational arts of poetry, music, acting, and dancing" (Gadamer's emphasis, 155–57 passim).

27. The value of music, poetry and dance (the ancient *mousikè*) as play was usually held to be greater than that of plastic and visual arts such as architecture and painting. The execution of the former arts is namely ethereal, and therefore by definition more spontaneous and playful, than that of the latter, the static arts (Huizinga, chapter 10). And there is indeed an abundance of song and dance in Baroque festive performances, which greatly increases their playful character. In performances that combined the ephemeral première performance of a new "total work of art" (machine play or opera with lots of dance and with an allegorical program) with the inauguration of a new permanent, static locus, a link was made, somehow, between the ephemeral and the durable, as the visual and plastic arts were drawn into a game hitherto reserved for the performance arts. Renaissance celebrations, remember, were often movable, not restricted to one locale. My point is that the Baroque splendid festive performances attempted to unite the playfulness of the movable with the stability of the fixed locale. The linking of the ephemeral and the durable can be located in the exact moment of the inauguration, which coincides with the moment of the performance.

28. "Occasionality means that [the meaning and contents of certain art forms] are determined by the occasion for which they are intended, so that they contain more than they would without this occasion. . . . The important thing is that this occasionality belongs to the work's own claim and is not something forced on it by its interpreter. . . . Occasionality in the sense intended clearly lies in what the work itself claims to mean, in contradistinction from whatever is discovered in it or can be deduced from it that goes against this claim" (144–45).

29. Compare also with the "sacred" connotations of the ruler, probably derived from Burgundian court ceremonial, which attached many sacred connotations to the "first and only time." In Spain, for example, the clothes worn once by the king, as well as the mistress enjoyed by the king, became taboo (the ex-mistress usually being packed off to a nunnery for the remainder of her natural life).

30. For evidence, see the letters which Bussy-Rabutin (1618–1693)

wrote to Louis XIV from his country estate, to which he had been exiled (and where he stayed for seventeen years) for publishing his libertine *Histoire amoureuse des Gaules* (1665).

31. The crowd was, literally, given the crumbs to devour at one of the "Plaisirs de l'Ile enchantée" feasts in Versailles in 1664; opening the gates to the poor crowd that was gaping both from amazement and from hunger was part of the aristocratic entertainment. An indication of the sense of exclusivity that was characteristic of splendid performances is the fact that printed reports of première performances began to be widely circulated in the capital as well as in the provinces, no doubt because there was a great demand for this sort of information. Reports of public and private festive celebrations are to be found mainly in diaries, letters of ambassadors and other private texts, and private letters remain an important source of information on feasts and the private performances that were organized later in the century (for example, the letters of Mme de Sévigné to her daughter Mme de Grignan). The upper layers of the general public wanted to know more details of the majestic celebrations from which they were permanently excluded.

This need was served by such publications as the *Gazette de France*, or the *Mercure galant*—later the *Mercure de France*—which was published weekly by De Visé from 1672 on, and which reviewed not only plays in public theaters but often also the splendid private festive performances. (The complex relationships between courts and the press form a fascinating research topic. See Section 8: "Der Hof und die Öffentliche Meinung," ed. Elger Blühm, in August Buck, et al., eds., 3: 581–632.) Seventeenth-century novelists catered to the same taste with lengthy fictional descriptions. All these reports, true or fictional, fostered a sense of deprivation, or even jealousy and envy among those who could never hope to be present. Readers could not get enough of this sort of description, and reading about it gave one the illusion of participating. Thus a new employment was created: the intermediate party, the chronicler of the event, the faithful reporter, the eyewitness journalist, or the artist who engraved the stage sets for the published libretti. The middle classes were also fond of peepboxes with scenes of private aristocratic entertainments ingeniously fitted inside.

32. "My God, Miss, there is nothing that kings like so much as prompt obedience, and they don't like it at all when they find obstacles put before them. Things are good only precisely at the moment when they long for them, and to try to delay an entertainment is to take away all its attractions for them. They want instant pleasures, and the least prepared ones are always the ones they like best. We should never take ourselves into consideration in regard to those things they want from us; we only exist to please them, and when they instruct us to do something, then it is our task to make quick use of their current whim. Better to perform badly what they ask from us than to

perform it not quickly enough; and if we are ashamed because we did not succeed very well, then we can at least feel proud because we were so quick to obey their orders. However, let us get on with our rehearsals, please." Molière, "L'Impromptu de Versailles," *Oeuvres Complètes*, ed. Maurice Rat, Bibliothèque de la Pléiade 8 (Paris, 1962) 549–74, 553–54.

3

The Barberini Saint: *Sant'Alessio*

In 1623, Maffeo Barberini was elected to the throne of St. Peter; his papacy as Urban VIII was the high point in the illustrious Roman career of the Tuscan Barberini family. Within a few weeks, the new pope had begun to channel the energies and the very considerable talents of his extended family and those of his three nephews (*nipoti*) in particular. Their aim was singularly complex: to impose the Barberini stamp on the spiritual, aristocratic, intellectual, and artistic life in the Eternal City and the papal states. In 1632, the new family palazzo, still unfinished but already magnificent, was officially inaugurated with the festive performance of a new opera based on the legend of Alessio (Alexis). *Sant'Alessio* (1631), with a libretto by Giulio Rospigliosi—Barberini poet laureate and future pope [Clement IX] himself—and a score by Stefano Landi, is considered by historians of opera a milestone in the history of Roman opera, primarily, it seems, because it was the first of several influential Barberini operas.[1] The circumstances of the opera's initial performances (*hypocrisis*, or execution in the rhetorical scheme) have been very difficult to establish. It is now generally agreed that the première took place in 1631, a second series of performances in 1632, and a third series in 1634, all for primarily aristocratic and ecclesiastical audiences. Moreover, the 1631 performance was held in a different location than the succeeding ones, and the opera itself (its *dispositio* rather than its *topoi*) was considerably revised for the 1634 performance. The 1634 score was published in that same year.

The circumstances of the rise and fall of the Barberini dynasty have been amply documented,[2] and I will limit myself here to a few facts that bear directly on the present subject. Originally named Tafani, this rich merchant family had been established in Tuscany at least since the fourteenth century. All evidence points to the fact that they were, indeed, "an actively aggressive, adept group of highly intelligent men" (Carfagno 91). Maffeo Barberini (1568–1644) left Florence to study law in Rome and Pisa; he was also a gifted poet and Humanist.[3] Determined to rise, this ambitious man carved out for himself a brilliant career in the hierarchy of the Church, which was made possible in part by the prestige and wealth of an uncle at the papal court and by his own political and judiciary skills. His efforts were crowned with his complicated election, at the early age of fifty–six, to the throne of Peter. As Urban VIII, he had an unusually long tenure for the time, wielding the power of an absolute monarch from 1623 until 1644.[4] Upon his ascension, the fortunes of previous papal families, the Borghese (Paul V) and the Ludovisi (Gregory XV), declined correspondingly: from 1623 until 1644, the Barberini as a family were the most powerful aristocratic clan in Rome, the Eternal City's unchallenged arbiters of taste, and the undisputed directors of the many artistic and intellectual talents that flocked to Rome from the whole of Europe. Perhaps because constant intrigues made it somewhat of a necessity, popes, like other rulers, had taken up the habit of surrounding themselves with reliable kinsmen in high offices. Urban VIII may originally have intended to refrain from nepotism, as is sometimes said, but like his predecessors he, too, began very soon showering family members (especially his two brothers and his three *nipoti*) with lucrative offices and prebends, though refusing them any serious influence on his government. Maffeo made his brother Antonio, a Capuchin monk, Cardinal of Sant'Onofrio in 1624, and he charged his other brother, Carlo, with the command of the papal armies on land and at sea. Of Carlo's three sons (the *nipoti*), Francesco was the oldest and perhaps the most talented. He was made a cardinal in 1623, at age twenty-six; he received one rich prebend after the other and was generally regarded as the first personage after the pope himself, representing him, for example, as nuncio in Paris and Madrid. Like his uncle, he promoted book learning and became an avid collector of art and a generous Maecenas. His artistic and intellectual interests greatly outweighed his political-professional performance; for example, he founded the Barberini library, second in importance only to that of the Vatican itself. Francesco's brother Antonio, also a man of considerable learning, was made a cardinal at age nineteen, much to the displeasure of the Sacred College; he, too, was given several profitable prebends. One member of Antonio's household staff would greatly eclipse his master in fame and achievements: Giulio Mazarini, who served Antonio Barberini as secretary and general intendant for several years. Taddeo, the youngest of the *nipoti*, was not a man of the cloth: he succeeded his father Carlo as general of the armed forces of the Church in 1630. Even more ruthless and greedier than the other Barberini, Taddeo was made Prefect of Rome, the first to have that function since antiquity; stripped of any real function, the Prefecture carried nevertheless many honorary prerogatives.

In 1625, Cardinal Francesco Barberini bought a palace from Alessandro Sforza, which then became the original Roman residence of the Barberini. Located in the Via dei Giubbonari, on the slope of the Quirinal hill near Quattro Fontane, the building was handed over to Taddeo when Francesco left for Madrid as Urban's nuncio. But Taddeo acquired additional property on the Quirinal and ordered extensive reconstruction of its palazzo. Begun in 1626 or 1627, with the bulk of it finished by 1633, the new palazzo Barberini was the first great Baroque palace to be constructed in Rome.[5] The most distinguished architects and artists of the period contributed to make this residence worthy of Barberini ambitions. Although the famous architect Carlo Maderna (1556–1629) had provided the basic plans, construction began to get well under way only when Bernini took over after Maderna's death.[6] The celebrated painter Pietro da Cortona, another Barberini protégé, contributed significantly to the interiors. When completed, the new building distinguished itself from the typically Roman fortress-like palazzo because of its open courtyard with two projecting wings, and its impressive three-storied loggia with seven bays. Typically Baroque elements are the false perspectives and the highly ingenious, assymmetrical groundplans; indeed, the classical, elegant façade of the palazzo Barberini is rather like a theatrical décor of the period, cleverly dissimulating a complex, irregular interior arrangement. Just like *Sant'Alessio* itself, the new palazzo was part of the Barberini family's complex epideictic rhetorical strategies. It had the same function as the opera: to solicit praise, applause, and admiration; its criterion was beauty, and its principal argumentative strategy was, again, amplification or exaggeration. The rhetorical invention included the task of transforming a fortress-like city palazzo built on sloping terrain into a solid, but airy and elegant, and vast, but not overburdened palace with a country look. Taddeo Barberini lived but briefly in the palazzo, from the spring of 1632 until 1634, when he moved back to the old family residence in the Via dei Giubbonari, which he also enlarged considerably. By the end of the decade, Cardinal Antonio Barberini moved into the new palazzo. Cardinal Francesco's personal residence was the Cancelleria, which he turned into a sort of Academy, open to Italian and foreign scholars, literary men, and celebrities (even if they were not Catholic). His large-scale entertainments, however, would be given in the more majestic environment of the new palazzo.

A theatrical note is characteristic of many products of Bernini's Roman architectural activity during Urban's pontificate.[7] The map of Rome had been thoroughly redrawn at the end of the sixteenth century by Sixtus V, who envisaged a city of wide avenues, vast squares, and huge churches. In a way, such an architecture of open spaces that serve to connect neighborhoods, palaces, and churches is also a rhetorical undertaking, though the rhetoric is of a crude kind. No fewer than three popes ruled between Sixtus and Urban, but it was really only the latter (or rather, his architect Bernini) who became the next "great builder" of Rome. Most commentators agree that Urban's Rome looks like some vast décor. Within the blueprint of the city inherited from Sixtus V, Urban, aided by Bernini, stimulated ecclesiastical architecture and decoration to an unprecedented degree. The architectural rhetoric was adapted to serve the purpose of persuading the world and the city—which according to contemporaries abounded with freethinkers, atheists and cynical men—that all was still very well with the Faith (Haskell 33 n. 3). It has often been said that Bernini manipulated urban settings to create a theatricalized environment: the entire city can then be interpreted as a set in front of which the life of the polis went on as a continuous mise-en-scène, a permanently changing performance punctuated with stable, recurring events, a "lived" theatricality, which, however, was experienced mainly by the commoners. For if we except the commedia dell'arte (which *was* originally for commoners), "professional" theatricality did not take place outside on the square or against the backdrop of the façades, but inside: in the palazzi of the aristocratic families who created with the assistance of many artists their own scenography along the lines of artistic models and learned philosophical doctrines that had been provided by Antiquity and reworked by Renaissance philosophers and artists (Angelini 111–12).

The Barberini had operas performed in their palazzo before they had a theater proper. To this purpose they adapted the vast principal hall, which was two stories high. Indeed, on certain occasions, and during the carnival season in particular, Roman aristocratic families vied with each other to entertain guests—mostly secular and ecclesiastical dignitaries (*porporati*) as well as foreign visitors—to contribute to the ruling atmosphere of play in the polis, or to reaffirm at least the perception by the polis of their wealth, social status, and artistic taste. Thus *commedias*, *melodrammas*, and works of an operatic nature were performed with very little regard to expense in both the old and the new palazzo Barberini, as well as in the palaces of the Pamphili, the Corsini, the Ludovisi, the Colonnas and other principal Roman families. Such festive performances had also a historical and almost mythic significance, recalling the entertainments offered by the powerful families of antiquity: from the epic games offered by King Alkinoös to Odysseus, to the circus games offered by the Roman patriciate to the *plebs* during the Republic and the Empire. The famous Barberini theater, which was set slightly apart from the main palazzo building, was only completed by the end of the decade. (It must have been, again, a large facility, since in March, 1639, no fewer than 3,500 people were able to attend the performance of another Rospigliosi opera, the comic *Chi soffre speri*. This performance has gone down in anecdotal history mainly because John Milton was in the audience—perhaps he was among the extra six hundred lucky ones who could be accommodated when Cardinal Francesco personally made everyone squeeze up on the benches.)[8] So much operatic activity took place in the palazzi Barberini that the Barberini name has become inextricably connected with the history of Roman opera.

Apart from descriptions of textual revision, not much critical, nonmusicological material on *Sant'Alessio* exists.[9] Historians of opera and musicologists have generally praised *Sant'Alessio* for its considerable dramatic qualities, for its innovative musical solutions, and for its successful expression of the concrete feelings of a genuinely human protagonist. In other words, they interpret *Sant'Alessio* as a typical Roman opera, even as a sampler of the forms with which the Roman musical theater was experimenting in the early seventeenth century. For example, it contains long overtures before each act, *ritornelli*, *intermedi*, expressive recitatives, solos, lyrical ariosos, more formalized arias, prominent ensembles and choruses, and a grand finale with machines. In the orchestra, the (by then old-fashioned) viols were replaced throughout by the more modern violins and violin-cellos. (Since the term "opera" in the modern sense was not yet in general use, contemporaneous documents referred to *Sant'Alessio* with a variety of lables: *opera spirituale*, *rappresentatione in musica*, *rappresentatione tutta recitata in musica*, and even *commedia* or, simply, *rappresentatione* [Murata, Appendix 1-A].) Historians of music generally distinguish between typical Roman opera and its predecessor, Florentine Camerata opera; as we have seen, the Florentines considered the literary-allegorical program of the text more important than the actual performance itself, whereas the Romans highlighted music, drama, and performance. If opera became a more scenic art form in Rome, after its intellectual, aristocratic début as an art form among the Florentine Camerata, this development was due to a great extent to the influence and sponsorship of the Barberini, who were able to secure the assistance of an unusual concentration of superbly gifted artists, ranging from Bernini to the professional singers of Saint Peter's basilica. Thus opera, though still an élite art form, quickly became the most spectacular form of theatrical entertainment, in which the princes of the Church in particular played an active role. They organized performances and continually interfered with the libretti, the music, the choice of costumes, and the staging (for more examples, see Fagiolo dell'Arco 291–92). The Barberini in particular did their best to replace spoken theater with opera or at least to equate the two (in a form of *recitar cantando*), and furthermore, to make opera primarily an aristocratic as well as a spiritual form of entertainment. The juxtaposition of Florentine and Roman operatic types on this basis was canonized by Henri Prunières in his influential study *L'Opéra italien en France avant Lulli* (1913; Paris, 1949). Prunières claimed that

> par réaction contre les doctrines trop littéraires de la *Camerata*, les compositeurs romains ne verront bientôt plus dans le livret qu'un prétexte à expressions musicales variées, un thème à déclamation, un simple canevas sur lequel ils broderont des fleurs magnifiques. . . . Délaissant l'idéal florentin de noble beauté et de raison, les poètes et les musiciens de Rome chercheront surtout à flatter les sens d'un public avide de jouissances (5).[10]

It may well be the result of such generalizing and impressionistic criticism as Prunières' that little has been written about the textual aspect of Roman opera. In this chapter, I will argue precisely that the libretto of *Sant'Alessio* provides not merely "un simple canevas," a mere frame, upon which the composer can embroider beautiful melodies. First, its hagiographical subject was still rather unusual for the time.[11] Urban VIII is now particularly remembered for his efforts to promote Christian subjects in the various arts and to discourage the use of pagan-classical and mythological motifs.[12] It is partly for this reason that Roman opera, of which *Sant'Alessio* was one of the initial successes, did not generally represent mythological characters and pagan deities in the cardboard pastoral-arcadian or Olympian setting familiar from early-seventeenth-century Florentine Camerata opera. Barberini taste and Church ideology determined the political and cultural program, and hagiography provided the most frequent source of Roman operatic plots (including *Sant'Alessio*) between the 1620s and the 1660s—roughly, between *Sant'Eustachio* (1625) and *La Comica del Cielo* (1668).[13] Second, as we will see, the circumstances of the creation(s) and the performance(s) of the opera, and the publication of its text, indicate that *Sant'Alessio* was intended as a rhetorical discourse *ut doceat, moveat, delectat* with a very specific literary-allegorical textual program. For why would Rospigliosi and the Barberini select for the subject of their first "own" Roman opera the legend of Saint Alexis? True, Alessio happened to be the most popular Roman saint and his story can also be symbolically assimilated to the carnival setting of the actual festive performances.[14] But given the fact that the philosophical context of all early opera was Neoplatonism, according to which "meaning" is to be half revealed and half concealed, it is safe to assume that the Alessio legend contained a more specific and, at the same time, less ostensible element useful to the Barberini and their political and spiritual aspirations. For it seems incongruous that the immensely powerful and wealthy Barberini would celebrate their new status and their new palazzo with the legend of the patron saint of beggars and pilgrims.

Although Alessio proved a useful and adaptable pawn in the Barberini campaign, the saint, his legend, and Rospigliosi's opera were ultimately but means to an end. I have previously argued that the rhetoric of the Baroque grandiose festive performance was epideictic: not primarily persuasive or polemical but panegyrical; its emphasis was on praise (*"Art" of Rhetoric* I: 1358b). It is characteristic of epideictic rhetoric that its audience is mainly expected to applaud the orator or, in a more general sense, the artist. The audience does not really applaud the "theme," or subject, for the subject of epideictic rhetoric is usually already well-known, but rather its presentation, the technical handling of the aspects of invention, disposition, elocution, and action. Therefore, contrary to what one might expect, the saint—the ostensible subject of the discourse—is hardly the subject of the praise that the discourse attempts to solicit. Rather, the participants in the discourse of the performance are eligible for praise. These participants include, in rising order of importance, the singer-actors (who are responsible for the action), the librettist and composer (disposition, elocution), and ultimately, the Barberini themselves. Not only did the Barberini as sponsors provide lavish entertainment during the carnival season, but they also gained fame for conceiving the entire performance, for "finding" the clever, hidden theme (invention) and suggesting it to the librettist. It was then the latter's task to develop the best arguments for it. One other group of participants in this discourse was implicitly eligible for the audience's praise: the audience itself. That is to say, the audience merited praise to the extent of its relative understanding of the complicated matters that were presented to it, half revealed and half concealed, in the course of the performance. The legend of Alessio in itself is not at all complicated. But the same is not true for the Barberini adaptation of the legend. In the latter, the complexity was a matter of relative insight and initiation, and part of a game of disguise.

In brief, *Sant'Alessio*, the first Barberini opera and rather an artistic novelty for Rome, was designed as part of the early 1630s Barberini political strategy, which was aimed at soliciting "praise" and admiration, and at further solidifying Barberini power. The revealed meaning of the opera was the apotheosis of Alessio. The more important concealed meaning concerned the apotheosis of the Barberini, who were, more than Alessio himself, the protagonists of their own festive performance. The new art form of opera, by a simple manipulation of the principles of its Neoplatonic foundation, was turned into a rhetorical vehicle for the purpose of self-promotion, infinitely more subtle than open oratory could ever hope to be. Rhetorical methods were applied toward a Neoplatonic purpose. Given the fact that rhetoric is only a means to a goal, what was the goal of the Barberini? What was the subject of the *communiqué?*

Before developing this question, it may be useful to summarize the curious legend of Alessio, as it was set down in the thirteenth century by Jacobus de Voragine (Viraggio), Archbishop of Genoa, in the *Legenda aurea*.[15] Alessio was born in a wealthy family in fourth-century Rome, during the rule of the Emperors Arcadius and Honorius. His father Eufemiano gave him a solid education and then betrothed him to a girl of excellent family. On the eve of his wedding, however, after advising his "wife" to live in fear of God and keep her virginity, Alessio left Rome. Thus he arrived in Edessa in Syria, where he lived as a beggar and a very pious man for the space of seventeen years, informing neither his parents nor his wife of his whereabouts, though their messengers sought for him far and wide and also looked for him in Edessa. Then a voice that came from God identified Alessio as a man worthy to enter the kingdom of Heaven; when this miracle became known in Edessa, Alessio, out of humility, left the city, which was about to worship him. Abandoning himself to God's will, Alessio was brought back to Rome, where he decided to seek admission as a beggar in his father's household. He lived for another seventeen years, unrecognized among his family, under the staircase of the mansion, much humiliated and scorned by the servants, praying, fasting, doing penance, and taking the sacraments. Then, one Sunday, a voice from God was heard again in church after Mass, urging the people to search among them for a servant of God who was praying for all Rome. Soon after—Voragine specifies it was on Good Friday—Alessio died, after having written the story of his life on a piece of parchment. Told by God that the holy man was to be found in the house of Alessio's father, the people went there; Alessio's "wife" suggested that the poor beggar who lived with them might perhaps be the holy man. Alessio was found dead; his face was that of an angel, and the Emperor, along with the Pope, came to look at him. The letter was discovered, and Alessio's identity revealed and confirmed by some objects he had given to his wife thirty-four years earlier. His father, his mother, and his wife, incapable of understanding his motivations, wept long over the corpse, mourning his fate and also their own. The Pope had the body borne to a church, and sick people who touched it while it was being transported were miraculously cured. Alessio was enshrined in the church of St. Boniface on July the seventeenth, on which day his feast is still celebrated. Alessio seems to have been revered quite early. The title of a *lauda* or song of praise to Alessio was written down early in the fourteenth century (the music is missing) but the *lauda* may be much older (Carfagno 134–35, 144 n. 2).

Eufemiano's house may have become a church as early as the fourth century; in 1217 the Church of Sant'Alessio in the via di S. Sabina was reconsecrated by Pope Honorius III to receive the relics of the saint, and in the late sixteenth century (the early Baroque), Pope Sixtus V greatly increased the status of this church devoted to the patron saint of beggars and poor pilgrims.

Adapting the legend for theatrical performance, Giulio Rospigliosi chose to dramatize only the second half of the story. The first act begins with a conversation between Eufemiano and Adrasto, a soldier of his acquaintance who has just returned after a long absence abroad; to Eufemiano's despair, he has no news about Alessio other than that he heard rumors about a devout pilgrim who had suddenly left the distant shore ("lontano lido") where he was dwelling. Perhaps this was Alessio. Then Eufemiano tells the story of Alessio's sudden departure from the paternal house, much as it is outlined in the

Golden Legend. Adrasto pities the old man, which is about all he can do ("Il ciel pietoso i tuoi dolor consoli,/ Che ben merita pietade"). Alessio, who has returned to Rome a beggar and holds the second scene alone, ponders at length and with conventional Baroque imagery the vanity of earthly things ("O desir cieco," "o vanità mortale"). He is already living incognito in his father's house, because in the third scene Eufemiano's page Martio enters the stage muttering to himself, until he sees Alessio:

> Mà cola'mesto e solitario io vedo
> Qual pellegrin mendico
> Ch'in questo albergo il mio Signor mantiene.[16]

When Martio asks why he is so gloomy, Alessio talks again about the vanity of earthly things, but in the course of their conversation, the saucy Martio shrewdly suggests that Alessio may be hiding something, for,

> Alle parole, all'habito, al sembiante
> Tu rassembri un soldato.[17]

They leave, yielding the stage to the Devil and his Chorus of devils (whether the latter are visible or not is not entirely clear); after some general observations on Hell and the human condition, the Devil ("Io d'ogno frode autore," "I the master of all deceit") reveals his plan to pluck Alessio, who is insensitive to the sighs and tears of his relatives, off the heavenly path ("celeste sentiero"); the Chorus of devils ends the scene with a vicious call to arms, repeated three times: "alle pugne, alle stragi, all'armi, all'armi!" In the fifth scene, Alessio's mother, his wife, the nurse, and Martio sit together; the women lament bitterly: the lack of news about Alessio is a daily renewed martyrdom for them, his mother has visions in her sleep of Alessio "hor moribondo, hor morto," and his wife is equally inconsolable; it is a scene in which all the connotations of *pietà* are present: pity, piety, compassion, and mercy. To conclude the first act, the Chorus of "Cortigiani d'Eufemiano" begs sweet Jesus ("Dolce Giesù") to protect Alessio on his way, wherever he may be.

The second act opens with the Devil gloating over his sinister plan: to draw Alessio out of his incognito by inspiring the wife to leave, ("Per ricercar il suo marito errante," "to look for her wandering husband.") In the second scene, we see the wife already dressed in her pilgrim's clothes, announcing her departure to the nurse; then the mother, Martio, and Alessio himself come on stage; when the latter learns his wife's intention he is flabbergasted ("Che sento, o ciel, che veggio?"), especially when his mother, too, becomes inspired by that example of boundless love and decides to join her daughter-in-law in the hope that future ages will not forget such splendid "Amor di Genitrice, amor di sposa." Whereas Martio offers some cheeky remarks, Alessio tries to dissuade them, but fails. In the fourth scene, he sincerely doubts (which is precisely what the Devil wants him to do) whether he has been doing the right thing:

> Alessio, che farai?
> . . .
> Tu, che per Dio cercar, fuggisti il mondo
> . . . Ah quale io provo
> Nel teatro del cor dura battaglia.[18]

Then the Devil enters disguised as an old hermit and introduces himself very aptly as "Humil servo, et indigno/ Del ciel son io" ("I am a humble servant, and unworthy of Heaven"). Posing as God's messenger, he has come to convince Alessio to give up his foolish fervor ("folle zelo") and reveal himself, but he is forced to flee because an Angel descends, the real "Celeste messaggiero," who informs Alessio of the Devil's deceit and that he is nearing his destiny, the heavenly martyr's crown. As the Angel departs again, Alessio sings a hymn in praise of the death that will free him "dal carcere humano," ("from this human prison."). In the seventh scene, Eufemiano and Adrasto exchange pious remarks following Eufemiano's revelation that a voice told him that "E morto Alessio, il tuo figlio è morto." An unspecified Chorus sings a hymn on hope, and a Chorus of festively costumed Roman nobles concludes the act with song and dance.

The first scene of the third act mirrors the first scene of the second: the Devil sits in his gloomy den with his Chorus of devils, but now he is singing a different tune:

> Non può forza infernale
> D'un alma trionfar, che il ciel difenda.[19]

In the second scene, a messenger, reinforced by a Chorus, informs Adrasto of the stupendous marvels that have the city enthralled: the voice of God, the revelation of God's elected servant living in Eufemiano's house, Pope Innocent and Emperor Onorio going there and finding Alessio dead, the identification of the corpse as the saint and the long-lost loved one. Then the decor changes to show a different room ("una stanza," but perhaps the family tomb is meant) and we see Alessio's corpse, surrounded by his parents, his wife, Martio and Adrasto, sharing their grief and mainly lamenting their own unhappy fate. Eufemiano produces the letter that Alessio has left and reads it, several times interrupting himself to air his grief. Suddenly, a Chorus of Angels is heard: "Lasciate il pianto" ("Leave off your lamentation"), for Alessio is in Heaven, wearing a crown of stars and a golden mantle; a second Chorus of Angels joins in, and the act, and the opera, conclude with a hymn to Rome, "Felice Roma." The Elect are now rejoicing, and so let there be feasts in the city also, for it is now blessed with a most resplendent advocate in Heaven.

It is not impossible that the story summarized above was fleshed out with dances appropriate to the carnivalesque setting (Pirotta 1982: 279). In 1634, additional visual effects, dances, and comic scenes were added (for instance, the Devil/pseudohermit is transformed into a bear and chases the insolent Martio offstage). Choruses were expanded: there are no fewer than four singing choruses (consisting of slaves, members of Eufemiano's household, angels, and demons) and four dancing choruses (representing demons, country men, young Romans, and the Virtues). In the summary of the libretto, I have indicated some of the Baroque stylistic features with which Rospigliosi's adaptation is replete: the play with oppositions of emotions (grief alternated with decent comic relief), clever motifs that are at the same time parallels and oppositions (the homecoming of the soldier Adrasto versus the homecoming of Alessio), the paradoxical motif of presence/absence, and the direct interference of the supernatural.

Rospigliosi chose to focus on the human side of the Alessio character (for example, by omitting the miracles after his death), pruning the legend to emphasize what has remained its most curious aspect: Alessio's stubborn incognito, his refusal to alleviate the emotional and psychological suffering of his family while continuing to live under their roof. In a superficial but valid interpretation, it is precisely this play with incognito that makes the Alessio legend an ideal subject for performance during the carnival season. Usually, the carnival was celebrated exuberantly, and people, regardless of their station in life, delighted in going about masked and disguised, turning illusion into reality and vice versa. The celebratory carnival spirit that customarily moved the polis of Rome made the unusual the norm, turned work into play, and bestowed prizes on the most successful untruths (masks, costumes). In this context, pressure to remain incognito imposed a taboo value on such markers of reality as names and identities. Alessio's actions, during the seventeen years that he lives unrecognized under his father's roof in Rome, correspond quite closely to what the Roman revellers would do in the carnival season: he reverses in his own person the social order (the aristocrat places himself below the servants), he suspends work (since he is a recognized beggar, others must feed him), and he maintains a highly effective disguise. Actually, Alessio's actions cannot be considered forms of "play" in the post-Platonic sense, since they constitute a heavy task that must be performed permanently. Still, the success of his masquerade is stupendous. In the legend, Alessio's staunch fortitude is supposed to move people to grief and repentance. In the performance, it seems rather designed to elicit *admiration* in the French (Cornelian) sense of that term: bewildered amazement, and stupefied approval.

Like the two buildings in which it was performed, *Sant'Alessio* was "renovated" and expanded in a process that lasted several years. In fact, *Sant'Alessio* can be said to have had not one, but three premières. In the unusual carnival season of 1631, a first version was performed in the old palazzo; no score or libretto was printed. Like any Italian city during the carnival, Rome should have seen a varied round of festive activities, which would typically have included comedies, tumbling, juggling, parades, races, masquerades, among other events. But because of several calamities (plague, famine, war), public carnival festivities were suspended in Rome in 1631 (Murata 19). Several noble families, however, ignored the general sobriety and proceeded with their private entertainments; among them, the Barberini, who, according to the *Avvisi di Roma*, had "the life of the glorious Roman Saint Alexis [. . .] represented in music." The carnival season of 1632 was quite the opposite of the previous year's bleak affair. A great number of performances of all sorts, balls, and masquerades kept the city busy and entertained for a whole month. Each of the households of the Barberini *nipoti* contributed to the social swirl, with balls, a comedy, and spiritual operas. Francesco had *Sant'Alessio* performed at least twice, in the vast main hall of the new palazzo, where a stage, tiered seating accommodations, and arrangements for machinery could be easily installed (Donington 212). A gala performance was held on Wednesday, February 18, for the Habsburg prince Hans Ulrich Fürst von Eggenberg, the season's most distinguished visitor to Rome. At least one other performance was held the next week, on Monday the 23rd: since the performers had rehearsed and were prepared, and since the sets were painted, the machines working, and the hall decorated, the munificent Barberini could well afford to console with a repeat performance deserving guests of second rank. A record of this second performance has survived in the form of an expanded entry in the diary of the Frenchman Jean-Jacques Bouchard, who fortunately also held on to his copy (numbered 285) of the printed *Argommento* that Francesco Barberini had had distributed.[20] It is from Bouchard that we know, for example, that the walls of the great hall were completely covered with red, yellow, and blue satin. There were four scene changes, which offered in succession a perspective of the city of Rome with its palaces, a view of Hell with a number of devils, the tomb of Alessio, and a *gloire* of Paradise showing Alessio with a number of angels.[21] It is said that *Sant'Alessio* was given again in 1633, but I have found no records that substantiate this claim. During the 1634 carnival, Francesco gave *Sant'Alessio* once again, but the opera had been revised: Rospigliosi and Landi had added new comic scenes and spectacular effects. Again, the first 1634 performance was designed as a gala for an important foreign prince: Alexander Charles Wasa (1616–1634), youngest brother of King Ladislaus IV of Poland. It is not clear, however, whether Alexander Wasa was really present; he appears to have left the city earlier than expected, perhaps for religious reasons. For example, he did not attend the splendid carousel, or mock-medieval joust, which the Barberini had planned especially in his honor and which took place on the Piazza Navona, February 21, 1634 (Haskell 55; Bjurström 1966: 34). It is possible that Rospigliosi had revised *Sant'Alessio* in Alexander Wasa's honor; the comic scene in which the devil-hermit-bear chases Martio offstage may have been inserted to please a young prince. As was often the case with such grandiose festive performances, the artists had worked on short notice, too. Landi remarked in his preface to the printed text that, given so little time to work on the opera, he felt he was throwing it together rather than composing it ("nel quale fu più tosto precipitata questa opera, chè composta," Carfagno 62). And Rospigliosi was apprehensive about the proper functioning of the new machines, which had been made rather hastily, and for which there was not much room. Although Bernini is often credited with these rather conventional machines (one made angels appear flying in midair, another brought forth the allegorical figure of Religion on a chariot of clouds), it is by no means certain that he actually made them. But apparently everything added up to a tremendous success.

Even with such scant data on the performances of *Sant'Alessio*, the beginning of a pattern can be traced. The opera seems to have been reserved for gala performances for visiting dignitaries of the highest rank, each time with repeat performances for select courtly audiences consisting of *porporati*: "Cardinali, Prelati, et altri Signori," as well as "delle principali Signore, e Dame di questa Corte." Since the opening of the new palazzo in 1632 would have provided additional justification for a new work symbolically related to that occasion, we may assume that *Sant'Alessio* was retained for specific reasons. For example, a case can be made that the patriotic connotations of the legend were an important consideration to retain it as a showpiece for foreign princes. The stirring prologue ("Roma son'io . . .") sung by the allegorical figure Roma before a painted backdrop representing the Eternal City, as well as the concluding Chorus of Angels ("Felice Roma . . ."), point in this direction.

But in what follows, I will entertain another hypothesis: the legend of Alessio was excellently suited to be rigged out with a subtext in favor of the Barberini, and its grandiose performance in a festive context was the ideal vehicle to solicit praise for the Barberini as the first family of the Eternal City. There is no doubt that the Barberini actively sought to assert their position through allegory and rhetorical strategies in various media. One such medium of self-expression, and a fairly commonplace one, was the grandiose Palazzo Barberini itself. The Barberini began to project their own image as the wealthiest and the most powerful family of Rome, the worldly city, by building the most grandiose private mansion within its walls; with the palazzo, they fixed their name, literally, on the city map. Still, a building, regardless how impressive, is only a building, and subject to the ravages of time. A much more powerful medium of self-expression was the papal throne, which guaranteed its occupant access to immense worldly power as well as a niche in the continuum of the history of the Eternal City. At the very beginning of his tenure Urban VIII himself had some problems with using the papal throne as a symbol of Barberini power (some admonishing poems from his hand addressed to the *nipoti* suggest this), but the nephews never seem to have shared these reservations. Yet, the Barberini were doubtlessly aware that even the papal office does not come with a guarantee of perpetual or popular esteem, and that few popes permanently mark the imagination of the faithful. Boldly taking the process of self-representation as far as they could take it, the Barberini therefore attempted to associate themselves with the very spirit of the Eternal City, that is, with Alessio, the symbolic embodiment of Rome and her personal intercessor at the eternal court of God. In this sense, the creation and the performances of the opera *Sant'Alessio*, held in the two Barberini palazzi during the tenure of Maffeo as Urban VIII, truly mark the "carrying out completely" of the grand project that had begun in a way already when the ambitious Maffeo left Florence as a young man.

As I mentioned earlier, the choice of Alessio's legend for a Barberini opera does indeed seem strange, even paradoxical. Alessio's abject, self-imposed poverty versus Barberini wealth and splendor? Alessio's humble incognito as a pilgrim versus the Barberini papal arms dotted with bees, which could be observed painted or sculpted everywhere in Rome? And yet, the Barberini appropriated the Alessio legend via the medium of operatic representation, and they strove to be assimilated with his name and his achievement via a rhetoric of reconcilable opposites. It would be naive to hypothesize, as modern middle-class interpreters hostile to fundamental principles of the Baroque sensibility well might, that the Barberini intended to claim sainthood for themselves and present themselves to the City and the World as contemporary "reincarnations" of the *person* Alessio, as the archetypally Roman saints. Though the Barberini were doubtlessly among the least modest princes ever to lead the Church, such intolerable vanity was not part of even the widest interpretation of the Baroque taste for ostentation and self-promotion. It would have been generally derided and condemned as blasphemous, and not only by the usual critics of the Church and the papacy. That the Barberini were careful to avoid *this* type of self-glorification is illustrated by a significant detail, pertaining, interestingly enough, to the decoration of the great hall of their new palazzo. Francesco Ubaldini's original plan called with an exaggerated sense of flattery for a series of frescoes, each illustrating one of the chief events of the pontificate of Maffeo Barberini (Pastor vol. 29: 501–02). This plan was not carried out. If it had been, the hall would undoubtedly have called to mind Trimalchio's villa in Petronius' *Satyricon*, with its vulgar self-glorifying murals, and it would have cheapened the real merits of the papacy of Urban VIII. Barberini good taste prevailed, and a series of gobelins representing scenes in the life of Christ was ordered to decorate the hall.[22] However, the ceiling of the Gran Salone, next to the hall, was later decorated by Pietro da Cortona with a vast and magnificent allegorical fresco extolling the virtues and achievements of the Barberini. But in the early 1630s, the performances of *Sant'Alessio* proved a more discreet way for the family to celebrate itself in a social context.

Some assimilation of the Barberini with the saint did occur, but subtly, as a matter of metaphor, or translation. The metaphor, in typically Neoplatonic manner, can be read on various levels. On a fairly simple level, readily available to many members of the audience, the opera seems intended to praise the persistence of a pious man, or to persuade the audience that the Barberini deeply admired the determination of a man, born in a social class very comparable to their own, to set eternal, spiritual values above the worldly advantages of his birth. It is, in fact, every Christian's advised duty to do the same. It is fair to say that most among the audience would at least privately reflect on the immense difference between Alessio and their Barberini hosts. Evidence surrounded the audience even in the very fact of the grandiose performance that Urban's *nipoti* were eagerly pursuing everything that Alessio consistently rejected: power, wealth, advancement through family nepotism, fame. It is simply inconceivable that the Barberini sponsors were not aware of the glaring discrepancy between the subject and the setting of the performance. In the context of approaching Lent, it is even possible that Alessio's legend was intended in part as a public confession of Barberini inadequacies by means of the very comparison the audience was invited to make. Quite obviously, Alessio's poverty and humility expose Barberini wealth and pride. At the same time, the *revision* of the legend as performed for the Barberini sponsors—that is, the focus on the second half of the legend—made another point, more difficult to understand but even more relevant to the sponsors. This point is, briefly, that even though the Barberini could or would not claim to be like the *person* Alessio, they were doing the same sort of thing that he did: they fulfilled some of his *functions* for the City and the World.

This argument requires some clarification. It is essential to emphasize here again the invention (in the rhetorical sense) that distinguishes *Sant'Alessio* the opera from the legend. The Barberini opera exclusively stages the second half of the legend, which is set in Rome and which deals with the overcoming of pride by means of a tenaciously maintained incognito against all human reason and emotion. The same action that today would be condemned as a perverse deviation from filial piety, the Baroque sensibility would praise as heroic fortitude in the face of temptation. We are exposing here the central point of interest in the Baroque interpretation of the legend. True, Alessio practises the theological virtues of Faith, Hope, and Charity toward God and his neighbor, as well as the cardinal virtues of Prudence, Justice, Fortitude, and Temperance. But what really wins him his sainthood is his superhuman refusal to yield to the human temptation of self-revelation in his father's house. He is a Christian hero, surpassing by far the classical hero Odysseus, whose only reason for the long sustained incognito is to gain a strategic position from which the defeat of his human adversaries seems plausible and possible. Alessio, by contrast, would lose at once all the advantages (the indulgences, to use a popular seventeenth-century idea), so diligently and painfully acquired in the course of his seventeen years of beggary abroad, if he were to betray his identity. More than to one's wordly parents, a Christian's duty is, first and foremost, to God. It is from God that Alessio takes his cue to return to his father's house in Rome and face the ordeal waiting for him there—an ordeal so inhuman that it must be divine. Neither the humiliations stemming from the constant mockery by lowly and impious people, nor the vicissitudes attendant upon extreme poverty provide the saint's true martyrdom—for these are discomforts that everyone must expect to suffer in the course of the pilgrimage of life, as art and literature from the Middle Ages throughout the seventeenth century inform us constantly. Rather, Alessio's true martyrdom consists in resisting temptation, specifically the temptation to say who he is, and he earns the status of saint (a Christian equivalent to classical heroism) by overcoming his human pride; that is, by blotting out his personal identity and his human past and by submitting himself unconditionally to the will of God. The legend makes it clear that, in spite of the words spoken by the voice from Heaven, Alessio's family does not understand the true value of his actions, unlike the Emperor and the Pope, who realize immediately that they are dealing with a saint.

Alessio's life, his constancy to his calling, and the heavenly interventions are "admirable" events (again, in the Cornelian sense of "amazing" and worthy of praise), comparable to many episodes in Scripture and pagan-classical epic, as well as in Baroque art (heroic drama, painting, sculpture, sermons, sacred poetry). More specifically Baroque, the voices from Heaven, the display of grandiose emotions and violent spiritual experiences, and the beams of heavenly light bursting through the clouds, are to Alessio and his fellow–citizens the indices of immediate Grace. Through their constant repetition (especially by Bernini) in public places, these motifs or tropes were part of a rhetoric which was familiar to many then, but again unfamiliar to us. For example, Alessio's action must be understood with the seventeenth–century obsession with *gloire*, virtue, duty, and heroism in mind. Numerous stage heroes of the period (Corneille's Polyeuctus among them) quite simply *insist* on a personal martyrdom, scorning any other solution to their dilemma. Therefore, Alessio's abandoning his wife and especially his parents against all filial, natural and worldly inclination, but inspired by a sense of sublime duty, must be interpreted as a heroic sacrifice in the true spirit of Corneille, or of Christianity in general.

This "heroic fortitude," stemming from the duty of obedience, is the central issue of the legend, when it is interpreted in terms of the Baroque sensibility. Milton treats no different theme in *Paradise Lost*. Alessio's legend is about remaining true to one's calling in the face of temptation. Rospigliosi brilliantly dramatized Alessio's fortitude by staging the basic premise of the legend in the form of two attempts, theatrical plots really, mounted by the Devil to tempt Alessio's resistance and to make him forsake his calling. These episodes are central to the opera. First, the Devil deceives Alessio's mother and wife, prompting them to leave the house in order to search high and low for their son and husband. Their decision is heroic in human terms (for they agree to suffering a terrible and uncertain fate as begging pilgrims) but not in God's terms (since they do it only to retrieve a human loved one and not unconditionally for the love and greater glory of God). The Devil is not really interested in the mother and wife, though; he merely creates the situation in the hope that Alessio will succumb to his human love for them and reveal himself in order to prevent their hardship and resolve their plight. Of course, the shrewd plot fails. The Devil, running out of ideas, then appears to Alessio disguised as a pious hermit. With a characteristic Baroque taste for dramatic juxtapositions, Rospigliosi immediately counters the infernal presence with a heavenly one: an Angel appears to chase the Devil away and to inform Alessio that he has suffered enough and will die soon. In such a context, to die means to be born again, but in a better form. Rather than confirming the pessimistic scepticism that was characteristic of contemporaneous philosophical speculation and worldly courtly art, Rospigliosi and Landi celebrated eternal time in their spiritual courtly art. The grandiose vision of Paradise at the end of the opera reminds us that Alessio's true life has only just begun. To the Christian philosopher, time is not an utterly negative force, but rather the great apocalyptic vindicator which lays to ruin the vanity of people and their works and which guarantees a reward for the just. Viewed as such, the present is only part of eternity and must be considered *sub specie aeternitatis*.

It is useful to remember here that the favorite procedure of epideictic rhetoric is *amplification*. The orator, who is after all exposing well-known facts, must enlarge them, magnify them, and highlight with maximum efficiency what it is that makes these facts beautiful, or grandiose, and worthy of the praise of the polis (*"Art" of Rhetoric* I:1368a). Hyperbole, repetition and metaphor are among the tools at the disposal of the orator, or artist, to achieve this goal. To the Baroque sensibility, Alessio's fortitude, and his resistance to the temptation of revealing his identity (an analogue to the effects of trompe l'oeil so beloved by Baroque artists), were the beautiful aspects worthy of praise and deserving of sanctification. These motifs were clearly the ones that Rospigliosi selected for amplification. But why? What were the ulterior motives of the Barberini sponsor?

A principal function of praise, including praise of the self, is to avert blame, and epideictic rhetoric is often used to make the audience swallow an inciting message, as well as to create a consensus, a communion of social values. The Barberini absorption of power and wealth was heavily criticized in Rome. The following ratiocination posits that the opera was intended to avert at least some of this blame. The Barberini opera *amplifies* Alessio's resistance of temptation by the Devil and his total submission to the will of God. Logically then, the intended purpose can only be to *persuade* the audience that the Barberini, too, were submitting to the will of God, just as Alessio did, but that the testing conditions were different, and, indeed, given their era and their hierarchical position, far more complicated. For some, submitting to the will of God may imply submitting to poverty, humility and anonymity; for others, the test may imply the exact opposite: the far more difficult task of properly administering power and wealth. In the rhetoric of the harmonious opposite, the function of the grandiose performances of *Sant'Alessio* was to persuade the audience (at least those with the appropriate level of understanding) that, though the *accidental* conditions were exactly the reverse, the Barberini wanted to be thought of as doing, in *essence*, the same thing that gained Alessio his sainthood: they were overcoming the temptations of their high offices and their power, they felt that they had been rewarded with power and wealth, and they were fulfilling well the obligations that come with the reward. For Alessio, the reward is sainthood, which implies the power and the duty to meet the requests of worthy supplicants with magnificence and largesse. With each satisfied supplicant, the saint's status rises, at least in our world and in Rome, his own city, in particular. For the Barberini, the reward was the possibility of acting as "sponsors" to Rome and the World, an office different from that of Alessio not so much in type as in magnitude. This is the "half revealed, half concealed" content of the operatic adaptation of the legend, and of its Barberini assimilation. Given the preoccupation of the period with the analysis of pre- and postfigurations of Christ, with the *imitatio* of Christ and his Saints, and similar theological matters that seem remote to us, the Barberini assimilation with Saint Alessio then seems not so extravagant anymore. It has also been said often that the subject of Rospigliosi's *Sant'Alessio* is historical, but that "the persons and scenes . . . are obviously drawn from the contemporary life of seventeenth-century Rome" (Grout 69). This statement may be more true than it appears at first sight.

But a nagging doubt remains; all of the pious "explanations" given above seem just a bit at odds with the known Barberini character. Presenting the following remark, then, not as the final "solution" to the Barberini motivation for *Sant'Alessio* but merely as a provocative thought, I would like to return briefly to the notion of potlatch as presented in the Interlude. Let us posit that with the festive performance of the legend of Sant'Alessio, the Barberini flung in the faces of their audience, the richest and the most powerful elite of Rome and her visitors, a brilliantly applied example of the most intensely agonistic potlatch expenditure that could be imagined: that of the Christian hero, of which type Christ himself is the noblest representative. It has been posited that when Christianity entered the social warfare that has always existed between the rich and the poor, between the powerful and the unempowered, it brought a new dimension to that warfare by empowering the powerless to hurl their very lack of power and wealth into the faces of their opponents—an attack of unproductive expenditure which the rich and powerful could not possibly withstand unless they were themselves to yield up their wealth and power to the poor and powerless, and so on and so forth. Except for a very few cases (as supposedly in the case of Alexis), the rich and powerful are not likely to do this, and therefore end up the losers (from Bataille 1970, vol. 1: 316–18; it is questionable, of course, whether Christianity was actually exclusively the religion of the unempowered). After all, in the social game of potlatch as it is played in this passing world, the player with the most chips left loses; the same is true on an immeasurably grander scale in the eternal world as it is projected by Christianity. In a way, having deliberately thrown away his inherited wealth and position, becoming the most steadfast of beggars, Alessio became upon his conversion a compulsive gambler with the dirt and humiliation of Christianity, the "immondice indispensable à ses tourments extatiques" ("the filth that is indispensable to its ecstatic torments;" Bataille 1970, vol. 1: 317). It can been argued that Christ himself introduced this supreme form of potlatch-poker, which one might, in the most negative reading, actually consider a rather annoying occupation; for being one of his better pupils, Alessio entered Heaven as well as the Golden Legend. Consequently, the Barberini, by throwing a potlatch performance in which they related themselves functionally and thematically to Alessio, did present themselves like Alessio, and by *tertium comparationis* like Christ. The wealthiest and the most powerful family of the City offered freely, arrogantly, to the most distinguished audience ("Cardinali, Prelati, principali Signore, e Dame di questa Corte"), in the most beautiful room (hung from ceiling to floor with blue, red, and yellow satin!) of the most grandiose palace of the most renowned city of the Christian world, and with the most splendid performers available (including the singers of Saint Peter's) a spectacle that could not, at least for a while still, be rivalled by anybody: "le délire propre à la fête s'associe indifféremment aux hécatombes de propriété et aux dons accumulés avec l'intention d'étonner et d'aplatir" (Bataille 1970, vol. 1: 310).[23]

For the time being, who could possibly give more? Moreover, given the carnival setting, who could argue with them, who could claim that anything serious was intended? Whatever was sung or presented, whatever was thought to be implied, might just as well mean its opposite!

The last recorded performance of *Sant'Alessio* in Barberini Rome was in 1634. The opera was published in the same year.[24] Had *Sant'Alessio* outlived the functions for which it was designed? But the conscious decision to "release" the opera in 1634 may have been prompted by the idea that the work was now complete. The last phase in the rhetorical construction of a festive performance is the creation of *memoria*, permanent reminders of the performance. As a printed text, *Sant'Alessio* was relegated to permanence. The publication of the libretto and the engravings of the four scenes effectively terminated two very important aspects of *Sant'Alessio* as a Baroque festive performance: first, the private status of the work as something to be controlled by the sponsors; and second, the ephemeral, transient quality of the work. Upon publication, therefore, *Sant'Alessio* ceased to be subjected to, and to represent, the rhetoric of the Baroque festive performance.

In the light of the above, the fate of the Barberini, following the death of Urban VIII in 1644, seems ironic. On July 2, Maffeo Barberini died an exhausted man. Rome and the Papal States had suffered badly from a war against the League of Italian Princes, that is, Modena, Tuscany, Venice, and Parma. The treasury was in shambles, taxation enormous. From a political and economic point of view, Maffeo Barberini's grand plans for Rome had largely failed. In fact, Rome had become "a backwater dammed by the policies of France and Spain and stagnant in diplomatic ceremony," while "the Counter Reformation, the resident Jesuits, papal nepotism, and a wealthy Curia were comfortably entrenched in the Eternal City at an almost provincial level" (Murata 1). But comparatively speaking, the rest of Italy fared much worse. The bubonic plague had caused a million deaths in Italy by 1630; in the first half of the century, the population of central and south Italy declined by ten percent and that of the Po valley by twenty. The population of Rome was at about 100,000, making it only the fourth largest city in Italy after Naples, Venice, and Palermo (Bonnefoy 168). Yet, Rome's powerful position as the ceremonial center of the Christian world assured its rulers great wealth until just into the second half of the century. But by the 1660s, many upper- and middle-class residences stood empty, abandoned.

Urban VIII was succeeded by Cardinal Pamphili (Innocent X), who represented a family hostile to the Barberini. Charges of nepotism were openly made, and, more seriously, accusations that the Barberini had used the pontificate to enrich themselves beyond any reasonable measure. When an inquiry into Barberini financial policy seemed inevitable, the *nipoti* fled Rome one after the other, taking with them much of the artistic talent that they had sponsored so lavishly. But they would soon return; meanwhile, in Paris, they were offered refuge by Richelieu's successor: Cardinal Mazarin, fellow-Italian and opera lover, who as Giulio Mazarini had been in the service of Francesco Barberini in 1632 and who had perhaps been involved in that year's production of *Sant'Alessio*.[25] In chapter 5, we will return at greater length to Mazarin and his involvement with splendid performances.

Notes

1. It may also have been the first opera in which the titular role was sung by a *castrato*; see Hermann Kretzschmar, "Die venetianische Oper und die

Werke Cavalli's und Cesti's," *Vierteljahrschrift für Musikwissenschaft* 8 (1892): 1–76, 17. Further, see, first and foremost, Romain Rolland, "La première représentation du *San Alessio* . . . à Rome," *Revue d'histoire et de critique musicales* 2 (1902): 29–36, 74–75; Margaret Murata, *Operas for the Papal Court, 1631–1668*, diss., U Chicago, 1975 (Ann Arbor, 1981); and the relevant sections in Donington, and Grout. See also Nino Pirotta and Elena Povoledo, *Music and Theatre from Poliziano to Monteverdi*, trans. Karen Eales (Cambridge, 1982).

On Rospigliosi, see Giovanni Canevazzi, *Papa Clementa IX poeta* (Modena, 1900) and Abd–El–Kader Salza, *Dramma inediti di Giulio Rospigliosi, poi Clemente IX* (Turin, 1907). On Landi, see Simon Albert Carfagno, "The Life and Dramatic Music of Stefano Landi, with a Transliteration and Orchestration of the Opera *Sant'Alessio*," diss., U of California at Los Angeles, 1960; and Silke Leopold, *Stefano Landi. Beiträge zur Biographie*, 2 vols. (Hamburg, 1976).

2. See Alfred von Reumont, *Beiträge zur italienischen Geschichte* (Berlin, 1853–1857), 5: 117–71; Oskar Pollak, *Die Kunsttätigkeit unter Urban VIII* (Vienna; Augsburg; Cologne, 1928), vol. 1; Alberto Cametti, *Christina di Svezia, l'arte musicale e gli spettacoli teatrali in Roma* (Rome, 1931); Freiherr Ludwig von Pastor, *The History of the Popes*, trans. Ernest Graf (London, 1938), vols. 28 and 29; Francis Haskell, *Patrons and Painters: A Study in the Relations between Italian Art and Society in the Age of the Baroque* (London, 1963); Per Bjurström, *Feast and Theatre in Queen Christina's Rome* (Stockholm, 1966); Yves Bonnefoy, *Rome 1630: L'horizon du premier baroque* (Paris, 1970); Marilyn A. Lavin, *Seventeenth–Century Barberini Documents and Inventories of Art* (New York, 1975), docs. 99 and 429; S. Carandini, "La festa barocca a Roma," *Biblioteca teatrale* 15–16 (1976): 276–308; and Volker Reinhardt, "Der päpstliche Hof um 1600," in August Buck, et al., eds., 3: 709–15.

3. A fairly prolific poet early in his career, Maffeo liked to insist that he wrote not for personal fame but to foster piety and morality in the hearts of his readers. His poems attack the vices (especially Greed, Envy and Pride) and praise the virtues (especially Charity).

4. The ruthless Sixtus V had already turned papal power into an absolute dictatorship in the 1580s and early 1590s.

5. See Victor Tapié, *Baroque et classicisme* (Paris, 1957; 1980), 141; Anthony Blunt, "The Palazzo Barberini," *Journal of the Warburg and Courtauld Institutes* 21 (1958): 256–87; and Angela Negro, ed. *Guide Rionali di Roma: Rione II-Trevi*, part 1 (Rome, 1980): 140–214. See also Pollak for documents pertaining to the building of the "Quattro Fontane" palace (251–338).

6. In these years (from 1624 until 1633), Bernini was also working on the celebrated *baldacchino* for the Saint Peter's basilica.

7. See Valerio Mariani, "Bernini regista e scenografo," *Studi di bibliografia e di argomento romano in memoria di Luigi de Gregori* (Rome, 1949) 254–64; and M. Fagiolo dell'Arco, *Bernini: una introduzione al grande teatro del barocco* (Rome, 1967) 179–212.

8. See Alessandro Ademollo, *I teatri di Roma nel secolo XVII* (1888; Bologna, 1969) 28–31, on the subject of Milton's visit to the Barberini.

9. My source text was Giulio Rospigliosi, *Sant'Alessio* (C1632, item #6, from R. Vat. Codex Ottob. Pat. 2259. vols. 329–57), of which I obtained a xeroxcopy through the kind services of the Archivio Segreto of the Vatican, Vatican City State, 00120 Rome, Italy. I also used Murata 279–301.

10. "In reaction to the overly literary doctrines of the Camerata, the Roman composers soon began to consider the libretto nothing more than a pretext for a variety of musical expressions, a theme for declamation, a mere canvas on which they could embroider gorgeous flowers. . . . Discarding the Florentine ideal of noble beauty and reason, the Roman poets and musicians sought above all to flatter the senses of a public eager to enjoy themselves."

11. Musical drama had been performed for the Barberini previously to *Sant'Alessio*, of course—such as Tronsarelli's *Sirena* on the occasion of Taddeo's wedding in 1629. In the same year, Cornachioli's *La Diana schernita* ended with a symbolic apotheosis of the Barberini.

12. One aspect of Urban VIII's theatrical policy was quite unusual and ahead of the times: he allowed female singers to perform in public. But in *Sant'Alessio* all female roles were taken by castrati, which emphasized the carnivalesque transvestism motif. Later popes, such as Alexander VII, were not as tolerant, though women could continue to perform in private performances (Bjurström 1966: 30).

13. Although such operas could include comic elements (*Sant'Alessio* did), they deliberately avoided the scurrilous aspects of the commedia dell'arte (Donington 207ff; Pirotta 1982: 270, 273). See also by Pirrotta, "Commedia dell'arte and Opera," *The Musical Quarterly* 41 (1955): 305–24.

14. Prunières claimed, not unreasonably, that the choice of subject and Landi's musical treatment of it were "peu faites pour être appréciées par la foule enfiévrée et joyeuse qui remplissait la salle" ("it was very much in doubt whether the feverish and joyous crowd that filled the hall would appreciate them;" 11). But his argument that Rospigliosi introduced the scenes with the comic page Martio as well as a ballet of peasants simply to remedy that defect is not very convincing.

15. Jacobus de Voragine, *The Golden Legend*, trans. William Caxton (1483), ed. F. S. Ellis (1900; New York, [s.d.]) 6: 205–12: "Of S. Alexis."

16. "But over there I see, sad and lonely,/ that pilgrim and beggar/ whom my master has given shelter in his mansion."

17. "In your way of speaking, your manner, and your general aspect/ you appear much like a soldier."

18. "Alessio, what now?/ . . . You, who to seek God, have fled the world/ . . . Ah! such fierce battles/ do I feel raging on the stage of my heart."

19. "The forces of Inferno cannot/ triumph over a soul that Heaven defends."

20. The manuscript of Bouchard's journal is in the Bibliothèque de l'Ecole Nationale Supérieure des Beaux Arts, Paris (MS 502). See Jean–Jacques Bouchard, *Oeuvres de Jean-Jacques Bouchard*, ed. Emanuele Kanceff, 2 vols. (Turin, 1976) 1: 139–55.

21. These scenes were still fairly static, with a quite severe central perspective: city scene, an exotic landscape, same city scene but adapted for the tomb, and same city scene but with Heaven opening; engravings of the four scenes (now in the Gabinetto Nazionale delle Stampe, Roma) are reproduced in Mariani 1949: 254–64. They influenced the scenes of *Il pomo d'oro* (see chapter 6, "Ne Plus Ultra").

22. The cartoons were made by Pietro da Cortona and others. The tapestries were not finished when the Barberini fled Rome in 1644–1645. In 1663, Francesco did order a series of tapestries on the life of Urban VIII; the work lasted more than twenty years (Pastor vol. 29: xxx; Haskell 59–60).

23. "The delirium characteristic of the feast is associated indifferently with the hekatombs of possessions and with gifts that have been accumulated in order to astonish and crushingly humiliate."

24. *Sant'Alessio* was revived in 1674. Perhaps the following reference from the *National Union Catalogue* Supplement, vol. 728, 100 (a reference which I was unable to track down any further) may prove useful in this regard: Pier D. Gentilucci, *Sant'Alessio* (Fermo: Bolis e frat., 1731) 15 pp.

25. Cardinal Francesco came back as early as 1648; immediately after the return of Antonio (1653), the Barberini theater was reopened, and the powerful family once again began sponsoring festive celebrations, both public and private.

4

EL REY PLANETA: *EL MAYOR ENCANTO, AMOR*

Cosme (Cosimo) Lotti and Pedro Calderón de la Barca created *El mayor encanto, amor* for the celebration of Saint John's night (Midsummer Night's eve), 1635, at the court of Philip the Fourth. Plays, sometimes augmented with extra music, had been organized for years in Madrid to mark the summer solstice, the moment of the year when the sun has reached its peak and cannot rise higher.[1] This event was given cosmic and mythic importance and was a splendid occasion to celebrate the power of the king. After all, he was the fourth to be named Philip, just as the sun is the fourth planet. Philip and his *privado*—the Count-Duke Olivares, the driving force behind the king—shared a keen interest in astrology. One of Philip's titles was *el rey planeta*, the Planet King, and court propaganda made extensive use of solar symbolism to illustrate Philip's status as absolute ruler over vast possessions that, still, spanned the world. The significance of *El mayor encanto, amor* as a sophisticated astrological *laudatio* of the *rey planeta* has been convincingly demonstrated.[2] But in 1635, Philip had an additional reason to celebrate: the completion of the magnificent and exorbitantly costly throne room, the Hall of Realms, in the Buen Retiro, Philip's new pleasure palace.[3] Not all was well in the realm, however. In June 1635, the usual Saint John's night celebrations were suspended, primarily because Spain and France had just seriously begun the war that was to last until 1659. In that year, the Peace of the Pyrenees was sealed with the symbolic marriage between Louis XIV of France and the

Habsburg Maria Theresa, daughter of Philip IV and Isabella of Bourbon. The (provisional) conclusion of the war and the royal wedding were celebrated in 1662 in Paris with the grandiose festive performance of *Ercole amante*. But in 1635, the political situation was very different, and a consideration of *El mayor encanto, amor* makes sense only in the historical context of its performance, which took place somewhat later than originally planned.[4] Given the circumstances, it is remarkable that the play was performed at all.

El mayor encanto, amor stages Ulysses' encounter with the beautiful witch Circe. It was the first of many mythological plays which Calderón wrote for festive occasions (*fiestas*) at court.[5] Following the death of Lope de Vega, also in 1635, Calderón became the court dramatist to Philip IV. He was to the Spanish court what his contemporary Giulio Rospigliosi was to the Barberini: a faithful servant who could for many years be counted upon to deliver appropriate play texts for the delight, amusement, and instruction of the ruler and the court. *El mayor encanto, amor* was first performed before the king, with magnificent effects of lighting and with spectacular machines, on an island stage raised in the middle of the large artificial pond in the famous Retiro palace gardens. Not so much the nominal subject of the performance and the fantastic setting, but especially the fact that Philip was seen enjoying himself when his country, in full recession, had just begun a war that promised to be lengthy and very costly, contributed to the mounting discontent in Spain with the Count-Duke and his power over the king.[6] *El mayor encanto, amor* manages to praise *and* criticize Philip *and* Olivares, undoing the *laudatio* with the *vituperatio*, and yet softening the blame with the praise. In the context of the Baroque festive performance as rhetorical discourse, *El mayor encanto, amor* is a masterpiece of diplomatic rhetoric.

The 1630s were not the most propitious time for the Spanish monarch to build a pleasure palace and indulge in its temptations. The old-fashioned, Anglo-Saxon view that the reign of Philip IV (and of Olivares) was a period of absolute decadence is trivial and largely irrelevant.[7] Yet, this reign undeniably marked the irremediable decline of the political, military, and economic power of the once unchallenged Spanish Habsburg empire.[8] Ever since the defeat of the Armada in 1588, Spain had steadily been losing much of her significance as a major European power; this continuing process was counterbalanced by the rise, first of England in the sixteenth, and then of France and the Netherlands in the seventeenth century. The profoundly troubled state of affairs in Spain was certainly not visible, however, in the realm of aesthetics and court entertainments. Especially in Madrid, at Court and in the houses of the grand nobles, painting (the school of Velázquez), theatrical performances and feasts, and art collecting (by patronage, purchase, and simple confiscation) flourished as never before.[9] Thus, a parallel can be drawn between the situation of Spain under Philip IV and that of Rome under Urban VIII. On the one hand, an enormous expenditure of funds and energy at Court satisfied the tastes of the rulers, allowed a generation of gifted artists to create its masterpieces, and constructed a dazzling façade of opulence and magnificence to silence some critics at home and abroad. On the other hand, this façade alone could not entirely make up for the loss of concrete power in the larger historical and geopolitical context.

Much has been written about the responsibility of the Count-Duke Olivares for this state of affairs. At the same time secretary, prime minister, and general confidant, Olivares succeeded in making himself indispensable to the young king. When Philip IV (1605–1665) succeeded his father in March, 1621, he was one week short of his sixteenth birthday. Trained in the use of arms, he also became a man of letters, thus excelling in the "two professions" that were so important to Spanish Golden Age thought.[10] It is interesting to speculate what Philip would have made of his tenure on the Spanish Habsburg throne without the domineering shadow of Olivares hovering over him. As it turned out, Olivares engineered his kingship, much like a bear was once thought to lick her formless cub into shape. Like the Barberini (or any other) pope, Olivares surrounded himself with his own appointees, many of whom were close relatives; until his fall in the mid 1640s, Olivares allowed the members of his clan to use their power to enrich themselves. Quickly becoming the most hated man in the nation, he had the power to make or break others, to give offices and take them away. Olivares was considered ruthless, overbearing, arrogant, and prone to theatrical gesticulation. An avid sermon-goer, he indulged increasingly in an appetite for devotional exercises. He took in hand the formal education of the young heir to the throne, trained him in the technical, bureaucratic aspects of the kingship, and converted him to his own plans for the nation: the restoration of Castile and the reconstruction of the monarchy, the tightening of public and official morals, the cleaning up of the royal finances, and the engagement in many ambitious modernizing schemes, none of which were carried out successfully: irrigation projects, the closing of brothels, tax reforms, a greater political and military union in the peninsula. All these and many other projects collapsed (Brown and Elliott 18ff). Olivares had become famous for his strict personal discipline, and infamous for the taxes and austerity policies which he imposed upon the nation. And then the Retiro was conceived. Planned down to every detail by Olivares, the pleasure palace was interpreted by critics in Spain and abroad as the living contradiction of Olivares' public policy. Rather than admiration, the palace turned out to generate scorn and hostility: for its own sake, because it was badly planned and rather unimpressive on the outside; for Olivares, who built it with public funds obtained through ruthless and selective taxation; and for the king, who succumbed to its charms at a time when it was thought that he should be with his armies in the field or with his fleets at sea.

The whimsical conception, speedy construction and costly furnishings of the Buen Retiro palace provide an excellent example of Baroque rulers' often spurned disregard for economic and political realities in times of crisis.[11] The absolutist age expressed itself in elegant palaces whose sheer size, design and location made them wholly indefensible, and whose very vulnerability was intended as an arrogant symbol of the ruler's claim to unchallenged power (perhaps also a sort of potlatch). More than a convenient dwelling, such a royal residence was mainly a statement in the service of internal and foreign policy. The palace also allowed the ruler to act as magnificent patron and host, capable of supporting large numbers of artists and craftsmen and even larger contingents of guests. In brief, it enabled the ruler to practice the courtly-heroic virtue of largesse, aristocratic generosity. Philip II made Madrid the fixed court, and it continued as such, with the exception of a period of less than a decade under Philip III. Yet, the Spanish kings retained also a travelling court system, making use of various royal residences for short or more extended periods of time. In the Spain of the *rey planeta*, the creation of the capital as a cosmic space for court and the designation of the central palace at its permanent center occurred virtually at the same time. Madrid became, for all practical purposes, the official capital in 1606. It was then still a small and relatively unimportant city, and, at least in the early part of the century, its subsequent development was largely haphazard, mainly responding to the needs and the growth of the court. Most new houses were mean, low constructions built with inferior materials; and at least on the outside, the new mansions for the nobility appeared merely severe rather than grandiose. The quite gloomy Alcázar functioned as the royal palace; it was a converted fortress from Moorish times, located at the west end of the city. Near to Madrid were other royal residences or pavilions with splendid gardens, such as the Pardo and the Casa de Campo.

What ultimately became the plan to build a new palace began modestly enough with the enlargement of the small royal apartment in the San Jeronimo monastery, just outside the east gate of the city (1630–31). Olivares then envisaged the construction, starting from this humble extension, of an Italian-style suburban villa with a theater. From those beginnings, the idea became an obsession that soon also affected Philip. Construction of the Retiro palace began, probably in 1632, on large tracts of land next to the royal monastery. The size of the project increased continually, as new gardens, stables, courtyards, halls, hermitages (to be occupied by officially appointed hermits!) were included. The project was characterized from the beginning by an astonishing lack of planning and an unexplainable (but "typically Baroque") desire to work at lightning speed. As a result, modifications had to be carried out regularly (newly completed walls or gardens were torn down because the latest version of the plan had no use for them, and so forth). Olivares was highly ingenious in finding new ways to fund the whimsical project at public expense. The new taxes that were thus added to the already intolerable burden on the middle and lower classes (the nobility was tax exempt) only added to the general hostility to the project. If asked, the tax payers would probably have preferred their money to feed the starving troops or to build warships to fight the French, or the English, or the Dutch. Olivares' feeble excuses did not succeed in overcoming the public anger, but construction went on undisturbed nevertheless, day and night. The building materials (brick and wood) were humble and not of very good quality, and the exterior of the palace, when completed, was considered anything but impressive by independent observers. For one, it was much too low and plain. The two strong points of the Retiro were undeniably its fabulous furnishings (paintings, tapestries, and furniture, much of it confiscated from subjected territories abroad, such as Flanders) and its extended gardens, filled with the most diverse plants and exotic animals. Upon its completion, artists rallied to praise the Retiro and, through the palace, the ruler. Lope de Vega wrote a poem on the occasion of the magnificent opening spectacle, "A la primera Fiesta del Palacio nuevo" (published 1637) and Calderón wrote an *auto sacramental* (a religious one-act play on the subject of the Eucharist) adapted to the occasion, *El nuevo palacio del Retiro* (1634).[12] Scores of panegyric poems were written, and in 1635, Diego de Covarrubias published his sycophantic anthology *Elegías al palacio real del Buen Retiro*. In stanza 95 of his long poem "Upon Appleton House," Andrew Marvell mentions the Retiro gardens among a great number of famous and mythological gardens:

> For you *Thessalian Tempe's Seat*
> Shall now be scorn'd as obsolete;
> *Aranjuez*, as less, disdain'd;
> The *Bel-Retiro* as constrain'd;
> But name not the *Idalian Grove*,
> For 'twas the Seat of wanton Love;
> Much less the Dead's *Elysian Fields*,
> Yet nor to them your Beauty yields.[13]

Needless to say, Marvell prefers the Appleton gardens. The Retiro palace, along with its grounds, was also painted numerous times in the seventeenth century. Most of the complex was destroyed in the Peninsular war (1808); a substantial part of the gardens, though drastically altered, survives in our time as a municipal park. From the beginning, the Retiro was intended as a pleasant retreat, as a pleasure palace. And that is exactly how it was used, for the Alcázar at the other side of Madrid remained the working palace. Councils were occasionally held at the new palace, but the Retiro served primarily for brief holidays and for festive celebrations of all kinds. Thus, the royal household was at the Retiro only for limited periods of time, from a few days up to, at most, a month. The setting, with its gardens and its courtyards, lent itself best to the production of charming and large-scale festive events: bullfights, pageants, and theatrical spectacles.

Unlike his grandfather and even his father, Philip IV had a genuine passion for the theater. The austere Philip II did not support the theater materially. Under Philip III, a stage for private performances (*particulares*) was constructed in one of the Alcázar's saloons—perhaps to please the Queen. (The Alcázar, including its theater, was later destroyed by fire.) Philip III also had a theater installed in the Casa del Tesoro, in the vicinity of the Alcázar, where their Majesties could watch *comedias* such as they were performed in the public playhouses (*corrales*).[14] It was of course inconceivable that they would attend a performance in a real *corral*. What was a mere interest in theatrical entertainment on the parent's part became a passion at the son's court—a passion, however, that benefited pretty actresses more than it did playwrights.[15] Philip had *comedias* performed by various companies in the Alcázar, in the private apartments of the king (*el Cuarto del Rey*) or more often in those of the queen (*el Cuarto del Reina*, where, for example, no fewer than forty-five *comedias* were staged over a period of just four months in 1622–23), as well as in the other royal residences—such as in the gardens of Aranjuèz (Rennert 237); the staging of *particulares* in the Alcázar continued even when the Retiro became available.

At Philip's court—to which the rigidly maintained etiquette and rituals (Burgundian in origin) lent a theatrical air—the propaganda value of festive performances was fully understood. Just as the Barberini had their Bernini, Philip had in his service a creative genius who could work miracles on the stage: Cosme Lotti. Lotti was brought to Spain from Tuscany in 1626; he was an engineer who specialized in fountains and garden waterworks, and was asked in that capacity to develop the gardens of various royal residences. His mechanical skills were soon to be applied to the theater; and in fact, building *tramoyas* (machines) and decors for spectacular plays was his principal activity throughout the 1630s and until his death in 1643.[16] From 1635 on, the Retiro palace became the official setting for court celebrations and all sorts of performances. The various courtyards and gardens saw performances of *comedias* with *entremeses* on a movable stage, pageants, out-of-door spectacles, bull-fights, puppet shows, and masques, and on some occasions the Hall of Realms, too, became a theatrical space. The official palace theater, equipped with up-to-date machinery, opened in 1640; one of its impressive features was the removable back wall of the stage, which allowed the beautiful park itself to serve as setting.[17] Lotti did not need a theater proper, however, to create his effects: an artifical island in the largest garden pond was created to form a theatrical space. Such was the case on the opening night of *El mayor encanto, amor*.

The performance began with a glorification (*loa*) of Madrid by the nymph Galatea rather than by the goddess Aqua—regardless, what a difference from the paltry, cliché-ridden glorification of Rome by the stiff, allegorical figure "Roma" with which the performance of *Sant'Alessio* began! Precisely on which date this magic was first worked is not entirely clear. Some confusion was created by the discovery of the undated manuscript *La Circe*, which claims to describe the "Fiesta que se representó en el Estanque grande del Retiro . . . la noche de San Juan" (see also Shergold 1958: 24 n. 3). The description of the performance clearly points to *El mayor encanto, amor*. But *La Circe* is not Calderón's first draft of *El mayor encanto, amor*, as has long been assumed.[18] Rather, the manuscript is Lotti's blueprint for the entire performance, containing a proposed outline of the plot and emphasizing the use of machines. Lotti presumably submitted this document for approval to a court official in charge of festivities; when the approval was granted, Calderón was asked to fill in the outline with dialogue. Considerably annoyed at this humiliating (although hardly unusual) lack of artistic freedom, Calderón rejected Lotti's plot as poetically stifling and too spectacular, as all effects and no substance (de Armas 1986: 140). Such conflicts—essentially debates whether the verbal or the visual should be given preeminence—were frequent between performance architects and poet-playwrights in Europe at this time. A comparable conflict arose in England between Inigo Jones and Ben Jonson.

The early performance history of *El mayor encanto, amor* is, just as that of *Sant'Alessio*, fairly confused. Most likely, the première was given for the king and Olivares late in June, 1635; it had been postponed a few days, so Jesuit newsletters inform us, because of growing public concern over the war.[19] Three more performances were given immediately after: for the Councils (*los Consejos*), for the Queen (Isabella of Bourbon), and for a paying audience. It was not altogether unusual to admit the general public to some performances in the palace grounds; later in the 1630s, Olivares made the practice part of his (futile) strategy aimed at increasing his popularity. One source claims that the performance lasted six hours, until 1 A.M., another source mentions four hours; at any rate, "la riqueza de los vestidos fué increíble, y la variedad de las cosas prodigiosa" ("the splendor of the costumes was incredible, and the variety of its spectacle prodigious"), and the magical effect of the many lights on the water was breathtaking. The cast was operatic in its size: Ulysses had eight companions (including Lebrel, a buffoon anticipating his namesake Leporello in Lorenzo da Ponte's libretto for Mozart's *Don Giovanni*), while Circe's retinue included five ladies, two attendants, and two nymphs, all with classical-pastoral names; in addition, there were two princes, a giant, the ghost of Achilles, Greek and Sicilian bands of soldiers, and, for the concluding ballet, Tritons and Sirens. Lotti was generally thought to have outdone himself. The length of the performance can be explained, in part, by the fact that, according to established custom, *El mayor encanto, amor* was accompanied by an *entremes*—in this case, *Las dueñas*, written by the most distinguished *entremesista*, Luis Quiñones de Benavente. There is evidence that a second performance or series of performances of *El mayor encanto, amor* was given a month later, around July 29, but it is not certain whether these differed in any way from the June performances (Shergold 1958: 24). *El mayor encanto, amor* was first printed in the second volume of Calderón's *Comedias* (Madrid, 1637; second edition Madrid, 1641).[20]

A plot summary of *El mayor encanto, amor* will prepare the reader for the discussion of the work to follow. Act one opens with a howling tempest at sea ("Ese monstruo de cristal,/ Sierpe escamada de espuma," "This cruel crystal monster rude,/ This azure serpent scaled with foam" [35]), in front of the island; when it calms down, the Greeks land safely. As the island seems a dreary and uninhabited place, the crew members depart to investigate:

> Todo el sitio es rigor.
> Todos es espanto.
> Todo horror. Todo asombro.
> Todo encanto (25–26).[21]

These men will not return soon. Ulysses, left with Clarín on the beach, meets with a lion who signals them to leave. Antistes returns alone: he describes a rich palace in the labyrinthine forest, where nymphs and their beautiful mistress have turned the crew into beasts:

> Vimos un rico palacio,
> Tan vanamente soberbio,
> Que embarazando los aires,
> Y los montes afligiendo,
> Era para aquellos nube,
> Y peñasco para estos,
> Porque se daba la mano
> Con uno y con otro extremo
> Pero aunque viciosos eran,
> La virtud no estaba en medio (28–29).[22]

Ulysses prays to Juno, and, wrapped in the song of a chorus of voices "within," Iris the rainbow brings the conventional antidote to Circe's spells:

> Este ramo, que te traigo,
> De varias flores cubierto,
> Hoy contra Circe ferá
> Triaca de sus venenos (33).[23]

In front of Circe's palace, Ulysses is welcomed by singing and playing musicians and he meets its denizens; after long compliments, Circe offers Ulysses the magic cup ("Bebe y brinda al dios de Amor," "Drink and pledge the God of love" [36]), but the latter overcomes its power: as he dips the branch in the goblet, flames rise up from it. All flattery ends, and Ulysses, drawing his sword ("Verás, mágica, este acero/ En tu púrpura teñido," "Sorceress, thou shalt feel this steel/ With thy crimson blood imbued" [37]) orders Circe to transform the men again. Upon her request, Ulysses tells Circe his story; she replies in kind. As a sign of goodwill, Ulysses asks her to undo the spell on two trees: as a result, the lovers Flerida and Lysidas emerge, which is a cause for celebrations. The jealous Arsidas is introduced: he is a passionate suitor, whom Circe has perversely punished by permitting him to live in sight of her. In an aside, Ulysses reveals that he will feign love for Circe to rid the island of her.

The second act begins in the palace. Circe is in love with Ulysses but wants to dissemble her feelings for reasons of decorum. She suggests that Flerida feign love for Ulysses; if he responds and they meet secretly at night, Circe can substitute herself for Flerida. In the beautiful garden, Ulysses confesses to himself that he is in love with Circe. A complicated courtship begins, with each lover feigning false feelings and dissembling genuine ones. The jealousy of Arsidas and Lysidas complicates the development. When Ulysses and Arsidas almost come to blows, Circe orders a contest: Ulysses, whom she thinks hates her, must feign passion for her, while Arsidas, whom she knows loves her, must dissemble his passion. Obviously, Ulysses has the easier task. The climax of this game comes when Ulysses describes his passion with the metaphor of the heron, an emblem of the harmonious union of two opposites (water and air):

> Luego que tú te retiraste de una
> Guarnecida laguna,
> Espejo de la hermosa primavera,
> Se remontó una garza, que altanera
> Tanto á los cielos sube,
> Que fue á un tiempo aqui pájaro, alli mube;
> Y entre el fuego y el viento,
> Arbitro igual, (o válgome su aliento!)
> De fuerte se interpuso, que las alas
> En la diáfana esfera, en la suprema,
> O las hiela, ó las quema,
> Cuando las enarbola, ó las abate,
> Tan á compas entre las dos las bate,
> Que aqui elevadas é inclinadas luego,
> Aqui dan en el aire, alli en el fuego.
> Geroglífico era
> La garza entre la una y otra esfera
> De alguno, que aqui osado, alli cobarde,
> Se hiela á un tiempo, y arde,
> Y entre el aire y el fuego se embaraza (88–89).[24]

As Ulysses develops the image still further (he sets two falcons loose upon the heron, which in its attempts to escape first resembles a boat and then descends like "una encarnada estrella," "a incarnate star" [91]), Circe keeps interrupting him, for she well understands his metaphors. By the middle of the play,

Circe and Ulysses have comprehended one another's true feelings; but they must still dissemble and feign in front of the others. A splendid supper for Circe, Ulysses and Arsidas appears on a magical table, soft music is heard but suddenly drums announce war: the rude giant Brutamonte has incited the remaining Cyclops to attack the feasting nymphs and Greeks. It turns out to be a false alarm, a trick devised by Circe to see which of the two heroes would prove his love most valorously; her innocent trick backfires, for the act ends with a genuine battle, fought in the dark in a thunderstorm, between the jealous rivals: Ulysses with his men, and Arsidas with the beasts of the island.

In the third act, which is set several months later, we gradually learn that Arsidas and Lysidas have yielded to Ulysses and have left the island, no doubt plotting revenge. A depressed Antistes sums up the situation to the Greeks: as Aeneas fell for Dido, so Ulysses has become addicted to Circe and the soft life, spending all his time with Circe and her ladies in a beautiful, fairy tale-like setting:

En esta florida márgen,
Desde cuya verde estancia
Se juzgan de tierra y mar
Las dos vistosas campañas,
Tan contrariamente hermosas,
Y hermosamente contrarias,
Que neutral la vista duda,
Cual es la yerba, ó el agua,
Porque aqui en golfos de flores,
Y alli en selvas de esmeraldas,
Unas mismas ondas hacen
Las espumas y las matas,
A los suspiros del noto,
Y á los alientos del aura . . . (109)[25]

The setting recalls the Retiro itself. Antistes proposes to rouse Ulysses from his stupor by producing sounds of battle. Then the scene shows Ulysses and Circe in their wonderful, very operatic duet, the leitmotif and refrain of which is the phrase "el mayor encanto, amor" (111–12). At the end of the duet, Ulysses dozes off—fit emblem for his new role—but his enchantment is broken by the Greek trumpets and drums. An operatic duel between the island women and the Greeks follows: the former counter the Greek shout "guerra, guerra" with their battle cry, "amor, amor." *Gloria* (rapture) wins it from *honor*, for Ulysses declares love and Circe the winners of the duel:

Esclavo tuyo he de ser.
No hay mas fama para mí
Que adorarte, no hay mas gloria
Que vivir en tu memoria (116).[26]

As the islanders burst out again in strains of "el mayor encanto, amor," however, new martial noises are heard approaching: the forces of jealousy (Arsidas and Lysidas with an army) invade the island. Circe, with her girls (who have doffed the silken robes of Venus and donned the armor of Mars) and a magic army of phantom soldiers, goes off and defeats the invaders. Meanwhile, Ulysses is again asleep; Antistes places Achilles' armor at his side, in the hope that the mere sight of it will shame Ulysses out of his dishonorable passion (129). The armor wakes him up all right, but Achilles' ghost has to put in a personal, highly Baroque appearance ("tú, afeminado Griego," "you, effeminate Greek" [132]) to get him going. Ulysses obeys Achilles' order and, with his crew, secretly embarks and is already at sea when Circe enters in triumph; at the news of Ulysses' departure, she collapses. When he calls out to her from his ship that he has triumphed over the many seductions of her island:

> Yo fui de vuestros venenos
> Triunfador, Teseo felice
> Fui de vuestros laberintos,
> Y Edipo de vuestra esfinge.
> Del mayor encanto amor
> La razon me facó libre . . . (136)[27]

Circe begs him to come back, then tries to raise a tempest and set the sea on fire; this is prevented by the nymph Galatea, who appears magically from the sea to rescue Ulysses. Lamenting that she is powerless—love, the greatest enchantment, has proven too strong even for her—Circe destroys her own palace: the scenic milieu devours itself:

> . . . Estos palacios,
> Que mágico el arte finge,
> Desvanecidos en polvo,
> Sola una voz los derribe.
> Su hermosa fábrica caiga
> Deshecha, rota y humilde . . . (140)[28]

In its place, a horrible volcano emerges from the island. Circe dies, and the scene closes with a ballet of Tritons and Sirens. Calderón's very operatic play bears some similarities to Shakespeare's *The Tempest*, but these are in all likelihood coincidental or the result of shared conventions of courtly romance, as well as a comparable performance context.[29]

Calderón is one of the few post-medieval European dramatists whose plays consistently celebrate the religious origins of western drama. Many of his plays are openly religious or spiritual, and all are allegorical to some extent. The (few) critics who have discussed *El mayor encanto, amor* at some length suggest that Calderón, in this play as in his other mythological *comedias*, uses a classical-pagan fable and its characters to illustrate a Christian moral point.[30] As we have seen previously, the idea that aspects of classical myth and fable could serve to illustrate moral allegories was a crucial interpretative strategy of medieval and Renaissance thought. Book XV of the *Reductorium morale* (better known as the *Ovide moralisé*), by the fourteenth-century Benedictin monk Pierre Bersuire, greatly reinforced this tendency by its wide dissemination. The application of pagan ideas and forms to Christian doctrine received a fresh impetus with the writings of Renaissance Neoplatonists, who repeated the call to interpret on various levels—principally, Boccaccio, Ficino, and Juan Perèz de Moya (*Filosofía secreta*; Madrid, 1585). The latter work exercised great influence on Calderón's mythological plays. When the Circe fable and its protagonists reached the seventeenth-century creative imagination, a complex Christian and Neoplatonic apparatus of moral interpretation had been applied to them. The drastic extent of the resulting changes can be gauged from comparing the loci classici: Homer's *Odyssey* (X: 135–574 and XII: 8–141); Apollodorus' *Bibliotheca* ("Epitome" VII: 14–17); Ovid's *Metamorphoses* (XIV: 246–440); the *Ovide moralisé*; Dante's "Inferno" (XXVI: 91); Ariosto's *Orlando furioso* (VI); and perhaps, most of all, Tasso's *Gerusalemme liberata* (XVI: 37). The moral allegory that the Christian interpreters illustrated by means of the fable is a complex one, because it combines ideas relevant to the classic heroic ideal as well as to Christian moral doctrine.[31]

The medieval debate whether the principal quality of the hero is *sapientia* or *fortitudo*, for example, is very relevant to the fable, and obviously also to Calderón's play.[32] If Ulysses is usually taken to represent *sapientia*, Achilles is interpreted as the embodiment of *fortitudo*. In the play, Ulysses' proverbial wisdom alone clearly does not suffice to escape the embrace of Circe. What Ulysses lacks in the third act is not cleverness but will power and determination: literally, he lacks the strength to remove himself physically from the island. After failed experiments, some members of his crew can administer an effective shock treatment. When Ulysses sees Achilles' armor and hears the voice of Achilles' ghost, he is in fact injected with a strong dose of *fortitudo*. This shot provides instant will power, and, coupled with his native wily resourcefulness, it enables Ulysses to escape Circe's arms and her island. Thus he becomes, once again, qualified to receive divine help or sponsorship.[33] The moral of this seems to be that in order to fight Circe successfully, the hero must possess both archetypal epic qualities (*sapientia* as well as *fortitudo*), or be a Ulysses and an Achilles at the same time. In the context of Calderón's oeuvre, Ulysses' infatuation with Circe seems related to themes in other plays (*La vida es sueño* in particular).[34] The events of the fable can be used to illustrate, if one wishes, man's struggle against his own dark, beastly impulses. Viewed in this light, Ulysses, in act 3 of the play, is arguably in a state of suspended animation: yielding to sensual temptations, he allows his lower appetites to get the upper hand and is content to merely "exist" in a state of *acedia*, or sinful indifference, sloth.

Then what about Circe? The classical tradition has not much to say about her, but from the sparse facts we can deduce that she is the daughter of the Sun, very beautiful, industrious, and obviously rather sweet and good-natured. If men approach her in the wrong way, however, she will habitually change them into beasts. Since she uses a philter to this purpose, she must possess some learning. When Ulysses announces the decision to depart, she does not attempt to hold him back and does not argue with him. The medieval Christian interpretation of her fable, however, gave Circe the same negative treatment it extended to other lovable and loving women of antiquity, such as Helen, Cleopatra and Dido. In the allegorical tradition, Circe thus has come to embody *voluptas*: sensuous temptation that dangerously appeals to man's lower appetites and intends to drown man in his own lusts. A Platonic text was appropriated to serve as authority for this new, un-Homeric idea, and the Platonic argument lifted out of context to substantiate it. Early in *Symposium*, Pausanias distinguishes between two aspects of Aphrodite—two different Aphrodites, actually: the young Aphrodite Pandemos, who affects the senses, and the older, superior Aphrodite Urania, who affects the intellect. To each Aphrodite corresponds a different Eros. Christian and Neoplatonic writers applied the distinction to their topos that reason must overcome sensuality and to their version of the dualism between the sensuous love for earthly matters and the more exalted, spiritual love that affects reason and the soul. For example, the warning that reason is superior and that the senses are deceptive is especially repeated for the benefit of courtiers in Castiglione's *Libro del Cortegiano* and again in Ficino's *Convivium Platonis Commentarium* (Valbuena-Briones 1982: 77 n. 6 and 7). Ficino in particular recapitulates the Platonic distinction between the two Aphrodites, or Venuses, in the second "Oratio" of his *Convivium*. In the fable, Circe temporarily immobilizes Ulysses. Arguably, Circe is thus really like Venus-Aphrodite, for, unless overcome, she will effectively prevent the Greeks from reaching their homeland. Since she does so by means of her beauty and love, she can serve as an illustration of Venus Pandemos's destructive effects upon the heroic "soul" or status of Ulysses as well as upon the entire social structure. Ulysses must overcome the temptation she represents in order to recover his *virtù* and reach his goals—both his present goal (staying alive and returning home) and his future goal (an "afterlife," or an eternal life as the admirable hero whose story is forever on the lips of men). The allegorical application of all this in a Christian context is obvious—perhaps even too obvious to be convincing. In fact, we have already seen a related Christian application in *Sant'Alessio*: Alessio's apotheosis is brought about by his triumph over the temptation of self-revelation, although the cost, in human terms, is heavy. At first sight, Calderón's play yields itself very well to an allegorical reading along these lines (Valbuena-Briones 1982: 81): Circe represents the "dishonest love" associated with Venus Pandemos, which turns its more active victims into wild and fierce animals and the more passive ones, those insensitive to honor and reputation, into plants and stones. The former represent the instinctive life without election, the latter the merely vegetative life. Ulysses himself symbolizes the spirit that must exercise free will in the choice between the lower and the higher passions, after Providence has helped to counter the first attack or temptation of the lower passions.

Supposing this reading is valid, does this traditional and rather mechanical allegorical interpretation also support the thesis that the play, the circumstances of its performance, and the occasion of the performance must be seen as an (epideictic) rhetorical discourse between artists, sponsors, and audience? We can approach the problem by establishing a hypothetical connection between the world that is presented in the play with the world in which the play is presented. In terms of physical setting, the analogy between these two worlds is fairly obvious. Lotti's detailed instructions emphasize rather than obscure the fact that "Circe's island" is, literally, located in the Retiro gardens. For the time of the performance at least, the artificially raised stage in the middle of the large artificial pond is the focal point upon which all eyes watching from across the separating waters converge. During the performance, therefore, the Retiro itself does not exist—except in concentrated form, transplanted, on or as the island. To the inhabitants of Madrid outside the Retiro walls as well, the pleasure palace always appears as an area of separation, a world apart, impossible to penetrate except by special grace or an exceptional stroke of luck or fate. Like Circe's island, the pleasure palace is rather plain and unimpressive on the outside, but within, the senses are gratified at every turn: protected by vast, elaborate, and labyrinthine gardens, the interminable art galleries and spectacular festive entertainments (such as the performance of *El mayor encanto, amor* itself) delight the beholder. The Retiro, in other words, *is* Circe's island. That Calderón intended the audience to make this association seems to follow from the fact that *he* left out the Giant Hermit "Buen Retiro," whom *Lotti* had introduced in his *memoria* precisely to *avoid* an association or identification of Circe's palace with the Retiro.

But the Retiro is more than Circe's island. Built around an ancient royal monastery, crammed full with luxurious objects, buzzing with pleasant entertainments, and further distinguished for its whimsical construction history, the Retiro stands as an emblem of Philip himself. The palace embodies his love of beautiful objects, his lack of planning and resolve, his unsystematic mind, his wavering between extremes of spirituality and sensuality. The pleasure palace to which Philip is irresistibly drawn is also the emblem of Philip's *voluptas*: the Retiro, quite simply, is Philip's Circe. As such, it presents a sharp contrast to the stern Escorial palace, which was the emblem of the *fortitudo*, the rigid determination of his grandfather Philip II. The Retiro, as a place of enchantment and transformation, is, with its endless court rituals and its strictly observed etiquette, no less a theater than is the island in the palace pond. When Calderón's Circe tries to "sell" her island to Ulysses, her promises are those of the Retiro itself:

> Con músicas y festines
> Te espero, porque la ausencia,
> Y memorias de tu patria
> Entretenido diviertas (64).[35]

And like Philip at the Retiro, Ulysses is left asleep by Circe when the war between the Greeks and the forces of Arsidas breaks out (120).

Similar to this island (or theater), the Retiro is not an arcadia but an oasis for indulgence in the mortal sin of *acedia*. Olivares' role in creating this situation should not be underestimated; he, too, is Philip's Circe, for he was generally perceived as having spun the web that imprisoned the king.[36] Many aristocrats, members of the regional feudal nobility or of old families, all of whom hated the Count-Duke Olivares, did indeed perceive the king as a slave to the Retiro, Olivares' creation. Many commoners shared this view. They criticized the palace's ever increasing hunger for money—although contemporaneous scandal stories may be exaggerated or based on a inaccurate perception of facts. And they criticized Philip's inability to use to Spanish advantage the winds of economic and political change that were blowing over Europe in the 1630s. It remains to be seen whether Philip's infatuation with the Retiro and its many pleasures actually had something to do with these failures. Regardless though, it was obvious already in 1635, when *El mayor encanto, amor* was produced, that the country was basically on the verge of collapse and that its internal unity, already so fragile, was threatened both from within and without, while the locus of power was shifting rapidly, to France and to the Netherlands, and moreover, that Spain was unable to do anything about it. Especially important was the fact that the war with France was beginning to assume serious proportions early in 1635, right before the performance took place. In the historical context of the première of *El mayor encanto, amor*, then, the moral lesson illustrated by Ulysses' departure from Circe's island of love and pleasure was a very timely reminder to the king of his duties. The performance can thus be considered a rhetorical discourse of the epideictic kind, whose objective is not to praise, however, but to blame. Philip should interpret the events of the play as an illustration of his own situation: he is the victim of his *voluptas* no less than Ulysses is the victim of the seductions of Circe. Disguised as a festive entertainment, the play thus acts like a moral allegory, or like a councilor warning the king that prompt action is needed to save not only his country but also his status as a hero.

Appealing though this moral-allegorical reading of *El mayor encanto, amor* may be, it is, in a sense, anachronistic and must be supplemented with contemporaneous ideas. For example, the very context of the grandiose festive performance itself, with its dependence on machines and spectacular effects, betrays a happy indulgence in sheer visual and aural beauty that is hard to reconcile with the "negative" moral-allegorical reading that has just been provided. In fact, this interpretation assigns a negative intention to the work, and seems derived from an exclusive, misdirected emphasis merely on the play's text rather than on the performance of the play as a "total work of art." Surely, this interpretation is anachronistic for that reason alone. Problematic also is the contradiction inherent in the moral-allegorical reading. It is difficult to accept that Lotti and Calderón would produce a grandiose spectacle for Philip and his court in order to blame Philip and his court for liking grandiose spectacles; should the king "reform," the first people affected adversely would be, precisely, Lotti and Calderón and their colleagues working in various artistic media. Moreover, the allegorical interpretation reflects the anthropological anxieties of medieval Christian and Neoplatonic ideology (as well as more modern, social-utopian ideologies)—the "view from below"—while excluding some fundamental concerns of the Baroque sensibility—the "view from above."[37]

It is true that Cosme Lotti, judging from his *memoria*, did envisage Circe as the opposite of heroic *virtus*, but Calderón's text offers evidence for a more positive, Baroque interpretation of the "witch." The negative view of Circe as the embodiment of destructive *voluptas* is a product of the medieval mind, which the Renaissance adopted. It is not a strictly classical motif, and it is not really part of the Baroque sensibility either. From the late sixteenth century onwards, the Circe motif underwent a considerable shift in its applications (admittedly, primarily in France), as Circe began to appear prominently and positively in courtly festive performances or events, such as ballets. Thus, Circe meant something else to the Baroque mentality than it did to the medieval and Renaissance mind (see Rousset 1954, chapter 1). The element of the fable that was specifically selected for Baroque amplification was Circe's power of metamorphosis—after all, the Baroque sensibility was deeply fascinated with movement in all its forms. In Circe, the Baroque recognized and represented itself. Circe was in effect the operative power of movement, the force that makes movement in nature possible and that guides it. Most often, movement in nature can be reduced to some kind of metamorphosis: an egg becomes a bird, water becomes air, hot becomes cool. In a reading of *El mayor encanto, amor* that is sensitive to the Baroque sensibility, Circe must therefore be seen not as a negative but as a positive, creative, and playful power: she is the driving cause of metamorphosis, translation, and metaphor.

On Circe's island, complex language, influenced by Góngorism and conceptism, is a means of transformation and metamorphosis. By means of wit and language, Circe beautifies ordinary things and concepts, and thereby transforms her island into a more beautiful, gracious, and elegant place. For example, Circe's sophisticated use of conceits is part of a Baroque attempt to transcend the limitations imposed by nature, principally the division into the three realms of sea, land, and sky—such as when she ceremoniously addresses Ulysses:

> Retórico Griego, á quien
> Ese escollo cristalino,
> Ese peñasco de nieve,
> Esa campaña de vidrio
> Náufrago huésped te tuvo
> Tantos años . . . (41)[38]

Like the speakers in Góngora's *Polifemo* and his *Soledades*, she interchanges these realms: sea, dry land, and air exchange qualities and properties, as do fish, ships and birds, natural and manmade objects, soft and brittle things—for example, when birds become "ramilletes vivos" ("living nosegays" [43]) or surf is transformed into "Blanca espuma, que al azul/ Camelote de aguas hace/ Bella guarnicion de plata" ("foam white fair, which on the azure/ Camlet of the sea made lovely/ Broidery of netted silver" [119]). The result can, indeed, be called, an "enchanted" world, or, to use Rousset's phrase as explicated by Genette, a "reversible universe."[39] But language is Circe's only power of enchantment (besides sex appeal, of course), and moreover, she shares it with Ulysses—and with no other character. It is only proper that Ulysses, too, has the same power of changing the world through metaphor, such as when he addresses his delapidated boat,

> . . . Descoge
> O surto delfin, que vuelas,
> Varado neblí, que corres,
> Las alas, porque otra vez
> La plata del agua cortes,
> O con la quilla la rices,
> O con el buque la entorches (41).[40]

He is, after all, the smoothest talker of the Greeks and the quickest wit; it is through language that he wins Circe's love, for in language he proves himself her equal. The turning point in their relationship, and in the play, comes precisely in the middle, with Ulysses' beautiful conceit of the heron as emblem of the harmonious union of opposites. Before she falls in love with Ulysses, Circe has supposedly used magic on men (and women) who professed to be in love. This is a difficult point. The island seems to be crowded with intelligent beasts (such as the lion who nods to Ulysses and Clarín that they should leave, in act 1) and trees (Lysidas and Flerida), all of whom were once, supposedly, people. But are they now truly animals, or trees? Why does

Ulysses never follow up on his promise to have Circe release them? Does Calderón's Circe really possess a magic agent other than her language? The drink that according to Antistes' report turns the crew into a menagerie is presumably the same she offers to Ulysses ("el generoso/ Néctar, que los dioses beben," "the reviving/ Nectar that the great Gods drink" [35]). What nourishes the gods, however, dehumanizes mortal men and deprives them of their form. Here Calderón remains close to the classical motif. Does Circe, with her superior knowledge, perceive that the love-starved sailors begin to harbor swinish thoughts when they see her? Does she wish to create a harmony between the men's inner thoughts and their outer appearance?

Besides, what can we really believe on this island? Things are never what they seem. The play is full of brisk, unforeseen and unaccountable reversals. In this realm of fleeting appearances, perception is questioned continually. What some deem a rock, is to others a cloud (29); the "wild beasts" do not really come to devour Ulysses and Clarín (26). Paradoxes, drunkenness, and dreams contribute to the confusion. In a world where nothing is defined or definable, who can say that Circe really transforms people at all? In fact, various characters throughout the play continuously use their intellect or ingenuity to produce effects that are far more enchanting than whatever can be attributed to magic. The intellect is stronger than any philter, and far from being merely a super-sensuous, physical being, Circe in particular indulges in ingenious games—which makes her all the more dangerous but also much more attractive (the proposed switch with Flerida, the idea of the contest, the various tricks to see whether Ulysses or Arsidas loves her most). In this sort of activity, as in the use of language, Ulysses is at least her equal, and is able to enchant Circe by means of his own intellectual magic (his feigning performance in the contest, his secret escape from the island).[41] The net result of all these stratagems is confusion: "nothing is what it seems, yet is exactly what it seems" (DiPuccio 732). The audience should learn that the same holds true for the "real" world, and that they, too, are prone to being enchanted in the theater of the world, and in the theater of the court in particular.

The most important change that does take place in the play, because it is a complex process and because it is certifiably real, is the transformation of the two protagonists. Indeed, Calderón's Circe transforms Ulysses—more specifically: she is the catalyst of a transformation that takes place within Ulysses himself—but, and this is absent in the conventional interpretation of the motif, she herself is also and simultaneously transformed by him. No magic is involved in this process; all comes from within the characters. Let us begin with Ulysses. Ulysses enters the play as a soldier disinterested in love (act 1) and becomes a soldier capable of loving and being loved (act 2). In the second act, Ulysses is forced by the terms of the contest with Arsidas to feign (*fingir*) a passion, and he falls more in love in the course of his performance.

The heron speech in the second act (89–92) marks the moment of the transition; his situation closely resembles that of the actor-martyr-saint Genesius in Lope de Vega's *Lo fingido verdadero*, in that the more he speaks the truth, the more his audience thinks he is feigning or acting and the more they applaud what they interpret as a increasingly convincing, verisimilar performance.

Ulysses' first transformation is thus certainly due to Circe, who makes his change possible—though hardly with magic. Circe herself goes through a similar process. Calderón allows Circe much time to explain who she is and why she does what she does. At the beginning of the play, Circe is clearly disinterested in male-female love: she narrates how she turned from a frustrated girl into a man-hating, "misandric" woman. Her frustration and present attitude are explained by her experience that men deny women the possibility of pursuing the two professions (arms and letters) because men fear that the women, given this possibility, might equal or outperform them. Hence also the two conventional and repulsive emblems of female superiority in either profession: the Amazon and the Sphinx. In her actions, Calderón's Circe transgresses male-female role patterns just as much as she transgresses the three realms of nature in her language—her wit and extensive knowledge make her a Sphinx (31), her skill and courage in battle make her an Amazon (act 3). In order to realize her ambitions, she withdraws to Trinacria with some handmaidens and creates her own utopia, growing increasingly spiteful against men who profess love for women (and against women who respond to them). She can be likened to Diana for her learning, her skill at arms and the hunt, and her chastity. By the end of the second act, however, she, too, will have developed into a person capable of loving and being loved. This transformation is effected in the course of a playful and originally inconsequential game (the contest between Ulysses and Arsidas). Circe turns from a Diana into a Venus at the same moment that Ulysses turns into a lover. This transformation in both protagonists, and Ulysses' original resistance to his new role and identity, recall an important theme in Renaissance and Golden Age literature and iconography: the struggle between Mars and Venus. Renaissance Neoplatonists often sought to illustrate the mystery of harmony by portraying the subjection of Mars by a benevolent Venus: Love is more powerful than Strife.[42] If Circe becomes Venus, then the soldier Ulysses naturally becomes Mars, whom Venus traditionally tries to subject (de Armas 1981).[43]

In the third act, which is set considerably later in time, Calderón shows how both protagonists have changed again. Has "Venus" conquered her "Mars?" It seems so: from an active lover, Ulysses has become not a passive but rather a compulsive lover, wholly consumed by a relationship that some might call unhealthy. But it is all too easy and unfair to blame Circe for this state of affairs, and the play does not support such an interpretation. Circe, too, has again developed in the time span between the second and the third act: from a rather timid Venus who was very concerned with decorum, she has turned into a very happy, very fulfilled woman—exactly the opposite of her initial state. She is simply too strong for Ulysses—an interesting reversal of Ulysses' initial mastery over her. Trinacria has developed with her: from a rather grim and forbidding island, it has become a playful world (a setting for practical jokes) in which—strangest of all—humble secondary characters share the fortunes of the powerful protagonists (humble men find love as well as riches). The kingdom of love is threatened only by jealousy (a crucial theme in seventeenth-century drama and fiction), by the rejected lover (Arsidas) and by those who are as impervious to (hetero)sexual love as Ulysses was thought to be at first (Antistes, Achilles). The very fact that Ulysses can be persuaded to change again, at the end of the play, suggests that Circe has no real magic at her disposal. When Ulysses leaves the island, he is, in terms of love, again the man he was before he arrived. He has no regrets, no kind word or thought for Circe. It is different for the latter, however. Circe, who has obtained a very high level of happiness, is trapped; when she loses everything, she cannot, unlike Ulysses, simply go back to the starting point. Instead, she carries her transformation a drastic step further, and destroys her palace as well as herself (*nada*).

In short, it is not really important whether Circe really transforms anyone specifically by magic. What matters is that she transforms a world, a court, a person and herself. It is an illusion (a form of madness, or enchantment) to think that Circe's so-called magic can enchant or enslave Ulysses on her island; similarly, it is an illusion to think that the many attractions of the Retiro really enslaved Philip IV. Besides blame, Calderón's epideictic rhetoric thus seems also to bestow praise on the king and the palace; by extension, if anything is blamed, it is the hostile criticism directed against the palace. What is Circe then? Circe, quite simply, is the "spirit" of the Retiro. She is able to turn her island (the palace) into a civilizing place, which is able to give real happiness to those who play by the rules, and in which play is taken very seriously. Without Ulysses to share it with her, Circe has no more use for the island.

Without Philip, what would be the point of the Retiro?

Notes

1. Norman D. Shergold, *A History of the Spanish Stage from Medieval Times until the End of the Seventeenth Century* (Oxford, 1967), 277–78.

2. Frederick de Armas, *The Return of Astraea: An Astral-Imperial Myth in*

Calderón (Lexington, 1986) 139–49, 141–47. I have used this edition of *El mayor encanto, amor*: Pedro Calderón de la Barca, *Comedias*, facs. ed., D. W. Cruickshank and J. E. Varey (Westmead: Gregg International Publishers; London: Tamesis Books, 1973) vol. 5. See also the bilingual edition of Denis Florence Mac-Carthy referred to in the Prelude; all quotations and translations from the play refer to the Mac-Carthy edition.

3. See Jonathan Brown and J. H. Elliott, *A Palace for a King* (New Haven, 1980).

4. See Norman D. Shergold, "The First Performance of Calderón's *El mayor encanto, amor*," *Bulletin of Hispanic Studies* 35 (1958): 24–27.

5. More precisely, it was the first such play that he wrote alone. *Polifemo e Circe*, written in collaboration with two other authors, was performed in 1634. See W. G. Chapman, "Las comedias mitológicas de Calderón," *Revista de Literatura* 5 (9–10) 1954: 35–69; Sebastian Neumeister, *Mythos und Repräsentation. Die mythologischen Festspiele Calderóns* (Munich, 1978); and Susan Fischer, "Calderón's *El mayor encanto, mayor* and the Mode of Romance," in William C. McCrary and José A. Madrigal, eds., *Studies in Honor of Everett W. Hesse* (Lincoln, Nebraska, 1981) 99–112. See also Margaret R. Greer, who (briefly) discusses Calderón's first court spectacle (*El mayor encanto, amor* for Philip IV) in conjunction with his last (*Hado y divisa de Leonido y Marfisa* for "the mentally and physically feeble" Charles II in 1680; 329).

6. Philip spent a month (an unusually long period) at the Retiro in May and June, 1635. See also Gregorio Marañón, *El Conde-Duque de Olivares* (Madrid, 1965). Margaret R. Greer quotes interesting examples of plain speech—"loyal criticism" or "loyal opposition" (her phrases)—that were directly addressed to Philip IV on this and other occasions (330).

7. Very characteristic is Martin A. Hume, *The Court of Philip IV. Spain in Decadence* (New York, 1907).

8. J. H. Elliott, *Imperial Spain 1469–1716* (New York, 1970) 96.

9. Since many cities in Spain had flourishing theaters, and since there were numerous travelling companies—in the middle of the seventeenth century, more than three hunderd were counted—the theater as an institution was far less dependent on royal patronage than it was in contemporaneous England or in France. Baur-Heinhold 46 describes the types of companies that were active.

10. In his famous "Autosemblanza," Philip wrote on the importance of the two professions (see Brown and Elliott, 41–42 n. 21). The theme is also relevant for *El mayor encanto, amor*: both Ulysses and Circe practice the two

professions of arms and letters. The theme of the two professions is prominent in Cervantes' *Don Quijote* (part 1, 1605).

11. The Retiro archives were lost during the Peninsular war (1808); Brown and Elliott did an outstanding job combining materials from various Spanish archives and the scattered reports of contemporaneous witnesses.

12. Described by Hans Flasche, "Die Struktur des Hof-Laudatio in den 'Loas' der 'Autos' Calderóns," in August Buck, et al., eds., 2: 277–85, 278.

13. Andrew Marvell, *The Poems & Letters of Andrew Marvell*, ed. H. M. Margoliouth (Oxford, 1952), vol. 1: 82.

14. Hugo A. Rennert, *The Spanish Stage in the Time of Lope de Vega* (1909; New York, 1963) 230–31 n. 1.

15. The most famous actress-mistress of Philip IV was "La Calderona" (Don Juan of Austria was their son), perhaps not the most beautiful but probably the most loved of those like her who had shared the royal bed. Philip's patronage of playwrights seems to have been less marked than was usually thought; Calderón was his only real protégé, and Philip did very little for Lope de Vega (Rennert 232 n. 1). See also Charles V. Aubrun, "Nouveau public, nouvelle comédie à Madrid au 17e siècle," in Jean Jacquot, et al., eds., *Dramaturgie et société. Rapports entre l'oeuvre théâtrale, son interprétation et son public au XVIe et XVIIe siècles*, 2 vols. (Paris, 1968) 1: 1–12.

16. J. E. Varey, "Calderón, Cosme Lotti, Velázquez, and the Madrid Festivities 1636–37," *Renaissance Drama New Series* 1 (1968): 253–82; Norman Shergold, "Documentos sobre Cosme Lotti, escenógrafo de Felipe IV," in Karl-Hermann Körner, et al., eds., *Studia Iberica: Festschrift für Hans Flasche* (Bern, 1973) 589–602; and Ruth Lamb, "La influencia italiana en la scenografía española del Siglo de Oro," (which I have not been able to see) in Manuel Criado de Val, ed., *Lope de Vega y los origines del teatro español* (Madrid, 1981).

17. An eyewitness report of the première of Calderón's *La fiera, el rayo y la piedra* in the Coliseo theater of the Buen Retiro, on the occasion of the birthday of the queen in May, 1652, gives us an idea of the sort of theatrical activity that took place in this theater. The performance, illuminated by faggots, lasted seven hours and was performed, first, three days in a row for the dignitaries, and then thirty-seven days for the paying general public. See Pedro Calderón de la Barca, *Obras completas*, ed. A. Valbuena-Briones, 3rd ed. (Madrid, 1966) 1: 1592ff.

18. Rennert was mistaken when he considered *La Circe* a separate, previous play, performed at court around June 24, 1634 (241–42). Calderón did write another play on Circe, *Polifemo y Circe* (1630?), in collaboration with

Mira de Mescua and Juan Perez de Montalvan. The Circe motif was also treated by Lope de Vega in "La Circe," a poem of 3,000 lines (1624).

19. It is reported that as the king and the courtiers were watching the première performance from their gondolas, sudden heavy winds upset the boats and extinguished the lights; there was also a rumor that the king had been "seasick." Everett W. Hesse, *Calderón de la Barca* (New York, 1967) 15.

20. In the seventeenth century, *El mayor encanto, amor* was twice translated into Dutch; one version was performed as a *Hofspel* (court play) in Brussels (1668), the second, with added music and ballets, in the renovated public Schouwburg in Amsterdam (1670, 1690). The Dutch translations are by Claude de Grieck, *Ulysses in 't eylandt van Circe, oft geen grooter toovery als liefde*, and by Adriaen Bastiaensz, *De Toveres Circe* (subtitled "Treurspel met Kunst en Vliegwerken, nieuw Muzyk en Balletten," "Tragedy with Various Machines, new Music and Ballets"). On these Dutch translations, and on the Dutch influence on Germany, see J. A. van Praag, "Les traductions de *El mayor encanto, amor* de Calderón en néerlandais," in *Neophilologus* 7 (1922) 8–19.

Via the Dutch translations, Calderón's play reached the German-speaking world. A German translation by August Wilhelm Schlegel, *Über allem Zauber Liebe*, was published in 1803 and performed as a *singspiel* under the title *Ulysses und Circe* in Berlin (1807). The Spanish play is also at the basis of the opera *Circe* by Werner Egk (1948), a new version of which was produced in 1966 under the title *Siebzehn Tage und Vier Minuten* ("Seventeen Days and Four Minutes"). See Sebastian Neumeister, "Vom Nachleben Calderóns: Aspekte aus der Geschichte einer schwierigen Rezeption am Beispiel von *El mayor encanto, amor* ('Über allem Zauber, Liebe')," *Maske und Kothurn* 24 (1978): 326–38.

21. "All here is gloomy./ All is full of fear./ Horror./ And terror./ And enchantments drear!"

22. "A rich palace we beheld there,/ So superbly proud and haughty,/ That embarrassing the zephyrs/ And the mountains' sides oppressing,/ It to those a vast cloud seemeth,/ And to these a rock as mighty:—/ Since at once to earth and heaven/ Each of its extreme ends reaches/ But unlike the extremes of vices/ In its midst no virtue dwelleth."

23. "See this floral branch I bear/ Gemm'd with buds that Flora tended,/ It will be the antidote/ Against Circe's poison'd secrets."

24. "You scarce had gone, when near/ The margin of a lake, that crystal-clear/ Seem'd a smooth mirror for the beauteous Spring,/ A heron rose, so sudden its quick wing/ Bore it amid the sky elate and proud,/ That at one moment it was bird and cloud,/ And 'twixt the wind and fire,/ (Would that

such courage had my heart's desire!)/ So interposed itself, that its bold wings/ Wheeling alternate near,/ Now the diaphanous, now the higher sphere,/ Were burnt or froze,/ As down they sank or upward soaring rose,/ In all the fickleness of fond desire,/ Now in the air and now amid the fire./ An emblem as it were,/ This heron was, betwixt each opposite sphere,/ Of one who is both cowardly and bold,/ Can burn with passion, and yet freeze with cold,/ And 'twixt the air and fire still doubts his place."

25. "On this flowery margin here,/ From whose green slopes softly slanted,/ The two lovely level plains/ Of the land and sea expand them,/ So contrasted in their beauty,/ In their beauty so contrasted,/ That the neutral vision doubts/ Which is grass and which is water,/ Since in bright bays here of flowers,/ In green groves of emerald glass there,/ The same waves together make/ Now the foam-wreaths, now the branches,/ When the sunny south wind sigheth,/ When the softer zephyr panteth . . ."

26. "From this hour I am thy slave;/ To adore thee be my fame,/ All my glory, my reward,/ But to live in thy regard."

27. "I was o'er your many poisons/ The triumpher, of your circled/ Labyrinth the happy Theseus,/ Oedipus of all your sphinxes;/ From thy greatest of enchantments/ Love, hath reason me deliver'd . . ."

28. "This palace,/ Which by magic art I builded,/ Let it vanish into dust,/ Let a single word, to shivers/ Shake this beauteous fabric down,/ Ruin'd, broken, rent, made little."

29. The most obvious parallels between *The Tempest* and *El mayor encanto, amor* include the dramatic staging of the storm in the opening scene; the protagonist who is an exiled magician; the comic-ironic subplot with secondary characters whose adventures mirror and comment on the main plot; difficulties of communication and skewed relationships due to faulty perceptions of reality; the abundance of songs and other musical forms; the appearance of Iris on a rainbow machine, and the presence of an island monster; and, the implied self-destruction of the island, the site of the performance, together with the magician's cessation of the practice of magic.

30. See especially Angel Valbuena-Briones, "Eros moralizado en las comedias mitológicas de Calderón," in Michael McGaha, ed., *Approaches to the Theater of Calderón* (Washington, D.C., 1982) 77–93.

31. For an alternative reading of Circe, see Levin 81–82.

32. On the debate, see Curtius 170–77; it is applied by Frederick A. de Armas, "Metamorphosis in Calderón's *El mayor encanto, amor*," *Romance Notes* 22 (1981): 208–12.

33. Calderón inverts a classical tradition: when the youth Achilles,

whom his mother Thetis had disguised as a maiden, was idling in safety at the court of Lycomedes of Scyros, it was Ulysses who roused Achilles' martial appetites by putting armor in front of him and sounding a bugle (see Apollodorus, *Bibliotheca* III.13:8). Compare also Ariosto, *Orlando Furioso*: Rinaldo has the courage to break free from Armida when he sees armor.

34. In his edition *La primera versión de "La vida es sueño"* (Liverpool U P, 1992), J. M. Ruano de la Haza has argued that Calderón wrote two versions of *La vida es sueño*, the first about 1630 and the second in 1635 (when it was approved for publication); hence the play antedates *El mayor encanto, amor*. I am indebted to Margaret R. Greer for this information.

35. "Here with songs and festive music/ I await thee, that the absence/ And the memory of thy country,/ Thus amused, may not *unman* thee" (my emphasis: Mac-Carthy's translation is really too free; Calderón merely writes "may entertain thee").

36. See Brown and Elliott for evidence (234); see also De Armas 1986: 144–45.

37. For example, Neumeister 1978: 337, introduces the allegoresis of the Frankfurter Schule (Horkheimer and Adorno) in this context. I must point out here that the interpretation of Circe (that is, Circe as a finally positive figure), which I am about to develop, departs from the conventional, exclusively negative representation and interpretation of the Circe figure in the Spanish tradition. Margaret R. Greer has suggested that Calderón-Lotti were in fact criticizing the king, much like Louis XIV was criticized by means of *Ercole amante* (see next chapter); I refer the reader to Greer's essay "Bodies of Power in Calderón: *El nuevo palacio del Retiro* and *El mayor encanto, amor*," in *Conflicts of Discourse, Spanish Literature of the Golden Age*, ed. Peter Evans (Manchester, 1990). My response is that *vituperatio* and *laudatio* are often very difficult to separate in this sort of performance, and that particular details that strike one observor as blame can very well impress another as praise—such ambiguities may well have been built in deliberately by the makers of performances, who were, as able courtiers, certainly up to the mental gymnastics and delicate rope-walking that this *vituperatio-laudatio* near-symbiosis required (the real question being whether their spectators were up to distinguishing the finer shades of meaning). I acknowledge Greer's point as valid but stand by my reading nevertheless.

38. "Eloquent-tongued Greek King [sic] whom/ Yonder rippling realm of crystal,/ Yonder liquid hills of snow,/ Yonder plains of glassy glitter,/ Have a shipwreck'd guest detained/ Such a length of years . . ."

39. Gérard Genette, "L'Univers reversible," *Figures* I (Paris, 1966) 9–20.

40. "Be then unfolded,/ Flying dolphin, anchor'd there—/ Stranded-falcon so swift-footed,/ Thy white wings, for thou once more/ Must cut through the silver-molten/ Surface of the sea, thy prow/ Dashing up the curling foam-wreaths,/ And thy keel wave-woven braid."

41. For an elaboration of this theme, see Denise DiPuccio, "The Enigma of Enchantment in *El mayor encanto, amor*," *Hispania* 70 (1987): 731–39.

42. See de Armas 1981, and de Armas 1986: 83, 147–49; see also Edgar Wind, *Pagan Mysteries in the Renaissance* (1958; New York, 1968) 89.

43. Interestingly, Philip IV was born on April 8, 1604; this makes him an Aries, a sign ruled by Mars (pointed out by de Armas 1986: 147).

5

HERCULES AND THE SUN KING: *ERCOLE AMANTE* AND *LA PRINCESSE D'ELIDE*

Louis XIV expressly ordered the first performance of *Ercole amante* for February 7, 1662; following the première, four more performances were given before Lent, and again six after Easter. Composed by Cavalli on a libretto by Buti, *Ercole amante*, which shows the tragic death of the lustful Hercules, was one of Mazarin's last grandiose projects. Three years in the making, the opera necessitated the construction of a vast court theater and of big machines capable of raising and lowering many people simultaneously; it had also required intense activity on the highest political and diplomatic levels, and numerous intrigues had finally brought a brilliant team of (virtually exclusively Italian) designers and performers together in Paris. Yet, in spite of the enormous budget and the pool of talent which its makers commanded, *Ercole amante* is generally considered a failure. After the last performance, early in May, 1662, the ad hoc company definitively disbanded. Deeply disappointed by his Parisian experiences, Cavalli headed back to Venice, where he was cherished and showered with gold as he had been before the French venture. But more important than Cavalli's personal grievances was the fact that, henceforth, Italian opera in its original form was out of favor at the court of Louis XIV.

In a sense, *Ercole amante* came too late in history, and it is mainly for this dubious distinction that the opera is mentioned in musical-historical textbooks. The wedding of Louis XIV and Maria Theresa, which the work was supposed to celebrate, had taken place two years earlier; the queen had already produced an heir, and, as we will see, the king himself had just entered a distinctly new phase in his long career as absolute monarch. Even at court, where Italian-style spectacular operas had been sponsored for decades, the latter were being systematically replaced with entertainments that were considered more authentically French, such as the *ballet de cour*. And in the arts in general, official classic taste, which was in the ascendant, made the Baroque form and content, and even the very concept of *Ercole amante* seem irrelevant, obsolete, and curiously anachronistic to contemporaneous observers.[1] It is ironic, moreover, that Mazarin (b. 1602), the driving force behind *Ercole amante*, did not live to see the première; the cardinal, who was hated as much in France as Olivares had been in Spain, died on March 9, 1661. After the death of their principal protector, Italian musical professionals were publicly harrassed as his "creatures:" they had been dealt a blow from which they could not possibly hope to recover. By the 1670s, they had either left Paris or had become totally frenchified. In the shadow of the Sun King, one representative of the latter category reigned supreme: Jean Baptiste Lully. *Ercole amante* was thus an end, a climax—not only, it seemed, of a genre, but certainly also of Mazarin's rhetorical, political and artistic control over three successive French courts. Even in death, however, Giulio Mazarini can be said to have participated in the première of "his" grand opera, for he was allegorically represented on stage by the Roman river Tiber. In theory at least, *Ercole amante* is a brilliant example of the genre that forms the subject of this study. The intention of the spectacle was festive, and its execution grandiose; its program was complex and directly related to important dynastic affairs. And the opera was designed to function as a political-rhetorical signifier. One might call it, perhaps, a final, loud statement testifying to Mazarin's influence over the French dynasty. I will also argue that the opera signalled a crucial hinge in the personal career and the political-rhetorical perception of Louis XIV. It was probably no coincidence that the official inauguration of the cult of Louis XIV as the Sun King concurred with the conclusion of the series of performances of *Ercole amante*.[2]

Italian-style musical-dramatic entertainments—though not yet "operas" proper—had been regularly organized at the French court since the late sixteenth century.[3] But by the middle of the seventeenth century, Italian musical drama was flourishing at court, mainly through the personal influence of Mazarin, whose French career had begun in 1634.[4] Mazarin's own predilection was clearly for Roman opera.[5] It has been argued that he attempted to introduce the genre in Paris for political-rhetorical purposes.[6] Consequently, from mid-1644 onward, more Italian professionals sought to perform in France. Throughout that decade and the next, Mazarin's power and the Queen

Widow's musical interests allowed Italian composers, actor-singers and stage designers to reap great successes in Paris (Mazarin's enemies fruitlessly attempted to perpetuate the rumor that audiences were bored), although very few established themselves permanently and the French musical professionals generally remained their bitter enemies. *Nicandro e Fileno* (*poemetto dramatico per musica*) may well have been the first Italian opera to be performed in the Palais royal, during the carnival season of 1645.[7] On December 14 of the same year, the Italian comedians performed Strozzi and Sacrati's *Finta Pazza*, with ballets by Balbi, in the great hall of the Petit Bourbon, which had been equipped with Torelli's machines. This comedy was performed for a much larger (though still private) audience than *Nicandro e Fileno*; contemporaneous observers made much of the machines and scenes, the ballets and costumes, while remaining virtually silent on either the story or the music.[8] But the first truly grandiose opera to be represented in France was Buti and Rossi's *Orfeo*. Its première took place on March 2, 1647, in the rather small Hall of the Palais royal.[9] With Torelli's machines, with its scene changes and ballets, this opera was apparently a tremendous success at court and a great personal triumph for Mazarin, who had been actively involved also with this production from the very beginning. Yet, the consideration of the vast sums spent on the Italian performers and on the machines caused great scandal, and fueled the Parisian public's vivid dislike of Mazarin and the Italian music scene that he was so avidly promoting. Castrati in particular were ridiculed, in France as elsewhere in Europe. At this time, the native French stage was still unable to produce the complex designs and visual-aural spectacle of a work like the *Orfeo*, although efforts in that direction were beginning to be made at the public Marais theater.[10]

The two periods of violent riots and civil disorder known as the Frondes (1648–1649; 1651–1653) temporarily put an end to splendid courtly entertainments and spectacles. But after the definitive defeat of the second Fronde and Mazarin's return from self-imposed exile in February 1653, both the ballet and Italian-style musical drama soon flourished again. Determined to gain even with the Italians and to compete with Italian-style opera, French composers and other artists set out to create complex machine plays and spectacular ballets (Prunières 1913: chapter 7).[11] No doubt the most splendid performance at court prior to *Ercole amante* was the première of *Le nozze di Peleo e di Theti* by Buti, Caproli, and Torelli. The libretto of this opera-with-dance-and-mime suggests that Mazarin himself may well again have had a hand in its design (Prunières 1913: 163). It has been said that the cardinal had engineered the interesting fusion of Italian-style opera and French court ballet in *Nozze* for rhetorical-political purposes, that is, to counter the continuing hostility against Roman opera proper and to accommodate simultaneously Louis' well-known fondness for the ballet, in which the new king liked to perform personally. *Nozze*, which contemporaries thus typically described alternatively as *grand ballet royal* and *comédie à musique*, was first performed in the vast hall of the Petit Bourbon on April 14, 1654, for a large but nevertheless still private audience. It was given many times afterward, and for the final two performances in May, the general public was admitted.

After the relative success at court of *Nozze di Peleo e di Theti*, Mazarin sought to create a permanent Italian operatic company in Paris for political, practical, and economic reasons. But his efforts met with great hostility among Parisians, who continued to despise Italian performers. Whereas at court the anti-Italian faction had been virtually silenced after the defeat of the Frondes, the French musical profession, as well as the general public, had now begun to rebel openly against what was perceived as an Italian musical dictatorship.[12] But to Mazarin, Italian opera would always remain the supreme genre—even if it had to be padded with French-style court ballets. Thus, Mazarin used the first truly splendid events that affected the French monarchy since the defeat of the Frondes—the Peace of the Pyrenees (1659) and its planned outcome: the dynastic union of the previously warring factions—as the occasion for a new grandiose performance at court. The conception of *Ercole amante* as the opera that was to eclipse anything that had been seen or heard before was launched as early as the summer of 1659 (Prunières 1913: 213).[13] And its production began at a time when the continuation in France of Italian opera as a genre was clearly in jeopardy.[14] Yet, once more Mazarin managed to impose his taste: librettist, composer, architect and stage designers, and most of the performers were Italians. Even the harpsichords were imported from Rome.

Mazarin entrusted his secretary, the experienced librettist Buti, with the libretto and, equally important, he convinced the veteran stage designer and *machiniste* Gaspare Vigarani to leave his patron, the Duke of Modena.[15] Vigarani constructed a new theater, the Salle des Machines, which was appended to the left wing of the Tuileries palace. It was a very large and ornate rectangular building, with two galleries running round three sides.[16] And as soon as Buti and Vigarani were well at work, Mazarin set in motion a difficult campaign aimed at luring the celebrated Cavalli from Venice to Paris to compose the opera and direct its production.[17] This undertaking proved more difficult than the cardinal had expected.[18] When Cavalli finally arrived in Paris (July, 1660), Buti had long finished his libretto. The Venetian Cavalli never got along with the Florentine Lully, to whom the ballets had, of course, been assigned; these ballets were a significant concession to French (or let us say, Louis') taste, and they added drastically to the length, complexity, and visual appeal of the work. Lully had been providing the king since the latter's adolescence with the chance to dance as the centerpiece of a complex programmed arrangement of moving figures, all contributing to represent something higher than the sum of its parts. Establishing himself as composer for festive ballets by Benserade and Beauchamp, Lully became Louis' favorite; in 1653, the Florentine, then twenty-one years old, was already appointed "compositeur de la musique instrumentale" and danced with the fifteen-year-old Louis in the famous *Balet de la Nuit.*[19] (At that time, Molière and his company were still touring the provinces; Lully was known to the court much earlier than Molière and would remain in Louis' favor much longer.) In 1654, Lully and Louis danced again together, in *Les Noces de Pélée et Thétis* and in *Le Balet du Temps.*[20] The culmination of the court ballet was the grandiose *Balet de Flore* of 1669, again by Benserade and Lully; in 1670, Louis stopped participating personally in the dances, which began a new phase in the grandiose entertainments at Versailles.[21] Therefore, in 1660, the perhaps overly ambitious Lully had absolutely no reason to fear any competition of the elderly Cavalli: the Venetian never expressed any desire to settle in Paris and, unlike Lully, he certainly never planned to make any significant concessions or contributions to French musical taste. Yet, given the now open French resistance to and scorn of the resident Italian performers, the recruitment of the most outstanding Italian singers and instrumentalists proved an even greater headache to Mazarin and Buti than Cavalli's hiring had been. Gradually, however, the artists who were to create the greatest operatic performance ever finally came together in Paris, from Rome, Turin, Florence, Venice, Vienna, and elsewhere (Donington 277). Numerous intrigues, accidents, small fires, and, apparently, inebriated workmen caused repeated delays so that neither the opera nor even its new theater was ready for the grand occasion for which it was originally intended.[22] By the beginning of 1662, singers, instrumentalists and dancers were rehearsing, although the crucially important machines were still neither finished nor reliable.[23] Meanwhile, in the city and at court, critics grumbled ever more loudly at the money that was, it seemed, forever being wasted on this cursed opera.[24] Irritated by the endless delays and excuses, Louis himself ordered *Ercole amante*—ready or not—to be performed on February 7.[25] And so it came to pass.

The lengthy Prologue was performed against a backdrop showing the sea and a rocky shore.[26] A chorus of Fourteen Rivers, with a solo by the Tiber, glorifies Hercules-Louis, praises the dynastic union ("ne'beati Imenei Di Maria, e di Luigi"), and concludes that Gaul is truly the most fortunate nation ("O Gallia fortunata"). Cynthia-Diana descends from the heavens, accompanied by a representative of each of the fifteen Houses from which the French royal line claimed to descend; singing the praises of the new dynastic union, she directly addresses Anne of Austria in the auditorium: "Ed io m'inchino ad Anna, Anna la gran Reina" ("And I bow before Anna, the great Queen Anna"). The general idea is that Louis has shown such heroic valor that he must now be rewarded with the peaceful enjoyment of beauty ("che di goder in pace alma beltà"), for Hercules, too, had married Beauty after winning heroic honors ("della beltà fu sposo Ercole alfine").

The first act consists of three scenes and is set in a Greek landscape with a perspective of woods, representing the countryside outside the fictional capital of Occalia (Oechalia).[27] Beginning with the plaintive line, "Come si beffa amor, del poter mio!" ("How love laughs at my strength!"), the brutish lout Hercules soliloquizes about his infatuation with princess Iole, the daughter of his most recent victim, King Eutyro. But Venus descends from heaven in her chariot, borne by clouds and accompanied by the chorus of Three Graces. She promises Hercules that he will be able to satisfy his love, for

Scoglio si rigido,
Mostro si frigido
Non regge il mar
Ch'amato al pari non deva amar,[28]

which is easy for her to say, since she has magical arrows with which she promises she will force Iole to love him; then she reascends; Hercules leaves, reassured. Juno, seated on a peacock, has overheard everything from within a cloud; she now comes out and, characteristically, vows that Venus and Hercules will not succeed. To emphasize her point, she unleashes thunder and lightning; then, various Winds and Forces of Nature dance a ballet.

The second act, which consists of seven scenes, begins in the main courtyard of the royal palace of Occalia.[29] Iole and Hyllo (Hercules' son) pledge eternal love in a duet:

Amor ardor più rari
Accesi mai non ha
Che quelli onde del pari
Le nostr'alme disfà.[30]

They are interrupted by a page, who informs Iole of Hercules' amorous desires and instructs her to meet the murderer of her father in an adjacent flower garden. Though most distressed and apprehensive, princess Iole consoles her desperate lover. The page is then left alone, to muse upon the nature of true Love: "E che cos'è quest'Amore" ("What then is this thing called Love"), only to conclude "Egli é qualche ciurmadore" ("He is some sort of trickster") who torments and yet fascinates everybody. The next character to enter is the pastoral buffoon Licco (a role comparable to Lebrel in *El mayor encanto, amor*). Faithful retainer to Hercules' wife Dejanira, he soon finds out from his fellow-servant what is afoot. Then Dejanira arrives, and when she hears the evil tidings, she is gravely affected and laments her own fate ("Misera; ohimè ch'ascolto?" "Wretch; alas, what have I just heard?"), Hercules' violent passions, and her son's dark future.[31] Then the scene shifts to the Cave of Sleep (Sonno), where Pasithea (Sonno's wife) and the chorus of Zephyrs and Brooks guard over the sleeping deity ("Mormorate, fiumicelli,/ Sussurate, o venticelli," "Murmur, then, little brooks,/ Rustle then, o soft breezes;" and

"Dormi, dormi, o Sonno dormi," "Sleep, sleep, o Sleep, sleep"). But Juno descends anyway to take Sonno away with her in her chariot. Characters impersonating Dreams then dance a ballet.

As the third act (which has ten scenes) commences, we see Hercules waiting for Iole in the flower garden—a magical place, with many once-living persons transformed into garden statues (the motif of Circe's island returns). Venus descends from the heavens to help Hercules—her last appearance in the opera. Hercules, delighted to see her, wishes there were more monsters for him to slay so he could offer them up to her, but Venus tells him that she will be rewarded enough if Iole can be made to return his passion. To that end she conjures up an "incanto seggio," an inviting, magic seat of grass and flowers: by sitting on it, Iole will be enchanted and yield to Hercules. This done, the two conspirators, very satisfied with themselves, sing a duet in a contrived defense of their artifice (*arte*): since the pleasures of love are not controlled by reason (*ragione*) or mercy (*pietà*), but rather by cruelty (*crudeltà*) and severity (*rigor*), it is perfectly justified for the imperious (male) lover to use artifice to satisfy his "ardente desio," his burning desire. Next, the page appears to inform Hercules of the results of his embassy, and immediately after, princess Iole and Hyllo enter the garden. Iole first rebuffs Hercules (after all, he has killed her father and the corpse is, so to speak, still warm), but she cannot resist the effect of the magic seat:

> Che mai?
> Sento spuntar entro il mio petto,
> Per te improvviso involontario affetto![32]

Although she still loves Hyllo as well, her surprising words have a devastating effect on the latter, and when he declares his own passion for the princess, he is immediately chased away by his father; unable to bear his fate, Hyllo decides to end his life by jumping off a rocky cliff. Left alone, Hercules approaches Iole with lustful intentions, but in the nick of time Juno's chariot appears once more in the sky. To protect the maiden, Sonno quickly puts Hercules to sleep, and Juno hands Iole a dagger, urging the princess to avenge her father. Hyllo, she says, has not jumped off the cliff at all but has seen and heard everything from a thicket where he had hidden himself; Iole should kill Hercules, "quest'empio tiranno," before he returns. The magic love seat is about to be transformed into a sacrificial altar, when Hyllo enters with the page, just in time to wrest the dagger from Iole's hands. But then Mercury descends, and with his flapping wings wakes Hercules. Seeing Hyllo with the dagger, Hercules immediately assumes that his son was poised to murder him in jealous rage; the hero is about to kill Hyllo, when Dejanira intervenes. The raving Hercules is blind to reason by now, and only Iole's hasty promise to yield to his desires restrains him from killing both his wife and son: "Ma s'egli vive: spera" ("But if he lives, you may hope"). Thus he exiles Dejanira and has Hyllo incarcerated. In a moving duet, the wife and the son of the lustful hero sing their adieux: "Ah voglia il ciel che questi/ Non sian gl'ultimi amplessi" ("Alas, may it be Heaven's will that these/ are not our last embraces"). The page and Licco remain behind. The garden statues are returned to their human form, and they dance the ballet.

The opening scene of the fourth act (consisting of seven scenes) shows a rocky coast, lined with towers; presumably it is night. Hyllo has been locked up in one of the towers and bemoans his fate. But a frail vessel appears with the page, who, as soon as he comes within hearing distance, cries out that he brings a sad letter from Iole, confirming the news that she will submit to Hercules so as to save her true love Hyllo. But then a sudden storm whips up the waves and destroys the little boat; the little page drowns, and his final cry to the gods goes unheeded. Now in utter despair, Hyllo throws himself from the window of his tower into the wild waves, crying out "Iole, Iole" as he falls. Unlike the humble page, however, he is protected by the Olympians, probably because of his rank. Seated on her splendid throne, Juno appears in midair, imploring Neptune not to be as negligent as he was the time he caused Leander to drown, but instead to save Hyllo, "quel troppo ardito giovane" ("that overly intrepid youth"). Stung by the reproach, Neptune emerges from the depths in his great shell chariot drawn by seahorses; having deposited Hyllo on the coast, and after some good advice ("Per chi vive il ciel gira/ E non sempre un sospira;" "The heavens turn only for him who lives,/ and a sigh does not last forever"), he disappears again in the wavy deep. Juno, too, consoles the royal youth. As the Sun returns, the Zephyrs dance a joyous ballet.

Then the scene changes to a cemetery with cypresses, royal tombs, and more statues.[33] Hercules' wife and her servant are on stage. While the despairing Dejanira laments, Licco fruitlessly tries to cheer her up. Then Iole enters, leading a funeral procession and a chorus of Priests to her father's tomb, where she begs the dead Euryto's forgiveness for the fact that she must submit to fate and yield her body to the "iniquo tiranno." Her words are hardly cold, when dull noises emerge from the tomb, which starts to tremble and shake ("Ah ch'esser ció puote?/ Tutto trema e si scuote," sings the Chorus). The wrathful ghost of the slain king appears and, enraged against Hercules, denounces Iole's intentions as "prieghi ingiuriosi" and "voti obbrobiosi" ("insulting prayers" and "infamous desires"). Even dead, so he claims, he is still able to protect Hyllo against Hercules. Dejanira, who saw Hyllo jump from the tower but not how he was rescued, brings the news of his death to the company. At this new shock, the royal ghost sinks back in his tomb, silenced, and princess Iole weeps uncontrollably, vowing to follow Hyllo's example. Licco suggests that Dejanira try to lead her husband back to the right path and win back his love by means of the magic shirt once given to her by the Centaur Nessus. Iole, Deianira, and Licco then sing a trio of anguish, expressing "una stilla di speme," "a ray of hope" that, perhaps, Hyllo came back to his senses upon falling in the cold water and decided to swim back to shore. As this tragic act comes to an end, other ghosts leave their tombs; their dance frightens away the living characters.

The fifth act has four scenes. The first is set in one of the circles of Hades, where the ghosts of Hercules' recent victims, Eurytus, Clerica, Laomedon, and Busiris cry out at great length for revenge, accompanied by a Chorus of Dead Souls ("anime infernali"). The scene then switches to the portico of the temple of Juno Pronuba, where Hercules and Iole are about to get married. A Chorus of Priests presides. The trembling Iole ("Ecco il mio viver giunto/ A un formidabil punto," "Here the course of my life has reached/ a most frightful point") offers Hercules the shirt of Nessus. Hercules has never been so close to the fulfillment of his desires ("in vista dei contenti") but as soon as he puts on the shirt, he suffers indescribable torture, as if his blood were burning and twisting in his veins. Unable to rid himself of the magic garment, he throws himself in the flames of Hell: "Addio cielo, addio Iole, eccomi Pluto" ("Farewell heaven, farewell Iole, Pluto here I come"). Licco reacts rather stoically ("Che dici?/ Il mio non fu rimedio tardo," "What do you say of that?/ My remedies work rather fast"); he considers Hercules' horrible death not a tragedy but an instance of just retribution and an occasion for celebration. Deianira, by contrast, grieves even more, now having lost both her son and her husband ("A dolor su dolore," "Grief follows upon grief")—that is, until Hyllo reappears, to everybody's surprise and joy. Mother, son, and princess Iole are finally joyfully reunited, and they decide to honor Hercules' ashes with a most splendid funeral, with immeasurable "lagrime e di fiori," "tears and flowers." But then Juno reappears in the heavens, accompanied by Heavenly Harmony, and reveals, rather surprisingly, that Hercules is not in Hades but resides among the immortal Olympians as the new spouse of Beauty:

> Non morì Alcide
> Tergete i lumi
> Non morì, no!
> Su nel ciel ride
> Che lo sposò
> Il Re dei numi
> Alla belleza.[34]

Juno reascends, and the duo Hyllo-Iole, to which Dejanira then adds her voice, responds to her message with joy, singing that no force is stronger than reciprocated love.

In the epilogue, the skies open. Hercules and Beauty are revealed to be in heaven; assisted by the chorus of Seven Planets, they sing in honor of the royal couple Louis and Maria-Theresa, prophesying that

> Così un giorno avverrà con più diletto
> Che della Senna in su la riva altera
> Altro gallico Alcide arso d'affetto
> Giunga in pace a goder bellezza ibera.[35]

For the grand finale, stars and planets descend in a gigantic cloud machine and dance the final ballet, in glorification of Hercules-Louis and of the principle of "suffering virtue" which he has so admirably represented.[36]

The performance lasted at least six hours; no fewer than eighteen rather unrelated ballet entries by Lully, who as usual provided the king and members of the Court with ample and indispensable opportunities to shine, had been added to the opera proper. Most contemporaneous observers liked what they had seen and heard; others, obviously, did not. For one, the acoustics of the Salle des Machines were found to be very poor.[37] Moreover, apparently only few members of the audience could follow the Italian text—or, probably more truthfully, were willing to try. Still, much of the plot of *Ercole amante* was based on classical sources and thus somehow familiar to many in the audience. The costumes and the machines proved a success (though the machines squeaked rather badly), and the ballets were admired most of all—not in the least, we may presume, because of Louis' participation. Contrary to common opinion, *Ercole amante* did not fall into total oblivion after the series of grandiose performances in 1662. Nevertheless, it is a rather unusual fact that the décors of *Ercole amante* were not engraved.[38] And the opera itself was not staged again in its entirety until May 4, 1979. Interestingly enough, this modern performance took place in Lyon, the same city where the very first courtly musical-dramatic splendid performance in the Italian style on French soil was held.

To date, the most exhaustive discussion of *Ercole amante* is still to be found in Henri Prunières' book. Prunières, a historical musicologist, describes the opera as a disastrous affair. He is especially hostile to Buti's work; without analyzing the libretto in detail, he dismisses it as a clumsily conceived and constructed text, insipid and difficult to follow, lacking any genuine attempt at even rudimentary psychology, and merely presenting a string of silly intrigues and a concatenation of extravagant situations. Briefly, it is the shoddy product of a tired, uncreative man.[39] By contrast, Prunières argues, Cavalli's genius appears from the fact that he was able at all to breathe life into such a feeble frame: "Sa musique traduit avec intensité les sentiments les plus faiblement exprimés par Buti" ("His music translates into something intense even the feeblest emotions expressed in Buti's text;" 1913: 289). Obviously, Prunières' final standard of judgment is the degree to which text, music and drama collaborate to express characterization, psychological veracity, and the strong emotions of an individual character. It is therefore understandable that, among the opera's characters, he singles out for praise the buffoonish Licco, the only character who, he says, seems not made out of cardboard. Prunières vividly resents the fact that Cavalli's music was apparently not particularly appreciated by the audiences; hence his melancholic vignette of the aged composer who left Paris irritated, badly remunerated, and vowing never again to leave the wealth and adulation to which he was used in Venice. A misunderstood artist? Yes, Prunières says unequivocally: of all the artists involved in this festive performance, the Venetian composer "importe seul," "was the only one who mattered."[40]

Prunières' judgment is narrowly focused and quite harsh on Buti, but it is well in line with the former French rejection (amounting to a misunderstanding) of Baroque art and the Baroque sensibility. The point is that a Baroque splendid festive performance is a political product in the service of the absolute ruler, subject to the constant demands of a very specific and codified rhetoric interwoven with play and power. In such a performance, unlike in a "regular" eighteenth- or nineteenth-century lyric opera, the music—no matter how brilliant by itself—is the servant rather than the mistress of a functional rhetoric incorporating the literary program, the architecture, the design of machines and sets, the choreography, and the general visual spectacle.[41] Contemporaneous sources (quoted by Prunières himself) confirm this fact. Among others, the gazetteers, the chronicler and court gossip Loret, the Venetian ambassador, and Mme de Lafayette found much that was worthy of praise in the performances of *Ercole amante*:[42] the technical expertise of vocalists, instrumentalists, and dancers; the abundance of sumptuous costumes; the design of the ten sets; and the grandeur of Vigarani's machines for raising and lowering large groups of people. Judging from the plot, these machines were indeed the crucial structural feature around which the entire visual experience of the performance was organized and that expressed its rhetorical design.[43] The dynastic and political relevance of the splendid performance was translated—as was customary—into its literary program and its visual rhetoric rather than presented by purely aural means. The role of music was to support, rather than lead, the interpretation of the visual and textual dynamic clues that made the interpretation of the rhetorical program possible. In short, splendid festive performances at Baroque courts were not created by one single artistic genius, and least of all by the composer. Rather, they were made by a conglomerate of performers, the first and foremost of whom was quite naturally the royal presence, who provided the occasion for the performance, the material means and the impetus to make it possible, and the ultimate sanction to carry it out. In a performance of this kind—and in that of *Ercole amante* in particular—everything ultimately turns around this royal presence, the center to which everything points and from which everything radiates. Throughout his discussion, Prunières remains insensitive to this crucial aspect of the opera, although his insights as to Mazarin's role are very important.[44]

To place *Ercole amante* in its proper context, as a splendid festive performance in the service of the dynasty at whose court it was performed, we must thus reject Prunières' harsh condemnation of the literary program. It is true, at first sight, that the tragic tale of a criminally lecherous Hercules, who hurls himself into the flaming mouth of Hell and dies in agonizing pain, seems rather grotesque and quite inappropriate for the two joyous occasions that were to be celebrated jointly. But the oddity resides not so much in the tragic connotations as in the subject of Hercules' lustful appetites and death.[45] During Mazarin's tenure, Louis was customarily associated with Hercules.[46] Of all epic and mythological heroes, Hercules is arguably the most fallible and therefore also the most human character.[47] The legends and fables attribute many moral failings to him.[48] He is represented as deserving blame (*vituperatio*) in equal proportion to praise (*laudatio*). The harmonization of these contradictory qualities in a context in which Hercules—in his double role as an undeniably great hero but also an unreasonably lustful lover—was (we may safely assume) read as Louis, leaves much room for epideictic rhetorical-allegorical play. We can examine, therefore, if and how the makers of the grandiose performance managed to balance the extremes of flattery with a sense of discretion and even criticism. For after all, the ostensible subject of *Ercole amante* is not so much Hercules the hero as Hercules the scoundrel: an immoral and jealous monomoniac who forgets his innate heroic qualities and who is rescued from perpetual infamy only by a mysteriously intervening force.

Buti's libretto is a family romance, which, like the aristocratic guessing games of the time, demands to be unscrambled,[49] and its "representational" mythological program must likewise be decoded. As is so frequently the case in Renaissance and Baroque courtly art, the mythological theme of the text and of the visual performance aspects (machines, scenes, costumes) is particularly important insofar as it contributes motifs of political, historical, ethical, religious, and human or personal relevance to the context in which these motifs appear. In *Ercole amante*, motifs of all these kinds are represented. Let us assume that the fourteen rivers of the prologue represent the kingdom of France, or even a wider, pan-European landscape. Roman Tiber, most venerable among the European rivers, pays homage to Seine—implying that Greco-Roman antiquity admits the superiority of French culture and its ruling dynasty. After all, a fabricated myth perpetuated the notion that the French kings descended from the early kings of Rome.[50] The early appearance of Cynthia (Diana) anticipates a chaste, rational, and "positive" ending. Then Hercules is shown, sighing for princess Iole, the betrothed of his own son. Few in the audience can have failed to realize that Hercules—not accidentally also the best rhetorician among the cast—was the representation of the young Louis. Nobody was ignorant of the fact that Louis, who had already proven his mettle on the battlefield, was sincerely in love with the ambitious, rather *précieuse* Marie Mancini, one of Mazarin's nieces, to Mazarin's great chagrin.

(In fact, at Fontainebleau in 1659, Louis and Marie carried on a fairy-tale summer romance, which at least gave the monarch a civilizing passion for Renaissance romance epics and Baroque novels. This taste was soon to be translated in a persistent sponsorship of splendid performances at his court, of which "Les Plaisirs de l'Ile enchantée" was to be the first manifestation.)[51] Venus, who descends from heaven in order to fuel Hercules' passion, may well represent the sensuous "Princess Palatine" (Mme de Longueville), who was connected with some leaders of the Fronde and who had once made a great personal impression on Louis. Feeding "Hercules' " lustful but inappropriate desire for "Iole," "Venus" represents great danger for the king, the future of his rule, and the destiny of his country. "Venus" is therefore to be stopped. To that purpose, she is immediately contradicted by a maternal Juno figure, who represents morality, respectability and honest marriages—and who might therefore be considered an ally of Mazarin. She might well be taken to signify Louis' mother, Anne of Austria, whose objections to the Mancini affair were reinforced by those of Mazarin. The identification of Hyllo presents no real problem. Given the still semifeudal organization of the French nobility, Hyllo (Hercules' son) represents one of Louis' most prominent retainers; he might well be the Duke de Nemours, with whom it was once rumored Marie Mancini was in love. Thus, Hercules' dangerous and violent jealousy is a reflection on Louis' own feelings. The ill-advised liaison, which Hercules-Louis sought solely to satisfy his personal amorous inclination but which violated various ethical and probably also political codes, is ultimately aborted by Hercules-Louis' enforced plunge in the painful but redemptive fire, from which he emerges purified and sanctified as the worthy groom of placid Beauty herself—a rather lame representation of the Infanta. Hercules-Louis has overcome his own limiting passions for good and is properly married before Heaven. Having earned his place among the immortals, only the sky itself is now the limit.

The lesson that Louis and the court were supposed to derive from the opera's representational rhetoric, and especially from its surprising but flattering conclusion, seems therefore obvious. It is pointed out for all to see that the young monarch has sacrificed his personal desire to the advantage of the State. After some pressing by Anne and Mazarin, Louis was able to transcend one of his weaknesses. His marriage to the Infanta was intended to signify that the king had applied sound political judgment and had reflected seriously on the vital matter of dynastic unions.[52] Thus, the staged events do not really lead up to tragedy. On the contrary, the glorious epilogue confirms that, although Hercules dies in agony, the final effect of his death transcends its manner. Given the contemporaneous Christian moral and didactic framework, Hercules has achieved something very similar to the reward of Alessio in Rospigliosi and Landi's *Sant'Alessio*—an opera that Mazarin in all likelihood had seen performed in Barberini Rome.

In the seventeenth-century courtly world, artistic events and products were part and parcel of historical and political developments. The rhetoric of official art was in agreement with the absolute ruler's manipulation of his newfound role as god of play. As part of political history in the making, art—which includes the seriously playful art of the splendid performances—did not only record but could potentially provoke historical developments. I argue that *Ercole amante* fulfilled precisely these two functions. I would like to remind the reader of my argument (suggested by the etymological definition of "performance" as "a carrying out *completely*") that a truly splendid festive performance at a Baroque court actually constitutes the required culmination of an entire *series* of events, rather than a celebration of a single occasion. Thus, Mazarin ordered *Ercole amante* not so much to celebrate the marriage of Louis and Maria Theresa, but rather to crown with a *lieto fine* the complex series of political-historical events that culminated in the marriage. This series of events, which took decades to develop, was generally centered around the task of reducing Habsburg power in Europe. The strategy to accomplish this goal had taken off seriously with the Franco-Spanish war, which began in 1635 and ended with the advantage for the French. An initial peace treaty, the Treaty of Paris, was signed on June 9, 1659. The definitive treaty, the Peace of the Pyrenees, was concluded in November, with Mazarin acting as plenipotentiary of France.[53] From the very beginning, the cardinal envisioned the marriage of the young king Louis and the Infanta as part of his strategy to strengthen the position of France on the Continent and reduce that of the Habsburgs; in this matter, Mazarin could count on the full support of Anne of Austria.[54] But Louis was in love with Marie Mancini. This attachment, though flattering, was a source of irritation for the cardinal. The alliance would be hardly productive in the larger scheme of things. The cardinal's simultaneous creative adaptation of the Hercules mythology was intended to represent to the king the fact that, given the context of the European power game, his private passion was unacceptable. For, as we have seen, Mazarin began planning the creation of *Ercole amante* as early as the spring and summer of 1659: he charged Buti with the libretto and Vigarani with the construction of the theater and the machines a full year before the wedding took place (on June 9, 1660, at Saint-Juan-de-Luz in the Pyrenees). In other words, Mazarin originally intended to direct dynastic and national history by means of a festive performance, by representing to the king how behavior deserving *vituperatio* could be turned into behavior worthy of *laudatio*. Aided by Anne, Mazarin succeeded rapidly. He cannot really have doubted that Louis would quickly give up Marie Mancini, to the obvious disappointment of the latter.[55] The festive performance *had* to be grandiose because it was to serve the necessary ritual function of "carrying out completely" a complex series of political and military events. But in a way, the opera contains an interesting layer of epideictic rhetoric in praise of Mazarin's own political manipulations.

For who but the cardinal could have been the unseen, anonymous force that ultimately directs the outcome of the plot? Mazarin was the force responsible for rescuing the lustful Hercules-Louis from the flames of Hell and for raising him to immortal Olympian status as the spouse of Beauty-Maria Theresa. In fact, the literary-rhetorical program of Buti's libretto confirms that, up to this point in history, Louis' triumphs in general were realized through the cardinal and that it was the prime minister, rather than Louis, who had been ruling France. Likewise, Mazarin, and not Louis, filled the function of "god of play" by ordering the opera for the wedded couple and by tirelessly promoting its grandiose performance. The royal couple's triumphant installation began with a series of formal Entries in each major city on the road from Saint-Juan-de-Luz to Paris and achieved, as was suggested in chapter 1, a first apotheosis in the grand Entry in Paris, on August 26, 1660. The splendid festive performance of *Ercole amante* was intended as the crowning event, a magnificent visual spectacle as well as a finely tuned, ambivalent rhetorical statement in praise of the king and his chief minister.[56]

But as we will see in the rest of this chapter, the repeated delays of the performance undermined its rhetorical validity, because history itself has a tendency to move more rapidly than art. The representational function of a specific work made for a grandiose festive performance is not neutral, but is rather determined by very specific circumstances. As these circumstances evolve, the rhetoric of the representation becomes invalid or incomplete. *Ercole amante* provides a good example of an opera whose rhetoric had been overtaken and rendered ineffective by the course of history itself. In spite of the opera's intended happy ending, its actual implications, when it was finally performed, were rather tragic. I mean that the subject matter which had been designed in 1659 to be interpreted as an ultimate *laudatio*, could by 1662 only be interpreted as a *vituperatio*. Rather than a celebration, the opera was now an embarrassment—not so much because the Salle des Machines had poor acoustics or because the French audience despised the Italian performers, though these were doubtlessly important factors—but rather because the represented myth was now so very obviously at odds both with the real Louis XIV *and* his newly created mythic identity. The 1662 performance of *Ercole amante* represented Louis as depending for "salvation" on some higher force and as going through a learning stage. This characterization may have been useful, interesting, or even valid in 1659, but it was no longer so in 1662. The herculean symbolism itself had become outdated and inadequate. True: the performance still showed Louis achieving relative virtue and wisdom as well as immortality, but two other, related elements had come to interfere with the opera's rhetorical-allegorical program.

The first of these was the change in Louis' public persona: having risen in status, his representation required a proportionally more grandiose level of allegory and symbolism (let us not forget that the main figure of epideictic rhetoric is *auxeisis*, amplification). The year 1661 was a turning point for the French dynasty and its court: Mazarin was dead, and Louis, free from the cardinal's domineering presence, began to rule personally.[57] (Let us mention in passing, also, that 1661 and the following year were miserable famine years for the vast masses of the population.) It is interesting to note that, of the four flattering medals struck to commemorate the beginning of this personal rule, one represented Louis XIV as Apollo, and another depicted him as Phoebus in the Sun Chariot bringing light to the World (medals described by, and reproduced in, de la Hode 3: 10–11). Diplomatic incidents with Spain in 1661 almost led to a new war, which was only (temporarily) avoided when an envoy of Philip IV was forcibly humiliated into acknowledging, in a famous encounter before the other Powers on March 14, 1662, Louis' status as the first monarch of Europe. This international humiliation of her father—at a time when *Ercole amante* was still being performed—was yet another mortification, one of many, for Maria Theresa.[58] Thus, by 1662 Louis had definitely shown himself the sole master of his country. Although he surrounded himself continually with entertainments, he worked hard, concluding complex treaties with most European powers, dealing with difficult intrigues in France itself, and carrying out rather drastic reforms in the diplomatic, military, administrative, and civil services. In general, he aimed at tightening the reins and definitively curbing what little power the Fronde had left the hereditary nobility.

The second element that had changed since the 1659 conception of the program of *Ercole amante* was Louis' private persona. It is necessary to introduce, at this point, two important characters close to the young monarch: Nicolas Fouquet, and Louise de la Vallière. In 1661, the powers of Nicolas Fouquet, Surintendant of France, were immense, not only in matters of politics and economics but also in the domain of "culture" and "art"—concepts then inextricably linked both with politics and economics. Indeed, since the death of Richelieu in 1642, France and her court had lacked an official cultural policy. Throughout the 1650s, for example, Mazarin's interest in that area was rather limited, as we have seen, to the promotion of Roman-style opera and the importation of Italian artists and performers. The production of *Ercole amante* was the last manifestation of that particular phase in cultural-rhetorical policy. Perhaps it is fair to say that, by the end of the regency, only the immensely wealthy Fouquet came close to having both the vision and the material resources to conduct a "cultural" policy of sorts on his own, by providing financial support to French writers (Scudéry, Corneille, Scarron, and many others) and artists in various media, as well as numerous craftspeople. Fouquet's power as the patron of those "artists" who could glorify the realm and serve as its historiographers was obvious, and, in 1661, the twenty-two-year-old Louis was reduced to asking his surintendant to put on an entertainment for him. Fouquet made the fatal error of offering too much (a splendid example of ill-calculated potlatch-poker) and thus of outperforming his assigned role in the order of the state.

On the evening of August 17, 1661, he staged an hitherto unsurpassed grandiose entertainment against the background of his new château, Vaux-le-Vicomte. The main festivities, which lasted approximately ten hours, combined the talents of some of the greatest living makers of feasts. Moulded around ballets choreographed by Beauchamp (the most important among the contributors), décors painted by LeBrun, scenography and fireworks designed by Torelli, and music composed by Lully, Molière's three-act *comédie-ballet Les Fâcheux* was performed with an unusually large cast of musicians, dancers, and mimes.[59] It was on this occasion that Molière and Lully first worked together (though not as equals: Molière was only appointed to join the production at the last moment). It has been argued that Fouquet at this time already knew that he was a doomed man, and about to become a political victim; if so, his staging of the grandiose entertainment can be construed as either a politically defiant or a politically desperate act, amounting, in fact, to a (futile) confrontation between minister and king.[60] Indeed, the conclusion of the grandiose performance at Vaux-le-Vicomte was the beginning of the "affaire Fouquet," which Louis used to his best advantage and to clean house. In his *Histoire de la vie et du règne de Louis XIV*, de la Hode reflects at length on the sordid trial (3: 137–63), which reached its climax only in December, 1664. According to our chronicler, the complicated trial failed to substantiate the charges against the former Surintendant of Finances—charges including corruption, misappropriation of funds and, above all, *lèse-majesté*. In fact, so de la Hode argues, the entire *affaire* was trumped up by Colbert and by Louis; the latter's hatred of Nicolas Fouquet had grown such that he even commuted the court's sentence of perpetual banishment to perpetual imprisonment—a highly unusual step—"sous prétexte, qu'il ne convenoit pas, qu'un homme, qui avoit une connoissance particulière des affaires les plus importantes de l'Etat, sortit du Roïaume" ("under the pretext that it would not be appropriate for a man with such intimate knowledge of the most important matters of State [to be allowed] to leave the Realm" 3: 161). In the wake of the patently unjust trial, Fouquet's relatives, former friends and allies suffered greatly in a general house-cleaning campaign that affected almost the entire court. Finally, de la Hode confesses that, having searched high and low, he could find no genuine motif to account for Louis' unusually harsh persecution of Fouquet, other than the alleged proposition "que ce Ministre voluptueux avoit faite à Mademoiselle de la Valière [sic] de lui donner vingt mille pistoles" ("that this voluptuous Minister had made to Mlle de la Vallière, namely to offer her twenty thousand pistoles" 3: 163).

In 1661, Louis began his noted affair with Mlle Louise de la Vallière, then hardly sixteen.[61] At first, he—along with the Queen-Mother—may have tried to hide the liaison from the pregnant queen—perhaps, may we assume, even out of consideration, since the shock of the royal spouse's infidelity might provoke a miscarriage.[62] But the unhappy queen quickly became aware that Louis loved elsewhere, and repeatedly.[63] (It is doubtful whether Louis ever loved the Infanta Maria Theresa, and the point is, of course, hardly relevant.[64]) Many prominent courtiers disapproved of the liaison, siding openly with Maria Theresa and the Queen Mother, and slighting the young favorite. If this social condemnation was at all apparent to the amorous potentate, it did not immediately seem to bother him—not yet. Regardless, Fouquet's deliberate and fated extravagance on August 17, 1661 was probably not so much the original cause of his persecution by the jealous Louis—as has traditionally been assumed—as, more likely, the straw that broke the camel's back. Fouquet was not only allegedly vying with the king for the royal mistress, but he was also seen to be competing, in public, for the royal prerogative of controlling the rhetoric of organised play. Both efforts cannot, of course, be dissociated.

What all this means is that the rhetorical program of *Ercole amante* had become not only irrelevant but even hideously inverted when the splendid performance was finally allowed to take place. Mazarin had wanted to show, after the Louis-Mancini affair, that a king should not only be able to perform physical (perhaps even intellectual) deeds of heroism but should also be able to overcome moral temptation. The young absolute monarch should be reasonable, ethical and juridicial. But Hercules-Louis was none of the above: when *Ercole amante* was finally produced with all its pomp and splendor, it was blatantly clear to all who saw it that Louis, far from having repented his passions, had actually begun to resemble more and more the lustful scoundrel Hercules. The opera's epideictic rhetoric can be said to have backfired in the most grotesque fashion; History herself was adding a crucial layer of meaning to *Ercole amante* even as the preparations for the production itself were still underway. Praise had become blame as historical circumstances had evolved: instead of being shown as furthering the true interests of the State—that is, the balance and equilibrium in the use of force and power—Louis was accused before his court of being too passionate and all too easily the absolute slave of another—whether mistress or minister.[65] The main problem was not so much the fact that Louis loved entertainments and feasts so much.[66] What mattered primarily was the fact that, only a few months into the personal reign, Louis had proven unable to control his voluptuous and passionate nature.[67] The queen had good reason to be thoroughly distressed. The fact that Louis allowed the performance to take place, and even insisted on it—imagine a Dorian Gray insisting on exhibiting his hideously deformed portrait—suggests that the obvious moral implications of the representation did not matter to the king—or else, that he was playing potlatch poker, too. Or: with Mazarin dead, Philip IV publicly humiliated, Louis recognized (so he liked to think) as the first among European monarchs, and Fouquet in jail, Louis was no longer simply Hercules but had moved far beyond that role.

When the 1659 rhetoric of the spectacle had been neutralized by history, in 1662 only its value as a grandiose spectacle mattered. And as we have seen, contemporaneous observers duly expressed their admiration for the many spectacular elements without commenting much, if at all, on the music or the text. With the graduation of Louis from the role of human-born Hercules to the persona of Phoebus Apollo, to whom the rules that govern social humankind do not apply, a new, more grandiose epideictic rhetoric was beginning to take shape in the service of the king, who had, moreover, become the god of play himself. For example, from 1663 onward an increasingly powerful stream of eulogies began to course through all modes of French writing, encouraged by Fouquet's successor, Jean-Baptiste Colbert, and controlled by the latter primarily by means of a complex system of official pensions and grants (Ferrier-Caverivière 1985: 50–52). (In 1665, Colbert was also made responsible for the administration of a wide range of crucial affairs, from finance and the national economy to colonial policy, architecture and the organization of "culture" [see Voss 123–32].) One will find evidence of the new official epideictic rhetoric, aimed at "making" Louis XIV in artifacts such as the theater of Corneille, the fables of de La Fontaine, philosophical or doctrinal papers, and Racine's historiographical projects (Marin 1988).

But Colbert, who may originally have tried to instill hatred for dissipation and waste in the heart of the young king by fanning his hatred of Fouquet, apparently only succeeded in fanning the tendency toward dissipation—which I have chosen in this study to associate with festive play—in the king's temperament. The new festive cycle was officially initiated, once again primarily by means of visual rhetoric, at the famous *carrousel* of the Five Nations that was performed, near the Louvre, on the 5th and 6th days of June—the month of the Summer solstice—1662. This *carrousel*, held only weeks after the final performance of *Ercole amante*, officially confirmed the beginning of the cult of Louis as the Sun King.[68] The fitting theatrical locus for a new festive cycle—of which the 1662 *carrousel* was only the first event and which continued almost without interruption until 1682 (thus spanning the entire first half of the personal reign and constituting an integral part of it)—was the "new" palace of Versailles.

One of several important things that Louis learned from Fouquet's exuberant, self-destructive display on that splendid evening in August, 1661, was the fact that a house, its grounds, and the way these are put to use constitute so many rhetorical statements about the master. Thus, in the first year of Louis' personal rule, Le Vau was ordered to undertake the (first) enlargement of Versailles. Gradually, the charming, rosy-brick hunting château of Louis' father became unrecognizable, metamorphosed into a complex solar allegory that, in spite of its regular geometrical patterns, was actually allowed to burst out of its seams. For the economical Colbert, the unchecked growth of Versailles and the extravagance of "Les Plaisirs" that we are about to discuss were probably not a very pleasurable matter. Yet, the continuous expansion of Versailles was a crucial part of the new rhetoric aimed at forging the myth of Louis the Sun King and sustaining it with concrete evidence, and the architectural project was at least as important as the official historiographical texts that were produced to the same purpose. Its completion became the personal objective and obsession of Louis XIV, to which everything had to give way—to the disappointment, perhaps, of Colbert, who would have preferred to develop the Louvre. The most sympathetic reading that one can extend to the project of Versailles is that the Sun King not only wished it but that the expanding culture of serious play, of which Louis was the focal point and the centerpiece, required such a stage to express itself fully.[69] A charming and fairly innocent episode in the saga of Versailles occurred at its very beginning, in May, 1664, with the performance (or, to use an anachronistic term, the thematically controlled "happening") of "Les Plaisirs de l'Ile enchantée."

De la Hode begins his chronicle for 1664 with a partly idyllic, partly tart passage that is very characteristic of that author's style. With the arrival of spring, so de la Hode notes dryly, the court left Paris for Versailles, "ce lieu désert, pour l'embellissement duquel on avoit déjà commencé & on continüa de dépenser depuis des sommes prodigieuses. Là, plus libre, & excité par la beauté de la saison, on donna quantité de Fêtes galantes, qui produisirent bien des chagrins" (3: 119).[70] The château and its grounds were still under (re)construction at this time: the main building was essentially still the Renaissance hunting lodge of Louis XIII and not yet recognizably the handiwork of Le Vau, Mansart and their able assistants. The hunting grounds and woods were only partially cleared, Le Nôtre's designs for the gardens existed mainly on paper, the grand avenues were hardly traced, only the basins for the fountains were dug out, and, most likely, there were not yet any marble statues. But the Sun King, characteristically, could not wait. Although unfinished, the new Versailles was splendidly inaugurated with "Les Plaisirs de l'Ile enchantée," the official name of the "quantité de fêtes galantes" to which de la Hode so briefly refers. Indeed, these feasts can stand as a splendid example of the quality of impatience, of the tendency to rush things that is such a marked characteristic of the Baroque sensibility and that we have witnessed in action before. For example, Molière and his company, the "Comédiens de Monseigneur le duc d'Orléans," left Paris to join the other makers of "Les Plaisirs" in Versailles on April 30—hardly a week before the actual festivities began in earnest. And it is well known that Molière was given such a tight deadline that he was unable to finish the versification of the original prose text of *La Princesse d'Elide*; except for the first act and part of the first scene of the second, which were in verse, the *comédie* was performed in prose.

Part of the reason for the production of these "Plaisirs" was doubtlessly the king's desire to "outdo" (in the rhetorical-topical sense) Fouquet, and to punish—with a pathetically mean-spirited gesture, perhaps—by means of a complex contrapasso his disgraced ex-minister, who was then still awaiting trial. Officially, the festivities were given in honor of Louis' mother and his wife, Maria Theresa. In reality, few of the six hundred or so hand-picked courtiers who were allowed to attend the events—the "chagrins" de la Hode mentions so diplomatically probably refer to the resentment of the many courtiers and aristocrats who found themselves without an invitation to what might be the grandest social occasion of the decade—would have been ignorant of the fact that Louis was offering "Les Plaisirs" to Louise de la Vallière.[71] This dedication, in addition to the very pleasant weather, may well have been the principal reason why Louis was so impatient to have the festivities take place. Indeed, following the opening passage quoted above, de la Hode's chronicle for 1664 continues with a lengthy discussion of la Vallière's social ostracism up until that time. The gist of it is that Louise bitterly complained regarding this ostracism to her royal *Amant* early in the spring of 1664, upon which the imperious Louis vowed that he would no longer tolerate such a lack of deference toward his mistress. This firm stand, which in effect virtually isolated Maria Theresa, brought about several quarrels with his mother as well as the inevitable court intrigues, which resulted in the disgrace of a few prominent persons who chose to remain faithful to the queen and to "decency." (To emphasize his independence, the king would even spend part of that same summer with la Vallière in Villers-Cotterêtz, a property of Monsieur his brother—Molière's patron—where the queen was prevented, diplomatically, by the late phase of her pregnancy from accompanying them [de la Hode 3: 121–22].)

Thus the opening of Versailles as Louis' pleasure palace—as distinct from the Louvre, the work palace which signified his duties toward the state—and the public confirmation of Louise de la Vallière as Louis' mistress—as distinct from his awareness of the duties following from the contractual alliance with the queen—became, in essence, one and the same issue. As Versailles and Louise were officially inaugurated together, Louis sent a powerful message to the Nation that conventional guidelines regarding the separation of "duties" and "pleasures" were henceforth not to be applied to himself. The deliberate confusion of the king's realms of duty and pleasure (*ananke* and *eros*) was from now on sustained in an atmosphere of serious play. Let us now examine in greater detail how "Les Plaisirs de l'Ile enchantée" and *La Princesse d'Elide*, which has been called "the only play in Molière's repertory in which the romantic interest is predominant," functioned as a rhetorical construct in this important development.[72]

"Les Plaisirs" was conceived as a gigantic ballet, the realization of a dream inspired by Renaissance *romanzesco* epic. The "enchanted island" is, of course, Versailles itself, or, to be more precise, those parts of the future park connected (or separated) by the *Allée royale* (today the *Tapis vert*). "Les Plaisirs" proper was supposed to encompass three nights but was allowed, in typical Baroque fashion, to linger and to spill over in time, detaining the revellers for about a week. The permanent *relation* of these ephemeral events, printed by special order of the king immediately after the actual feasts, defines them as "Les Plaisirs de l'Ile enchantée, Course de bague, Collation ornée de Machines, Comedie meslée de Danse & de Musique, Ballet du Palais d'Alcine, Feu d'Artifice: Et autres Festes galantes & magnifiques; faites par le Roy à Versailles, le 7. mai 1664, & continuées plusieurs autres Iours."[73] The lengthy title reflects the composite nature of the events. It must be remembered that for almost a century the chief festive event at the French court had been the *ballet de cour*. This form of organized play, which often had the king at its epicenter as Jupiter, as the Sun, or in a comparable role, was taken very seriously by its amateur participants, who could not afford to deviate in the slightest from the set patterns, the "hieroglyphs," lest the finer points of the final allegorical meaning be turned into chaos. Beaussant is surely right when he defines such a court ballet as "une cérémonie: la cérémonie solenelle par laquelle l'homme baroque célébrait sa dignité," "a ceremony: the solemn ceremony whereby the baroque individual celebrates his dignity" (39). Indeed, the ballets set to music by Lully in the course of the 1650s were usually so intricate that libretti were distributed in advance to assist the audience (who often watched them from above) in connecting Signifier and Signified and making sense of the figures.

But "Les Plaisirs" was an unusual enterprise in the sense that within its artistic setting, there was room not only for ballets and much music, but also for costume parades, mock combats, plays, banquets, concerts, lotteries, and fireworks—briefly, a dazzling combination of all known ancient and modern forms of aristocratic communal enjoyment. In addition to many artists and participants, vast numbers of anonymous cooks, candlemakers, dressmakers, carpenters, upholsterers, gardeners, and fire-works makers, among others, were involved in the execution of these feasts. The principal collaborators included Carlo Vigarani (the engineer, and therefore perhaps the true inventor of "Les Plaisirs") with his technicians, Molière and his company, Lully with his musicians and dancers, LeBrun with his painters and decorators, selected members of the court led by the king, and, let us not forget, the spectators themselves.

Thus, one can truly speak of "Les Plaisirs" as an anthology of pleasures, as a true discourse of festive rhetoric of which the punctuation marks were the royal appearances. The festive events themselves were ephemeral, but they achieved a considerable degree of permanence, not only by means of the printed *relation* but also because of the transformation that they effected in the self-willed mythistorical perception of the king. The story line of the three-night *Gesamtkunstwerk* that constitutes the core of "Les Plaisirs" allowed the monarch to cast himself into the roles of, subsequently, chivalric-epic hero (first night), princely lover (second night), and white magician (third night). These three roles are the quintessential, even archetypal, constructs in the western concept of play. Moreover, by providing the inspirational context, the practical locus and the material means for linking these constructs together in a virtually continuous illusionary chain of festive *gestae*, Louis can be said to have graduated via the *Gesamtkunstwerk* to the status of a patron of Feasts, a deity of Play. The story line was suggested by Louis to the Duke de Saint-Aignan, First Gentleman of the Chamber, who was made producer-in-chief and charged with providing the general script, the *liaison*, for the various entertainments. Besides Tasso's pastoral *Aminta*, which Louis had read in the long pleasant summer with Marie Mancini, Ariosto's romance-epic *Orlando furioso* (Books VI-VIII) served as the basis for Saint-Aignan's script.[74] The general outline of that story celebrating martial glory, love and magic was well-known. The beautiful witch Alcine holds the hero Ruggiero (Roger in the French translation) and his good knights emprisoned on her enchanted island of pleasure. They while the time away with dances, tournaments, banquets, plays, music, and other such pleasant entertainments until Roger, with the help of Angelica's ring, can finally break the spell. The role of "Roger" (*roi*) was appropriately reserved for Louis himself.

Thus the first night opened with a brilliant *défilé* on horseback by the monarch and his "enchanted cavaliers" along the *allée royale* toward the circular space where the four avenues of the park-to-be converged.[75] Louis' lifelong obsession with fanciful costumes was satisfied to the full: he appeared masked, wearing a helmet with extravagant red plumage, and clad in a pseudo-Greek silver harness covered with gold and diamonds. The costume not only served to link the monarch with the fabled heroes of Antiquity, but was, more importantly, a rhetorical expression of his ability to forge a harmony between opposite ways of conducting a nation. The martial harness signified the chivalric valor of ancient times. The armor's costly accouterments represented the accumulated wealth of the Nation which this monarch embodied: the riches produced by his warfare and by the diligence and skills of his subjects: diplomats, laborers and artisans, and tradesmen (Apostolidès 1981: 96). The symbolic meeting space—symbolic as a crossroads, combining the cruciform and the circular—had been turned into an arena, closed off by a dais and equipped with raised benches that could accommodate several hundred spectators. Innumerable flambeaux and candles were suspended in the trees around, making the area as bright—so the *relation* insists—as at the noon hour, thereby signifying that, under the auspices of the Sun King, the natural sun herself could be reduced to the status of a replaceable commodity.

A reconstruction of the fabled royal Entry, the *défilé* now served also as the prologue to the rhetorical discourse of the festivities. The parading knights were followed by many symbolic figures and machines. Most conspicuous was the Sun Chariot manned by Apollo, which was surrounded by allegorical representations of the four Ages, the four Seasons, the Hours, the Signs of the Zodiac, each of which was equipped with its respective sets of symbols, allegorical devices culled, still, from Ripa's *Iconologia* (Apostolidès 1981: 96). Thus the whole cosmos was represented at this *défilé*. Molière's actors, parading along on animals or seated on the machines, delivered flattering speeches addressed to the Queens.

After this procession of fantastically accoutered figures, a *course de bague* (riding at the ring)—an event supposedly ordered by Alcine in honor of the queen—was run in the circular space. The king participated but, with typical chivalric largesse, he did not compete for the prize: a golden sword studded with diamonds, which was awarded, of course, to the brother of Mlle de La Vallière. Potlatch? This *course de bague* was followed by a ceremonial entry of musicians led by Lully, to consecrate the locus for the meal to follow. Servants impersonating the Four Seasons brought in the dishes. Among the acolytes of the concelebration were Molière and Madeleine Béjart, disguised as Pan and Diana, whose function it was to address further prayer-like verses to the monarchs. The guests were seated at a huge crescent-moon table, which was dressed in the same circle where the contest had taken place, lit by masked figures—reified servants—holding candelabra, and was totally closed off by a thick hedge of richly costumed officers, who guarded against intrusion (or, alternatively, to prevent escape). Again, the *relation* emphasizes that the abundant lights eclipsed the sun; indeed, the imitation or amplification of the sun and the representation of stellar symbolism were the principal points of these arrangements. After the dinner, the concelebrants enacted a sacramental superstition or ritual by retreating through the *portique* opposite to the one through which they had entered the sacred space.

On the night of May 8, the centerpiece of the festivities was the première performance of Molière's *comédie-ballet La Princesse d'Elide*—an enchanting spectacle ordered, according to the argument, by Alcine to entertain the captured Roger and his knights. Thus, at dusk, the spectators entered a circular space prepared for the performance: the *rondeau des Cygnes* at the very end of the *Allée royale* opposite from the château. Again, this circle was enclosed with a palisade and covered with a fabric dome to protect the numerous *flambeaux* and candles from the wind. As a curtain was drawn in the leafy theatrical space, an orchestra began to play. *La Princesse d'Elide* will be discussed at greater length below, but the artistic form of this production, the *comédie-ballet*, merits some explanation at this point. Upon the disgrace of Fouquet, Louis confiscated not only his former minister's material assets but also, first, his idea of inaugurating his glorious mansion with a splendid feast, second, the services of the same artists and craftsmen who had made Fouquet's feast possible, and third, even the artistic form that was introduced on that occasion: the *comédie-ballet*, of which *Les Fâcheux* had been the first example. Having long been neglected in Molière scholarship and criticism, or else condemned as *bagatelles* and unoriginal circumstantial products, these dramatic hybrids do deserve closer attention (Béhar 321ff).[76] Attempting to fuse poetry (drama), instrumental and vocal music, and choreography in a combination of elements of which the total effect is more significant than that of each individual element, the designers of the *comédie-ballet* tried to link up with a lost tradition: the supposed union of the performance arts of the ancients, which had also set the Florentine Camerata on the road to opera (see chapter 2). Indeed, in his *Avertissement* to the published text of *Les Fâcheux*, Molière specifically draws attention to the antique precedent.[77] An essential feature of the *comédie-ballet* is the alternation of spoken play acts and thematically connected ballet entries (the *intermèdes*) in a continuous performance (Gethner, passim). Thus, the textual program remains very significant—a major difference from later, genuinely "lyrical" opera. Lully wrote all the music for and occasionally also danced or acted in the series of *comédies-ballets* that Molière wrote (following *Les Fâcheux* of 1661) for Louis and the court at Versailles until *Psyché* (1671). To provide such *divertissements* was in fact Molière's primary task. As an employee of the court since Louis had applauded the performance of his farce *Le Docteur Amoureux* in October 1658, Molière's function was to assist Lully in satisfying the king's taste for ballets and music. In the decade or so that Lully and Molière collaborated, the former was always the more important of the two in the eyes of the royal sponsor. After all, Louis had known and protected Lully, who had made it possible for him to express in dance his favorite roles—and perhaps even the essence of his personality—for many years before he met Molière.[78] In brief, what has for long been considered Molière's truly important work—such plays as *Tartuffe*, *Le Misanthrope* or *L'Avare*—constituted at that time an activity in which Molière was allowed to indulge despite occasional opposition.[79] During the 1660s, Molière and Lully were keen on collaborating on the new art form of the *comédie-ballet* after the première of *Les Fâcheux* had proven its validity. They each seemed to welcome the interpenetration of their respective fields, and the symbiosis of theater-play and ballet-musical spectacle. After all, Lully had considerable dramatic talent, and, vice versa, Molière was far from ignorant in matters musical, singing (bass-baritone) and increasingly incorporating music into his plays.[80] As a *comédie-ballet*, *La Princesse d'Elide* was a more balanced hybrid of the three performative arts (comedy-poetry, vocal music, and ballet) than *Les Fâcheux*, with its primary emphasis on ballet, had been.

Let us now examine more closely the second night's entertainment: the première performance of *La Princesse d'Elide*. The plot focusses on a "misandric" and misogamistic princess who is tricked into love and marriage. It was hardly an original story: Molière borrowed it from the translation of a Spanish play by Augustin Moreto (*El Desdén con el Desdén*; *Dédain pour dédain*).[81] This fact has sparked the predictable critical controversy whether Molière's adaptation was an improvement or an impoverishment in dramatic terms of the Spanish play.[82] Molière's main addition to the original was the crucial character Moron (whose role he performed himself): the uncourtly servant who—like similar characters in other Molière plays—parodies his master while yet advancing the latter's cause.

The first *Intermède* is set at dawn. The scene shows a group of four men (*valets de chiens*) asleep on the grass. In the first *entrée*, the allegorical Aurora delivers the *dévis* of the following entertainment: to a young, *aimable*, and attractive girl, there is nothing like being in love; such a person must encourage honest suitors and at all cost avoid the reputation of being a tease, a *cruelle*:

> Dans le temps où l'on est belle,
> Rien n'est si beau que d'aimer. (621)[83]

While this solidly patriarchal message is being delivered, three of the *valets* wake up; when Aurora has done, they try to rouse their colleague Lyciscas (also played by Molière) with a cheerful, teasing song: "pour la chasse ordonnée, il faut préparer tout," "we must prepare everything for the commanded hunt" (621). But the lazy, buffoonish Lyciscas first rails at them and then starts clamoring loudly. Six more *valets de chiens* then dance onto the stage to the music of violins, brass, and hunting horns.

Although Lyciscas and the *valets* are not part of the cast of *La Princesse d'Elide* proper, their preparations for the hunt form a connection both with the previous day's entertainments (that is, a comparable aristocratic competition in the open air, aimed at displaying one's agility to the ladies) and with the main argument of the play to follow. Indeed, *La Princesse d'Elide* forms a *liaison*, a linking element in the context of "Les Plaisirs:" it was performed on the second night of the three-night *Gesamtkunstwerk* and thus served, structurally if not thematically, as a hinge. The general argument of the play is simple. To overcome the "misandry" and misogamy of his daughter (whose role was played by Armande Béjart), Iphitas, Prince of Elide, has invited many young princes of Greece, including these of Ithaque (Euryale), Messène (Aristomène) and Pyle (Théocle) for a hunting party and related courtly entertainments. But this young woman—who remains nameless throughout—proves to be a genuine Diana, who is interested only in the hunt, remains cold toward all suitors, and even equates marriage and death. Thus the first act opens with a courtly discourse between Euryale and his *gouverneur* Arbate; their equally long speeches alternate neatly. Euryale reveals that he loves the proud princess but fears a rejection; Arbate argues that one must reveal one's passion if one wishes to succeed in love. The prince replies that his clever servant, the buffoonish Moron (Molière) will take on that job with the princess. As they are speaking, Moron runs onto the stage, terror-struck by a furious wild boar. An anti-heroic poltroon, he looks for safety with his master and wonders why noblemen insist on searching out such dangerous game instead of chasing harmless little rabbits. He admits that furthering Euryale's cause with the princess was more difficult than expected, because,

> l'office de bouffon a des prérogatives,
> mais souvent on rabat nos libres tentatives.
> Le discours de vos feux est un peu délicat,
> et c'est chez la Princesse une affaire d'Etat. (633)[84]

Then the princess enters with Euryale's two chivalrous rivals, Aristomène and Théocle; both lay claim to having saved her life from the boar. But the princess is angry: she would rather have killed the monster herself, and her suitors have thus harmed their cause instead of furthering it. Hence Euryale's decision to approach this Diana in quite a different way. In the second *intermède*, Moron wanders off by himself into the woods, to reflect on his own unrequited passion for Philis (played by Mlle Béjart), a shepherdess and maid of the princess, who remains as cold to him as her mistress to Moron's master Euryale. He comes across a huge bear, which he tries to appease by petting, "Ah! Monseigneur, que Votre Altesse est jolie et bien faite! . . . Ah! beau poil! belle tête! . . . Ah! beau petit nez! belle petite bouche! petites quenottes jolies! Ah! belle gorge! belles petites menottes! petits ongles bien faits!" (638)[85] But in spite of all this hilarious flattery, he ends up in a tree nevertheless. Eight armed peasants enter, followed by yet another bear; loudly encouraged by the poltroon, the hunters slay one bear, and the second one runs off. Moron descends and joyfully kicks the dead animal while the hunters dance.

The second act begins with the princess singing the praises of "nature"—an obvious reference to the gardens of Versailles with their manicured artifice, the setting of the performance:

> Oui, j'aime à demeurer dans ces paisibles lieux;
> On n'y découvre rien qui n'enchante les yeux,
> Et de tous nos palais la savante structure
> Cède aux simples beautés qu'y forme la nature.
> Des arbres, ces rochers, cette eau, ces gazons frais
> Ont pour moi des appas à ne lasser jamais. (640)[86]

Aglante remarks that one usually comes here to flee the bustle of court and find solitude, but that,

> . . . dans ces jours éclatants,
> Vos retraîtes ici me semblent hors de temps,

> Et c'est fort maltraiter l'appareil magnifique
> Que chaque prince a fait pour la fête publique, (640)[87]

another reference to the festivities of "Les Plaisirs" (although those were hardly "publique"). The "appareil magnifique" refers to the chariot race ("spectacle pompeux") which is being prepared for the three suitors to show off their agility and splendor.[88] Cynthie tries to tell the princess that she should love, because the gods, too, have loved often, at which the princess replies that it is erroneous to attribute human failings to the gods—another loaded reference to the intentional context of "Les Plaisirs." Iphitas again begs his daughter to accept the suitor of her choice, but the princess remains as adamant as before. Yet, to her cousin and confidante Aglante she reveals that Euryale's aloofness has hurt her pride. Indeed, having been advised by Moron to feign utter indifference, Euryale now appears to her the most interesting of the suitors. The wavering princess even decides, against her inclination, to seduce this unusually cold prince. The third *intermède* shows Philis expressing discontent with Moron's ungraceful *caquet*; Moron engages a satyr as a singing master, but this wonderfully operatic scene ends without him having learnt much. Again, the *intermède* concludes with a dance.

When the third act begins, Euryale has already won the chariot race; and although the princess has tried her best to charm him with her skillful singing and dancing, he pretends to remain as impervious as ever to this modern Siren. Moron failing her, she finally talks directly to Euryale—who pretends to care only about his own pleasures; no woman, he claims, will ever charm him—so she should be the one to understand him best. Stung to the quick, the princess confesses to Moron that, should Euryale ever give in to her, she will humiliate him with a show of supreme coldness. In the fourth *Intermède*, Moron surprises his Philis in the company of the great singer and more successful suitor Tircis; he, too, sings for her, but to no avail. Bored with Moron's attempts, Philis suggests that he die for her to prove his love in courtly-chivalric fashion. As the ridiculed Moron gets himself off stage to do so, Philis and Tircis continue to celebrate love in song.

At the beginning of the fourth act, the princess tests Euryale's jealousy by pretending that she loves Aristomène, but to her surprise, Euryale encourages her, pretending that he himself has, after all, fallen in love with Aglante. The jealous princess rushes to her astonished cousin, to whom she admits that she cannot bear seeing Euryale happy with someone else. Then Aristomène enters to claim the princess as his prize, for Euryale had immediately passed on to him what she had said; to the great confusion of the latter, he is sent packing. When Moron asks the princess to admit to herself that she loves Euryale, she chases him away, and, now alone, sadly muses that "j'ai méprisé tous ceux qui m'ont aimée, et j'aimerais le seul qui me méprise," "I have despised all those who loved me, and now I just have to love the one who despises me!" (661). The fifth *Intermède* is very brief; in a duet, Clymène and Philis agree that being in love is the best way of finding out what love is about; they are interrupted by the princess.

In the fifth act, Euryale, in the presence of Moron, Aglante, and Cynthie (another cousin of the princess), asks Iphitas for the hand of his daughter. When the Prince of Elide gladly accepts the Prince of Ithaque as his son-in-law, it appears to the princess, who has entered unexpectedly, that her father has just approved of the union of Euryale and Aglante. She throws herself at his feet, begging him to rule out this wedding, because, so she says, she hates Euryale for having despised her. Iphitas immediately grants her wish, adding that the only way for her to prevent Euryale from marrying Aglante is to wed him herself. When the latter then finally and publicly reveals his true feelings, the confused princess begs for some time to reflect on the strange outcome, and, in fact, her defeat; but it is clear that she will accept Euryale. The princes Aristomène and Théocle are betrothed on the spot to the princesses Aglante and Cynthie. To crown the universal joy, Philis announces that the shepherds will celebrate Venus' many triumphs with dance and song. This spectacle takes place in the sixth *Intermède*, when four shepherds and two shepherdesses summarize the theme of the entertainment in their song:

> Usez, mieux, ô beautés fières,
> Du pouvoir de tout charmer;
> Aimez, aimables bergères;
> Nos coeurs sont faits pour aimer.
> . . .
> Il n'est rien qui ne se rende
> Aux doux charmes de l'Amour. (668–69)[89]

They are soon joined by everybody on the stage in a celebration of the promised cosmic order. During the dance, an artificial tree rises up through the floor of the theater, carrying on its branches eight flute-playing fauns and eight violinists.[90] A hidden orchestra, comprising yet another thirty violins, six harpsichords and theorbos responds. While shepherds and shepherdesses dance, the fauns descend from the tree to join in the grandiose ballet.

The hinge function of *La Princesse d'Elide* is confirmed by the fact that this sixth and last *intermède* of the ballet prepares for the third night of "Les Plaisirs," which was devoted primarily to ballet. On the night of May 9, the spectators assembled near the large Apollo *bassin* situated at the very end of the *Allée royale* and the park. In the middle of this artificial lake, a rocky island constructed by Vigarani accommodated the magic castle of the witch Alcine; smaller rocks on either side provided a perspective arrangement. Once again, the entire scene was brilliantly lit. When the guests had taken their seats, the small islands came alive with the music of brilliantly costumed musicians: violins on the one, trumpets and kettledrums on the other. Alcine, warned in a dream that the Heavens had conspired to liberate Roger and his noble knights from their enforced repose, is determined to prevent this outcome. She appears from behind her castle-rock, seated on a huge sea creature and flanked by two nymphs on whales (*baleines*). The beauties address the Queen Mother with lengthy eulogies and glorify the son Louis through his mother:

> Disons qu'au plus haut point de l'absolu pouvoir,
> Sans faste et sans orgeuil sa grandeur s'est fait voir,
> Qu'aux temps les plus fâcheux sa sagesse constante
> Sans crainte a soutenu l'autorité penchante,
> Et dans le calme heureux, par ses travaux acquis,
> Sans regret la remit dans les mains de son fils;
> Disons par quels respects, par quelle complaisance,
> De ce fils glorieux l'amour la récompense;
> Vantons les longs travaux, vantons les justes lois
> De ce fils reconnu pour le plus grand des rois, (672)[91]

after which they return to the castle to prepare for defense. As the front of Alcine's rock splits open, it reveals her army of four giants and four dwarfs. In the course of the series of entries that constitutes the *Ballet du palais d'Alcine*, the knights do battle with monsters of various kinds but fail to escape, until in the sixth and last entry the good witch Mélisse appears, disguised as Atlas. She manages to slip Angelica's ring, the magic agent which undoes enchantments, on Roger's finger. Thus, the spell is broken, and thunder, lightning, and a gigantic fireworks display contrive to destroy Alcine's castle. As this magic island is reduced to ashes, the three-nights' entertainment comes to a climactic end.

In addition to the (admittedly, flimsy) thematic *liaison* given above, one can discern two other technical connections between the elements of this *Gesamtkunstwerk*. First, the various events were tied together by Lully's music and the numerous performers. Seven famous soloists, a chorus, and at least fifty-two musicians were constantly involved in the event: walking along in the *défilé*, sitting in the *fossé* or in the *machine*-tree, participating on stage, performing during the banquets. Briefly, Lully's musicians were everywhere, hidden or visible, peripatetic or seated, dressed in exotic and costly costumes, playing a wide range of instruments in a great variety of musical modes and forms. Indeed, "Les Plaisirs" was especially an aural experience (Dufourcq 73).[92]

Second, attention should also be drawn to the structural function of the *Allée royale* in this three-nights' entertainment, for it served as an architectural *liaison*, tying the events as well as the palace and its grounds together. In addition to providing a setting, the "royal road" was in a sense also a key protagonist, establishing, procession-wise, a direct spatial connection for the participants in the feast between the extreme ends of a spectrum of pleasure, with Louis' real pleasure palace and Alcine's illusionary pleasure island at opposite ends, and allowing them to return to reality once the witch's spell was broken and her island destroyed.

I have suggested earlier that Alcine's enchanted realm was very much like Versailles itself. The witch tries her best to charm Roger and his knights and detain them with fabulous entertainments, but she must ultimately give way to the superior power of Angelica's ring on Roger's finger. It is therefore also possible to refer to Alcine's island as an early competitor of Versailles, very much, perhaps, like Fouquet's Vaux-le-Vicomte, which is able to detain Louis for a while but which will quickly burst into flame and immolate its creator. Once free, Roger-Louis will leave the ashes of Alcine's pleasure palace behind to lead his knights to another, more realistic world. Indeed, the events related so far were followed by several days and nights of less outlandish and perhaps more cathartic festivities. For example, an important event, on May 12, was the première of the first three acts of *Tartuffe*, which were performed in the vestibule of the small marble courtyard.[93] The shock value of the intruding villain Tartuffe must have been primarily visual: his contemporaneous black robe sharply contrasted with the fantasy costumes that had, for days on end, sustained the illusionary mythistorical world of "Les Plaisirs" (see also Apostolidès 1981: 97). The festivities ended with the première, on Tuesday the 13th, of Molière's *comédie-ballet Le Mariage forcé*.[94] Then, the king commissioned Robert Ballard, the usual printer of such documents, to publish a complete *relation* (as quoted above), with engravings by Israël Silvestre.[95] Besides the full narrative of the events, this *relation* also contained new verses written for the publication by Benserade and others. Another contemporaneous account of the festivities was given by Jacques Charpentier de Marigny, *Relation des divertissements que le Roi a donnés aux Reines dans le parc de Versailles, écrite à un gentilhomme qui est présentement hors de France* (Paris, 1664).

All in all, Louis liked few works by Molière better than *La Princesse d'Elide*. It was performed four times in July at Fontainebleau, when Molière's company stayed there for three weeks. Parisian audiences first saw the play, in a stripped-down version, on November 9, when the controversy over *Tartuffe* was still raging. *La Princesse d'Elide* was given no fewer than twenty-five times at the Palais Royal before the end of the year. And in August 1669, Vigarani staged it four more times at Saint-Germain. It was revived in 1722, probably in February (Oliver 351). *La Princesse d'Elide* was first published separately (that is, out of the context of "Les Plaisirs") in 1734. In 1785, one "V.C.D.V." created a little known version of the play entirely in alexandrines, hoping that this effort to finish Molière's work would revive interest in the play.[96] In spite of the fact that it obviously fulfilled the function of festive entertainment for which it was created (or precisely because of this fact), *La Princesse d'Elide* has received little critical attention. "V.C.D.V."'s effort was futile and doomed from the start, not merely because he committed the fatal error of isolating the play text from its several contexts as a splendid festive performance, but more importantly, because the late eighteenth century—the era of the Encyclopédistes—did not foster the contexts necessary for an appreciation of the splendid private festive performances of the Baroque.

Some discussion has been devoted to the theme of "the outsider" that runs through the play (Gethner). It is, at first sight, an important theme, given the fact that so many courtiers and members of the Sun King's entourage were excluded from attending "Les Plaisirs de l'Ile enchantée" altogether. But why argue, for example, that the *intermèdes* and the main plot are connected because both explore primarily the "dichotomy between spectator/outsider and participant" (Gethner 215)? It is rare to find courtly-theatrical Baroque productions that do not explore or overcome this dichotomy in some way or other. Neither is it very rewarding to examine specific characters of the play as "outsiders" in the physical realm of Elide, for most of them obviously qualify in some way for that designation. Should one wish to pursue this argument of the "outsider," it might be more productive to turn it around and say that instead of "exclusion" (of individuals), these festivities celebrate "inclusion," namely of all possible festive forms, which in its turn necessitates the incorporation of all possible forms of the arts and crafts. The six hundred or so aristocratic guests (passive participants called upon to applaud the Sun King) were no doubt highly representative of their class and status and therefore need little individual attention. By contrast, the concrete execution of "Les Plaisirs" was almost totally in the hands of talented and highly skilled professionals, recruited from the vast labor pool of the realm and representing not only the "fine arts," but also the more mundane crafts, and even trade. Thus, the "outsiders" were first and foremost the members of the court aristocracy, whereas the true "insiders" were, actually, working people. The conceptualization of "Les Plaisirs" mirrored, in a sense, the redistribution of the responsibilities of practical power that had been taking place in France in the course of the seventeenth century.

Perhaps the most interesting approach to the play—besides locating it in its context—is to study first its events or narrative functions and via these, its characters. It has been argued that the play "focusses on the rites of initiation and challenge prevalent in many myths" and that it "follows the general upward movement of numerous fairy tales in which seemingly insoluble problems are overcome" (Alsip 231). This approach via myth respects the context of *La Princesse d'Elide* in "Les Plaisirs de l'Ile enchantée," which was the creation and promotion of a new great myth: that of the creation of the Sun King. It is useful to recall that the Greek country region of Elide (Elis) is traditionally a place for games with a serious purpose, a time-hallowed locus for sacred mythic play, or *agon*.[97] It is therefore in keeping with a cultural tradition that the events taking place in Molière's Elide are rites, necessary elements in a mythic context. Not unlike Barberini Rome during the carnival season, Elide is the place for distinguished foreigners to come together and to engage in the kind of serious play that is associated with rites of passage: an adolescent's development toward adulthood, preparation for leaving one's paternal home, the competition for the hand of a generally desired bride, and so forth—the culmination of such play being the appointment of a new ruler (and spouse). The association of Elide with Versailles (and Louise de la Vallière) is therefore significant.

But it is doubtful whether the titular but anonymous princess is the principal subject of this fairy tale, as has been argued, and whether she has, indeed, by the play's end, grown up, learned to love, and gained an identity (Alsip 227). In the context of the politicized Baroque-courtly attitude toward Eros, the princess, by caving in to Euryale in the fifth act, throws in fact away all chances of ever gaining a personal identity; she never acquires a personal name, and from "princess of Elide" she will merely become (so we are led to assume) "queen of Ithaca." She is not truly clever, for she fails to resist Euryale's *feintes*; unable to imagine that someone else might turn her own ruse against herself, she is defenseless when Euryale does precisely that. Her personal story has always been one of negation, and the promise of marriage to Euryale fails to turn that into a positive. Indeed, one may well argue that the princess merely serves a necessary narrative function in the folk tale of the hero's rite of passage: she is the required object of the quest for a foreign bride that Euryale and his two competitors each have to undertake, the necessary counterforce to be overcome in the *agon* of which the projected outcome is the hero's coming of age as man and ruler. Thus, the nameless princess has not really grown from girl to woman. It is, rather, Euryale who grows from adolescent to adult, from youthful prince to ruler with a duly conquered spouse. He succeeds, first, by means of purely physical skill and strength (for instance, by winning the chariot race), and, more importantly, by a cunning game of sustained role-playing and deliberate *feintes* (recall *El mayor encanto, amor*).

But Euryale is a problematic protagonist because of his intimate connection with his buffoonish, anti-courtly servant Moron. It is suggested that Moron, who serves as a correcting agent to Euryale's personality, is less of a fool than he appears and is perhaps even related to Euryale as the latter's illegitimate half-brother. In the opening scene, Euryale warns Arbate not to underestimate Moron:

> Par son titre de fou tu crois le bien connaître;
> Mais sache qu'il l'est moins qu'il ne le veut paraître,
> Et que, malgré l'emploi qu'il exerce aujourd'hui,
> Il a plus de bon sens que tel qui rit de lui. (630)[98]

And in the next scene, Moron himself reveals to his master that

Ma mère, dans son temps, passait pour assez belle,
Et naturellement n'était pas fort cruelle;
Feu votre père alors, ce prince généreux,
Sur la galanterie était fort dangereux;
Et je sais qu'Elpénor, qu'on appelait mon père
A cause qu'il était le mari de ma mère,
Contait pour grand honneur aux pasteurs d'aujourd'hui
Que le Prince autrefois était venu chez lui,
Et que durant ce temps il avait l'avantage
De se voir salué de tous ceux du village. (634)[99]

Contradicting one another on each issue, but inseparable, they form but a single character, Janus-like, facing opposite sides at once. What matters most is that both eye the courtly value system, and the courtly entertainment values in particular—hunting, parades and races, courtly-chivalric literature, music and dance— from diametrically opposite angles. In the acts of the play proper, the courtly Euryale celebrates these values and achieves whatever he desires; by contrast, in the course of the *intermèdes*, the anti-courtly Moron attempts to deny their importance and consequently achieves nothing for himself. Thus, *La Princesse d'Elide* does far more than reduce "to a harmonious coexistence" "the inherent tensions between the order of the ballet and the disorder of farce, between the stylized world of princes, kings and gods and the commonplaces of 'valets de chiens' and buffoons" (Coe 114). On the contrary, the inherent tensions are strengthened rather than reduced in the course of the performance, where *all* we ever hear or see is order and stylization—including the pseudo-farcical elements, which, after all, are represented by means of ballet and carefully orchestrated music. Although the *intermèdes* may well be *about* farce and disorder, they are themselves every bit as subjected to careful artistic stylization as the acts of the play themselves. Instead of a mere "harmonious coexistence," we can rather speak of a complete victory of the courtly entertainment values—the values of order and stylization—and of festive play over the forces that would deny these values. The former are imaginative and creative, the latter are neither. With Euryale's victory, the Janus-face that shines on festive play carries the day; with Moron's defeat, the Janus-face that would deny such play is reduced, at least temporarily, to closing its eyes.

We do not have to read Louis into the courtly Euryale and the merchant's son Colbert into the anti-courtly Moron—Euryale's level-headed and inseparable other half—in order to allegorically justify the première performance of *La Princesse d'Elide* and "Les Plaisirs de l'Ile enchantée" in their mythistorical context of the creation of Louis as the Sun King and "the god of play." The epideictic rhetoric that "made" Louis XIV into the Sun King from 1663 onward was organized to promote the notion that Louis best furthered the true interests of the State by his judicious equilibrium in the use of force and power. Since France was at peace in 1664 (being engaged only in a few minor conflicts abroad), Louis—also a Janus-figure, uniting in himself the two contradictory but inseparable powers to engage either in martial agon or in festive play—was not only able but in a sense also obliged to rally all the powers at his disposal toward the celebration of the latter. And indeed, in "Les Plaisirs" he offered all the previously existing but separated forms of courtly entertainment in a veritable anthology of pleasures. Thus establishing himself as the only possible purveyor of such wealth, the king commandeered all the riches, all the artists, all the foodstuffs, all the commodities of the kingdom, accumulating all of it within the walls of an artificial setting for the pleasure of dependents who were admitted at his own discretion (potlatch).

Moreover, since the festive events spanned the centuries (antique parade, medieval tournament, contemporaneous ballets and *comédie-ballet*), one can truly say that the resulting *Gesamtkunstwerk* incorporated *everything* known that related to festive activity. It was thus an amplification (in the rhetorical sense) of the very Idea of "the Feast." The fact that this *Gesamtkunstwerk* was, moreover, organized in a rhetorical way—with unifying links between the parts, the part subordinated to the whole—suggests that what mattered most for its total meaning was not the performance of the individual participants, but, in an Aristotelian sense, the unified plot: the combination of manifold forms of festive play in "the Idea" of festive play. In other words, Louis established a precedent for the notion that the Idea of the feast and of festive play *could* actually be realized, but, because of the material resources involved, *only* through the mediation of the State, which was itself by that time, needless to add, embodied in the person of the monarch. Since any further attempt to concretely realize the Idea of festive play would have to incorporate at least the same (but ideally more) expense and material resources as this precedent, none other than the monarch himself could propose such an undertaking. In other words, when "le roi tente donc de s'octroyer le monopole festif" ("when the king attempts to award himself the festive monopoly" Apostolidès 1981: 94–95), he inaugurated himself as the tutellary deity of play. If "Les Plaisirs" constituted an anthology of all arts and all festive forms, the political-allegorical program of the entertainment was, likewise, an anthology of the roles (to be) enacted by the god of play by whom and for whom it was created. On the one hand, Louis was Roger, who performed on the stage as the active incarnation of three essential archetypes of play in the western literary-artistic imagination: chivalric warrior, romantic lover, and white magician. On the other hand, Louis was the Sun King, outblazing the sun with his *flambeaux* and his reified servants, presiding passively over the entertainment.[100]

This last phrase is crucial, if we recall the development of the absolute monarch as "God(dess) of Play" outlined in the Interlude. Indeed, as the ruler-patron becomes the tutellary deity of play, s/he no longer participates actively in the festive play other than by his or her (passive) presence. "Les

Plaisirs" can be considered a significant moment of transition—itself a rite of passage—in this process. The ruler's personal participation signifies his or her self-indulgence in the pleasures of play; as the patronizing deity, however, the ruler must be able to transcend this pleasurable self-indulgence. It makes sense, therefore, to consider Roger—and Louis—a scapegoat of sorts: the hero of all forms of play, he assumes all their pressures so as to free his entourage from them and channel them in a desired direction.[101] As an anthology of licit pleasures, "Les Plaisirs de l'Ile enchantée" offered Louis the chance to live out his playful dreams completely and symbolically, in the starring role of an all-encompassing program crammed full with ludic entertainments. Or, in the famous paradox of Oscar Wilde, "the only way to get rid of a temptation is to yield to it. Resist it, and your soul grows sick with longing for the things it has forbidden to itself, with desire for what its monstrous laws have made monstrous and unlawful."[102] Roger can only be free from the tempations of Alcine and her island of pleasure when he has been given the opportunity to indulge in these pleasures. Once Louis has been allowed to play out his fantasies to the full—of course only by means of extremely carefully orchestrated play, in regulated ludic forms fuelled by established myth and canonized literature—he can, hopefully, get on with enacting his role as the dutiful administrator-king, and, perhaps, as the faithful spouse of the queen whose hand and possessions he had acquired in the course of yet another mythistorical, ritualistic social drama. Since Louis is Janus, his Colbert may temporarily face the other way or close his eyes, but he will never go away. Thus, one is left with a typically Baroque paradox: while everything in the composition and the execution of "Les Plaisirs" seems to strive toward linking things together, the total rhetorical effect is actually one of separation. It is with "Les Plaisirs" that an ultimate separation of play and work by and for the king is projected.[103]

When Louis ceased to dance personally in the court ballets in 1670, that form of courtly entertainment obviously lost, together with its principal participant, its principal function. Having evolved from the role of active ruler-participant in festive play to that of passively observing tutelary deity of grandiose festive play, Louis needed new ceremonial rites for his cult. Not Molière (who died in 1673) but Lully supplied these, when he combined aspects of the *comédie-ballet*—in which music had become the dominant element—and the *ballet de cour*—in which the textual program had become ever more important—in French lyrical opera.[104] Thus began the next and final stage of the grandiose courtly entertainments given at Versailles—until roughly 1682. Preceded by a prologue, each such opera was constructed both like an epic to recount the history of the reign to date, and like a "mass" to celebrate the cult of the absolute monarch (Béhar 324) in the setting of Versailles, which was by now an infinitely more grandiose construct than it had been in 1664.[105] Following the famous breakup between Molière and

Lully in 1670, Philippe Quinault (1635–1688) took over from Molière as Lully's more docile collaborator in the series of entertainments, which were officially called *tragédies en musique* rather than "operas." Together, they achieved what was essentially the transformation of French classical tragedy into French lyric opera, mainly by removing what had formerly been one of the principal French objections against Italian opera: the fact that the text was virtually incomprehensible. Quinault and Lully took the utmost care that their audiences could understand the words.[106] The first of these works was *Les Fêtes de l'Amour et de Bacchus* (1672), which was produced by special order of the king. With this opera, and other ones much like it (*Cadmus et Hermione*, 1673; *Alceste*, 1674; *Thésée*, 1675; *Atys*, 1676; *Isis*, 1677; *Persée*, 1682; *Phaéton*, 1683; etc.), Lully created on the royal stage that now belonged to him alone the mythistorical-heroic celebrations of the victories (real or aspired) of the king. Typically, the pastoral flutes and the violins of the days of the *comédies-ballets* were replaced with martial drums and trumpets.[107] In the early 1680s, just when the mythistory of the Sun King seemed solidly accomplished, the administration that had created it virtually ran out of funds to perpetuate it. Around 1682, Louis' narcissistic megalomania—which continued to manifest itself in Versailles projects (for instance, Charles LeBrun began the famous Hall of Mirrors only in 1679) and, by this time, also in incessant warfare—put an end to much of the artistic and festive activity at the court. Louis even stopped attending performances altogether—perhaps, as has been suggested, under the growing influence of Mme de Maintenon and the *parti dévot*. Thus, one might say that, in France at least, the rites of Louis as "god of play" and as the creator of Versailles, the ultimate "sacred place of play," fizzled out two decades before Louis died.

I have argued earlier that any further attempts to concretely realize the Idea of festive play would have to incorporate at least the same (but ideally more) expense and material resources as this precedent (the *Plaisirs de l'Ile enchantée*), and that Louis wanted to emphasize that none other than the Sun King himself could propose such an anthologizing undertaking and thereby monopolize the rhetorical discourse of play. In the next and final chapter of this study, we will see how thoroughly mistaken Louis was in his belief that no monarch could compete with him in this arena. For barely a few years later, Louis' perpetual rival, the Austrian emperor Leopold, soundly beat Louis at his own game. Let us therefore now turn to Vienna.

Notes

1. See especially Prunières 1913 (re-ed. 1949), whose lengthy criticism can be reduced to the argument that the grandiose festive performance of

Ercole amante was an ill-planned, expensive, and troublesome mistake, and that Louis XIV wisely saw to it that it was not performed many times. See also the bibliographical notes to E. Gros, "Les Origines de la tragédie lyrique et la place des tragédies en machines dans l'évolution du théâtre vers l'opéra," *Revue d'Histoire littéraire de la France* 35 (1928): 161–93. See also Donington 271–80.

2. On the relationship between music, representations and power at the court of Louis XIV, see, in addition to studies mentioned in previous chapters or in the present one: Robert M. Isherwood, *Music in the Service of the King: France in the Seventeenth Century* (Ithaca; London, 1973); Christa Schlumbohm, "De la Magnificence et de la Magnanimité: Zur Verherrlichung Ludwigs XIV. in Literatur und bildender Kunst," *Romanistisches Jahrbuch* 30 (1979) 83–99; and, in addition to his 1981 and 1985 studies already mentioned, also Jean-Marie Apostolidès, *Le Prince sacrifié. Théâtre et politique au temps de Louis XIV* (Paris, 1985).

3. The first grandiose musical-dramatic performance in the Italian style took place in Lyon, at the court of Hippolyte d'Este, Count-Archbishop of Lyon and Cardinal of Ferrara, in September 1548 on the occasion of the visit of King Henri II, Queen Catherine de'Medici, and the royal mistress Diane de Poitiers. The court saw an Italian comedy with musical and choreographic *intermedi*, and with pagan-mythological figures and Neoplatonic emblems, devices and properties. A few decades later, Italian composers and instrumentalists were quite regularly employed at the court in Paris. Among them were the poet Baltazarini, who later changed his name to Beaujoyeux and created the famous and seminal *Balet comique de la Reyne* in 1581, and, since 1604, the musician Caccini, a specialist of the *stile rappresentativo*, who promoted a more natural musical declamation and the subjection of the music to the text (see also Donington 267).

In addition, professional companies of Italian comedians occasionally performed at court, where they introduced the fairly complex musical-dramatic forms (with pastoral, mythological, or allegorical intrigues) which directly preceded Roman-style opera. For example, a company of Italian actors, the Fideli led by Giambattista Andreini, had been in intermittent residence in Paris since 1613; they had been brought there by Marie de'Medici (1573–1642; Donington 273). Still, few Italian opera-singers (this holds true for castrati in particular) performed in France until well into the early seventeenth century, and, likewise, Italian opera proper was not well known in Paris until the 1640s. Nevertheless, the dramatically expressive and mimetic singing techniques of the Italians were known much earlier to French musical theoreticians and singers, who were influenced by them, mostly, probably, via freely circulating manuscript copies of vocal chamber music (Donington 269).

4. In 1634, the Jesuit-educated Mazarin was first appointed vice-legate in Avignon and then nuncio in Paris. By the end of the decade, and against the background of the Franco-Spanish war, Mazarin had become a French citizen. He became a cardinal in 1641, and succeeded Richelieu the following year. Throughout his illustrious career, he remained intensely disliked by most Frenchmen. Putting to work his numerous correspondents in the cities of the Italian peninsula, and using his connections both with aristocratic patrons and with the composers and performing artists whom they sponsored, he tried to establish Italian music in Paris, thus not only satisfying his own taste but also that of Louis XIII, Anne of Austria, and Richelieu, who were all great lovers of music. See also François Moureau, "Les Comédiens italiens et la Cour de France," *Dix-Septième Siècle* 33 (1981): 63–81.

5. While still a Barberini protégé in Rome, Mazarin reportedly performed the part of Saint Ignatius of Loyola in an opera on the life and works of Ignatius and St. Francis Xavier, on the stage of the Jesuit "Collegio romano" (Prunières 1913: 39). This opera was composed by Johannes Hieronymus Kapsberger, who preceded Rospigliosi as the offical Barberini composer; the score is preserved in the Hofbibliothek, Vienna (ms. 16013). Mazarin's education by the Jesuits had included a strong musical component.

6. Mazarin was in the habit of employing musicians and composers both as spies and as diplomatic agents. Following the death of Richelieu in 1642 (whom Mazarin immediately succeeded as chief minister), and that of Louis XIII in 1643, Mazarin had famous Italian composers and performers appear at court to please the Queen Widow (to whom, it was alleged, he was secretly married). Immediately following the official period of mourning, he attempted to bring an entire operatic company to Paris—Anne of Austria, it was well known, loved both comedy and music—a difficult and time-consuming task which involved delicate negotiations on the highest diplomatic levels. In 1644, Pope Urban VIII (Maffeo Barberini) died. In chapter 3, we have seen that the *nipoti* temporarily fled Rome soon after Urban's death. When Mazarin's former patron, Cardinal Antonio Barberini, sought refuge in Paris (January 11, 1646), he brought a good deal of the cultural energy of the Barberini papacy with him, including the taste for Roman opera (Prunières 1913: 43ff). See also Marie-Françoise Christout, "L'Influence vénitienne exercée par les artistes italiens sur les premiers spectacles à machines montés à la cour de France durant la Régence (1645–1650)," in M. T. Muraro, ed., *Venezia e il melodramma nel seicento* (Florence, 1976) 131–43; and Per Bjurström, *Giacomo Torelli and Baroque Stage Design* (Stockholm, 1962).

7. Unlike the more usual *comédies* and *ballets*, this pastoral musical-dramatical spectacle was performed for a very intimate audience (Prunières

1913: 60–62). *Nicandro e Fileno* may thus well have been the first truly private opera-like work to be performed at the French court and to create an appetite for the genre. New Italian professionals were sent for, including singers, choreographers, and a stage designer, Giacomo Torelli, who arrived from Parma in June 1645. Like other foremost *machinistes*, such as Inigo Jones in England and Cosme Lotti in Spain, Torelli was prone to considering the creator of marvellous effects an artist superior to poet and actor.

8. Actually, *Finta Pazza* was not a new work; it had served earlier to inaugurate the "Teatro novissimo" in Venice (1641; Prunières 1913: 77).

9. Both the librettist and the composer were in the service of Cardinal Antonio Barberini. The circumstances leading up to the performance of *Orfeo*, as well as the plot and music of the opera, are described in great detail by Prunières 1913: 86–150. Performances of *Orfeo* continued until May 8, 1647, except during Lent.

10. Partly for patriotic reasons—to showcase French talent—the public Théâtre du Marais revived *Orphée aux Enfers* in 1648. The play dated from 1640 but had been reconstructed in order to accommodate machines that had apparently been imitated from Torelli. It was from this date that the Marais theater began to specialize in spectacle plays and became known as the "Théâtre des Machines." The scenery used for *Orphée aux Enfers* was very expensive by the standards of a public theater, and efforts were made to use it again. Thus Corneille was commissioned to write another play expressly for the same sets: his *Andromède* was first published in 1649, and performed, with the scenes of *Orphée aux Enfers*, in 1650. Written in alexandrines, *Andromède* was perhaps the first real splendid *French* musical-dramatic spectacle; the music, of which very little has survived, was by Dassoucy, a friend of Rossi.

In his 1928 article, Gros, a cultural patriot, traced the history of the *tragédie lyrique* and French opera, arguing that Italian opera (which was generally disliked by the French) was not the only and not even the principal direct influence on French opera. In fact, Gros claimed, such grandiose Italian-style operas as *Orfeo*, *Finta Pazza*, and *Ercole amante* mainly served to remind French writers and composers of their own musical-dramatic heritage; the mid-seventeenth-century artists began to seriously develop the foundation laid by their predecessors in the genres of machine plays, ballets, and spectacular performances that incorporated ballets. By the middle of the century, machines had certainly become more complex and the musical element more important, and court performances of all types in particular became more luxurious and sumptuous. Richelieu, too, says Gros (173) understood the usefulness of spectacle. Thus, the French national dramatic tradition was not simply dependent on Italian models but contained in itself many of the seeds that, from the 1670s on, developed into full-fledged French operas: the so-called *tragédies lyriques* of, especially, Lully and Quinault (see further in this chapter).

11. On the ballets, see Claude-François Menestrier, *Des Ballets anciens et modernes selon les règles du Théâtre* (1682; Genève, 1972); Henri Prunières, *Le Ballet de cour en France avant Benserade et Lulli* (Paris, 1914); Marie-Françoise Christout, *Le ballet de cour de Louis XIV, 1643–1672* (Paris, 1967); and Allan Boase, "Leçons sur le ballet de cour," *Neohelicon* 7 (1979): 61–144. On other theatrical forms, including machine plays and spectacles, see Menestrier, *Des Représentations en musique anciennes et modernes* (1681; Genève, 1972); M. Horn-Monval, "La grande machinerie théâtrale et ses origines," *Revue d'Histoire du Théâtre* 9 (4) 1957: 291–308; Walter G. J. Langlois, "The Evolution of Scenic Spectacles in France (1600–1673): National and Italian Origins of the Machine Play," diss., Yale U (1955); Francis Bondino, *Présentation des pièces à machines au XVIIe siècle* (Paris, 1971), which I have not seen; and Pierre Béhar, "Rolle und Entwicklung des Theaters am Hofe Ludwigs XIV.," in August Buck, et al., eds., 2: 319–27.

12. French composers had begun to prepare the French genre of the *mélodrames*, building on the foundation of the machine plays and musical pastorals (see Prunières 1913: 212). For example, in 1658 Molière founded the Théâtre du Petit-Bourbon, the ancestor of the Comédie française. (Yet, a crew of workmen started demolishing the theater of the Petit Bourbon, in which Molière's company was actually rehearsing, on October 11, 1660. When Molière complained, the company was allowed to use the theater of the Palais royal instead.)

13. Already in the summer of 1659, Mazarin was concerned about the locus for the grandiose performance; he did not consider any existing hall or theater space at court vast or impressive enough to stage the spectacle appropriately. The libretto, on the one hand, and the construction of theater and machines, on the other, were, together, his first priority.

14. Among the many reasons why French audiences supposedly disliked Italian opera, Gros mentions, besides the ever-active anti-Italian *cabale*: religious objections to the "pagan" subjects, the Italian language, which many did not (or were unwilling to) understand, the extravagant length of the representations, the confusing intrigues, the lack of verisimilitude and psychological "truth," the uncomfortable mixture of the comic and the tragic, and the dubious taste of some comic elements (176–77). Though this is not the way Gros phrases it, one might conclude that, briefly, Italian opera was condemned because it was so unlike French neoclassical tragedy.

15. Gaspare Vigarani was then seventy-one years old! He had to his credit the Teatro Ducale in Modena, which could seat close to three thousand

spectators (1654). He arrived in Paris in the summer of 1659 with his sons Lodovico and Carlo; he profited from the fact that Torelli, resident architect and creator of the *Orfeo*, had become a victim of political intrigue. As a supporter of Fouquet, the great Torelli was (already) disliked by Colbert and Buti; following Fouquet's disgrace and imprisonment, he would even be ordered to leave France. Immediately upon their arrival, the Vigaranis began working on the building and on the machines. Their correspondence shows that they had the latter planned in detail as early as October 10, 1659, although neither the libretto nor the music was finished by that time (see a letter reprinted in Prunières 1913: 218). Very optimistic, or simply devious, they repeatedly gave out totally impossible deadlines for the completion of the theater. See also Gabriel Rouchès, *Inventaire des lettres et papiers manuscrits de Gaspare, Carlo et Lodovico Vigarani, 1634–1688* (Paris, 1913).

16. The principal distinguishing features of this theater (besides the secret corridors, and the royal dressing rooms) were its size and its ornate decorations. Consequently, the acoustics were immediately found to be abominable; moreover, few of the several thousand spectators had a really good view of the stage. After the series of performances of *Ercole amante*, the Salle des Machines was probably not used again until 1668, when Molière's *Amphytrion* was performed there. Although de Pure's contemporaneous description of the Salle des Machines is very interesting, his observation that the theater was much admired may not be entirely truthful (311–17). His description of the theater concludes the last chapter of the book, which is mainly devoted to the ballet. Did de Pure then, too, think of *Ercole amante* in the first place as a ballet? I have not been able to see Albert Babeau, "Le Théâtre des Tuileries sous Louis XIV, Louis XV, et Louis XVI," *Bulletin de la Société de l'Histoire de Paris et de l'Ile de France* (22) 1896, nor his *Le Jardin des Tuileries au XVIIe et au XVIIIe siècle* (Paris, 1902).

17. Cavalli, student and successor of Monteverdi, was the towering figure in Venetian musical circles and the principal composer of Venice's specialty: public opera. Cavalli acquired fame as singer, composer of sacred music, and organist. He became the first organist of San Marco's, and in 1668, he was promoted to the post of *maestro di capella* of that cathedral. His master Monteverdi had occupied this office—arguably the most important musical post in Italy—before him. But Cavalli especially gathered fame as the foremost Italian opera composer. Venice played a key role in the rise of opera as a cultural phenomenon. For Venetian opera houses were public, and the performances drew widely varied audiences. By contrast, in Florence—the birthplace of opera—performances had characteristically remained restricted to the private-aristocratic sphere.

It was in Venice that opera became first "popular" in the common meaning of the term; from Venice the art first spread to Naples, where a special school was established, and then all over Europe. Soon, many Italian composers and musicians as well as entire companies were touring the Continent, or had relatively fixed appointments at various courts. The tremendous influence of these Italian composers, musicians, singers, dancers, choreographers and engineers on musical and musico-dramatic theory and practice throughout the seventeenth century has been amply documented by historians of opera. And as I have shown, the Italians, and their operas in particular, were originally well received at the French court. Cavalli had been working for the San Cassiano theater (the first public opera house anywhere) from 1639 onward; over a period of thirty years, he composed no fewer than thirty-two operas to be performed there. These operas, but also his other work (sacred music in particular) and his proficiency as an organist, assured his fame abroad. One solid reason for his success was the fact that the quality of his work was matched by the intensity, speed and efficiency with which it was delivered. See further Jane Glover, *Cavalli* (New York, 1978); and Bruno Brunelli, "L'impresario in angustie," *Rivista italiana del dramma* 19 (1941): 311–41.

18. For example, the composer was hardly impressed with the suggested remuneration, especially because of the strict terms of his contract with the San Cassiano theater (Prunières 1913: 227): during his absence from Venice, San Cassiano would almost forcibly have to remain closed, in which case Cavalli would personally be held responsible for lost profits. See also Gordon F. Crain, "Francesco Cavalli and the Venetian Opera," *Opera* June, 28 1967: 446–51.

19. Born Giambattista Lullio, Jean-Baptiste Lully (1633–1687) worked diligently to rid himself of the stigma that the public mind eagerly attached to Italian musical professionals. He entered the service of Louis XIV in 1653, as composer of instrumental ballet music and chamber music (*intendant de la musique instrumentale*), although on occasion he also composed vocal music in the fluid, smooth Italian manner, suitable both for Italian and French texts. He was considered to excel in both styles, and, though practising mainly the Italian style, he made many concessions to the French. An example of the conscious rivalry of the two styles is provided by the musical duel between Italian and French music in the *intermède* between the sixth and the seventh entries in Lully's *Balet de la Raillerie*, which was performed at the 1659 Carnival (Prunières 1913: 208). In 1661, Lully was promoted to *Surintendant*. Almost a century later, Yves-Joseph La Motte (1680–1730), who used the pseudonym "Monsieur de la Hode" to chronicle the life and reign of Louis XIV in six fascinating volumes, still remarked that Lully "a passé & passera longtems pour le prémier homme du monde dans son Art" ("has since long been considered the best man in his Art in the world, and will remain so for

a long time to come;" *Histoire de la vie et du règne de Louis XIV, Roi de France et de Navarre* [Frankfurt; Basel, 1741], 3: 13).

In 1653, Louis danced the role of the "Soleil levant" in Lully's *Balet de la Nuit*. Two years later, Louis was already passionately in love with Marie Mancini (see further); Lully made it possible for the king to act out his passion in public by having him dance and play a guitar serenade under the window of an Italian *belle* (a proxy for Marie Mancini, one might say) in the *Balet de la Galanterie du Temps*.

20. In fact, the importance of the dance to Louis can hardly be exaggerated, and the ballets furnish an invaluable key to an understanding of the regency as well as to the early period of the reign. It has even been written that Louis "n'a eu jusqu'à vingt ans pour unique plaisir, unique occasion de paraître, de se sentir valoir et de se faire valoir, que la musique et la danse. Lully à cette époque fut le seul homme qui fît faire au Roi ce qu'il aimait vraiment et qui lui donnât, non seulement du plaisir, mais le plaisir beaucoup plus grand d'être content de soi. Lully est l'homme qui a eu le génie de faire danser Louis XIV son propre mythe; qui lui a sans cesse renvoyé, dans un miroir musical, sa propre image, ou plutôt l'image qu'il voulait avoir de lui-même, et voulait renvoyer à la face du royaume et à la face du monde" ("Until his twentieth year, [Louis] knew no other pleasure than music and dance, and had no other occasion to show himself, to feel self-worth and have the esteem of others. During this time, Lully was the only person who gave the King the chance to do what he really liked to do and who gave him not only simple pleasure, but the much greater pleasure of being proud of himself. Lully was the genius who had the vision of letting Louis XIV dance his own myth; who constantly let him see, in a musical mirror, his own image—or rather, the image of himself that he wanted to have and that he wanted to project onto the kingdom and onto the world"; Philippe Beaussant, *Versailles, Opéra* [Paris, 1981] 101). Lully became even more indispensable to Louis (certainly more so than Molière ever was) in the early phase of the personal rule.

21. It is from this date onward that Lully "invented" French grand opera (*tragédie lyrique*) as the substitute festive vehicle to celebrate the cult of the now passive Sun King as the deity of play.

22. The queens must genuinely have feared that a catastrophe was likely to happen in the Salle des Machines, since they expressly had an iron, fireproof gallery installed to ensure a quick exit. Due to the delays, the royal wedding was celebrated on November 22,1660, with the performance of *Xerse*, a widely known opera of Cavalli's (on a libretto by Minato, 1654) in the Galerie des Peintures in the Louvre palace. It was produced with ballets by Lully inserted between the acts. Though it had been a tremendous success in the Italian cities, *Xerse* was apparently not very well received in Paris.

23. Vigarani's original *coup de théâtre* called for an apotheosis of the royal family by means of a huge flying machine; understandably, the design and testing of this contraption was a matter of intense concern and scrutiny.

24. *Ercole amante* was then promised for the carnival season of 1661. In the meantime, another spectacle was mounted in the Louvre to satisfy the impatient public, the aptly called *Ballet de L'Impatience*, by Lully and Benserade (February 19, 1661). And then Mazarin died (March 9, 1661), involuntarily causing another delay to the realization of what had become less a pet project than an obsession.

25. From a letter, dated February 14, 1662 by the Venetian ambassador (mentioned in Prunières 1913: 282 n. 1).

26. *Ercole amante*, by Francesco Buti. Bilingual ed., textsheet of record Musical Heritage Society Stereo 834719A. Introductory essays by Jean-Louis Martinoty. All quotations refer to this edition. The ms. of *Ercole amante*, together with those of twenty-six other operas of Cavalli, is preserved in the Biblioteca Marciana, Venice.

27. An early reference to Versailles, just outside of Paris?

28. "No such hard rock,/ no such frigid monster/ that inhabits the sea/ that, when loved, it must not equally love."

29. A palace of enchantment crafted by Hephaistos-Vulcan; compare Ovid's Palace of the Sun (*Metamorphoses*, I–II), and certainly Marino's Palace of Venus (*L'Adone*, VIII).

30. "Never has Love stirred up/ a more burning passion/ than that with which/ he has smitten our two hearts."

31. In the complex web of Hercules myths, Dejanira was his second wife. In a fit of madness provoked by Hera, he had killed his first wife, Megara of Thebes, as well as their children. Having purified himself of that crime (in one version of the myth, by performing the twelve labors imposed upon him by Eurystheus, king of Tiryns), he married Dejanira, daughter of Oeneus of Calydon, whom he won from the river-god Achelous in a wrestling match. As the newlyweds tried to cross a flooded river, the centaur Nessus abducted Dejanira and tried to rape her, but Hercules shot him with a poisoned arrow; before he died, Nessus tricked Dejanira into preserving some of his blood on a shirt. She believed the centaur's promise that it would help her to win back Hercules' love should she ever lose it.

Paul Fréart de Chantelou, prominent courtier of Louis XIV, owned a painting by Poussin entitled "Hercules carrying off Dejanira;" now apparently lost, this painting was admired by Bernini during his sojourn in France in 1665 (John Rupert Martin, *Baroque* [New York, 1977] 277).

32. "But what now?/ I feel how within my heart are suddenly surging/ strong, involuntary feelings for you."

33. Such drastic scene changes at the end of an act were fairly unusual.

34. "Alcides did not die./ Prepare the torches./ He did not die, no no!/ He is now smiling in heaven,/ because the King of the gods/ has married him/ to beauty."

35. "And so an even more delightful day will come,/on which, on the noble bank of the Seine,/ the next Gallic Hercules, aflame with passion,/ Will in peace enjoy an Iberian beauty."

36. The scene distribution of the principal characters is interesting. Hercules occurs in no fewer than twelve scenes (he sleeps through one of these), but he is absent from the entire second act. His wife Dejanira only has seven scenes, whereas Licco, her servant and the obligatory buffoonish character, has as many as nine. Hyllo, son of Hercules and Dejanira, appears in more scenes than any other character, that is, thirteen. His beloved, Princess Iole, whom Hercules lusts for, has twelve scenes—the same number as Hercules himself; yet she first appears in the second act, when Hercules is absent (an act which she clearly dominates), and she does not have a single duet with Hercules. Among the goddesses, Juno, goddess of legitimate married love and morality, manifestly outweighs Venus, with six scenes over Venus' two. Among the other divinities, Mercury, Neptune, and Cynthia-Diana (Prologue) appear in only one scene. Iole's page has eight scenes.

37. During his stay in Paris (1665), Bernini, a highly qualified observer, criticized the auditorium as acoustically deficient (Prunières 1913: 302). See Cecil Gould, *Bernini in France: An Episode in Seventeenth-Century History* (Princeton, 1982).

38. Apparently, Louis had ordered Henri de Gissey to draw the decors and have them engraved, but for unknown reasons, this order was not carried out. See Jacques Vanuxem, "La Scénographie des fêtes de Louis XIV auxquelles Molière a participé," *Dix-Septième Siècle* 98–99 (1973): 77–89, 78–79.

39. Prunières seems to forget that it was not so much Buti as Mazarin himself who had designed the program for the opera and who had asked Buti, then his secretary, to write it out. Some of Prunières' arguments are seriously flawed—such as his claim that the audience did not understand the text. Courtiers had many occasions to attend rehearsals (especially if they participated in the performance) and bilingual libretti were distributed. Moreover, the dramatic quality of Buti's text should not be underestimated. Buti's Licco is obviously a direct ancestor of Lorenzo da Ponte's legendary Leporello. In other interesting scenes as well (such as the scene in which the cemetery

statues come to life) and details of characterization, Buti's libretto clearly anticipates da Ponte's libretto for Mozart's *Don Giovanni* (premièred in Prague, 1787).

40. From a musicological standpoint, *Ercole amante* is indeed an impressive work. The opera has no fewer than eighteen singing parts—though some singers took double roles—and no fewer than eight choruses. Cavalli followed Buti's text closely, emphasizing the required musical variety throughout the entire opera. In terms of aural rhetoric, for example, the fifth act presents a magnificent apotheosis of the characters, the royal actors and the audience, with its astonishing palette of ensembles: the composer introduced, in rapid succession: a quartet, a trio, a duet, then a quintet, a double chorus, another duet, and, to top it all, an eight-part chorus. One of the Baroque hallmarks of *Ercole amante* is precisely its great variety of choruses (though they probably featured the same group of singers). It has been noted that Cavalli, who had abandoned large-scale choruses in the 1650s as being too costly for the Venetian public opera, quite clearly felt like splurging on them now that financial considerations were irrelevant. See also Prunières, *Cavalli et l'opéra vénitien au XVIIe siècle* (Paris, 1931). For a further musicological analysis of the opera, see Kretzschmar 53–59.

41. Prunières' irritation at the apparent lack of interest in Cavalli's ingenious music for its own sake reflects his post-Romantic conviction that the composer is the opera's principal creator. This is of course incorrect; we have seen that Mazarin was concerned first of all with the music and the theatrical locus, that Buti had finished his libretto and that the construction of the building and the machines were well under way before Cavalli even arrived in Paris.

42. For instance, Mme de Lafayette in *Histoire de Madame Henriette d'Angleterre* (quoted in Prunières 1913: 301). Regarding Henriette: Louis XIV married his brother, the Duke of Orléans, to this English princess, the sister of Charles II (March 31, 1661). Monsieur de la Hode, commenting on the dowry that Charles provided for his sister, sneers that Mazarin had given practically three times that amount to his nieces upon their marriages (3: 9).

43. Indeed, *Ercole amante* has been called a culminating point in the development of the French *opéra en machines*. Of the ten vast, costly sets, the most impressive were strategically placed toward the end: the storm at sea, the view of Hades (probably complete with flames), and the cemetery scene. In fact, these sets offered the usual stock scenes of opera at the time, only they were probably bigger than any used before. The same sets were to be used again for the production of *Psyché* (by Molière, Corneille, and Quinault; produced 1671), a work which may have been written specifically to use these

expensive sets again. Racine wrote his *Orpheus* to compete with *Psyché*, but Molière's play was chosen. Interestingly enough, it was via Shadwell's *Psyche* (1675), an adaptation of Molière's play, that the sets (in an adulterated version) reached the English Restoration stage.

44. For example, Prunières seems hardly aware that the relative success of an opera that was specifically produced for a splendid festive performance at a Baroque court cannot really be determined on the basis of its commercial success or the number of its performances. So what if *Ercole amante* was not performed often? The exclusivity of the private grandiose performance was precisely one of its principal and most attractive characteristics.

45. Setting aside modern standards of decorum, we must accept that seventeenth-century courtly convention apparently did not consider it problematic to celebrate a joyous occasion with a tragic performance. After all, had not Aristotle himself argued that a tragedy can give pleasure? "A work of imitation [*mimoumenon*], such as painting, sculpture, poetry, and all that is well imitated [is pleasant], even if the object of imitation is not pleasant; for it is not this that causes pleasure or the reverse, but the inference that the imitation and the object imitated are identical, so that the result is that we learn something" (from *"Art" of Rhetoric* I.xi: 23–24).

46. In fact, it was partly because the analogue Hercules-Louis had become so commonplace that the king was gradually associated with the Sun and with Alexander the Great. On the long-standing association of Hercules-Louis, see also Strong 1973: 24ff.

47. Bakhtin mentions Hercules as the subject of much popular comedy and parody; see *The Dialogic Imagination* 54–55.

48. The *loci classici* of the Hercules mythology are found in Greek, Latin, medieval, and Renaissance literature. Among the most significant texts and references are: Hesiod's *Theogony*; Homer's *Iliad* and *Odyssey*; the Homeric Hymn 15; Pindar's Odes 1, 3 (Olympian), 4 (Isthmian), 9, and 10; Sophocles' *Trachiniae*; Euripides' *Alcestis* and *Heracles*; Aristophanes' *Frogs*; Xenophon's *Memorabilia*; Aristotle's *Poetics*; Theocritus' Idyll 25; Pausanias' *Description of Greece*; Athenaeus' *Deipnosophistae* 38–39; Virgil's *Aeneid* 8 and *Eclogue* 6; Ovid's *Heroides*, *Metamorphoses*, and *Amores*; Plutarch's *Parallel Lives of Noble Grecians and Romans*; Horace's *Odes*; Juvenal's Satires; Seneca's *Hercules Furens*; Herodotus' *History* 2; and further references by Dante and Ariosto.

49. By the middle of the seventeenth century, the aristocratic and upper-middle class readers of French epic-historical *romans de longue haleine*, who also largely made up the audiences of grandiose performances, would expect nothing else. The majority among the audience wanted, first of all, a great spectacle, and secondly, an entertaining guessing game. See also Barbara Ives

Beyer, "Baroque Representation," *Journal of Aesthetics and Art Criticism* 12 (3) 1954: 360–65.

50. The myth that the French royal house descended from the early kings of Rome was propagated by a genealogical prologue which was written by Camille Lilius and duly reprinted in the libretto of *Ercole amante*.

51. See Francois Régis Chantelauze, *Louis XIV et Marie Mancini, d'après de nouveaux documents* (Paris: Librairie académique, 1880).

52. The arrangement of this dynastic union will be discussed in greater detail in the next chapter.

53. See for example, Henri Vast, *Les grands Traîtés du Règne de Louis XIV* (Paris, 1899), vol. 1. Of course, history itself would soon disprove the validity of such teleological and limited viewpoints. For it is characteristic that the grand reconciliation of the one-time foes harbors in itself the seeds of a new social breach and a new series of conflicts. Partly because Maria Theresa's dowry of half a million gold crowns remained unpaid, Louis had an excuse to invade the Spanish Netherlands so as to make up for it, which brought about the so-called "War of Devolution" (1667–1668). Thus, like its predecessor, this complex social drama, too, must be seen in a political context.

54. See Alfred F. Pribram, "Die Heirat Kaiser Leopold I. mit Margaretha Theresia von Spanien," *Archiv für Österreichische Geschichte* 77 (1891): 319–75, 322ff. See also further in chapter 6.

55. "En exécution des dernières volontés du Cardinal [Mazarin], Marie Mancini sa nièce fût mariée avec le Connêtable Colonne. Loüis quatorze lui fit des présens magnifiques; mais il la vit partir sans émotion, & parut ne plus se souvenir de la passion violente qu'il avoit euë pour elle. Cette personne partit fort mécontente de tout le monde; du Cardinal, qui ne lui laissoit que cinq ou six cent mille écus, & qui l'avoit déshéritée, disoit-elle, pour laisser son bien à un étranger; de ses soeurs, qu'elle méprisoit & haïssoit; de Colbert, qu'elle n'avoit jamais pû souffrir; de la Reine-mère, qui s'étoit opposée à ses folles & ambitieuses prétentions; enfin du Roi, qui la laissoit partir sans se soucier d'elle" ("According to the last wishes of the cardinal, his niece Marie Mancini was married off to Commander Colonna. Louis XIV gave her magnificent presents; but he saw her depart without emotion and seemed not to remember the violent passion that he had once felt for her. That little lady left quite displeased with everybody: with the cardinal, who had only willed five or six thousand écus to her and who had disinherited her, so she said, to leave his possessions to a foreigner; with her sisters, whom she despised and hated; with Colbert, whom she could never suffer in the first place; with the Queen Mother, who had put herself squarely against her crazy and ambitious

pretensions; and finally, with the King, who let her go without caring in the least for her" de la Hode, 3: 6).

Thus, Marie Mancini was married off to Commander Colonna (on April 11, 1661) and she moved to Rome.

56. The story of the opera had an interesting, indirect afterlife (illustrating also very well the circular nature of its dynastic context), since Fénelon included it in *Télémaque* (1694), a book written for the Dauphin. The Abbé thus recycled the gruesome story that had served to celebrate the wedding of the parents for the moral education of their son.

57. In 1661, Louis XIV supposedly declared that "il ne pouvoit approuver la vie des Rois fainéans. Il ajoutoit, qu'on pouvoit lui reprocher d'avoir fait lui-même ce qu'il condamnoit; mais il attribüoit sa conduite passée à l'estime qu'il avoit euë pour l'habileté du Cardinal [Mazarin], & à la dépendance à laquelle son enfance l'avoit accoûtumé" ("he could not approve the way of life of idle kings. He added that one might well reproach him as having been guilty himself of what he condemned now; but he attributed his past conduct to the esteem he had had for the skills of the cardinal and to the dependence to which his youth had accustomed him" de la Hode, 3: 1–2).

58. In this period, the young Spanish queen "pleuroit continuëllement, dans la crainte que ces divisions n'achevassent de lui enlever le coeur de son Epoux" ("wept ceaselessly, fearing that all these ruptures might eventually cause her Spouse to cease loving her" de la Hode, 3: 26).

59. See Claude Abraham, *On the Structure of Molière's Comédies-Ballets* (Paris; Seattle; Tübingen, 1984), chapter 1; see also Beaussant 18ff. The most significant artistic component of *Les Fâcheux* was dance; the (instrumental) music was of secondary importance, and the only function of the play (poetry) was to hold everything somehow together. It was Molière's first *comédie-ballet*, and his last one without any vocal music; the title can be translated as "The Blocking Characters."

60. See Perry Gethner, "Comedy-Ballet and Court Festivities: Three Extreme Scenarios," *Cahiers du Dix-Septième* (3) 1989: 207–23 for a reading of *Les Fâcheux* as a petition to *and* a triumph of the monarch. See also Beaussant 41.

61. In spite of his obvious sympathy for the unhappy queen, de la Hode tactically considered that "[s]i jamais il y a eu un vrai amour, c'étoit celui dont elle [Mlle de la Vallière] brûloit pour son Amant" ("if ever there has been true love, then it was that which set [Mlle de la Vallière] aflame for her Lover" 3: 14).

62. The Dauphin was born November 1, 1661; the birth almost cost

Maria Theresa her life. Hardly ten months later, in August 1662, the queen gave birth again, to a daughter, who only lived a few months.

63. Monsieur de la Hode piously remarks that, in attaching himself to de "aimable" la Vallière, Louis, "amant respectueux & timide," committed "sans doute un crime, marié comme il étoit à une aimable Princesse, dont il étoit adoré, & que peut-être il eût aimée si elle n'eût pas été son Epouse" ("was doubtlessly guilty of a crime, considering that he was married to a lovable Princess, who adored him and whom perhaps he could have loved in return, if only she had not been his Spouse" 3: 15).

64. In 1661, "la jeune Reine étoit belle, vertueuse & remplie de piété," says de la Hode who sympathizes with her throughout his chronicle ("the young Queen was beautiful, virtuous, and pious to the core" 3: 12).

65. Compare Nicole Ferrier-Caverivière, "Le siècle de Louis XIV et le problème du pouvoir: témoignages littéraires," *Travaux de Linguistique et de Littérature* 23 (1985): 45–57, 53ff.

66. Indeed, for Louis XIV, festivities were part and parcel of the rule. He had been trained to think that way; for example, in his *Discours des Divertissements, Inclinations, & Perfections Royales* (Paris, 1644), a heroic-galant and pedagogical novel specifically written to educate the young Louis for his future role as absolute ruler, Potier de Morais mentioned that the same skills are needed to construct and sponsor a grandiose feast as to conduct an army in the field. See Volker Kapp, "Die Beschreibung des idealen Königs aus der Sicht höfischer Gesittung im 'Discours' von Potier de Motais (1644)," in August Buck, et al., eds., 2: 235–38, 237.

67. "La jeunesse, le pouvoir suprême & la modération dans les plaisirs sont presqu'incompatibles. Les passions s'y mêlent & ne manquent point d'y répandre l'amertume. Peu à peu, non content des plaisirs du jour, les repas & les promenades dans les bois jusqu'à deux ou trois heures après minuit, commencèrent à s'introduire & à se pratiquer d'une manière, qui avoit un air plus que galant, & dont la volupté paroissoit être le principe." Perceiving Louis' tendencies, "la Reine, uniquement attachée au Roi, fût dans de continuëlles inquiétudes. La Reine mère, sans entrer tout-à-fait dans ses sentimens, parla, fit des remonstrances; on ne se rendit point, & les divertissemens continüèrent de la même force" ("Youth, supreme power, and moderation in pleasure are virtually incompatible. Then the passions start to play a role, too, and do not fail to add some bitterness. Bit by bit, the pleasures by day[light] do not suffice anymore, dinners and outings in the woods until two or three A.M. begin to become customary, even in a manner that is more than just gallant and of which voluptuousness seems to be the ruling principle. . . . The Queen, attached only to the King, suffered in continual anxiety.

The Queen Mother, without entering totally into his state of mind, talked to him, protested [faintly]; but nothing happened, and the entertainments continued on the same scale" 3: 13). Interestingly enough, although de la Hode says that Louis surrounded himself continually with entertainments, he does not once refer specifically to *Ercole amante*.

68. The *carrousel* was described extensively by Charles Perrault (with engravings by Silvestre and Chauveau, colored by Bailly, all eminent specialists of this kind of subject); the unique copy is in the Versailles library. See also de la Hode 3: 37–38, and, at length, Moine 24ff. Its near-operatic features included the grandiose music and the exuberant costumes; contrary to custom, no heavily allegorical chariots or machines were employed. Just as for the 1660 Entry, program brochures were made available a week in advance.

69. See also André Félibien, *Description sommaire du château de Versailles* (1673), as discussed by Marin 1988: 180–92.

70. "this far-off wasteland, on the embellishment of which they had already begun to spend prodigious sums and continued to do so. There, more freely, and excited by the beauty of the season, numerous gallant Feasts were organized that caused quite some chagrin."

71. In his report of the year 1663, de la Hode notes that Louis never really intended to hide his passion for la Vallière, in spite of the reproaches and chagrin of the two queens. Following a plot orchestrated most likely by the latter, Louis' mistress was sent—with supreme irony—to a "retreat" in the Convent of the Visitation, but Louis immediately had her brought back to Paris, where he installed her in a richly equipped *Hôtel* (3: 117).

72. *La Princesse* has been called such by Barbara W. Alsip, "Myth and Fairy Tale in Molière's *La Princesse d'Elide*," *Papers on French Seventeenth-Century Literature* 18 (1983): 221–32, 221.

73. Title given *Oeuvres complètes de Molière* ([S.l.]: Imprimerie Nationale de France, [1947?]) 4: 133. For the complete texts, see Jean-Baptiste Molière, "Les Plaisirs de l'Ile enchantée" [incl. *La Princesse d'Elide*], in *Oeuvres Complètes*, ed. Maurice Rat, vol. 1 Bibliothèque de la Pléiade 8 (Paris, 1962) 601–78. 2 vols. All quotations refer to this edition.

74. Published in 1516; trans. as *Le divin Arioste ou Roland le Furieux* by F. de Rosset (Paris: de Sommonville & Courbé, 1643–44).

75. See, for example, Pierre de Nolhac, "Les premières fêtes de Versailles," *Revue de Paris* 15 April 1899: 841–58.

76. For serious attempts in this direction, see Lila Maurice-Amour, "Rythme dans les comédies-ballets de Molière," *Revue d'Histoire du Théâtre* 26

(1974): 118–30; Ada Coe, " 'Ballet en comédie' or 'comédie en ballet'? *La Princesse d'Elide* et *Les Amants magnifiques*," *Cahiers du Dix-Septième* 2 (1988): 109–21; and Charles Mazouer, "Il faut jouer: Les intermèdes des comédies ballets de Molière," *Dix-Septième Siècle* 165 (1989): 375–81.

77. Georges Mongrédien, "Molière et Lulli," *Dix-Septième Siècle* 98–99 (1973): 3–15, 5.

78. In 1661, the same year Lully met Molière at Vaux-le-Vicomte, he was naturalized and appointed "Surintendant de la Musique." When he married in 1662, Louis himself signed the contract (see Mongrédien 4–5).

79. A. Richard Oliver, "Molière's Contribution to the Lyric Stage," *Musical Quarterly* 33 (1947): 350–64, 359.

80. See Norbert Dufourcq, "Les Fêtes de Versailles: La musique," *Dix-Septième Siècle* 98–99 (1973): 67–75.

81. On Moreto's play, see Mabel M. Harlan's study (which I have not seen), *The Relation of Moreto's "El Desdén con el Desdén" to Suggested Sources* (Bloomington, 1924).

82. Lawrence 108ff argues that Molière improved upon the Spanish model.

83. "In the season when one is beautiful,/ Nothing is so beautiful as to be in love."

84. "The office of fool has its prerogatives,/ but our free attempts are often curtailed./ The argument of your passion is a bit delicate,/ and for the Princess it is a State affair."

85. "Ah, Milord, how beautiful, how well turned out your Highness is! . . . Ah! nice coat! pretty head! . . . Ah! nice little nose! pretty little mouth! those cute little teeth! Ah! pretty throat! pretty tiny little hands! pretty nails, ah, how well manicured!"

86. "Yes, I love to dwell in these peaceful surroundings;/ nothing can be found here that does not delight one's eyes,/ and the complex structures of any of our palaces,/ must give way to the simple beauties that nature has created here./ These trees, these rocks, this water, these fresh lawns/ I find so charming, I'll never tire of them."

87. "while such splendor is staged these days,/ it seems that you're retreating here at the wrong moment,/ and it is not right to disdain all this magnificent equipment/ that each prince has contributed toward the public feast."

88. It is in the middle of this scene (II.i) that the verse changes to prose.

89. "Make better use, oh proud beauties,/ of your universal, charming power; love, lovely shepherdesses;/ our hearts are made for love/ . . . / There is absolutely nothing that can resist/ the soft embracing charms of Love."

90. In terms of scenography, *La Princesse d'Elide* has been called a regression as compared to *Ercole amante* (see Vanuxem 80). True, there are no astonishing architectural effects, the *Allée royale* itself forming the main backdrop. Yet, to see this big tree with its sixteen musicians rise up from beneath the stage must have been interesting.

91. "Let us reveal, then, that at the zenith of absolute power,/ her grandeur shone forth without pomp and without pride,/ that in the most perilous times her constant wisdom/ kept her authority stable, without fear when it hung in the balance,/ which, when all her labors had achieved a happy calm,/ she handed on to her son without regrets;/ Let us reveal, then, with what respect and with what courtesies/ the love of this glorious son rewards her for it all;/ Let us praise the lengthy labors, let us praise the just laws/ Of this son who is acclaimed the greatest of all kings."

92. Dufourcq also argues that celebrations such as "Les Plaisirs" provided an excellent training for Lully and his performers in view of the creation of French lyric opera in the course of the next decade.

93. "Nothing authorizes us to assert positively either that the five-act *Tartuffe* we possess is a substantially revised, different play or that it represents simply the completion of the unfinished piece with, perhaps, a few minor changes" (Lawrence 109).

94. Molière and his company returned in Paris on May 22, having earned 4,000 *livres* from participating in "Les Plaisirs;" Molière personally received another 2,000 *livres*.

95. First edition, 1664; second edition, 1665; reprint of the 1664 edition in 1673–1674.

96. See Spire Pitou, "L'Autre version en vers de *La Princesse d'Elide*," *Dix-Septième Siècle* 97 (1972): 105–9. Pitou remarks that Voltaire showed (predictably enough) little enthusiasm for Molière's play.

97. Elis is situated in the northwest Peloponnese; Olympia was located in that region; from the fifth century B.C. onward, the Eleans were officially in charge of the Olympian rites.

98. "You think you know him well enough by his title of fool;/ but know that he is much less of a fool than he likes to pretend,/ and that in spite of the job he holds at present,/ he has more good sense than those who mock him."

99. "When she was young, my mother passed for a beauty,/ and naturally enough she was not much of a tease;/ well then, your late father, that generous prince,/ was quite redoubtable in matters of gallantry;/ and I know that Elpénor, whom they called my father/ because he was my mother's husband,/ kept telling the shepherds of his day, as if it were a great honor,/ that the Prince had once stopped at his place,/ and that in those days he had the good fortune/ of seeing himself greeted with respect by the entire village."

100. Compare Philippe Beaussant's comment on "Les Plaisirs:" "C'est là que Roger s'est incarné en Louis, et voilà pourquoi dans ce lieu s'est fixée (comme on parle, en psychologie, de la fixation d'une obsession) l'image héroïque, galante, amoureuse à la fois, et tout en même temps royale et politique, de Louis. Le narcissime royal se développe comme une pièce de théâtre," "It was on that occasion that Roger was incarnated in Louis, and that is why in that setting the image of Louis: heroic, gallant, and amorous all at the same time, but equally royal and political, was fixed—much like psychologists speak of the fixation of an obsession. Royal narcissism was developing like a play" 69).

101. Compare Apostolidès 1981: 99. Apostolidès examines this notion in the Christian context of the motif of the king-thaumaturge, as symbolic body.

102. Oscar Wilde, *The Picture of Dorian Gray* (1891; Harmondsworth: 1985), 41–42.

103. Compare Apostolidès 1981: 100. Another feast was staged in the gardens, on June 12, 1665, for which Vigarani constructed a new, bigger theatrical space (Molière's company performed *Le Favori*, by Mlle Desjardins, on that occasion). No doubt the most splendid feast ever to be given at Versailles was concentrated in one single night, on July 18, 1667: Vigarani had built a bigger, more permanent looking theater, with statues and columns, and Molière's *Georges Dandin*, also a *comédie-ballet*, was performed on that occasion. For a description, see de Nolhac 851.

104. See Béhar 323ff; and see also Jérome de la Corce, "L'Opéra français à la Cour de Louis XIV," *Revue d'Histoire du Théâtre* 35 (4) 1983: 387–401.

105. On the physical–symbolic arrangement of Versailles, see Schlumbohm. The cult of Louis XIV as Sun King started from the idea that Louis was the bright sun bursting through the clouds of civil war (the Frondes) and restoring the peace of the realm with his sunshine triumphant. The construction of Versailles continued the allegory: it was built to the West of Paris—like the Garden of the Hesperides, which is located in the remote West into which the sun-Helios-Apollo descends to rest; architectural rays emanate from the palace; the palace and the grounds are replete with light symbolism and

with the motif of reflection (water surfaces, fountains, Hall of Mirrors); exuberant use is made of gold (especially in the heart of the palace, the royal bedroom, which is oriented toward the East); the *lever* and the *coucher* of the Sun King are transformed into quasi-mythic ceremonies. See further Hans Sedlmayr, "Allegorie und Architektur," in Castelli, ed. 197–208, 201–2. One of the most useful contemporaneous sources on Versailles is André Félibien, historiographer of the Royal Buildings under Louis XIV, who also wrote about festive performances held at Versailles (*Description du château de Versailles et de ses peintures, et d'autres ouvrages faits pour le Roy*; Paris, 1698). Apostolidès 1981 (87ff) discusses the planning and the construction of the palace in terms of a rhetorical discourse.

106. The counterreactions included Saint-Evremond's "Lettre sur les Opéras," in which he called opera "une sottise magnifique, mais toujours une sottise" (quoted in Béhar 325). Rousseau's famous "Lettre sur la musique française" is a famous un-musicological, revolutionary indictment of Lully's opera *Armida* (1686) but, beyond that, of Versailles itself (see Beaussant 131–33).

107. See also Lila Maurice-Amour, "Comment Lully et ses poètes humanisent dieux et héros," *Cahiers de l'Association Internationale des Etudes françaises* 17 (1965): 59–95, 65.

6

NE PLUS ULTRA: *IL POMO D'ORO*, THE HABSBURG APPLE

In the wake of the Thirty Years War, the fortunes of the Austrian branch of the House of Habsburg rose steadily, whereas those of the Spanish branch continued to decline.[1] The Treaties of Westphalia (1648) contained the seeds for the solidification of a coherent Habsburg Austria in the political, ethnic, linguistic, and religious crucible that was Central Europe. The ruler during whose tenure this development occurred was Leopold—an unhandsome man who gained the throne unexpectedly in 1657, at age seventeen, and who ruled until his death in 1705.[2] Many personal weaknesses have been attributed to him.[3] Yet Leopold, who was assisted by a cosmopolitan body of advisors, clerics, and professional politicians and soldiers, managed to forge a state that could, toward the end of the century, quite comfortably hold its own against Louis XIV as well as the Ottoman Empire.[4] This achievement would have been difficult to predict in the early decades of the reign. First, continuing Ottoman pressure in southeastern Europe resulted in several dramatic clashes, of which the 1683 siege of the imperial capital Vienna by Grand Vizier Kara Mustafa certainly serves as a memorable example.[5] And second, it seemed that in its old rivalry with the House of Valois-Bourbon (now represented by Louis XIV), the House of Habsburg was losing ground.

Indeed, just as the respective administrative structures of France and the

Austrian Empire were virtually diametrically opposite, so were the personalities of their rulers, although they were cousins as well as brothers-in-law. For example, the complex territorial history of Austria prevented Leopold from exercising "absolute" power in the strict sense of the term,[6] in that it did not fuse in his person the powers of justice, finance and administration over all the territories (Tapié 116ff).[7] Unlike Louis, the emperor worked with various councils that were still controlled by the upper aristocracy.[8] With their help, he conducted rather separate "Austrian" and "imperial" policies, although the two are often conflated and confused.[9] Also unlike Louis, Leopold took little personal interest in the military.[10] And he also did not design a palace-city comparable to Versailles to reflect his glory and serve as an embodiment of his status. (In fact, Habsburg Austria had no one city that served as a permanent center of power and administration until Leopold made Vienna his capital; his principal palace there, the Hofburg, was an old fortress on the ramparts of what was essentially still a medieval-looking walled city.[11]) Instead, like many members of the House of Habsburg from the end of the fifteenth to the end of the eighteenth century, Leopold was a talented creative and performing artist.[12] He served as patron to universities and libraries, and generally practised the musical-theatrical rather than the martial arts.

At the turn of the seventeenth century, musical culture, which flourished in Vienna, Graz (in Styria), and Innsbruck (in Tyrol), was controlled mostly by northern European, French, and Spanish musicians. But in Austria, as elsewhere, the prestige of Italian composers and musicians increased steadily in the course of the century.[13] During the reign of Leopold's father Ferdinand III (1636–1658)—who was himself a prolific composer and an amateur of Italian music—and partly because of the influence of Ferdinand's third wife Eleanora Gonzaga of Mantua, Vienna became the most active and the most italianate musical center of the realm. For example, Ferdinand's private opera house was built by the Venetian Giovanni Burnacini and it employed mainly Italians; he also sent German musicians to study in Italy. Dynastic events during the reign of Ferdinand III were celebrated with operatic *melodrammas* and allegorical ballets in which members of the imperial family participated.[14] The most important composers who became associated with Viennese opera were Cavalli, Bertali, Ziani, Andrea, Draghi, and Marc'Antonio Cesti.[15]

The relatively peaceful (for Austria) 1660s were also the gayest years at court during Leopold's entire reign. The carnival season was celebrated from Christmas till Shrovetide; and throughout the year, plays and operas were performed continuously—and not only on special occasions, as before Leopold's time. The ballrooms of the Hofburg and the "Favorita" palace of Leopold's stepmother Eleonora Gonzaga served as theaters,[16] as did, depending on the season, halls and gardens of the other imperial residences: Laxenburg and Ebersburg.[17] Ladies and noblemen of the highest rank took to the stage, and the emperor himself could be seen conducting the orchestra

(Baur-Heinhold 20). Leopold did not even forget the children: from 1672 onward, he supported the puppetshows of Johann Baptist Hilverding (Griffin [7]).[18] A large staff was maintained at court especially for these entertainments; Leopold's palace musicians and opera personnel were better organized and paid than most other branches of the imperial administration. Although the rigid Spanish court etiquette had been introduced and officially codified in Vienna since 1651 (Hadamowsky 24), the Spanish formal decorum did not subdue the natural temperament of the central Europeans, namely the "Austrians," Slavs, Magyars, and Bohemians, and it hardly interfered with the atmosphere of pleasurable play that pervaded the city and the court.[19] During these early years of the reign, Leopold may thus have shown less enthusiasm for international politics and matters of state, and more for play, than was expected of him. Wenceslaus Lobkovic, Leopold's prime minister during the 1670s, allegedly stated once to the French ambassador, the Marquis de Gremonville, that "the Emperor is not like your king, who does everything himself; but like a statue which is carried about and placed or moved at convenience" (Vehse I:481). Regardless: later in the reign, even Louis XIV had to recognize Leopold and his generals as formidable opponents. It is a commonplace that Austria, under Leopold's reign, gained marked international prominence, whereas France emerged from Louis' reign impoverished and enfeebled.

Yet, unlike the France of Louis XIV, the Austria of Leopold I has hardly been examined from a mythistorical perspective. It will have transpired from the previous chapters that this mythistory—which studies the artistically constructed function of the absolute ruler within the state and the ruler's fabricated personality that goes with this function, and which emerges, for example, in the rhetoric of the splendid festive performance—is hardly less relevant to an understanding of a realm in the seventeenth century than the "real," conventional history of dates, battles, treaties, and statistics of various sorts. After all, the makers of the splendid festivities served as historiographers of the ruler and as co-architects of the living memory of the reign. Starting from this premise, then, we will examine, in this final section, the performance context of *Il pomo d'oro* (The Golden Apple), a feast-opera (*teatrale festeggiamento*, *festa teatrale*) based on the story of the "Judgment of Paris." Originally commissioned in 1666 to celebrate the wedding of Leopold with his first wife, the Infanta Margareta Theresa, it was only performed in July, 1668, on the occasion of the empress's seventeenth birthday. Leopold was probably the least "absolute" (and the least solvent) of the rulers discussed so far; yet, *Il pomo d'oro* was the grandest of all the grandiose performances given in the service of seventeenth-century absolutism. A spacious wooden theater, the "auf der Cortina," was especially constructed near the Hofburg on the present site of the *Bibliothekshof*, near the *Nationalbibliothek*.[20] The performance of *Il pomo d'oro*, which was spread out over a three-day period, formed the conclusion of an exhausting, eighteen-month-long program of celebrations. And what an amplification (*auxeisis*) this ending was! In the last scene of the opera—before the Spirits of Air, the Cavaliers of Earth, and the Sirens and Tritons of the Sea perform a triple victory ballet—Leopold and Margareta Theresa are confronted with an amplified mirror-view of themselves and the courtly ceremonial that surrounds them, as they watch their effigies enthroned in the "Secret Chamber of Fate" high in the Heavens—higher even than the cloud ranges from which Jupiter and the Olympic pantheon survey the world and its stage. As an epideictic projection of imperial ambition, the epilogue (the flattering *licenza* typical of Venetian opera) remains unsurpassed: ignoring Juno, Pallas, and Venus, Jupiter's eagle deposits the golden apple in the lap of Margareta Theresa.

The magnificence of this opera, as well as the related festivities that preceded it, were in direct proportion to the length of the marriage negotiations and to the importance of the wedding for international politics. With the union of the twenty-seven-year-old Austrian emperor and his fifteen-year-old Spanish first niece, the main twin branches of the Habsburg dynasty were, once more, formally reunited. The affair had, again, pitted Leopold against Louis XIV. In the Prelude, I have suggested that the splendid performances given for dynastic occasions at the court of a Baroque absolute ruler were hardly ever isolated, whimsical play-moments or events in the life-rhythm of such a court. I argued, rather, that one could probably reconstruct much of the history of the Continent through the Baroque period by determining the personal, causal, chronological, and geographical connections between the numerous grandiose festive performances given at its courts. Such connections do indeed exist between, for example, the performance contexts outlined in the preceding two chapters and in this final chapter.

The eldest daughter of Philip IV of Spain (from his first wife, Isabelle of Bourbon) was Maria Theresa; already in 1646, Mazarin had begun to envision an alliance between the Infanta and her first cousin, the future Louis XIV. It was a union that Anne of Austria (Louis' mother, and Philip's sister) also warmly desired but which could not be seriously considered in view of the hostilities between the two countries. Maria Theresa was generally considered to be reserved for the elder son of Ferdinand III, Ferdinand IV, who was crowned king of the Romans in 1653. But death overtook the latter prematurely, hardly a year later, before the marriage could be arranged. The French court began to pursue again Maria Theresa's hand for the adolescent Louis. Philip, however, promised the Infanta to Ferdinand III's second son, Leopold, but he changed his mind in 1657, when, following the death of Ferdinand III, Leopold began to claim his father's various crowns (Pribram 325ff).[21] In 1658, the Infanta was assigned to Louis (then about to be wedded to Margareth of Savoy), to the great delight of Louis' mother and Mazarin. This union was projected as a *lieto fine* to the Franco-Spanish war that had begun in

1635; the wedding took place in 1660, and, as we have seen, provided the occasion for the creation, and belated performance, of *Ercole amante*.

Meanwhile, also in 1660, Philip had promised his youngest daughter Margareta Theresa (from his second wife Maria Anna of Austria, Leopold's sister) to Leopold. This princess, a consolation prize, was hardly nine years old. Negotiations for the marriage contract began in 1662.[22] And in 1663 the engagement was announced to the courts of Europe (Louis XIV sent warm congratulations to his cousin and rival). Leopold was kept informed of the princess' development by his ambassadors in Madrid and by means of Velázquez' portraits of her. But Philip was reluctant to let the Infanta depart for Vienna, citing her young age, the dangers of the sea crossing, and the Turkish troubles as reasons to postpone the departure again and again.[23] These repeated delays were due also to the incessant plotting and wrangling of anti-Austrian, pro-French forces in Madrid. Leopold's private correspondence indicates that he was happy with the prospect of the marriage and that he seems to have truly fallen in love with his child-fiancée. Philip's lingering illness in 1664 delayed the Infanta's departure by another year, and his death in 1665 almost enabled Leopold's enemies to cancel the match altogether, but the Queen Widow, his sister, ultimately proved more powerful than the pro-French party. The Infanta's departure from Madrid was scheduled for February, 1666, but by March, she still had not left—perhaps because of financial problems. Leopold grew ever more impatient, and he wrote his ambassador, in his characteristic polyglot style, that "Ich als ein Brauttigamb recht verliebt bin und die Worthe sagen, chi ama teme" ("as a Bridegroom I am squarely in love and I say those words, chi ama teme;" Pribram 361). Final preparations were underway by April, and on Easter Sunday (April 25), 1666, the proxy wedding took place in Madrid, where Duke Medina de las Torres represented the emperor. A few days later Leopold's bride left Madrid, never to return. While awaiting the embarkation in Gandia, she fell ill and was bled excessively, which postponed the departure again. Finally, on July 16, the royal vessel *Reale di Spagna*, gilded from stern to rudder, and her companion ships set sail from Barcelona; the fleet reached Finale, near Genoa, on August 20. Leopold's trusted general Count Raimundo Montecuccoli was waiting to escort the empress to Vienna.[24] The fact that Margareta Theresa arrived later than planned had direct consequences for the grandiose festivities and their critical fortunes. Leopold, though very much in love, was easily consoled and wrote, touchingly: "ma no importa, wann die Brautt hie ist, ist es Fest genung" ("But it does not matter: when the Bride is here, there will be Feast enough;" Pribram 367). Progress on land was also very slow, for the empress was well entertained in the cities and at the courts on the way.[25] Only on December 5 did Margareta Theresa make her grandiose Entry into Vienna (see description in Vehse I:495–96). After three hours, the procession had finally reached the Augustine church where the Papal nuncio pronounced the benediction.[26] A supper followed in the Hofburg. The dates of the actual arrival of the empress and the *de facto* wedding coincided with the beginning of the carnival season, which caused a greater profusion of celebrations than even this very festive city and court could normally expect.[27]

Let us now focus on the three most grandiose of the many events organized to celebrate this wedding (the enormous cost of which was borne, of course, by the loyal subjects of the realm): first, the fireworks display (more properly, a pyrotechnical play) titled "Von Himmeln Entzindete und Durch Allgemainen Zuruff der Erde sich Himmelwerts erschwingende Frolockungs-Flammen" on December 8, 1666; then, the equestrian ballet (*balletto a cavallo*) titled *La Contesa dell'Aria e dell'Acqua* (The Contest of Air and Water) on January 24, 1667; and, finally, the première performance of *Il pomo d'oro* in the "auf der Cortina" theater on July 12 and 14, 1668. The twenty-month time span between the first and the last event has obscured the fact that the pyrotechnical play, the equestrian ballet, and the opera were originally designed as the three facets of a pyramidal *Gesamtkunstwerk*—a crucial point confirmed by the planning chronology of the feasts. Already on February 20, 1660, Leopold had ordered the speedy construction of the theater for the performance of *Il pomo d'oro*.[28] Clearly, the opera itself had by then also been—or was being—commissioned from Sbarra and Cesti.[29] The première was scheduled for October of that year, by which time Margareta Theresa was then expected to have arrived in Vienna. The grandiose equestrian ballet was devised at about the same time: the participating cavaliers were told on March 10 to stand by for rehearsals. Meanwhile Sbarra was writing the libretto: on June 27, Cesti composed the last sections of *Nettuno e Flora festeggianti* (which was performed on July 12, to celebrate the birthday of the still absent empress); he also on that day wrote to the Venetian impresario Marco Faustini that he was now ready to start working on "l'Opera grande" (*Il pomo d'oro*)—which means that the text thereof must have been at least partly available to him.[30] During the summer, preparations continued at a brisk pace. On August 8, when the empress was well at sea, Cesti wrote that the performance of *Il pomo d'oro* would take place in October, that he had only finished the first half of the first act ("e sono cinque"!), and that the impatient emperor was urging him to work faster; on August 15, Cesti reported again that Leopold was keeping close tabs on his progress (Giazotto 510–11). At this point, the tight schedule collapsed and the festivities were put on hold. For example, the rehearsals of the equestrian ballet did not actually begin until August 30.[31] The first of many dress rehearsals in the Hofburg courtyard, with music and machines, took place on November 10. Leopold attended them regularly. With the complete libretto of *Il pomo d'oro* at his disposal, Cesti virtually finished the music sometime in the fall.[32] But Sbarra's and Cesti's achievement was made irrelevant by the fact that the construction of the theater—which was designed to have an ingenious stage allowing a flexible, dynamic use of space in depth and in height by means of several staging areas with interacting levels—was far behind schedule (Griffin [4]). The equestrian ballet was performed after three months' delay. *Il pomo d'oro* was almost two years behind schedule; it was promised thrice for 1667, but each time in vain (see Seifert 9–11, and Schmidt 1976: 386–87). Perhaps it was to assuage frustration at these repeated delays that in 1667 the libretto was published, lavishly illustrated with twenty-three engravings of captivating stage action and decors.[33] The period of mourning following the January 3rd, 1668 death of the three-month-old heir Ferdinand Wenzel caused yet another delay, until, finally, the birthday of Margareta Theresa in July, 1668, provided a suitable occasion to inaugurate the newly completed theater. Clearly, planning had been overly optimistic and technical problems kept interfering with the timely construction of the facility.

In the paradigm of splendid festive events available to seventeenth-century courts, the fireworks display, the (equestrian or regular) ballet, and the feast opera occupy the three most prestigious places. It is thus important to realize that the original plan called for the combination of *all three of these events* in a *contiguous*, allegorically orchestrated flow of light, color, movement, and sound. Indeed, the fireworks display/pyrotechnical play and the equestrian ballet can be said to relate as "thesis" and "antithesis" to one another, whereas the program of *Il pomo d'oro* functioned as a sort of synthesis (the Hegelian *Aufhebung*) of the two preceding events. Such a weighty, complex structure would provide the instrument for the creation of Leopold's mythistorical persona as *the* "God of Play"—a "playing god" who was able to outdo (*amplificatio*) the mythistorical construction of Louis XIV as Hercules-Phoebus. What a potlatch in the face of the French cousin and rival! Let us therefore ignore the actual delays and interpret the three grandiose performances as they were originally intended: as a programmatic *Gesamtkunstwerk*.

The display entitled "Von Himmeln Entzindete und Durch Allgemainen Zuruff der Erde sich Himmelwerts erschwingende Frolockungs-Flammen" was performed on December 8, 1666.[34] On the Bastion near the Hofburg, two artifical mountains—representing Etna and Parnassus—flanked the scaffolding for the fireworks display. In the Prologue, Mercury entered with a nuptial torch; as the Emperor lit it from the palace window, numerous flames rose to the sky and many shots were fired from nearby forts to proclaim the world's ardent enthusiasm at this dynastic union. The first act had three scenes: Vulcan and his tribe were shown forging arms in the bowels of Mount Etna; Cupid appeared, chased the Etnaeans away, and forged the golden wedding ring, which he then carried to heaven; then the nine muses on Parnassus (which was all ablaze with bonfires) celebrated Cupid's success with joyous song. In the second act, Hymen lit two hearts attached to the scaffolding: each flaming heart showed the letters *L* and *M*; then Centaurs brandishing burning torches stormed down from Etna but they were routed on Jove's command by Hercules; from two large towers (representing Austria and Spain, and each surmounted by the cryptogram *V A V H*: Vivat Austria Vivat Hispania) rockets rose into the sky, and from the Bastion many fireballs were shot from mortars, at which the fiery letters changed to *V L V M* (Vivat Leopoldus Vivat Margareta). In the third and last act, Jove's eagle lit a joyous fire on the altar of Hymen's pillared temple which was already ablaze with thirty-three pyramidal fires; then the Phoenix appeared in flames above the temple; and, finally, when the flames had engulfed the entire temple (pillars, statues and pyramids),[35] the cryptogram *A E I O U* was written in fire against the sky, the message of which (Austria Erit In Omne Ultimum) was reinforced by yet another immense number of explosions, rockets, and huge fireballs, each of which disintegrated into countless golden sparks. Clearly, much of the action of this festive event was freely visible to anyone who cared to look up. The cryptograms, written in blazing letters against the cold night sky, were intended not only for the amusement of the court and the Viennese crowd but served also, symbolically, as a warning for the world, the pantheon and the cosmos.

By contrast, the audience of the equestrian ballet was select. Originally intended for a late summer or early fall performance, the long awaited and much rehearsed *Contesa dell'Aria e dell'Acqua* was finally given on January 24, 1667, in the enclosed courtyard of the Hofburg.[36] It has been said that Leopold specifically intended with this ballet to emulate Louis' "Plaisirs de l'Ile enchantée" of 1664 (Solf 34). Leopold participated personally in the four-hour event, surrounded by the best among the Austrian nobility, and watched by the enchanted ladies from the palace windows that looked out over the courtyard. The program of this ballet was thus designed by Sbarra to be understood by spectators who had, quite literally, a "view from above." The music for the enormous orchestra (numbering more than a hundred string instruments, reinforced by trumpets and kettledrums) was by Schmelzer; Bertali had composed the choruses, and Carlo Pasetti had been fetched from Ferrara to build the stage (Wellesz 82ff). Already the Prologue alone consisted of many fanciful entries. First, Fame addressed the empress from atop an "Oriental" galley which was "rowed" into the arena by "Turkish" slaves and which represented the ship of the Argonauts.[37] Next, four companies (totalling more than one thousand performers) entered the arena: each company represented one of the elements, was led by an actual military commander of the highest rank, and entered with a huge float full of allegorical-mythological detail from which singers serenaded the empress in Italian.[38] Then an orchestrated battle ensued, presumably for the two treasures guarded by the Argonauts: the Habsburg Golden Fleece and the Holy Roman imperial crown. But the fray ceased at the sudden appearance of a huge cloud, which first filled the horizon and then dissipated to reveal a globe as well as the allegory of Eternity (Immortality) seated on the rainbow of Peace. Eternity bade the fighting to end, since the fleece and the crown rightfully belonged to Austria. As the globe split open, it revealed Eternity's temple within, and in this temple the effigies of the fifteen Roman emperors preceding Leopold, all in full regalia on horseback (thus splendidly outdoing the representatives of the fifteen Houses of the French royal family that descended from the Heavens at the beginning of *Ercole amante*). Then another large car, in the form of a silver shell, was wheeled into the arena; it contained, besides a huge pearl, Margareta Theresa's painted image as well as the effigy of Leopold.[39] And this shell, which represented the Chariot of Glory, was followed by a procession of subjected nations: captured Indians, Turks, and Tartars. Next, a large crowd emerged from the temple of Eternity, which was followed successively by twelve trumpeters, by the emperor dressed as a Roman Imperator on horseback, and by his retinue of cavaliers; as this large company rode around the arena, the chorus sang paeans. The arena was cleared, and only then did the "ballet" proper begin (that is, the emperor and several companies of splendidly accoutered cavaliers executed a series of complex geometrical figures and patterns). At the conclusion, a triumphal car, filled with singers in bejewelled robes, rode in to serenade the empress; and then all exited in a tight formation.

The première of *Il pomo d'oro* was planned in February 1666 to be held in October of the same year. Given the immense scope of the work, the number of people involved in its creation, and the complex requirements of its performance, such optimistic scheduling seems laughably naive. Everything about the opera was vast; because the entire affair was so taxing on the performers as well as on the audience, the performance was spread over two days.[40] On Thursday, July 12, the Prologue and acts 1 and 2 were given, and on Saturday, July 14, acts 3 through 5.[41] The number of acts—each of which was introduced by a sonata—was unusual: five instead of the normal three, and that after an extraordinarily long prologue. The cast included forty-eight roles, representing virtually the entire Olympic pantheon and many heroes.[42] In addition, there were various choruses (each act contained choral scenes) as well as ballets composed by Schmelzer, which were somehow linked to the main action—not to forget the grand triple ballet, the climax to the entire work.[43] For the sixty-six scenes (a large number of scenes was another characteristic feature of Venetian-style opera), no fewer than twenty-three different stage sets were designed. Most of these used complex machinery, and many featured excellent examples of Mannerist and Baroque grotesque motifs.[44] As mentioned before, of the twenty-five detailed engravings which illustrated the 1667 and 1668 editions of the libretto, twenty-three represent composite, synchronous pictures of several scenes each. The complete sequence serves (and was intended as such) as an excellent *memoria* of the action.[45]

The outline of the main plot follows the well-known *muthos* fairly closely.

The choral prologue is set in the "Theater of Austrian Fame," where Leopold's mounted effigy (a splendid example of the characteristically "moving" Baroque equestrian statue) is shown mounted on a heap of weapons and surrounded by the images of former Austrian emperors (engraving 3)—an emblem that recalls the central scene of the prologue to the equestrian ballet. Divided in two choruses but singing in many combinations, eight provinces and kingdoms (Spain, Italy, Hungary, the Empire, Sardinia, Bohemia, America, and the Austrian patrimonial states) establish the glorious festive mood, while Cupid with his bow and Hymen with the torch (both also recalling the fireworks display), and Austrian Glory on the winged horse Pegasus, express their joy at the wedding in arias and recitatives.

The first act consists of fifteen scenes. In the realm of Pluto, Proserpina laments her boring, gloomy existence, and Pluto orders Discord to begin the argument over the golden apple in Jupiter's palace (1.1–3; engraving 4).[46] In the heavenly realm of Jupiter, the gods are making merry; as the court jester Momo is making fun of them (especially of Mars), Discord appears on her cloud and throws the golden apple—with the well-known result (1.4–5; engraving 5). In a pastoral landscape on Mount Ida, we see the nymph Ennone (daughter of the river Xanthus) and her following; her lover Paris appears, and they sing a love duet; some of this is overheard by the shepherd Aurindo, but then Mercury descends from the heavens, appointing Paris as the judge of the goddesses; later, in the same setting, Aurindo, alone, laments his unhappy passion for Ennone until Filaure, Ennone's nurse, enters and mocks him (1.6–10; engraving 6). In the enclosed courtyard of the palace of Paris, Juno and Pallas descend separately from the heavens to bribe Paris, while Momo again ridicules Paris for the odd role he has to play (1.11–14; engraving 7). In a pleasure garden, Venus presents her case to Paris and bribes him with the promise of Helen, while Momo, Nereids and the Chorus of Beauty stand by; Paris decides in Venus' favor (I.15; engraving 8).

The second act opens with a view of a seaport with ships and ruinous towers. Paris is about to depart to claim Helen as his reward. First Aurindo convinces Filaura to help him obtain Ennone; then Momo informs Filaura of Paris' infatuation with Helen; as Paris sings solo about his new love, Ennone and Filaura enter to accuse him of treachery, upon which Paris falsely reaffirms his feelings for Ennone (2.1–5; engraving 9). Then, the setting changes dramatically: even this particularly sophisticated audience must have thrilled when the earth opened and a enormous, fire-snorting monster's head rose up; as its huge jaws opened, the scene within revealed the entrance to Hell, with Charon in his skiff on the Acheron and the walled city of Dis in the background.[47] The horror of this scene is comically contradicted when the rather grotesque ferryman complains about the lack of business in his realm; the three Furies appear flying overhead and ask Charon to ferry them across, which Charon will do if they will tell him a story. The Furies then announce the impending war on earth, and Charon is happy that this event will increase his power (2.6–7; engraving 10). The scene shifts back to the sea port, where we witness the departure of Paris. Venus and Cupid fly out with him (2.8–9). In the tent camp (a staple set of Baroque opera) of the Athenian warriors, the armed Pallas—hovering in the air on a chariot drawn by owls—appears to her priest Adraste and King Cecrops and orders them to avenge her slighted honor. Queen Alceste laments the frequent wars that separate her from her spouse, and Cecrops permits her to accompany him and the Athenian army (2.10–12; engraving 11—a particularly detailed and "painterly" one [Solf 73–74]). In a marshland, which represents the birthplace of Pallas, Athenian maidens are shown practicing the martial arts; again Pallas flies over their heads and requests her citizens to avenge her honor (2.13–14; engraving 12).

The first scenes of the third act are set in the gloomy cave of Aeolus, king of the Winds. Aeolus sits on a rocky throne and confers with the winds Eurus, Auster, Zephirus and Volturnus. Then Juno appears, with an order similar to that given by Athena; more specifically, she requests that the winds destroy Paris' ship at sea (3.1–2; engraving 13). In a very Austrian-looking valley shaded by pines, Ennone is anxious because, searching high and low, she cannot find Paris anywhere. Aurindo and Momo join her; after the latter prevents the desperate Ennone from drowning herself in the nearby Xanthus, he also gives the despairing Aurindo new hope: perhaps Ennone will return his love, for, after all, the world is a stage with "varie Prospettive et'apparati" which Fortuna, an able stage engineer, can change "in un tratto;" thus the play of life ("la favola") has many surprise scenes (3.3–5; engraving 14). In the next scene, Venus visits Mars in a high-ceilinged armory hung with trophies, banners, and martial gear, soliciting his help against the forces that her two rivals have been marshalling (3.6; engraving 15). Meanwhile, Aeolus has obeyed Juno. A howling tempest violently rocks Paris' ship, which is still dangerously close to the rocky shore; but Venus appears on a shell drawn by Nereids, and she bribes Neptune (who rides on a chariot pulled by sea horses), via the promise of the nymph Amphitrite, into calming the tempest so that Paris can continue his voyage. Filaura and Aurindo are still wandering around in search of Paris (3.7–10; engraving 16). In an amphitheater, the armies of Cecrops (Pallas) and Mars (Venus) are fighting; Mars wins ("Tanto ardito un 'huom mortale/Contro mè venir presume?"), and the Athenians are led away to shameful captivity (3.11–12; engraving 17).

The opening set of the fourth act is a quiet cedar grove; here Ennone grieves for not having found Paris. She is soon joined by Filaura (4.1–2; engraving 18). Then, in the ornate temple of Pallas in Athens, in front of the fabled gigantic statue of the goddess, Adraste and the other priests are in the midst of a sacrificial ceremony when the temple collapses in an earthquake caused, no doubt, by the furious Athena herself. Appearing again on her flying chariot, she tells the Athenians that their king is a prisoner and locked up in the same fortress where Mars and Venus have stored the golden apple (4.3–5; engraving 19). In the heart of the Milky Way, encircled by the sphere of fire, Venus sits enthroned as Cupid, on a flaming chariot, hovers between the sea and the heavens (he has come to replenish his supply of amorous ardor at the sphere of fire).[48] Juno flies in to confront Venus, but the latter sends her packing with the tart remark that Mars is now in charge of the apple. Furious, Juno orders Fire to destroy the realm of Neptune (to punish him for helping Paris to escape), but Fire refuses, saying that the Fates have forbidden him to interfere (we might rephrase this and say that Fire obeys the laws of nature; 4.6–9; engraving 20). Then we see the three Graces gathered in the forecourt of the palace of Venus, which is lined with rows of satyr-columns. On a huge triumphal car drawn in by two lions, Venus and Mars sit enthroned, while Victory holds a laurel crown and the golden apple over their heads. Cecrops and the Athenian prisoners march before them in chains, guarded by the soldiers of Mars. As Venus and Cecrops exchange insults, Cupid flies in, warning Venus and Mars that more Athenians are approaching (4.10–13; engraving 21). Indeed, led by Adraste and Alceste, the latter begin to besiege the castle; two turreted elephants participate in the battles, which are directed by Pallas in the sky (4.14–15; engraving 22).

At the beginning of the fifth act, it has become clear that the end of this war is not yet in sight. The stately pleasure garden of Paris, with its many pleasant country pavilions, is the setting for the beginning of the denouement. Juno rails at Jupiter for having appointed a mortal man to judge her, and she unleashes a dramatic thunderstorm to vent her frustration. Aurindo, too, is unhappy and nearly commits suicide because Ennone, still pining for Paris, keeps rejecting him—until Filaura and Momo inform her of Paris' betrayal, and slowly she realizes that she would be better off with Aurindo than with Paris (5.1–8; engraving 23). Tired of all this strife, Jupiter has now occupied a throne in what appears to be Mars' ruined fortress—although the tower with the golden apple is still standing. Pallas and Juno start quibbling again, and so forth, until Jupiter intervenes and angrily shatters the tower with a lightning bolt; he then sends his eagle to retrieve the apple (5.9; engraving 24). In the final scene, Jupiter allots the golden apple ("Premio divino") to Margareta Theresa ("grand Heroina"), for she combines the best qualities of each goddess. Leopold and Margareta Theresa will start a new, better human race ("Coniunta al Gran Leopoldo/ Per arricchir l'Europa/ de più famosi Heroi") and inaugurate a new Golden Age ("[I]l secolo felice,/ Che il Destin ne predice") for a world at peace ("con dolce Pace," "Il tranquillo seren d'un secol d'oro"). The scene shows Jupiter and the gods enthroned on an enormous cloud; uppermost, the Secret Chamber of Fate, with the effigies of Leopold and Margareta Theresa ("si bella Imago") in the center, surrounded by the past, present, and future members of the House of Habsburg. Venus, Pallas, Juno, and the Chorus of the Gods sing a final hymn in praise of this brave new world ("O bell'età") and its glorious future under this Imperial couple and its (hopefully numerous) offspring ("l'Austriaca Prole"). The opera is concluded by a triple ballet, featuring the spirits of Air, the cavaliers of Earth, and the Sirens and Tritons of Water (5.10–11; engraving 25).

With this libretto, Francesco Sbarra proved that he was capable of stretching a hackneyed fable to almost unbearable proportions, while yet allowing its tired story and protagonists to achieve new life in an interesting work of art. In this aspect, *Il pomo d'oro* rivals Marino's comparably long and also highly gilded epic poem *L'Adone* (which was dedicated to Marie de'Medici and Louis XIII). Sbarra's text may also justifiably be called an epic (for example, because the many intrigues and episodes do not really advance the action: their main function is to interrupt the plot development and show the hero in a different setting [Wellesz 57]), but whereas *L'Adone* was a poem designed to be performed in the theater of the mind only, *Il pomo d'oro* had to be realized on an actual stage. Indeed, it is likely that Burnacini was involved in the creation of the libretto, in the sense that he probably discussed with Sbarra such matters as the order of the scenes. For example, landscape settings alternate with city or battle scenes according to the rhetorical principle that alternation causes delight.

Besides amplifying the familiar story with an innovative epideictic-rhetorical ending and with ballets and choral scenes, Sbarra added a typically operatic-erotic pastoral subplot with "comic" characters in the conventional court-versus-country mode. The main plot, which stars divinities and princely heroes, and the subplot, which treats the amorous tribulations of shepherds, are connected mainly by means of the earthy character Momo, who functions in both. Momo is Jupiter's court jester (*buffone*, *matto*) and a stock character of ancient comedy. In addition to frequently addressing the audience directly, he also talks back to the gods, thus exposing and holding up for ridicule the vices of these authority figures—such as their incessant feuding and their petty vanities. At the same time, he functions as "the true force for ethical behavior in the play," for example by preventing Aurindo's suicide (Aikin 67). Furthermore, the poor shepherd Aurindo is obviously set up as the more reliable counterpart to the treacherous princely shepherd Paris; and Filaura, whose mockery Aurindo has to endure for most of the opera, may well represent a caricature of a certain type of courtier, with whom the original audience must have been familiar.[49]

I posited earlier that the accidental chronological separation of these three festive events has obscured the fact that they were intended as a triadic or pyramidal *Gesamtkunstwerk*, the culmination of which was the glorification of the effigies of Leopold and Margareta Theresa in the Secret Chamber of Fate. The allegorical-thematic framework of the opera was prepared by the respective programs of the pyrotechnical play and the equestrian ballet. In the course of the triad of performances, the audience's horizon of expectation was progressively expanded by means of two principal motifs (structural features, building blocks). I will define these motifs as, respectively, the interplay of the four cosmic elements and the allegoresis of the "spherical object;" together, they constitute a dialectic of War and Peace.

Let us first examine the presence of the four elements in the three events.[50] The pyrotechnical play was dominated, obviously, by the element of Fire, which was reconstructed in profusion by the rockets and the guns of large calibre that were fired from the Bastion and from nearby fortifications.[51] Fire emerges from Earth (Etna, Parnassus, the Bastion) to inscribe in Air the names of the rulers and the fame of the twin Habsburg branches in their pan-Christian unification (recall that Mercury forges the golden wedding ring in Vulcan's forge, deep in mount Etna). Thus, martial instruments do not produce a destructive but a festive and creative Fire. Water and Air dominate the equestrian ballet; note, however, that the programmatic title of the ballet is *not* "The Contest of Air and Water *against Fire and Earth*." In their ritualized struggle, the four elements do not contest ownership of the Golden Fleece (which is forged in Fire) or the Holy Roman crown (which represents Earthly territories)—for who can dispute that these icons are rightfully associated with the Austrian Habsburgs—but rather the claim to produce pearls (an allusion to the name Margareta). It should not come as a surprise that Air and Water are the favorites in this program. Leopold's birthday was June 9; thus, he was a Gemini (an Air sign); Margareta Theresa's birthday was July 12, which makes her a Cancer (a Water sign). Pearls are produced only in Water, and it is further noteworthy that Immortality, who appears to end the contest, does so seated on Iris, the Rainbow, an auspicious phenomenon resulting from the glorious combination of Water and Air. The victory of Water and Air signifies that the new dynastic union will bring wealth (pearl) and a message of peace and good hope (Iris). By contrast, Earth, Water, and Air are genuinely pitted against each other in the main plot of *Il pomo d'oro*. Indeed, Sbarra's elaboration of the conventional *muthos* includes the fact that the three goddesses each enlist one of the elements in her service. Not only did this addition to the plot allow the librettist to introduce a fair number of digressions and invented episodes, but equally importantly, it gave the architect-scenographer the opportunity to introduce his own solutions for such conventional epic and operatic settings as the underworld, fortresses, caves, and tempestuous seas. Thus, Neptune (Water) is bribed by Venus (which is only natural, since Venus was born from the sea); Aeolus (Air) supports Juno; and the Athenian Heroes (Earth) fight for Pallas. It is crucial that the element of Fire disobeys Juno's request to intervene and thereby contribute to the destruction of the world. The unique but significant participation of Fire comes when Jupiter's lightning bolt, the power of justice and divine retribution, shatters the tower of Mars; consequently, the golden apple can be given to Margareta Theresa, and the war of the goddesses and their enlisted elements becomes irrelevant. Thus, as in the pyrotechnical play, the destructive potential of martial Fire is channeled by the emperor (of the gods) toward a positive cause. Its intervention produces an immediate boon (the resolution of the dispute over the golden apple) as well as a future blessing (the most famous war of antique mythistory will not be fought). Thus, the opera posits "history" not as a predetermined, immutable sequence (that is, of wars and destruction), but rather as a flexible tool that a judicious "emperor" can use entirely at his own discretion: either for his own glory and the benefit of a grateful world, or to plague and destroy miserable humankind. The presence of the four elements in the wedding celebrations is designed to promote the theme that this dynastic union serves the cause of peace, not war. *Il pomo d'oro* shows it most clearly: when gods (or rulers) quarrel over trivial issues, when they are deficient in morality, then humankind suffers and the world is at risk of annihilation. It is not different when princes make wrong or illicit choices—such as, to lust rather than to love, or to conquer by war rather than to engage in responsible dynastic relationships. Those in high places, gods and princes alike, cannot act on personal desire but only according to their responsibility toward the realm and humankind. Often they can learn from the examples set by humble people, or from the scathing words of apparent fools. Paris' irresponsible and lustful choice of Venus could well have destroyed the world; by contrast, Leopold's gracious acceptance of Margareta Theresa avoids the need for further war and constitutes a blessing that, it is hoped, will materialize in peace and prosperity for all the nations of the realm.

The motif of the "spherical object" strengthens this allegorical program. Recall that the contest of the four elements in the prologue of the equestrian ballet ceased at the sudden appearance of a huge cloud, which first filled the horizon and then dissipated to reveal a globe and the allegory of Immortality on the rainbow of Peace. This globe represents the world, but since it splits open to reveal Eternity's temple, in which the effigies of the fifteen emperors preceding Leopold are displayed,[52] it is also, more particularly, the material symbol of the Holy Roman Empire itself: the *Reichsapfel*. Toward this globe (Leopold's terrestrial omnipotence sanctioned by Fame and Immortality) is drawn the chariot containing the colossal pearl (wealth and fortune), with which Margareta Theresa is associated via her name and portrait. The principal plot-motif of the opera is the struggle for yet another spherical object. The three vain goddesses were greedy for the precious golden apple, which becomes a *radix malorum*, the cause of cosmic strife. By contrast, Margareta Theresa, who has not even desired the golden apple, will receive it because her innate qualities transcend anyone else's claims. The new empress is the signifier of wisdom, beauty, and power, and, as Leopold's bride, the universal peace-maker. Thus, when in the crowning scene of the opera, the effigies of Leopold and Margareta Theresa are shown enthroned in the Secret Chamber of Fate, it is to be understood that they surpass the divinities of the classical pagan pantheon not only in a purely positional sense (by surmounting them in the Heavens), but also, and more importantly, on a moral level. The pan-Christian Idea, re-established as a political force through the reunion of the Habsburg branches, is represented as transcending the limitations and the shortsighted vices of pugnacious paganism. Thus, as the golden apple is permanently transferred at Jupiter's command from the pagan to the pan-Christian (Catholic) world, it changes function. From the cause of greedy strife, it turns into the signifier of peace and concord: again, the *Reichsapfel*. The *lieto fine* of the opera is, simply enough, rooted in the proposition that this dynastic reunion sets an example for resolving discord among Christian Houses—a most useful example in the face of the continuing Turkish advances in the region.[53]

The fact that most spectators of the première had already read the libretto and knew the outcome even strengthens the power of Sbarra's epideictic rhetoric—for in this type of argument, the audience is not presented with "new" information but with the *auxeisis* of a well-known "fact," which the allegorical lavishness of the representation and of its architectural framework made even more memorable. Indeed, the architectural framework is of the greatest importance. Küsell's detailed engravings of the sets and decors enabled Solf (40ff) to deliver a detailed exegesis of the intended allegorical program. Suffice it to confirm here that Burnacini's architectural devices and his stage "decoration" are not merely ornamental; rather, they constitute an integral part of the rhetorical program and reinforce the moral-allegorical significances of Sbarra's libretto.[54] If we consider, for example, Burnacini's sustained use of machinery in order to create effects of flight, descent, and horizontal movement;[55] his oxymoronic juxtaposition and even hyperbolic exaggeration (to the point of redundancy and grotesqueness) of specific motifs in the performance, the architecture, and the decoration; his careful alternation between scenes of "lightness" and "darkness," "quietness" and "violence," "amorous passion" and "warfare;" then we are clearly reminded of Tesauro's scheme, which was so important for the epideictic-rhetorical construction of the Baroque grandiose festive performance and of which the principal *figure ingegnose* were hyperbole, oxymoron, antithesis, anastrophe, metonymy, ellipsis, and metaphor. For example, special attention is due to the elaborate proscenium, which remained visible throughout the performance and which therefore framed everything that was sung or acted out on the stage. Much like an emblem, this proscenium offers its many allegorical riches for interpretation by each spectator according to his or her level of instruction. When we reduce the proscenium to the simplest of schemas (following Solf), we find that it is composed of a double series of triangularly disposed effigies, which are crowned by the two-headed imperial eagle, and which can be "read" as follows:

Imperial Eagle

Youth	*Young Woman*
(Leopold)	*(Margareta Theresa)*
Hercules	*Athena*
Apollo	*Fortuna*
Peace Compassion Constancy	*Merit Peace Justice*

The action of the opera is set within a frame that presents several of the most powerful Olympians—thus outdoing Louis, who invited comparison, first with Hercules only, and later with Phoebus Apollo only—as well as—closest to the ground and nearest to the audience—embodiments of Christian virtues. The spectators of the performance and the viewers of the engravings who were familiar with Ripa's *Iconologia* and similar sources are invited to detect the identity of each represented figure, its allegorical values and those of its selected attributes and accouterments, and the relevance of these values to the subject at hand, to the emperor and empress (their virtues and duties), and to the general dynastic relevance of the celebration. For example, Hercules is relevant to the nominal plot of the opera because he, too, plucked a golden apple which was to serve as a wedding present (to Juno) from the Garden of the Hesperides. But Hercules was equally significant as a model to rulers because of the choice between the two modes of life with which he was faced and because of the immortality which was his reward. The proscenium, briefly, constitutes a visual text, which remains constant throughout the performance and which is therefore intended to be impressed on the spectator's subconscious. Note, for example, that, among these parameters of permanence, Burnacini emphasized figures of peace and the arts rather than images related to war, which is entirely in line with the desired mythistorical representation of the rulers in question.

The splendid festive performance organized at the Baroque absolute court was the most synthetic and syncretistic event of its age. Essentially, such a performance sought to represent, as a philosophical program and by means of a multifaceted artistic praxis, the tensions of hierarchical relationships on various levels: the individual versus the state, the state versus other states, humanity versus the rest of the cosmic creation—in other words, tensions between the part and the whole, between the microcosmos and the macrocosmos.[56] Another way of saying this is that Sbarra's libretto, Cesti's music, and Burnacini's allegorical and illusionistic apparatus constituted a translation (metamorphosis) of external objects (figurative or textual emblems, political motifs, devices provided by the new science) into internal states, for the audience was invited to understand the motifs and applaud them wholeheartedly. Thus Burnacini's program, in collaboration with Sbarra's text and Cesti's music, followed from the central Neoplatonic metaphor: the human being is the small equivalent (microcosm) of what the universe is in large (macrocosm). Similarly, the festive celebration constitutes itself, again, a microcosm of the world, which signifies nothing else than that the sponsor-creator of the celebration is held up as the equivalent of the creator of the world. In theory, this holds true for many, if not all, of the grandiose festive performances at the courts of absolute rulers. But Burnacini/Sbarra/Cesti went further than any other makers of such performances in their pure explicitness.

I have argued earlier that, unlike the Renaissance ruler who participated in "play in performance," the Baroque ruler who sponsored grandiose festive performances was, in general, "merely" an observer of "performed play." Leopold and Margareta Theresa, however, combined both roles. On the one hand, they placed the spirit of play under their aegis and presided over a series of performances that metaphysically and symbolically represented them as fixed points of reference in the cosmos. On the other hand, Leopold participated personally in the equestrian ballet and created significant portions of the music for the opera; and without the empress' symbolic involvement in the climax of the opera, the latter would have had no point. At the same time, it was precisely in providing this surprising ending of the opera (*heuresis*) that Sbarra deviated from the standard interpretation of epideictic rhetoric and strove to affect the passions and the ethos of the audience by going beyond the judicious rearrangement and presentation (disposition and elocution) of existing matter. This invention, too, was a matter of amplification and magnification (*auxeisis*). Of course, the makers of the splendid festive performances discussed in the preceding chapters, likewise represented their sponsor-rulers as heroic, superhuman figures with the passions and expressions characteristic of the high genres (epic, tragedy). But who could hope to take the amplification any further, now that Sbarra had not only placed Leopold and Margareta Theresa above Jupiter but had even unequivocally associated the Austrian rulers with the Christian cause itself? For Christian motifs can be read in the arrangements and the decoration of the stage (Solf 44ff), and who could miss, moreover, the association of the golden apple with the *Reichsapfel*, symbol of the pan-Catholic dynasty? To go any further than the creators of *Il pomo d'oro* had done would be to risk the charge of blasphemy that the consistent, previous use of pagan imagery and settings had successfully avoided. To insist more strongly that the emperor and empress, the sponsor-rulers of these feasts, were "gods" in play and by means of play, would be indecent. In this play, the symbolic values of all its artistic components were combined harmoniously. The seriously playful union of these arts in a new creation was symbolic of the new union of the nation. Politics and the art of play are, indeed, closely related.

It is interesting to note, finally, that the "auf der Cortina" theater, which continued to serve after the performance of *Il pomo d'oro*, was one of the first victims of the Turkish siege of Vienna in 1683. An excellent target for enemy artillerists and a huge fire hazard, the wooden building was torn down on the orders of Vienna's valiant defenders, Burgomaster Liebenberg and Governor Count von Starhemberg. With this dramatic gesture, armor-clad Reality declared the absolutist cult of play irrelevant and its most recent temple a danger to the city. Leopold and Margareta Theresa did not witness the permanent destruction of this theatrical space, which had been dedicated to them as the "gods of play" of the realm. They had fled before the Turk pitched his innumerable tents before the city and did not return until Polish and German forces, who had arrived in the nick of time, had saved their city. Thus, the demolition of "auf der Cortina" under enemy fire forms a fitting conclusion (though hardly a *lieto fine*) to this study. In a sense, the event also signified the end of the cult of the gods of play in general. No *Gesamtkunstwerk* resembling the one of which *Il pomo d'oro* was the climax was ever attempted again. This festive cycle was actually designed to be unsurpassable ("ne plus ultra"), and its successful though delayed performance contributed perhaps as effectively toward the termination of the "genre" as any political and intellectual circumstance of the close of the century.

Notes

1. Following the abdication of Emperor Charles V (= King Charles I of Spain) in 1555, his son Philip succeeded him in Spain, Italy, Burgundy and the Netherlands as Philip II (grandfather of Philip IV). Charles' brother Ferdinand, who was already King of Hungary, King of Bohemia, and Archduke of Austria succeeded him as the German emperor. Hence the "separation of the branches" of the Habsburg dynasty. It is further important to note that the crowns of Hungary and Bohemia, previously separate, had been linked since 1490. Ferdinand became king of both in 1526. A very well documented historical introduction is R. J. W. Evans, *The Making of the Habsburg Monarchy 1550–1700: An Interpretation* (Oxford, 1979). His "select bibliography" is particularly rich. Equally interesting is Victor-L. Tapié, *The Rise and Fall of the Habsburg Monarchy*, trans. Stephen Hardman (London, 1971). A more popularizing, illustrated introduction is Edward Crankshaw, *The Habsburgs* (London, 1971). See also John Spielman, *Leopold I of Austria* (London; New Brunswick, 1977).

2. Born the second son of Ferdinand III in 1640, Leopold was trained for an ecclesiastical career by the Jesuits (he remained a lay associate of the order). But his brother Ferdinand IV—the Roman king elect—died of smallpox at age twenty-one in July, 1654; Ferdinand III followed his son in death three years later (April, 1657). Leopold was elected to the Roman

throne and crowned in Frankfurt on July 22, 1658; he was crowned King of Hungary in 1665 and King of Bohemia in 1666. It is interesting to note, in view of what follows, that the Roman throne came to Leopold in spite of initial French opposition to the Habsburg cause. Mazarin, who quickly abandoned his initial idea of boldly proposing the young Louis XIV for the vacant post, advanced the candicacy of the Elector Ferdinand Maria of Bavaria. I have not been able to see G. Zeller, "Les Rois de France candidats à l'Empire," *Aspects de l'ancien Régime* (Paris, 1963; reference from Tapié 137 n. 1), nor Paul Frischauer, *The Imperial Crown: The Story of the Rise and Fall of the Holy Roman and the Austrian Empires* (London, [1939]).

3. A caricatural portrait was drawn by the mid-nineteenth-century popularist historian Karl E. Vehse, who made selective use of contemporaneous sources (such as the memoirs of French ambassador Grammont and the Italian tourist Father Pacichelli) in his two-volume *Memoirs of the Court, Aristocracy, and Diplomacy of Austria*, trans. Franz Demmler (London, 1856; passages quoted from Vehse are in Demmler's translation). Leopold emerges from Vehse's pages as a dull, short man, with a very large mouth and hanging lip, and an exaggeratedly heavy Habsburg chin, which a little black beard vainly tries to hide. Dressed in Spanish fashion in red stockings and red shoes, bowed down under the weight of an enormous periwig, and sporting a red feather in his hat, the Emperor can usually be found on his knees in his court chapel—where, it is well known, he hears three masses in succession on festival days. Besides visiting places of devotion, he spends his time signing despotical orders in retaliation for insurrections or alleged crimes of *lèse-majesté*, scribbling virtually illegible letters in several languages at once to other crowned heads throughout Europe, and hunting (or angling), composing and performing music, playing cards, and collecting such curiosities as rare coins and gems, mechanical automatons, objects pertaining to the occult arts, and curious books.

In *The Making of the Habsburg Monarchy 1550–1770*, Evans paints a much subtler picture of Leopold. This modern historian detects in the artistically gifted emperor a "devoutness going with a disarming gaiety; friendliness and immediacy with conscientiousness and pride. Here is a man well-informed, intelligent, and curious, but no freethinker; honest and correct, but pusillanimous and irresolute; thoughtful, immensely hard-working . . . and heavily reliant on advice which he treats, however, with some independence of spirit and without sense of obligation" (143). There can be little doubt that Leopold was, above all, a genuinely pious man. On the famous Plague Column (*Pestsäule*) on the Graben in Vienna (a votive offering in commemmoration of the plague that struck Vienna in 1679; it was dedicated in 1692), Leopold is represented in a humble and kneeling position, rendering thanks to God for the delivery of his capital from the plague, with the caption "Ego Leopoldus humilis servus tuus."

4. Leopold is said to have been overly dominated by the Jesuits and his successive chief ministers. In theory, there was no such office as that of prime minister, although practice was different. The Italian count Portia, lord steward and chief governor of the young Leopold, became his first prime minister. After Portia's death in 1665, the generally disliked Prince Johann Weickard Auersperg succeeded him, but not for long; he fell over an alliance in the making between Leopold and Louis XIV and was exiled to his estates in 1670, where he died in 1677. Auersperg was succeeded by the Bohemian Prince Wenceslaus (Václav) Eusebius Lobkovic, archenemy of the Jesuits, protégé of the young empress Margareta Theresa, and, like his predecessor, an amateur of French manners and culture. Hated by the second empress and the Jesuits, Lobkovic was obscurely charged with "disclosure of secrets" in 1674 and exiled for the remainder of his life to his castle in Raudnitz, where he continued to satirize his enemies. His immediate successor was the Modenese count Raimundo Montecuccoli, a man of melancholy temperament, widely read in many subjects, and a military hero who had distinguished himself by inflicting the first defeat on the Ottoman Empire in two centuries (the Battle at Sankt Gotthardt in 1664). Evans lists more important counsellors to Leopold (144–45), none of whom, however, were as notable and as indispensable to the emperor as the brilliant Prince Eugène of Savoy (after 1700).

5. The siege of Vienna was a definitive turning point in the confrontation of Christianity and Islam, and the most important manifestation thereof since the legendary naval battle of Lepanto (1572); hardly four years after a catastrophic outbreak of the plague had ravaged it, the city was thus again hit heavily. Vienna had been besieged by the Turks earlier, that is, by Suleiman the Magnificent in 1529. "Fighting the Turk" was actually the dominant principle of Austrian foreign policy from 1660 (when the Ottoman empire invaded Transylvania) until well into the eighteenth century. See a contemporaneous document, *Glaubwurdiges Diarium und Beschreibung dessen was Zeit wahrender turkischen Belagerung {...} der Stadt Wien vorgangen*, which was published in an English translation "out of High-Dutch by his Majestie Command" as *Journal, or, A most particular account of all that passed in the late seige of Vienna written by a principal officer, who was in the town during the whole time of the seige, and sent by authority to the Imperial Commissioner at the Dyet of Ratisbonne* (London, 1684).

With the Turkish defeat before Vienna in 1683, the war against the Ottoman Empire, still well entrenched in the Hungarian Danube Valley, was far from over. A Holy League was formed by Pope Innocent XI which included the Emperor, the King of Poland, Venice, and the Czar of Russia—all of whom had had territories ransacked by the Turks. Together with forces from as far north as Sweden and as far west as Cataluña, the League reconquered a series of Turkish-occupied Hungarian fortresses. In 1686, its commander Charles Duke of Lorraine took Buda, and in 1688 Belgrade (which the Turks had taken in 1521) was reconquered. As was only to be expected, the contingents of this "imperial army" behaved as cruelly toward the populations which they "liberated" as, perhaps, the Turks had ever done (Tapié 145ff). When Hungary was reconquered, the military excesses curbed and some form of central authority substituted for the still feudal organization, the main problems were those of repopulation and economic restoration.

6. The large and complex patrimonial territory of the House of Austria was part of the generally Catholic southern part of the German Empire (that is, the part situated south of the Main Valley, though not including Bavaria and Salzburg). It was structurally organized around the valley of the Danube, which ran right through it, into the rebellious and largely Protestant Kingdom of Hungary, much of which it included. The patrimonial territory also included the Kingdom of Bohemia (with Moravia and Silesia) on one side of the Danube Valley, and the Alpine duchies (such as the Tyrol, with Innsbruck as its capital) and Innerösterreich on the other side (Tapié 116). The Austrian Habsburgs also controlled some territories outside the compact region formed by these three kingdoms and the Alpine duchies—such as Trieste and Fiume on the Adriatic. Thus, the Habsburg emperor was at the same time a German prince and Head of the Holy Roman Empire, and the prince of the various patrimonial states. The case of Hungary in particular proves that Leopold, though almost never independently, could on occasion act with fanatical and cruel determination. Several conspiracies of Hungarian nobles during the 1670s were not "resolved" (and then only partly) until the early 1680s (see Tapié 142ff). Following the defeat of the Turks at Mohács, the throne of Hungary became the hereditary possession of the Habsburgs. Besides Transylvania, Austria would gain more Hungarian territory after Prince Eugène's defeat of the Turks at Zenta (Peace of Carlovtsi, 1699; Tapié 158). One of the reasons why the Habsburgs coveted Hungary was the presence in that region of gold and silver mines.

7. The Habsburg lands still had their own regional dynasties, authority-conscious Estates, chancellors and systems of taxation. And as an immediate result of the Thirty Years War, the many dichotomies that historically existed in each land (and in some cases in different counties of each land) had become even more pronounced. These included (1) dichotomies between cities and feudal aristocracy. For example, the fact that some universities and other excellent institutions of learning continued to flourish in major cities did not prevent a marked regression of urban power, and the subsequent loss of status of the average city dweller. In the seventeenth century, Evans writes, "the towns of Central Europe ceased to be *bourgeois*. They lost any claim to represent distinct civic values and appeared as foreign bodies in an organic

rural-based society, an impression fostered best of all wherever townsmen had actually once immigrated from abroad and still spoke a different language from the surrounding countryside, as through much of northern Hungary and parts of Bohemia's Czech hinterland . . . the new order of the seventeenth century held little place for the towns or for serious use of urban resources. The average town-dweller became more or less a peasant, tending his small-holding as well as plying his trade, unable to raise credit, and dreading the descent of the next imperial garrison" (84–85]); (2) between the old and the new aristocracy; (3) between "redeemed" (land-owning) and "unredeemed" peasants (Tapié 120); (4) between Catholics and Protestants, and among "Protestants" themselves.

Like his father Ferdinand III before him, Leopold was actively engaged in counter-reforming the provinces. He encouraged the Jesuits as well as mendicant orders such as the Dominicans, the Franciscans, and the Augustinians to purge large areas as well as small pockets of provincial territory from Lutheranism and Calvinism. Thus, actively supported by the central government, "Reformation Commissions" consisting of priests, officials, and soldiers toured the countryside, threatening and occasionally chastising the people into submitting to the Church. Jesuits worked the countryside as individual missionaries, established networks of well-functioning schools and organized lay societies in the towns. Lower Austria and Bohemia were targeted in the 1650s; through the 1660s and 1670s more attention was given to Moravia and Silesia, and especially to Hungary where the Counter Reformation did not succeed in eradicating all kernels of Lutheranism and Calvinism. (For further details, see Evans 118–21). It is noteworthy that these preachers and clerics included foreigners who contributed much to the already very cosmopolitan makeup of the Empire.

8. These councils included the *Hofrat* (Aulic Council or Privy Council), the *Geheime Rat* (*Geheime Konferenz* or Privy Conference, which dealt with the most important matters, the *Hofkammer* (which controlled some of the emperor's revenues), and the *Hofkriegsrat* (the War Council, which was established in Graz, closer to the Turkish "front"). There was also a Council of Commerce, which was supposed to combine the economic policies of all the states but which failed to work because it consisted of members from the high aristocracy who had little if any grounding in economics and trade. Although these councils could also include professionals (in particular, jurists) from the middle class, they were controlled by the upper aristocracy.

Whereas Louis XIV deliberately excluded members of the high nobility from his councils and his government, "under [the Austrian emperor's] patronage and in his name, the central government was exercised by a juxtaposition of Councils, just as the territory of the dynasty itself comprised a juxtaposition of autonomous kingdoms and principalities. This was an empirical system; the structure of the State was not yet complete" (Tapié 118). In addition, it is to be noted that the emperor, clearly not an economist himself, did not have a Colbert to advise him. Several efforts at establishing *manufactures* on the French model failed, and luxury products continued to be imported from France; likewise, the individual interests of the patrimonial lands were often contradictory; and, finally, the system of taxation, tolls, state monopolies, revenues reserved for the personal use of the emperor, and the still feudal giving of lands or properties in return for services rendered to the emperor made a coherent economic policy difficult, if not impossible (see Tapié 151–54).

9. For instance, Leopold's government had two distinct executive chanceries, one for the Empire, the other for Austria; they rivalled one other and squabbled continuously.

10. Leopold was hardly ever in attendance at military reviews. Nonetheless, in the latter decades of the reign, he allowed Prince Eugène of Savoy to reorganize and modernize the Austrian military system into a model force second to none.

11. Leopold connected the Hofburg by means of a new wing with the sixteenth-century palace of Rudolf II (1576–1612). Vienna, which had well withstood the Thirty Years War, remained essentially a medieval city; by contrast, Prague in Bohemia was a more "modern" (Baroque) and a more impressive city. Not Leopold, but his sons Joseph I (ruled 1705–1711) and Charles VI (ruled 1711–1740) would carry out the architectural transformation of Vienna.

12. Leopold was a prolific and talented amateur composer. He wrote no fewer than seventy-nine Latin church compositions in a great variety of forms (including oratorios, motets, masses, hymns, psalms, and litanies) and much secular music as well: at least 155 songs and other contributions to plays and operas (arias for Italian-language operas and for two German-language comedies), contributions to nine theatrical celebrations (including compositions for several acts of *Il pomo d'oro*), and a vast number of compositions for ballet and dance. See H. V. F. Somerset, "The Habsburg Emperors as Musicians," *Music and Letters* 30 (1949): 204–15; and Robert Griffin, "The Burnacini Style in High Baroque Theatre," introduction to his edition of *Il fuoco eterno—Das Vestalische Ewige Feuer*, by Ludovico Burnacini (1674; New York, 1970).

13. Egon Wellesz, *Essays on Opera* (London, 1950) 54–81, 46ff. In the eighteenth century, Austrian musicians and composers rose in prominence, fusing their "sense of melody" with the Italian "feeling for form" and creating "the style of the pre-classical Viennese composers" which "helped materially to prepare for the arrival of the glorious epoch of Austrian music associated

with the names of Gluck, Haydn, Mozart, Beethoven, and Schubert" (Wellesz 48). See also Franz Hadamowsky's very detailed study, "Barocktheater am Wiener Kaiserhof. Mit einem Spielplan (1625–1740)," *Jahrbuch der Gesellschaft für Wiener Theaterforschung* 1951–52 (Vienna, 1955).

14. For example, in 1631, Ferdinand's first marriage to the Infanta Maria Anna was celebrated with the melodramma *Allegrezza del mondo* and with a ballet in which Archduchess Claudia danced the role of the Moon and several ladies appeared as planets. At Ferdinand's coronation on December 30, 1637, an allegorical ballet was performed, complete with the customary triumphal cars (Wellesz 33). On the occasion of his second marriage (to Archduchess Maria Leopoldina of Innsbruck, in 1648), the opera *I Trionfi d'Amore* was performed. In the prologue of this opera, Venus asks her son Cupid to show the world that her power is stronger than that of Diana and Pallas; the main plot features, once again, Ulysses on the island of Circe; a pastoral subplot is woven through the main plot; and the work ends with a testimonial to the power of Venus, and an homage (*licenza*) to Ferdinand and Maria Leopoldina. Structurally and thematically, *I Trionfi d'Amore* thus anticipates *Il pomo d'oro* on several counts.

15. Marc'Antonio Pietro Cesti (1623–1669), a Franciscan friar, was a younger contemporary of Cavalli. He had worked for the public opera houses in Venice, then in Rome and for the Habsburgs in Innsbruck before Leopold brought him to Vienna in 1666 as *Ehrenkapellmeister*. His early work includes the operas *Orontea*, *Cesare amante*, *La Dori*, *Tito*, *L'Argia* and *La schiava fortunata*; later in his career he composed *Il principe generoso*, *Nettuno e Flora festeggianti*, *La magnanimità d'Alessandro*, *Le disgrazie d'amore* (for the carnival of 1667; text by Sbarra, *licenza* composed by Leopold), *Semiramide*, and *Il pomo d'oro*. He died in Florence in 1669, one year after the production of *Il pomo d'oro*. His music has been characterized as "more facile than Cavalli's, less vigorous, more feminine; he excels in the setting of idyllic, tender scenes; his melodies are clearly defined and graceful; his harmony . . . sounds less bold and experimental [than Cavalli's], more like the style of the eighteenth century" (Grout 100; see also Kretzschmar 63–76). For further information on Cesti's career in Innsbruck before he came to Vienna, see Walter Senn, *Musik und Theater am Hof zu Innsbruck: Geschichte der Hofkapelle vom 15. Jahrhundert bis zu deren Auflösung im Jahre 1748* (Innsbruck: 1954) 256–61.

16. It was burned during the Turkish siege of 1683 and rebuilt by Leopold.

17. The first new genuine court theater in Vienna was built in 1659 and inaugurated in January, 1660; it served especially for commedia dell'arte performances (Hadamowsky 34). Thus, the "auf der Cortina" project was actually Leopold's second newly built court theater. According to Somerset,

merely sixteen operas and/or oratorios were performed between 1630 and 1657; by contrast, in the first twenty years of Leopold's reign alone (before the great plague of Vienna of 1679), as many as four hundred works were performed—and these much more elaborate and expensive than the productions under Ferdinand III (208).

18. It was also in seventeenth-century Vienna that children performed hobby-horse ballets at court (see a contemporaneous illustration in Baur-Heinhold 21).

19. The citizenry was not deprived of performances, either. The University of Vienna maintained a public theater in its aula, where the general public was admitted free of charge to the religious dramas directed by Nicolaus Avancini, and where it could also get a taste of operatic ballets. Leopold himself attended regularly (Griffin [7]).

20. It was sixty-four meters long, twenty-six meters wide, and fourteen meters high, and it could seat several thousand spectators (Hadamowsky 35). Very little information is available on the theater. See Peter Fleischacker, "Rekonstruktionsversuch des Opernhauses und des Bühnenapparates in dem Theater des L. O. Burnacini," diss., U of Vienna, 1965 (which I have not been able to see; reference from Solf 35).

21. A crucial factor in these marriage negotiations was the lack of a male heir to the Spanish throne, and the fear that the future husbands of the two Infantas would claim the throne upon the death of Philip IV. But in 1657 Felipe Próspero was born, which obviously influenced the consequent Spanish decisions. I am indebted to Margaret R. Greer for this observation.

22. The contract was read out to Leopold on December 18, 1663. As might have been expected, perhaps, Leopold did not receive a cent from the enormous fortune promised.

23. Via his trustee Pötting in Madrid, Leopold even tried to speed up the departure by assuring his future father-in-law that he did not intend to actually consummate the marriage until the girl were physically mature (in a letter dated April 21, 1664; in Pribram 347).

24. For reasons of etiquette, the emperor himself could not accompany her (although he came halfway to finally meet her). Even before she left Spanish soil, Margareta Theresa occasioned festivities at the Viennese court. Her birthday was celebrated there on July 12 with the première performance of *Nettuno e Flora festeggianti* (an allegorical drama in three acts about Margareta's sea voyage, by Sbarra and Cesti, who were by then already collaborating on *Il pomo d'oro*), which was followed by the ballet *Concorso dell'allegrezza universale*, composed by Johann Heinrich Schmelzer. The pro-

gram of this ballet was composed in the three vernacular languages in use at the court: German, Italian, and Spanish.

25. And Leopold was well aware that "willn der Herbst schon vorhanden, die Tag kurz sein und las señoras nit gern früe aufstehn" ("now that it is almost fall, the days are short, and las señoras do not like to get up early;" letter dated September 2, 1666; in Pribram 366–67).

26. An heir, Ferdinand Wenzel, was born on September 28, 1667, but the infant died on January 3, 1668. From then on, Margareta Theresa was continuously pregnant, which utterly destroyed her already weak constitution. In July, 1668, when *Il pomo d'oro* was performed, the empress was pregnant with Maria Antonia (who was born on January 18, 1669, and remained the only surviving child from this marriage). After several more disastrous pregnancies, and totally exhausted, Margareta Theresa herself died (in childbirth) in March, 1673; she was not yet twenty-two years old.

Leopold's private correspondence indicates (see Pribram 375) that his amazingly early second marriage was the result of political-dynastic pressure, and that he had to suppress his personal feelings. On October 15, 1673, he wedded the nineteen-year-old Princess Claudia Felicitas of Tyrol; and like his first wife, she, too, died prematurely at age twenty-two, in 1676, leaving him still without a male heir. Characteristically, Leopold composed the music for her funeral (which was also to serve for his own in 1705; Somerset 212). Whereas Leopold's first two spouses had shared his love for music and performances, his third wife, Princess Eleonora of Neuburg-Mantua, clearly did not. It was a subject for gossip that the "saintly" Eleonora detested the theater and, while attending operatic performances with her husband, secretly read the Psalms instead of the libretto (Vehse II: 10).

27. See Herbert Seifert, "Die Festlichkeiten zur ersten Hochzeit Kaiser Leopolds I," *Österreichische Musikzeitschrift* 29 (1974): 6–16. Seifert needs five pages to list all the celebrations organized at the Viennese court between July 12, 1666 and July 12-14, 1668 (10–15).

28. The construction of this theater was entrusted, of course, to Leopold's architect and stage engineer, Ludovico Ottavio Burnacini. Perhaps the most difficult role in musical drama of the genre that we have been discussing was reserved for such artists as Inigo Jones, Cosme Lotti, Giacomo Torelli, Gaspare Vigarani, and Ludovico Ottavio Burnacini, whose task it was to translate into a three-dimensional phenomenon the allegorical conceptualization of the sponsor-ruler and the corresponding fantasies of librettist and composer. Leopold went down in history as a "theatrical emperor," but considerable credit for this reputation is due to the talents of his devoted employee Ludovico Ottavio Burnacini.

He was the son of stage designer Giovanni Burnacini, who moved from

Venice to Vienna in 1651, with his brother Marc Antonio and with Ludovico. From 1652 on, the Burnacinis were employed by Ferdinand III; for example, they constructed the Cesarea Corte theater and introduced Venetian stage refinements to the Viennese operatic scene. At the death of his father in 1655, Ludovico inherited his office. However, when Leopold ascended the throne and appointed Giovanni Angelini as his theater architect, Burnacini returned to Venice. In 1658, he was recalled and reappointed; until his death in 1709 he worked uninterruptedly in Vienna, first for Leopold and after 1705 for Joseph I. He created over one hundred and fifty operas and oratorios, and in addition designed costumes, interiors, altars, triumphal monuments and buildings at the various country estates of the imperial family (Griffin [2]).

29. The Jesuit Francesco Sbarra was an imperial court poet from 1665 to 1668.

30. "Fatta quest'Operetta [*Nettuno e Flora festeggianti*], devo proseguire l'Opera grande che di già ho principiata, ma ad ogni modo vedrò di servire a V.S. e di nuovo ritornerò alla solitudine per poter operare con maggior quiete et applicatione." Quoted from R. Giazotto, ed. "Ventidue Lettere Ritrovate nell'Archivio di Stato di Venezia," *Nuova Rivista Musicale Italiana* 3 (1969): 496–512, 510. It was doubtlessly to allow Cesti to work full-time on *Il pomo d'oro* that his colleague, *Hofkapellmeister* Antonio Bertali, was appointed to compose the music for the equestrian ballet.

31. Rehearsals took place twice a week in the imperial riding school under the direction of Alessandro Carducci, chamberlain of the Grand Duke of Tuscany and the undisputed expert in the art.

32. Carl B. Schmidt, "Antonio Cesti's *Il pomo d'oro:* A Reexamination of a Famous Hapsburg Court Spectacle," *Journal of the American Musicological Society* 29 (1976): 381–412, 384.

33. The libretto *Il Pomo d'oro, Festa teatrale Rappresentata in Vienna per l'augustissime Nozze delle sacre cesaree reali maestà di Leopoldo, e Margherita, componimento di Francesco Sbarra* was first published in 1667 (octavo) and again, in a more lavish folio format, in 1668. Both editions were printed in Vienna by court printer Matteo Cosmerovio, and the illustrations had been done by Mathäus Küsell (see further). The 1668 edition includes also a "snapshot" engraving of the interior of the theater during the première of *Il pomo d'oro*. It is interesting also to note that the 1667 edition of the opera libretto was published in conjunction with the libretto of the equestrian ballet, which suggests, again, that these events were designed as the contiguous elements of a *Gesamtkunstwerk*. The musical score of *Il pomo d'oro* was not published at that time (see further).

The first translation of the complete Italian libretto was done, not surprisingly, into Spanish by Juan Silvestre Salvo; it was printed in Vienna, 1668, and two copies exist in the Sección de Raros in the Biblioteca Nacional, Madrid. A German translation was commissioned by Prince Duke Johann Ernst of Saxony-Weimar from the courtier-playwright Caspar Stieler. This translation ("Der göldene Apfel, Freudenspiel," 1669) was not published; the ms. copy is kept in the Zentralbibliothek der Deutschen Klassik, Weimar (see Aikin 62). Ilona Hubay was able to locate a German language ms. libretto (# 104) of *Il pomo d'oro* in the Coburg Landesbibliothek (*Die Handschriften der Landesbibliothek Coburg* [Coburg: Coburger Landesstiftung, 1962]), which is most likely the German summary of the text that was traditionally issued for those unfamiliar with Italian. A second, anonymous German translation of the complete text, *Der guldene Apfel: Schauspiel*, was published in Nürnberg, 1672; a facsimile edition was prepared by Margret Dietrich (Vienna, 1965), which contains the complete set of engravings. Finally, an English translation, not of the Italian original but rather of Salvo's Spanish translation, was published in 1671 (British Library 11726.a.15.[1]).

34. From Vehse I: 496ff. See also Alewyn and Sälzle 1959: 103.

35. According to Vehse who quotes from the *Frankfurter Relationen*, the number of lights in the temple was 73,000, "with at least 300 rockets, each charged with three pounds of powder" (I: 498).

36. From Vehse I: 499ff. A description of the event was also given in Wolfgang Geiger's *Theatrum Europaeum* (1677). An abbreviated repeat performance, without the emperor participating, was given on January 31. It has been suggested that the production of this ballet was far more expensive than the imperial court could actually afford (Wellesz 83; also Schmidt 1976: 385).

37. The Turkish galley with all its accouterments was so heavy that, unfortunately, the wheels of the car on which it was pulled around the arena broke, which must have spoiled some of the effect. When the equestrian ballet was repeated on January 31, the galley was left out (Vehse I: 499).

38. The floats featured Neptune riding on a whale; two elephants in a garden, carrying turrets on their backs on which the Earth rests; Air riding a dragon; Vulcan and the Cyclopes working in Mount Etna (Vehse I: 500–1).

39. Neither the chariot of Glory nor the pearl are mentioned in Wellesz's description of the event (85).

40. A note on the audience: besides numerous crowned heads and even a representative of the Ottoman Empire, honorable citizens made up part of the audience (Griffin [6]). The latter may have been admitted to compensate for the fact that they had been forced to lodge some of the numerous prominent guests in their homes, since the Hofburg was too small. This information is

from Guido Adler, ed., *Denkmäler der Tonkunst in Österreich* III/2 vol. 6 (1896; Graz, 1959) ix.

41. Schmidt quotes descriptions of the performance given in the *Theatrum Europaeum* 10 (1677): 803, and in the *Frankfurter Relationen* 1668: 61 (Schmidt 1976: 388 n. 33). In fixing the performance dates on Thursday 12 and Saturday 14 rather than on Friday 13 and Saturday 14, Seifert (9–10) and I follow the account from the *Frankfurter Relationen*. Indeed, on Fridays, usually only plays with religious subjects were performed at the court of Leopold. The opera was repeated on July 22 (?) and 23 (Seifert 10).

42. A great number of Olympian gods was a staple feature of Venetian opera (Kretzschmar 6). All roles were sung by males (including *castrati*). Cesti's orchestration called for six violins, twelve viols (alto, tenor, bass), two flutes (for the pastoral scenes), trumpets in two parts, a harpsichord, and other continuo instruments (lutes, theorbo). Scenes set in the realm of Pluto had their own group of traditionally "hellish" instruments, recalling, in fact, the orchestration of Monteverdi's *L'Orfeo* (two cornets, three trombones, a bassoon and a regale; Grout 103; Donington 257–58; Pirrotta 271). Donington even speaks of an "unbroken tradition" since Monteverdi's *Orfeo* sixty years earlier (257–58).

Yet, on a purely musical level, *Il pomo d'oro* also represents a transition to a more "lyrical" type of opera, in which the composer is a relatively more important contributor than the librettist. Although the allegorical-ideological value of the textual program of *Il pomo d'oro* was obviously very prominent, Sbarra attempted to give Cesti as free a rein as possible, for example by introducing such "pathetic" characters as Ennone, Alceste, Aurindo, and Proserpina. Wellesz 58–81 gives a musicological description of the opera. The ms. score of the Prologue and of Acts 1, 2, and 4 is in the Vienna Nationalbibliothek (Signature ms. 16844). It was edited and published by Adler in *Denkmäler der Tonkunst in Österreich* III/2 (vol. 6) and IV/2 (vol. 9) (1896–97; Graz, 1959). The score of Acts 3 and 5, long thought lost, was found in a ms. in Modena and published by Carl B. Schmidt, *Antonio Cesti: 'Il pomo d'oro.' (Music for Acts III and V from Modena, Biblioteca Estense, Ms. Mus. E.120)*, Recent Researches in the Music of the Baroque Era 42 (Madison, WI, 1982).

43. The *Ballettmeister* was Santo Ventura, and the numerous battle scenes were directed by *Fechtmeister* Agostini Santini.

44. Schmidt 1976: 384 speaks of "more than thirty-nine mechanical contrivances used to create storms, earthquakes, firespitting dragons, thunder, and lightning." On Burnacini's grotesques, see Solf 85ff.

45. The engravings by Küsell (Augsburg 1621—Vienna 1682) of Bur-

nacini's original sketches have been frequently reproduced. See the (small-sized) illustrations in Molinari 131–52; better, however, are the relatively large reproductions in Adler 1959. The Küsell engravings also provide an unusually clear picture of the splendidly anachronistic costumes, which were also designed by Burnacini. The costumes of minor characters are as elaborate as those of the principals; Küsell's engravings are so detailed that they allow the trained observer to distinguish between the various fabrics and the craftsmanship that went into their making; see Diane Hahn Shock, "Costuming for *Il pomo d'oro*," *Gazette des Beaux Arts* 69 (1967): 251–56. Moreover, Solf has been able to indicate details in these sets/engravings that seem directly influenced by motifs from contemporaneous painting, sculpture, and architecture (65). Finally, Carfagno pointed out that Burnacini might also have been inspired by some of the sets that were used for the production of *Sant'Alessio* (129).

46. The rulers of Hell are seated under a baldachin that seems an infernal travesty of Bernini's *baldacchino* in Saint Peter's in Rome (Solf 62).

47. This device recalls the amusing Mannerist fireplaces shaped like the mouth of Hades, such as the one designed by Alessandro Vittoria for the Palazzo Thiene, Vicenza. See John Shearman, *Mannerism*, Style and Civilization (1967; London: 1987) 122.

48. Solf considers this scene design a pagan-theatrical version of the Christian Humanistic motif that shows Christ as Pantokrater, as represented in the thirteenth-century Florence Baptistery and as adapted consequently by Dante in the thirtieth canto of "Purgatory," which features Beatrice flying in the center of the Spheres on a chariot representing the Church (105).

49. Filaura, a commedia dell'arte figure, serves "as a parody and thus a critique of the pretentious, avaricious courtier, a type which must have plagued the court in imperial Vienna, as elsewhere" (Aikin 67).

50. As far as I know, Aikin was first to suggest that the representation of the four elements forms a connection between the three grandiose festive events (66); however, she does not examine the point to the extent that it deserves.

51. The locus that hosted the apparatus of the fireworks display was the Bastion, a flat terrain near the Hofburg that served as a parade and exercise ground for the Imperial troops. Appropriately enough, the display was designed by Bartholomew Peissker, "master of the arsenal of the fortress of Glatz" (Vehse I: 499).

52. This motif is repeated in the Prologue of *Il pomo d'oro*. Indeed, the "motif of a room lined with the images of the illustrious ancestors of the

imperial house" recurs twice in the course of the opera to project political stability and historical continuity as the desirable outcome of the marriage (Aikin 68).

53. Predictably enough, "the apple of discord becomes the apple of concord, symbol of the *pax romana* the Holy Roman Empire wishes to impose on a pan-Christian Europe, and the imperial marriage is elevated to a symbol of the peace, stability, and dynastic continuity expected as a result of the union" (Aikin 65). The same motif was also very clearly present in the fireworks display (the acronyms in the air) and even more clearly in the equestrian ballet (the Temple of Immortality).

54. Solf summarizes the formative features of Burnacini's scenic design for *Il pomo d'oro* in five features: (1) the proscenium enframed the action as a carrier of allegorical-emblematic meanings; (2) classical mythological iconology was used profusely to refer to the emperor; (3) contemporaneous visual art served as inspiration for details of the stage decoration; (4) the system of sets embodied the symbolic form of perspective; (5) ornamental devices connected the scenes (61).

55. I would like here to recall a point made earlier: the operatic stage that was equipped with machines became a flexible geographical metaphor with, at least in theory, endless possibilities. A painted set was like a topos or commonplace, fixed in usage by certain conditions of decorum, determined by allegorical and mythological connotations, adding the power of the image to the power of the words. The task of the stage designer was to manipulate these topoi eloquently and efficiently, according to the required decorum of the context, and in order to affect the emotions and ethos of the audience.

56. Thus, in matters of thematics and formal presentation, the makers of Baroque feasts and festive performances explored what is essentially a metonymic concern. But in doing so, they not only represented a subject but also attempted to arouse the audience's emotions and direct its ethos. The most splendid festive performances were those of operas, because, as I have argued, opera was the most ideal medium for absolute monarch-sponsors to advertise and celebrate their new status (that is, their absolutism) in a festive, playful mode. The power of this new art form to combine an Idea-content (linked to allegoresis) and an ethical appeal (as determined by the rhetorical execution) was unparalleled.

Bibliography

Abraham, Claude. *On the Structure of Molière's Comédies-Ballets*. Biblio 17–19. Paris; Seattle; Tübingen: Papers on French Seventeenth-Century Literature, 1984.

Ademollo, Alessandro. *I teatri di Roma nel secolo XVII*. 1888. Bologna: Forni, 1969.

Adler, Guido. Ed. *Denkmäler der Tonkunst in Österreich* III/2 (vol. 6) and IV/2 (vol. 9). 1896–97. Graz: Akademische Druck & Verlagsanstalt, 1959.

Aercke, Kristiaan P. " 'An Odd Angle of the Isle:' Teaching the Courtly Art of *The Tempest*." *Approaches to Teaching Shakespeare's "The Tempest" and Other Late Romances*. Ed. Maurice Hunt. New York: MLA, 1992. 146–52.

Aikin, Judith P. *Scaramutza in Germany. The Dramatic Works of Caspar Stieler*. University Park, PA; London: Pennsylvania State U P, 1989.

Alewyn, Richard, et al. Eds. *Aus der Welt des Barock*. Stuttgart: Metzler, 1957.

———, and Karl Sälzle. *Das grosse Welttheater: Die Epoche der höfischen Feste in Dokument und Deutung*. Rohwolts Deutsche Enzyklopädie. Hamburg: Rowohlt, 1959.

Alpers, Svetlana. *The Art of Describing: Dutch Art in the Seventeenth Century*. Chicago: U of Chicago P, 1983.

Alsip, Barbara. "Myth and Fairy Tale in Molière's *La Princesse d'Elide*." *Papers on French Seventeenth-Century Literature* 18 (1983): 221–32.

Angelini, Franca. *Il teatro barocco*. Letteratura Italiana Laterza 29. Rome; Bari: Laterza, 1975.

Apostolidès, Jean-Marie. "Image du père et peur du tyran au XVIIe siècle." *Revue française de psychanalyse* 44 (1980): 5–14.

———. *Le Roi-Machine. Spectacle et politique au temps de Louis XIV*. Paris: Eds. de Minuit, 1981.

———. *Le Prince sacrifié. Théâtre et politique au temps de Louis XIV*. Paris: Eds. de Minuit, 1985.

———. "L'Entrée royale de Louis XIV." *L'Esprit Créateur* 25.1 (1985): 21–31.

Argan, Giulio Carlo. "La 'Rettorica' e l'arte barocca." See Castelli, Enrico, ed. 9–14.

Aristotle. *"Art" of Rhetoric*. Trans. J. H. Freese. Loeb Classical Library 193. 1926. Cambridge, Mass.; London: Heinemann, 1982.

Armas, Frederick A. de. "Metamorphosis in Calderón's *El mayor encanto, amor*." *Romance Notes* 22 (1981): 208–12.

———. *The Return of Astraea: An Astral-Imperial Myth in Calderón*. Lexington: U P of Kentucky, 1986.

Aubrun, Charles V. "Nouveau public, nouvelle comédie à Madrid au 17e siècle." See Jacquot, Jean, gen. ed. 1968. Vol. 1: 1–12.

Bakhtin, Mikhael M. *The Dialogic Imagination. Four Essays*. Ed. Michael Holquist; trans. C. Emerson & M. Holquist. U of Texas P Slavic Series 1. Austin: U of Texas P, 1981.

Baldinucci, Filippo. *The Life of Bernini*. Trans. Catherine Enggass. University Park, PA: Pennsylvania State U P, 1966.

Barnett, Dene. "La rhétorique de l'opéra." *Dix-Septième Siècle* 33 (1981): 335–55.

Bataille, Georges. "La Notion de dépense." "Premiers Ecrits 1922-1940." *Oeuvres Complètes*. Ed. Denis Hollier. Vol. 1. Paris: Gallimard, 1970. 302–20. 13 vols.

———. "Collège de sociologie." "Ecrits posthumes 1922–1940." *Oeuvres Complètes*. Ed. Denis Hollier. Vol. 2. Paris: Gallimard, 1970. 291–374. 13 vols.

———. "The Notion of Expenditure." *Visions of Excess. Selected Writings, 1927–1939*. Ed. introd. Allan Stoekl; trans. A. Stoekl, with Carl R. Lovitt and Donald M. Leslie, Jr. Theory and History of Literature 14. Minneapolis: U of Minnesota P, 1985. 116–29.

Batllori, Miguel. "Gracián y la Retórica barroca en España." See Castelli, Enrico, ed. 27–32.

Baur-Heinhold, Margarete. *Baroque Theatre*. Trans. Mary Whittall. London: Thames & Hudson, 1967.

Beaujoyeux, Balthazar de. *Le Ballet-Comique de la Reine.* Chefs-d'Oeuvre Classiques de l'Opéra Français 1. New York: Broude Bros. Ltd., [s.d.].

Beaussant, Philippe. *Versailles, Opéra.* Paris: Gallimard, 1981.

Béhar, Pierre. "Rolle und Entwicklung des Theaters am Hofe Ludwigs XIV." See Buck, August, et al., eds. Vol. 2: 319–27.

Beijer, Agne. "Vigarani et Bérain au Palais-Royal." *Revue d'Histoire du Théâtre* 2–3 (1956): 184–96.

Beyer, Barbara I. "Baroque Representation." *Journal of Aesthetics and Art Criticism* 12.3 (1954): 360–65.

Biach-Schiffmann, Flora. *Giovanni und Ludovico Burnacini: Theater und Feste am Wiener Hof.* Arbeiten des I. Kunsthistorischen Instituts der Univ. Wien, Lehrkanzel Strzygowski 43. Vienna, 1931.

Bjurström, Per. *Giacomo Torelli and Baroque Stage Design.* Nationalmusei skriftserie 7. 1961. Stockholm: Nationalmuseum, 1962.

———. *Feast and Theatre in Queen Christina's Rome.* Nationalmusei skriftserie 14. Stockholm: Nationalmuseum, 1966.

Blunt, Anthony. "The Palazzo Barberini." *Journal of the Warburg and Courtauld Institutes* 21 (1958): 256–87.

Boase, Allan. "Leçons sur le ballet de cour." *Neohelicon* 7 (1979): 61–144.

Bondino, Francis. *Présentation des pièces à machines au 17e siècle.* Paris: Centre d'Etudes Théâtrales-Univ. de Paris X, 1971.

Bonnefoy, Yves. *Rome 1630: L'horizon du premier baroque.* Paris: Flammarion, 1970.

Bossuet. *Politique tirée des propres paroles de l'Ecriture sainte.* Ed. J. Le Brun. Genève, 1967. X.1.1: 381.

Bouchard, Jean-Jacques. "Le Journal de Jean-Jacques Bouchard." *Oeuvres de Jean-Jacques Bouchard.* Ed. Emanuele Kanceff. Vol. 1. Turin: Giappichelli, 1976. 139–55. 2 vols.

Bradbury, Malcolm. "*Fanny Hill* and the Comic Novel." *Critical Quarterly* 13 (1971): 263–75.

Bragaglia, Anton. "Scenotecnica barocca." *Emporium* (1937): 608–14.

Brainard, Ingrid. "Der Höfische Tanz. Darstellende Kunst und Höfische Repräsentation." See Buck, August, et al., eds. Vol. 2: 379–94.

Braudel, Fernand. *The Mediterranean and the Mediterranean World in the Age of*

Philip II. 1949. Trans. Sean Reynolds. New York: Harper & Row, 1976. 2 vols.

Brown, Jonathan, and J. H. Elliott. *A Palace for a King*. New Haven: Yale U P, 1980.

Brunelli, Bruno. "L'impresario in angustie." *Rivista italiana del dramma* 19 (1941): 311–41.

Buck, August, and Georg Kauffmann, Blake Lee Spahr, Conrad Wiedemann. Eds. *Europäische Hofkultur im 16. und 17. Jahrhundert. Vorträge und Referate gehalten anlässlich des Kongresses des Wolfenbütteler Arbeitskreises für Renaissanceforschung und des Internationalen Arbeitskreises für Barockliteratur in der Herzog August Bibliothek Wolfenbüttel vom 4. bis 8. September 1979*. Wolfenbütteler Arbeiten zur Barockforschung 8–9–10. Hamburg: Ernst Hauswedell & Co, 1981. 3 vols.

Buffum, Imbrie. *Studies in the Baroque from Montaigne to Rotrou*. New Haven: Yale U P, 1957.

Buti, Francesco. Bilingual libretto. *Ercole amante*. Music by Francesco Cavalli. Cond. Michel Corboz. Musical Heritage Society Stereo 834719A. 1983.

Calderón de la Barca, Pedro. *Love The Greatest Enchantment; The Sorceries of Sin; The Devotion of the Cross*. Trans., introd. Denis Florence Mac-Carthy. London: Longman, Green, Longman & Roberts, 1861.

———. *Comedias*. Madrid, 1637. Facsimile ed. D. W. Cruickshank & J. E. Varey. Vol. 5. Westmead: Gregg International Publishers; London: Tamesis Books, 1973. 19 vols.

Cametti, Alberto. *Christina di Svezia, l'arte musicale e gli spettacoli teatrali in Roma*. Rome: Romano Mezzetti, 1931.

Carandini, Silvia. "La festa barocca a Roma." *Biblioteca teatrale* 15–16 (1976): 276–308.

Carfagno, Simon Albert. "The Life and Dramatic Music of Stefano Landi, with a Transliteration and Orchestration of the Opera *Sant'Alessio*." Diss. U of California-Los Angeles, 1960.

Castelli, Enrico. Ed. *Retorica e Barocco. Atti del III Congresso Internazionale di Studi Umanistici, Venezia 6/1954*. Rome: Fratelli Bocca, 1955.

Chapman, W. G. "Las comedias mitológicas de Calderón." *Revista de Literatura* 5.9–10 (1954): 35–69.

Charpentier de Marigny, Jacques. *Relation des divertissements que le Roi a donnés aux Reines dans le parc de Versailles, écrite à un gentilhomme qui est présentement hors de France*. Paris, 1664.

Chevallay, Sylvie. *Molière en son temps, 1622–1673*. Paris; Genève: Minkoff, 1973.

Christout, Marie-Françoise. *Le ballet de cour de Louis XIV, 1643-1672*. Paris, 1967.

———. "L'Influence vénitienne exercée par les artistes italiens sur les premiers spectacles à machines montés à la cour de France durant la Régence (1645–1650)." *Venezia e il melodramma nel seicento*. Ed. Maria Teresa Muraro. Florence: L. S. Olschki, 1976. 131–43.

Coe, Ada. " 'Ballet en comédie' or 'comédie en ballet'? *La Princesse d'Elide* et *Les Amants magnifiques*." *Cahiers du Dix-Septième* 2 (1988): 109–21.

Corce, Jérome de la. "L'Opéra français à la Cour de Louis XIV." *Revue d'Histoire du Théâtre* 35.4 (1983): 387–401.

Crain, Gordon F. "Francesco Cavalli and the Venetian Opera." *Opera* June 1967: 446–51.

Crankshaw, Edward. *The Habsburgs*. London: Weidenfeld & Nicolson, 1971.

Croll, Maurice. *Style, Rhetoric, and Rhythm: Essays by Morris W. Croll*. Ed. J. Max Patrick & Robert O. Evans, with John M. Wallace & R. J. Schoeck. Princeton: Princeton U P, 1966.

Curtius, Ernst Robert. *European Literature and the Latin Middle Ages*. 1948. Trans. Willard Trask. Bollingen Series 36. Princeton: Princeton U P, 1953.

Czapliński, Władysław. "Das Theater am Hofe des polnischen Wasas." See Buck, August, et al., eds. Vol. 2: 295–300.

Defaux, Gérard. *Molière, ou les Métamorphoses du Comique: De la comédie morale au triomphe de la folie*. French Forum Monographs 18. Lexington: French Forum Publishers, 1980.

DiPuccio, Denise. "The Enigma of Enchantment in *El mayor encanto, amor*." *Hispania* 70 (1987): 731–39.

Döring, Ulrich, et al. Eds. *Ouverture et Dialogue. Mélanges offerts à Wolfgang Leiner*. Tübingen: Narr, 1988.

Donato, E. "Tesauro's Poetics: Through the Looking Glass." *Modern Language Notes* 78 (1963): 15–30.

Donington, Robert. *The Rise of Opera*. New York: Charles Scribner's Sons, 1981.

Downer, Alan S. "Nature to Advantage Dressed." *PMLA* 68 (1943): 1002–37.

Dufourcq, Norbert. "Les Fêtes de Versailles: La musique." *Dix-Septième Siècle* 98–99 (1973): 67–75.

Ehalt, Hubert Ch. "Zur Funktion des Zeremoniells im Absolutismus." See Buck, August, et al., eds. Vol. 2: 411–19.

Elias, Norbert. *The Court Society*. 1969. Trans. E. Jephcott. New York: Pantheon Books, 1983.

Elliott, J. H. *Imperial Spain 1469–1716*. New York: Penguin, 1970.

Evans, R. J. W. *The Making of the Habsburg Monarchy 1550–1700: An Interpretation*. Oxford: Clarendon P, 1979.

Fagiolo dell'Arco, Maurizio. *Bernini: una introduzione al grande teatro del barocco*. Rome: Bulzoni, 1967.

———. "Lo spettacolo barocco." *Storia dell'arte*. Vol. 1. Florence: Nuova Italia, 1969.

———. *L'effimero barocco: strutture della festa nella Roma del '600*. Rome: Bulzoni, 1977. 2 vols.

Félibien, André. *Déscription du château de Versailles et de ses peintures et d'autres ouvrages faits pour le Roy*. Paris, 1698.

Ferrier-Caverivière, Nicole. *L'Image de Louis XIV dans la littérature française de 1660 à 1715*. Paris: PUF, 1981.

———. "Le siècle de Louis XIV et le problème du pouvoir: témoignages littéraires." *Travaux de Linguistique et de Littérature* 23 (1985): 45–57.

Flasche, Hans. "Die Struktur des Hof-Laudatio in den 'Loas' der 'Autos' Calderóns." See Buck, August, et al., eds. Vol. 2: 277–85.

Francastel, Pierre. "Limites chronologiques, limites geographiques [sic] et limites sociales du Baroque." See Castelli, Enrico, ed. 55–60.

Freud, Sigmund. "Civilization and its Discontents." *The Standard Edition of the Complete Psychological Works of Sigmund Freud*. Trans. James Strachey, with Anna Freud. Vol. 21 (1927–31). London: Hogarth P, 1961.

Füssel, Stephan. "Kaiserliche Repräsentation beim 'Wiener Kongress' 1515 im Spiegel der zeitgenössischen Darstellungen." See Buck, August, et al., eds. Vol. 2: 359–68.

Gadamer, Hans-Georg. *Truth and Method*. Trans. Joel Weinsheimer & Donald G. Marshall. 2nd. revised ed. New York: Crossroad Publishing, 1989.

Genette, Gérard. "L'Univers reversible." *Figures I*. Points 74. Paris: Eds. du Seuil, 1966. 9–20.

Gethner, Perry. "Comedy-Ballet and Court Festivities: Three Extreme Scenarios." *Cahiers du Dix-Septième* 3 (1989): 207–23.

Giazotto, Remo. Ed. "Nel CCC anno della morte di Antonio Cesti: Ventidue Lettere Ritrovate nell'Archivio di Stato di Venezia." *Nuova Rivista Musicale Italiana* 3 (1969): 496–512.

Glover, Jane. *Cavalli*. New York: St Martin's P, 1978.

Goldschmidt, Hugo. *Studien zur Geschichte der italienischen Oper im 17. Jahrhundert*. 2 vols. Leipzig, 1901. Facs. ed. Wiesbaden, 1967.

Gombrich, Ernst Hans. *Art and Illusion: A Study in the Psychology of Pictorial Representation*. 1960. 4th ed. London: Phaidon, 1972.

———. *Symbolic Images: Studies in the Art of the Renaissance*. London: Phaidon, 1972.

Gould, Cecil. *Bernini in France: An Episode in Seventeenth-Century History*. Princeton: Princeton U P, 1982.

Greer, Margaret Rich. "Art and Power in the Spectacle Plays of Calderón de la Barca." *PMLA* 104 (1989): 329–39.

Gregory, Tullio, et al. Eds. *Ricerche su letteratura libertina e letteratura clandestina nel Seicento. Atti del Convegno di studio di Genova (1980)*. Florence: La Nuova Italia, 1981.

Griffin, Robert A. "The Burnacini Style in High Baroque Theatre." Introduction. *Il Fuoco Eterno-Das Vestalische Ewige Feuer*. By Ludovico Burnacini. 1674. New York: Benjamin Blom, 1970.

Gros, Etienne. "Les Origines de la tragédie lyrique et la place des tragédies en machines dans l'évolution du théâtre vers l'opéra." *Revue d'Histoire littéraire de la France* 35 (1928): 161–93.

Grout, Donald Jay. *A Short History of Opera*. 1947. 3rd. ed., with Hermine Weigel Williams. New York: Columbia U P, 1988.

Hadamowsky, Franz. "Barocktheater am Wiener Kaiserhof. Mit einem Spielplan (1625–1740)." *Jahrbuch der Gesellschaft für Wiener Theaterforschung* (1951–1952). Vienna, A. Sexl, 1955.

Hanning, Barbara R. *Of Poetry and Music's Power: Humanism and the Creation of Opera*. Ann Arbor: U of Michigan Research P, 1980.

Haskell, Francis. *Patrons and Painters: A Study in the Relations between Italian Art and Society in the Age of the Baroque*. London: Chatto & Windus, 1963.

Hatzfeld, Helmut A. *Literature through Art: A New Approach to French Literature*. New York: Oxford U P, 1952.

Hawkins, Frederick W. *Annals of the French Stage from its Origin to the Death of Racine*. 1884. Grosse Point, MI: Scholarly P, 1969.

Hesse, Everett W. *Calderón de la Barca*. New York: Twayne, 1967.

Hode, Monsieur de la. Pseud. of Yves-Joseph La Motte. *Histoire de la vie et du règne de Louis XIV, Roi de France et de Navarre*. Vol. 3. Frankfurt: François Varrentrapp; Basel: Jean Christ, 1741. 6 vols. 1740–1743.

Hollander, John. "The Old Last Act: Some Observations on *Fanny Hill*." *Encounter* 21 (1963): 69–75.

Horn-Monval, Madeleine. "La grande machinerie théâtrale et ses origines." *Revue d'Histoire du Théâtre* 9.4 (1957): 291–308.

Houston, John Porter. *The Rhetoric of Poetry in the Renaissance and Seventeenth Century*. Baton Rouge; London: Louisiana State U P, 1983.

Huizinga, Johan. *Homo Ludens: A Study of the Play-Element in Culture*. 1938. Boston: Beacon P, 1955.

Hume, Martin. *The Court of Philip IV. Spain in Decadence*. New York: Putnam & Sons, 1907.

Isherwood, Robert M. *Music in the Service of the King: France in the Seventeenth Century*. Ithaca and London: Cornell U P, 1973.

Jack, Ronald D. S. "James VI and I as Patron." See Buck, August, et al., eds. Vol. 2: 179–85.

Jacquot, Jean. Gen. ed. *Les Fêtes de la Renaissance.*. Paris: Eds. du Centre National de la Recherche Scientifique, 1956–1957.

———. Gen. ed. *La Vie théâtrale au temps de la Renaissance*. Paris: Instit. Pédagogique National, 1963.

———. Gen. ed. *Le Lieu théâtrale à la Renaissance*. Paris: Eds. du Centre National de la Recherche Scientifique, 1964.

———. Gen. ed. *Dramaturgie et société. Rapports entre l'oeuvre théâtrale, son interprétation et son public aux XVIe et XVIIe siècles*. 2 vols. Paris: Eds. du Centre National de la Recherche Scientifique, 1968.

Jakobson, Roman. "Linguistics and Poetics." *Style in Language*. Ed. T. A. Sebeok. Cambridge, Mass.: Harvard U P, 1960. 350–58.

Javitch, Daniel. "Poetry and Preferment at Elizabeth's Court. Some Preliminary Observations." See Buck, August, et al., eds. Vol. 2: 163–69.

Johnson, Roger, Jr., et al. Eds. *Molière and the Commonwealth of Letters. Patrimony and Posterity*. Jackson: U P of Mississippi, 1975.

Kapp, Volker. "Die Beschreibung des idealen Königs aus der Sicht höfischer Gesittung im 'Discours' von Potier de Morais (1644)." See Buck, August, et al., eds. Vol. 2: 235–38.

Kindermann, Heinz. *Das Theater der Barockzeit*. Salzburg: Otto Müller Verlag, 1959. Vol. 3 of *Theatergeschichte Europas*. 10 vols. 1957–74.

Kivy, Peter. *Osmin's Rage: Philosophical Reflections on Opera, Drama, and Text*. Princeton: Princeton U P, 1988.

———. *Sound Sentiment: An Essay on the Musical Emotions*. Philadelphia: Temple U P, 1989.

Kretzschmar, Hermann. "Die venetianische Oper und die Werke Cavalli's und Cesti's." *Vierteljahrschrift für Musikwissenschaft* 8 (1892): 1–76.

Kristeller, Paul Oskar. *The Philosophy of Marsilio Ficino*. Trans. Virginia Conant. 1943. Gloucester, Mass.: Peter Smith, 1964.

Lancaster, Henri Carrington. *A History of French Dramatic Literature in the Seventeenth Century*. Baltimore: Johns Hopkins U P, 1929–1932. 5 vols.

Langer, Susanne K. *Philosophy in a New Key: Study in the Symbolism of Reason, Rite and Art*. Cambridge, Mass.: Harvard U P, 1957.

Langlois, Walter G. J. "The Evolution of Scenic Spectacles in France (1600–1673): National and Italian Origins of the Machine Play." Diss. Yale U, 1955.

Larson, Orville K. "Giacomo Torelli, Sir Philip Skippon, and Stage Machinery for the Venetian Opera." *Theatre Journal* 32 (1980): 448–57.

Lavin, Irving. Rev. *Fontana di Trevi*. By Bernini; ed. C. d'Onofrio. *Art Bulletin* 46 (1964): 568–72.

———. "Bernini and the Theater." *Bernini and the Unity of the Visual Arts*. Vol. 1. New York; London: Oxford U P, 1980. 146-57. 2 vols.

Lavin, Marilyn A. *Seventeenth-Century Barberini Documents and Inventories of Art*. New York: New York U P, 1975.

Lawrence, Francis L. *Molière: The Comedy of Unreason*. Tulane Studies in Romance Languages and Literature 2. New Orleans: Tulane U P, 1968.

Lawrenson, Thomas E. *The French Stage and Playhouse in the Seventeenth Century. A Study in the Advent of the Italian Order*. Manchester, 1957. Revised ed. New York: AMS, 1986.

Lazarowicz, Klaus. "Konzelebration oder Kollusion? Über die Feste der Wittelsbacher." See Buck, August, et al., eds. Vol. 2: 301–17.

Leclerc, Hélène. *Les origines italiennes de l'architecture théâtrale moderne: L'Evolution des formes en Italie de la Renaissance à la fin du XVIIe siècle*. Paris: Droz, 1946.

———. "Du Mythe platonicien aux fêtes de la Renaissance: 'L'Harmonie du Monde,' Incantation et Symbolisme." *Revue d'Histoire du Théâtre* 11 (1959): 109–71.

LeCoat, Gérard. *The Rhetoric of the Arts 1550–1650*. European University Papers, Series 18: Comparative Literature 3. Bern; Frankfurt: Peter Lang, 1975.

Lee, Renselaer. *Ut Pictura Poesis: The Humanistic Theory of Painting*. New York: Norton, 1967. Originally published in *The Art Bulletin* 22 (1940): 197–269.

Leopold, Silke. *Stefano Landi. Beiträge zur Biographie*. Hamburg: Wagner, 1976. 2 vols.

Levin, Harry. *The Myth of the Golden Age in the Renaissance*. Oxford: Oxford U P, 1969.

Lindenberger, Herbert. *Opera: The Extravagant Art*. Ithaca; London: Cornell U P, 1984.

Lippman, Edward A. Ed. *Musical Aesthetics: A Historical Reader*. New York: Pendragon P, 1986. 2 vols.

Loewenberg, Alfred. *Annals of Opera, 1597–1940*. 2 vols. Cambridge: Cambridge U P, 1943.

McCrary, William C., and José A. Madrigal. Eds. *Studies in Honor of Everett W. Hesse*. Lincoln, NE: Society of Spanish and Spanish-American Studies, 1981.

Magagnato, Licisco. "The Genesis of the *Teatro Olimpico*." *Journal of the Warburg and Courtauld Institutes* 14 (July-Dec.) 1951: 209–20.

Magne, Emile. *Les Fêtes en Europe au XVIIe siècle*. Paris: Martin-Dupuy, 1930.

———. *Les Plaisirs et les fêtes en France au XVIIe siècle*. Genève, Eds. de la Fregate, 1944.

Maiorino, Giancarlo. *The Cornucopian Mind and the Baroque Unity of the Arts*. University Park, PA: Pennsylvania State U P, 1990.

Marañón, Gregorio. *El Conde-Duque de Olivares*. 5th ed. Madrid: Espasa-Calpe, 1965.

Mariani, Valerio. "Il concetto architettonico nella scenografia del sei e settecento." *Rivista d'Archittetura e di Arti decorative* (1923): 97–110.

———. "Bernini regista e scenografo." *Studi di bibliografia e di argomento romano in memoria di Luigi de Gregori*. Rome: Fratelli Palombi, 1949. 254–64.

Marie, Alfred. *La Naissance de Versailles*. Paris: Fréal, 1968.

Marin, Louis. *Portrait of the King*. 1981. Trans. Martha Houle, foreword Tom Conley. Minneapolis: U of Minnesota P, 1988.

Marino, Giambattisto. *Adonis: Selections from "L'Adone" of Giambattista Marino*. Trans. Harold M. Priest. Ithaca: Cornell U P, 1967.

Martin, John Rupert. *Baroque*. Icon Editions. New York: Harper & Row, 1977.

Marvell, Andrew. *The Poems & Letters of Andrew Marvell*. Ed. H. M. Margoliouth. Oxford: Oxford U P, 1952. 2 vols.

Masson, Georgina. *Queen Christina*. London: Secker & Warburg, 1968.

Maurice-Amour, Lila. "Comment Lully et ses poètes humanisent dieux et héros." *Cahiers de l'Association Internationale des Etudes françaises* 17 (1965): 59–95.

———. "Rythme dans les comédies-ballets de Molière." *Revue d'Histoire du Théâtre* 26 (1974): 118–30.

Mauss, Marcel. *The Gift: Forms and Functions of Exchange in Archaic Societies*. Trans. I. Cunnison. New York: Norton, 1967.

Mazouer, Charles. "Il faut jouer: Les intermèdes des comédies ballets de Molière." *Dix-Septième Siècle* 165 (1989): 375–81.

Menestrier, Claude-François. *Traité des tournois, joustes, carrousels et autres spectacles publics*. 1669. Roanne: Horvath, 1975.

———. *Des Représentations en musique anciennes et modernes*. 1681. Genève: Minkoff, 1972.

———. *Des Ballets anciens et modernes selon les règles du Théâtre*. 1682. 1962. Genève: Minkoff, 1972.

Metzger, Erika A., and Michael M. Metzger. "Courtly and Anticourtly Literature." *German Baroque Literature: The European Perspective*. Ed. Gerhart Hoffmeister. New York: Ungar, 1983. 250–69.

Michel, Alain. "Le Théâtre et l'apparence: d'Euripide à Calderón." *Revue des Sciences humaines* 145 (1972): 9–16.

Millar, Susanna. *The Psychology of Play*. Harmondsworth: Penguin, 1968.

Miller, David. *Gods and Games: Toward a Theology of Play*. 1970. New York: Harper Colophon Books, 1973.

Moine, Marie-Christine. *Les Fêtes à la Cour du Roi Soleil 1653-1715*. Paris: Fernand Lanore, 1984.

Molière. "L'Impromptu de Versailles" and "Les Plaisirs de l'Ile enchantée." *Oeuvres Complètes*. Ed. Maurice Rat. 2 vols. Vol. 1. Bibliothèque de la Pléiade 8. Paris: Gallimard, 1962. 549-74; 601–78.

Molinari, Cesare. *Le Nozze degli Dèi: un saggio sul grande spettacolo italiano nel seicento*. Rome: Bulzoni, 1968.

———. "Delle Nozze medicee e dei loro cronisti," *Il Teatro dei Medici. Quaderni di Teatro* 2.7 (1980): 23–30.

Mongrédien, Georges. "Molière et Lulli." *Dix-Septième Siècle* 98–99 (1973): 3–15.

Monteverdi, Claudio. *Tutte le opere*. Ed. G. Francesco Malipiero. Asolo: [n.p.], 1930. Vol. 11.

Moureau, François. "Les Comédiens italiens et la Cour de France." *Dix-Septième Siècle* 33 (1981): 63–81.

Münch, Paul. "Haus und Regiment—Überlegungen zum Einfluss der alteuropäischen Ökonomie auf die fürstliche Regierungstheorie und -praxis während der frühen Neuzeit." See Buck, August, et al., eds. Vol. 2: 205–10.

Muraro, Maria Teresa. Ed. *Venezia e il melodramma nel seicento*. Florence: L. S. Olschki, 1976.

Murata, Margaret. *Operas for the Papal Court, 1631–1668*. Diss. U of Chicago, 1975. Ann Arbor: UMI, 1981.

Murphy, James J. *Renaissance Rhetoric: A Short-Title Catalogue of Works on Rhetorical Theory from the Beginning of Printing to AD 1700*. New York: Garland, 1981.

Nadler, Josef. "Das bayerisch-österreichische Barocktheater." *Deutsche Barockforschung*. Ed. Richard Alewyn. Köln; Berlin: Kiepenheuer & Witsch, 1966. 94–106.

Nashe, Thomas. *The Unfortunate Traveller and Other Works*. Ed. J. B. Steane. Harmondsworth: Penguin, 1985.

Neale, Robert E. *In Praise of Play: Toward a Psychology of Religion*. New York: Harper & Row, 1969.

Negro, Angela. *Guide Rionali di Roma. Rione II-Trevi*. Rome: Fratelli Palombi, 1980.

Neumeister, Sebastian. "Vom Nachleben Calderóns: Aspekte aus der Geschichte einer schwierigen Rezeption am Beispiel von *El mayor encanto, amor* (Über allem Zauber, Liebe)." *Maske und Kothurn* 24 (1978): 326–38.

———. *Mythos und Repräsentation. Die mythologischen Festspiele Calderóns*. Munich: Wilhelm Fink Verlag, 1978.

———. "Höfische Pragmatik. Zu Baltasar Graciáns Ideal des 'Discreto'." See Buck, August, et al., eds. Vol. 2: 51–60.

Nolhac, Pierre de. "Les premières fêtes de Versailles." *Revue de Paris* 15 April 1899: 841–58.

Oliver, A. Richard. "Molière's Contribution to the Lyric Stage." *Musical Quarterly* 33 (1947): 350–64.

Onians, R. B. *Origins of European Thought*. Cambridge: Cambridge U P, 1951.

Orgel, Stephen, and Roy Strong. *Inigo Jones: The Theatre of the Stuart Court*. Vol. 1. London: Sotheby Parke Bernet; Berkeley: U of California P, 1973. 105–14. 2 vols.

Palisca, Claude V. Ed. *Letters on Ancient and Modern Music to Vincenzo Galilei and Giovanni Bardi*, by Girolamo Mei. [n.p.]: American Inst. of Musicology, 1960.

———. *Baroque Music*. Englewood Cliffs, N.J.: Prentice Hall, 1968.

Panofsky, Erwin. *Studies in Iconology: Humanist Themes in the Art of the Renaissance*. 1939. New York: Harper & Row, 1962.

———. *Meaning in the Visual Arts*. 1955. Chicago: U of Chicago P, 1982.

Pastor, Freiherr Ludwig von. *The History of the Popes*. Trans. Dom Ernest Graf. Vols. 28 & 29. London: Kegan Paul, Trench & Trubner, 1938. 29 vols.

Pieper, Josef. *Leisure: The Basis of Culture*. Trans. Alexander Dru, introd. T. S. Eliot. New York: Pantheon Books, 1952.

Pirrotta, Nino. " 'Commedia dell'arte and Opera." *The Musical Quarterly* 41 (1955): 305–24.

———, and Elena Povoledo. *Music and Theatre from Poliziano to Monteverdi*. Trans. Karen Eales. Cambridge: Cambridge U P, 1982.

Pitou, Spire. "L'Autre version en vers de *La Princesse d'Elide*." *Dix-Septième Siècle* 97 (1972): 105–09.

Pollak, Oskar. *Die Kunsttätigkeit unter Urban VIII*. Vol. 1. Vienna; Augsburg; Cologne: Benno Filser, 1928. 2 vols.

Praag, J. A. van. "Les traductions de *El mayor encanto, amor* de Calderón en néerlandais." *Neophilologus* 7 (1922): 8–19.

Pribram, Alfred. "Die Heirat Kaiser Leopold I. mit Margaretha Theresia von Spanien." *Archiv für Österreichische Geschichte* 77 (1891): 319–75.

Prunières, Henri. *L'Opéra italien en France avant Lulli*. 1913. Paris: Champion, 1949.

———. *Le Ballet de cour en France avant Benserade et Lulli*. Paris: Laurens, 1914.

———. *Cavalli et l'opéra vénitien au XVIIe siècle*. Paris: Rieder, 1931.

Pure, Michel de. *Idée des spectacles anciens et nouveaux*. 1668. Genève: Minkoff, 1972.

Reinhardt, Volker. "Der päpstliche Hof um 1600." See Buck, August, et al., eds. Vol. 3: 709–15.

Rennert, Hugo Albert. *The Spanish Stage in the Time of Lope de Vega*. 1909. New York: Dover, 1963.

Reumont, Alfred von. *Beiträge zur italienischen Geschichte*. Berlin: Verlag der Deckerschen Geheimen Ober-Hofbuchdruckerei, 1853-57.

Rinck, Euch. Gottlieb. *Leopolds des Grossen Röms. Kayesers Leben und Thaten*. 2nd ed. Cologne, 1713.

Ripa, Cesare. *Baroque and Rococo Pictorial Imagery: The 1758–60 Hertel Edition of Ripa's 'Iconologia'*. Ed. Edward A. Maser. Dover Pictorial Archive Series. New York: Dover, 1971.

Rivers, Isabel. *Classical and Christian Ideas in English Renaissance Poetry*. London: Unwin Hyman, 1979.

Rogerson, Brewster. "The Art of Painting the Passions." *Journal of the History of Ideas* 14 (1953): 68–94.

Rolland, Romain. *Histoire de l'opéra en Europe avant Lully et Scarlatti*. 1895. Paris: Boccard, 1931.

———. "La première représentation du *San Alessio* de Stefano Landi, en 1632, à Rome, d'après le journal manuscrit de Jean-Jacques Bouchard." *Revue d'histoire et de critique musicales* 2 (1902): 29–36, 74–75.

Roloff, Hans-Gert. "Die höfischen Maskeraden der Sophie Elisabeth, Herzogin zu Braunschweig-Lüneburg." See Buck, August, et al., eds. Vol. 3: 489–96.

Rospigliosi, Giulio. *Sant'Alessio*. C1632 item #6. R. Vat. Codex Ottob. Pat. 2259. vols. 329–57.

Roth, Oskar. "Höfische Gesinnung und *honnêteté* im Frankreich des 17. Jahrhunderts." See Buck, August, et al., eds. Vol. 2: 239-44.

Rotondi, Joseph Emilio. "Literary and musical aspects of Roman Opera, 1600–1650." Diss. U of Pennsylvania, 1959.

Rouchès, Gabriel. *Inventaire des lettres et papiers manuscrits de Gaspare, Carlo et Lodovico Vigarani, 1634–1688*. Paris: Champion, 1913.

Rousset, Jean. *La littérature de l'âge baroque en France: Circé et le paon*. Paris: Corti, 1954.

———. *L'Intérieur et l'extérieur: Essais sur la poésie et sur le théâtre au XVIIe siècle*. 1968. Paris: Corti, 1976.

Sabbattini, Nicola. *Pratica di fabricar scene e machine ne'teatri*. 1637–38. Ed. Elena Povoledo. Rome: Carlo Bestetti, 1955.

Sbarra, Francesco. *Il Pomo d'oro, Festa teatrale*. Vienna: M. Cosmerovio, 1667 and 1668. (See Adler 1959 and Schmidt 1982).

Schlumbohm, Christa. "De la Magnificence et de la Magnanimité: Zur Verherrlichung Ludwigs XIV. in Literatur und bildender Kunst." *Romanistisches Jahrbuch* 30 (1979): 83–99.

Schmidgall, Gary. *Literature as Opera*. New York: Oxford U P, 1977.

Schmidt, Carl B. "Antonio Cesti's *Il pomo d'oro*: A Reexamination of a Famous Hapsburg Court Spectacle." *Journal of the American Musicological Society* 29 (1976): 381–412.

———. Ed. *Antonio Cesti: 'Il pomo d'oro.' (Music for Acts III and V from Modena, Biblioteca Estense, Ms. Mus. E.120)*. Recent Researches in the Music of the Baroque Era 42. Madison, WI: A-R Editions, 1982.

Schröder, Gerhard. " 'Courtisan' und 'honnête homme.' Zum Problem der Entstehung eines bürgerlichen Bewusstseins im 17. Jahrhundert." See Buck, August, et al., eds. Vol. 2: 245–48.

Sedlmayer, Hans. "Allegorie und Architektur." See Castelli, Enrico, ed. 197–207.

Seifert, Herbert. "Die Festlichkeiten zur ersten Hochzeit Kaiser Leopolds I." *Österreichische Musikzeitschrift* 29 (1974): 6–16.

Senn, Walter. *Musik und Theater am Hof zu Innsbruck: Geschichte der Hofkapelle vom 15. Jahrhunderts bis zu deren Auflösung im Jahre 1748.* Innsbruck: Wagner, 1954.

Seznec, Jean. *The Survival of the Pagan Gods: The Mythological Tradition and Its Place in Renaissance Humanism and Art.* 1940. Trans. Barbara F. Sessions. Bollingen Series 38. New York: Pantheon Books, 1953.

Shearman, John. *Mannerism.* Style & Civilization. 1967. London: Penguin, 1987.

Shergold, Norman D. "The First Performance of Calderón's *El mayor encanto, amor.*" *Bulletin of Hispanic Studies* 35 (1958): 24-27.

———. *A History of the Spanish Stage from Medieval Times until the End of the Seventeenth Century.* Oxford: Clarendon P, 1967.

———. "Documentos sobre Cosme Lotti, escenógrafo de Felipe IV." *Studia Iberica. Festschrift für Hans Flasche.* Eds. Karl-Hermann Körner, et al. Bern: Francke, 1973. 589–602.

Shock, Diane H. "Costuming for *Il pomo d'oro.*" *Gazette des Beaux-Arts* 69 (1967): 251–56.

Skrine, Peter N. *The Baroque: Literature and Culture in Seventeenth-Century Europe.* New York: Holmes & Meier, 1978.

———. "Court and Theatre in Restoration England." See Buck, August, et al., eds. Vol. 2: 329–34.

Solf, Sabine. *Festdekoration und Groteske. Der wiener Bühnenbilder Lodovico Ottavio Burnacini: Inszenierung Barocker Kunstvorstellung.* Baden-Baden: Valentin Körner, 1975.

Somerset, Henry V. F. "The Habsburg Emperors as Musicians." *Music and Letters* 30 (1949): 204–15.

Spariosu, Mihai I. *Dionysus Reborn: Play and the Aesthetic Dimension in Modern Philosophical and Scientific Discourse.* Ithaca; London: Cornell U P, 1989.

———. *God of Many Names: Play, Poetry, and Power in Hellenic Thought from Homer to Aristotle.* Durham; London: Duke U P, 1991.

Spielman, John. *Leopold I of Austria.* London: Thames & Hudson; New Brunswick, N.J.: Rutgers U P, 1977.

Stanley, Albert A. "Cesti's *Il Pomo d'Oro.*" *Papers and Proceedings of the Music Teachers' National Association* I (1906): 139–49.

Steadman, John. *Redefining a Period Style: "Renaissance," "Mannerist," and "Baroque" in Literature.* Pittsburgh: Duquesne U P, 1990.

Strong, Roy. *Art and Power: Renaissance Festivals 1450–1650*. 1973. London: Boydell P, 1984.

Tagliabue, Guido Morpurgo. "Aristotelismo e Barocco." See Castelli, Enrico, ed. 119–95.

Tapié, Victor. *Baroque et classicisme*. 1957. [Paris:] Librairie Générale française, 1980.

———. *The Rise and Fall of the Habsburg Monarchy*. Trans. Stephen Hardman. London: Pall Mall P, 1971.

Tauschhuber, Georg. "Kaiser Leopold I. und das Wiener Barocktheater." Diss. U of Munich, 1946.

Terza, Dante della. "Le corte e il teatro: Appunti e testimonianze sul congresso di New York (13 nov.-18 nov. 1978)." *Lettere Italiane* 31 (1979): 219–30.

Thierry, Edouard. "La Troupe de Molière et les 'Plaisirs de l'Ile enchantée'." *Bulletin de la Société des Gens de Lettres* August 1872.

Tintelnot, Hans. "Annotazioni sull'importanza della festa teatrale per la vita artistica e dinastica nel Barocco." See Castelli, Enrico, ed. 233–41.

Trevor-Roper, Hugh. "The Culture of the Baroque Courts." See Buck, August, et al., eds. Vol. 1: 11–23.

Turner, Victor. *From Ritual to Theater: The Human Seriousness of Play*. New York: Performing Arts Journal Publications, 1982.

Vaihinger, Hans. *The Philosophy of 'As If'. A System of the Theoretical, Practical and Religious Fictions of Mankind*. 6th ed. Transl. C. K. Ogden. 2nd ed. New York: Harcourt, Brace and Co., 1935.

Valbuena-Briones, Angel. "Eros moralizado en las comedias mitológicas de Calderón." *Approaches to the Theater of Calderón*. Ed. Michael McGaha. Washington, D.C.: U P of America, 1982. 77–93.

Vanuxem, Jacques. "La Scénographie des fêtes de Louis XIV auxquelles Molière a participé." *Dix-Septième Siècle* 98–99 (1973): 77–89.

Varey, J. E. "Calderón, Cosme Lotti, Velázquez, and the Madrid Festivities 1636–37." *Renaissance Drama New Series* 1 (1968): 253–82.

Vehse, Karl Eduard. *Memoirs of the Court, Aristocracy, and Diplomacy of Austria*. Trans. Franz Demmler. London: Longman, Brown, Green, & Longmans, 1856. 2 vols.

———. *Der Beginn des musikalischen Barock und die Anfänge der Oper in Wien*. Theater und Kultur 6. Vienna: Literarische Anstalt, 1922.

Vickers, Brian. "Figures of rhetoric/Figures of music?" *Rhetorica* 2.1 (1984): 1–44.

Voragine, Jacobus de. *The Golden Legend*. Trans. William Caxton, ed. F. S. Ellis. Vol. 6. London: Dent, 1900. Rpt. New York: AMS Press [s.d.]. 205–12.

Wagenknecht, Christian. "Die Beschreibung höfischer Feste. Merkmale einer Gattung." See Buck, August, et al., eds. Vol. 2: 75–80.

Walker, D. P. "Musical Humanism in the Sixteenth and Early Seventeenth Centuries." *The Music Review* 2 (1941): 1–13, 111–21, 220–27, 288–308; 3 (1942): 55–71.

Warnke, Frank J. *Versions of Baroque*. New Haven: Yale U P, 1972.

Weber, Max. *Protestant Ethic and the Spirit of Capitalism*. New York, 1958.

Wellesz, Egon. "A Festival Opera of the Seventeenth Century." 1914. Trans. Patricia Kean. *Essays on Opera*. London: Dobson, 1950. 54–81.

Wilde, Oscar. *The Picture of Dorian Gray*. 1891. Harmondsworth: Penguin, 1985.

Wind, Edgar. *Pagan Mysteries in the Renaissance*. 1958. 2nd. ed. New York: Norton, 1968.

Witeschnik, Alexander. *Wiener Opernkunst von den Anfängen bis zu Karajan*. Vienna: Kremayr & Scheriau, 1959.

Index